THE EUROPEAN
INHERITANCE

THE EUROPEAN INHERITANCE

EDITED BY

SIR ERNEST BARKER

SIR GEORGE CLARK

PROFESSOR P. VAUCHER

VOLUME II

OXFORD

AT THE CLARENDON PRESS

1954

Oxford University Press, Amen House, London E.C. 4

GLASGOW NEW YORK TORONTO MELBOURNE WELLINGTON
BOMBAY CALCUTTA MADRAS KARACHI CAPE TOWN IBADAN

Geoffrey Cumberlege, Publisher to the University

PRINTED IN GREAT BRITAIN

PREFACE

THE origin of this work goes back to the war of 1939–45, and, in particular, to the winter of 1942–3. At the end of 1942 the British Minister of Education convened a Conference of the Ministers of Education of eight allied governments, then resident and active in London; and this Conference of Allied Ministers of Education continued to meet regularly afterwards. In February 1943 the Conference appointed a Books Commission, with the primary purpose of arranging for the supply of English books and periodicals, at the end of the war, to the member countries of the Conference which were then occupied by the enemy,[1] but also with the further purpose of considering the possibility of producing a work on history, 'of an objective character', which might be available for general use in the member countries and elsewhere. In pursuance of this further purpose the Books Commission proceeded to appoint (in March 1943) a History Committee, containing scholars drawn from all the member countries, to plan the production of such a work. The general plan of these volumes is the result of the deliberations of this Committee.

The scheme of the History Committee, as it eventually emerged, and as it was adopted and confirmed by the Conference of Allied Ministers of Education, was a scheme for the publication of a history of European civilization, to be called *The European Inheritance*, in seven chronological parts (from the beginnings of prehistory to the middle of the twentieth century), each part accompanied by maps and illustrations and by a number of appropriate historical documents. In submitting the scheme the History Committee proposed, and the Conference of Allied Ministers of Education agreed, that *The European Inheritance* should be a work of independent scholarship, independently published by a university press, under the direction of an editorial board which would choose and invite the individual contributors, and would thus be freely and solely responsible, along with the contributors, for the form and substance of the work. The Clarendon Press was accordingly approached,

---

[1] That purpose was achieved; and owing to the work of the Books Commission from 1943 to 1945 the occupied countries were able to obtain a very large number of books and periodicals for their university and public libraries. (Note by Professor Paul Vaucher.)

and agreed to publish the work; and an editorial board was then appointed (in March 1944), which in its eventual form consisted of Sir Ernest Barker (who had acted as Chairman of the Books Commission and of its Historical Committee), Dr. G. N. Clark (at the time of his appointment Regius Professor of History in Cambridge, and afterwards Provost of Oriel College, Oxford), and Professor Paul Vaucher, at that time cultural counsellor of the French government in London and afterwards professor in the university of Paris. (Professor Odlozilik, of the university of Prague, was originally a member of the Board, but when he went to the United States for service in an American university he relinquished his membership.) When these arrangements had been made, the Conference of Allied Ministers of Education, which had originally suggested the work, decided to ensure its freedom from even the slightest shadow of any political control by disclaiming all responsibility for its form and substance; and they accordingly passed the following resolution, to be inserted in each volume:

'This volume originated in a suggestion made by the Conference of Allied Ministers of Education early in 1943. The Conference subsequently approved the scheme of publication, but decided to ensure the independence of the editors and contributors by dissociating themselves from the preparation of the volume. While, therefore, the Conference agreed to the insertion of this prefatory note explaining the origin of the volume, it will be understood that they had no responsibility for either the form or the substance of the present work.'

Just as it was, in its inception, internationally planned, or at any rate planned on a European basis, so too in its execution the work has an international width. Naturally some of the scholars who have made their contributions to a work originally planned in Great Britain (though many continental scholars were long concerned in the planning) belong to the British Isles. The first part, on prehistory, is written by Professor Gordon Childe, Director of the Institute of Archaeology in the university of London, who has also studied and taught in the universities of Sydney, Oxford, and Edinburgh; part of the second part, dealing with the Greek and Roman inheritance, is from the pen of a veteran Cambridge and Scottish scholar, Dr. Tarn, and another part, dealing with the Hebrew inheritance,

is written by a Cambridge Professor, originally trained in
Oxford, who has lectured and taught in several English and
several American universities, the Rev. C. H. Dodd; the fourth
part, dealing with the sixteenth and seventeenth centuries, has
been contributed by one of the two British editors. The contributors of three other parts all come from the continent of
Europe: Professor Ganshof, of the university of Ghent, has
written the section on the Middle Ages; Professor Vaucher (one
of the editors) and Professor Mornet, both of the university of
Paris, have collaborated in writing the part on the eighteenth
century; and Professor Vermeil, of the same university, has
contributed the part on the twentieth century. An American
scholar, Mr. Geoffrey Bruun, born in Canada of British and
Norwegian ancestry, has brought the perspective of the New
World to his contribution on the development of Europe during
the nineteenth century. The range of the contributors is wide:
the reader will judge the depth of their scholarship and the
lucidity of their exposition.

Two other things remain to be said in conclusion of this preface. The first is that the work has been planned to meet the
needs of students in the upper forms of secondary schools and
in the early years of university courses. (It is the hope of the
editors that the original English version may be translated into
other languages, and that the work may thus come to be used in
the schools and universities of many of the countries of Europe,
and even outside Europe). The second is that in the third and
succeeding parts the contributors have sought to deal not only
with the internal history of Europe, but also with the history
of Europe overseas, or, in other words, with the expansion of
Europe. The work is not a history of mankind. But it is, at any
rate, a history of European man, and of his influence on the rest
of mankind. This is not to say, for a moment, that it has a
European bias, or that it attempts to vindicate a particular
eminence for the continent of Europe over other continents. It
would not be 'objective history' if it had that bias or made that
attempt. It is just a record of Europe and the overseas growth
of Europe, set down by a number of scholars of European birth
or origin, with the intention of communicating to the youth of
Europe, as dispassionately and as justly as possible, some sense
of the inheritance of Europe and the spread and the influence of
that inheritance.

Detailed reference to authorities and sources is excluded by the plan of the three volumes, but the great debt which they owe to the labour of others will be apparent to scholarly readers, and this obligation the editors and authors gladly acknowledge.

E. B.

G. N. C.

P. V.

NOTE

THE original conception of this work was due to Sir Ernest Barker, who also took the initiative during the late war in carrying it out, and has throughout borne the heaviest share of the editorial burden. We think it right that these facts should be recorded here, and we take this opportunity of thanking Sir Ernest for all the generous help and kindness which we have received from him.

G. N. CLARK

PAUL VAUCHER

8 *April* 1952

CONTENTS

VOLUME I

I. PREHISTORY
by V. GORDON CHILDE

II. i. GREECE AND ROME
by W. W. TARN

II. ii. THE JEWS AND THE BEGINNINGS OF THE CHRISTIAN CHURCH
by C. H. DODD

III. THE MIDDLE AGES
by F. L. GANSHOF

VOLUME II
IV. THE EARLY MODERN PERIOD
by G. N. CLARK

V. 1. POLITICAL, ECONOMIC, AND SOCIAL DEVELOPMENT IN THE XVIIIth CENTURY

by PAUL VAUCHER

V. II. THE DEVELOPMENT OF LITERATURE AND CULTURE IN THE XVIIIth CENTURY

by DANIEL MORNET

VOLUME III

VI. THE NINETEENTH CENTURY (1815–1914)

by GEOFFREY BRUUN

DOCUMENTS
VOLUME I

VOLUME II

VOLUME III

LIST OF PLATES

VOLUME I

LIST OF PLATES   xxiii

VOLUME II

    This is one of the four miniatures painted, not earlier than 1477 and
    not later than 1482, for Mary of Burgundy in a Book of Hours which
    originally belonged to her father Charles the Bold. In the foreground a
    lady is reading—we must suppose that this is a portrait of the Duchess
    herself—and we see how a great lady lived, with her lap-dog, her
    large pearls, her brocaded work-bag, and her vase of cut flowers.
    The open window gives not on a natural scene but on her thoughts:
    there she is kneeling before the Madonna, who sits, attended by
    angels, before the altar of a church. The vertical lines of the late
    Gothic building and the overarching vault form a canopy; but the
    windows of the apse recede into the distance.

    In a spacious and expensively appointed room, such as were seen
    in Venetian palaces at the time when it was painted (1502–7), the
    saint is represented with the expression and attitude conventionally
    appropriate to one receiving an inspiration. No doubt he is composing
    sacred music, of which specimens are shown in the foreground. At
    the back is a recess with an altar and its vessels, and a mitre and
    pastoral staff, between two doorways of Renaissance design, through
    one of which various scientific instruments are visible. Among the

many objects in the room, three which deserve special notice are the statuettes, of a horse and of Venus, on the left, and the armillary sphere on the right. This is a skeleton celestial globe, made of metal hoops, revolving on an axis to represent the motions of the heavenly bodies. It was already a fashionable article of furniture, though the picture is intended to show St. Jerome (who lived in the fourth century), as he appears in legend, well versed in every science.

27. Albrecht Dürer, St. Jerome. Photograph by Mansell *facing page* 60
This work, by the greatest of the German engravers, is dated 1514 and represents St. Jerome as a Cardinal (the Cardinal's hat hangs on the wall behind him), absorbed in the work, presumably, of his Vulgate translation of the Scriptures into Latin, which was supposed to have occupied fifty-five of his eighty-eight years. In the legend his tame lion was an enterprising and able beast, but here it lies asleep, as benign as its master. The interior may well be appropriate for a distinguished ecclesiastic of the time, and, although Dürer knew Venice, it may perhaps be contrasted with that of Carpaccio as more northern. Among the things in it are an hour-glass and, on the window-sill, a skull, the emblem of mortality.

28. El Greco, St. Jerome as penitent. From the painting in the National Gallery of Scotland, Edinburgh 92
This represents an earlier stage of St. Jerome's life, when he was a penitent in the desert. It was painted about 1600 by Domenico Theotocopouli, called El Greco (the Greek), who painted this subject so many times that it has been called one of his obsessions. He was born in Crete, and though he studied painting in Venice, and did most of his work in Spain, he always retained something of the old Byzantine tradition, for which the exact representation of things seen was neither a means nor an end. Even in this fervid picture of a half-naked man in a cave there appear the hat, the hour-glass, and the skull.

29. Rembrandt, Faust in his study. Photograph by *Picture Post* Library 114
This etching, which was made in or about 1652, is usually named after the legendary magician Dr. Faustus, who sold his soul to the Devil; but there is nothing sinister or diabolical about it. It represents a moment of illumination in the search for truth. The books, the skull, the globe in the foreground are not mere scientific equipment. They are also symbols, and the thinker, who stands intent but not disconcerted, has performed some magical act to call up the shining shapes and the pointing hand. In the centre of the lettering there are the Christian initials I N R I.

30. Sébastien Leclerc, The Académie des Sciences in the Royal Library at Versailles in 1671. From J. Picard, *Mémoires pour servir à l'histoire naturelle des animaux. Mesure de la terre* 138
In this copper-plate engraving the official artist of Louis XIV shows how the search for truth was carried on under the auspices of his royal master. Again there is a globe in the foreground, an armillary sphere, and a whole skeleton instead of a skull. The magical element is supplied by the king, who wears his hat and listens to the explanation of his minister Colbert. Colbert points to the plan of a fortress. Outside the window may be seen a surveyor's quadrant in the formal garden, and something of the outlying building operations of the great palace of Versailles. This is said to be the earliest picture of a meeting of a scientific society.

VOLUME III

LIST OF MAPS
VOLUME I
I. PREHISTORY

II. 1. GREECE AND ROME

II. 11. THE JEWS AND THE BEGINNINGS OF THE CHRISTIAN CHURCH

III. THE MIDDLE AGES

VOLUME II
IV. THE EARLY MODERN PERIOD

V. POLITICAL, ECONOMIC, AND SOCIAL DEVELOPMENT IN THE EIGHTEENTH CENTURY

VOLUME III

VI. THE NINETEENTH CENTURY (1815–1914)

VII. 1914–50

VIII. REVIEW AND EPILOGUE

IV

THE EARLY MODERN PERIOD

By

G. N. CLARK

Sometime Regius Professor of History, Cambridge
Provost of Oriel College, Oxford

I

NEW AND OLD IN THE FIFTEENTH CENTURY

THERE are thousands of people who, although they have neither special historical training nor exceptionally keen perceptions, can judge correctly, nine times out of ten, whether a picture or a carving, or any other object of human workmanship that is set before them, did or did not originate in the western or central Europe of the fifteenth century. The civilization of that time and place had a character of its own which can be recognized in the things that have survived from it, and also in its literature and in much of what is known of its history. When, however, we try to describe such characters, we find them surprisingly elusive: it is far easier to recognize them when they are embodied in a particular product than to set out their essence in words. In a brief summary such as this it is impossible to do more than indicate a few salient points.

The first point is that for many generations the peoples had been used to fixed settlements. The main work of clearing the land, of draining it, and of breaking it in for cultivation had been done for them already by former generations. There were still many places where it could be pushed further, but the pioneering stage was over and the nomadic life was almost forgotten. Almost all the land had its owners. There were wandering flockmasters in Spain, drovers and pedlars everywhere, and armies of mercenary soldiers with no fixed abodes; but these, like the gypsies and the wandering scholars, were exceptional people, moving about in the interstices of a settled world. The population was very meagre by the standards of our time; but when some change in the conditions of livelihood caused a movement of migration, it ended not with the colonizing of empty spaces but with absorption into stable communities which could find work and maintenance for new-comers.

The outward aspects of life were much more diversified by contrasts, by local and regional peculiarities, than they are now, because travel and transport were so slow and difficult, and technology was so primitive, that the physical character of each plot of ground dictated, within very narrow limits, what kind of life could be lived upon it. The area of land which could be cultivated as a single unit, the tools which could be used, the crops which could be grown, the ways in which labour could be organized, depended on whether it was mountain or plain, light soil or heavy, in a wet climate or dry, near a navigable coast or river or far away, and not only on these great variations, which still count for much at the present day, but on far smaller physical accidents. There was little possibility of bringing fertilizers or equipment or even seeds and livestock from a distance; there was little choice of markets. Everything had to be done with local materials if possible, and so in most places farming, whether individual or communal, was not specialized but provided all the requirements of a neighbourhood. In many other spheres the same limitations caused a like variety. There were local styles of architecture, based on the available materials, timber or brick, hard stone or soft. In dress, tools, furniture, conveniences of every kind, the craftsmen of each town had their local fashions.

This variety went deep. It extended to the realm of thought, as may be seen from the instance of language. Each district had its dialect, and, although the dialects belonged to greater languages, such as French or Provençal, Low German or High German, not many people read books or needed to talk to anyone who came from more than a day's journey away, so that standards of correctness in speech scarcely existed. The man who lived at a distance of two days' journey was a foreigner. European man was a local animal.

In spite of all this variety there was one civilization. Below the diversities of systems of farming there was a similarity of social foundations. Almost everywhere individual property existed side by side with community rights. Systems of inheritance were found everywhere, and all ownership was based on the monogamous family. Women were in a state of dependence, though not in such complete subjection as in the oriental civilizations. The cultivators were free peasants in some places, serfs in others, while there were places in which serfs and freemen worked together in the same economy; but mere chattel-slavery did not prevail anywhere to any serious extent. Almost everywhere the division of classes in the countryside conformed to some feudal arrangement. There were distinctions of rank, more or less clearly marked by titles and forms of address, more or less strictly transmitted by inheritance. The higher his rank, the greater opportunities a man had of acquiring riches and surrounding himself with servants and possessions; but the degrees of rank were connected with differences of functions. Justice and the advisory and administrative work of government were largely in the hands of an upper stratum, who were rural landowners and had a military tradition.

The towns had grown up through manufactures and trade. There were many of them, but they were still very small. Paris had possibly 200,000 inhabitants; but most of the famous trading cities, such as Venice and London, were not half that size, while the market towns were proportionately smaller. The merchants and shopkeepers, apprentices and journeymen of the towns did not fit into the class-distinctions of the countryside. They had their own forms of organization. One of the distinctive features of European life was the number and vigour of the associations in which the townsmen combined together for economic, social, or religious purposes. According to the balance of strength between rural and urban elements, the towns were subject to the feudal lords in some places, in others independent of them, and in yet others, especially in Italy, they had overcome the country nobility, who now lived as citizens within their walls. But in the towns the fundamentals of the family and of inheritance were the same as in the country. In both alike the leading families formed aristocracies, that is bodies of men who had a claim to hold office not solely by reason of ability or by election or appointment, but by their inherited status. Their common life, their sense of ease and equality among themselves, and of superiority over those with whom they did not intermarry or share their opportunities, gave them habits of freedom. Many of them had ideals of courage, endurance, loyalty, consideration for women; at their best they recognized that service earned a right to protection, that weakness and inexperience ought not to be exploited, that it was wrong to ask another to run a risk which they would not run themselves. They also showed a harder side when they stood together in order to divide and keep under those who were less fortunate. But there were free men among these 'inferiors' also. There were some among the burghers and the peasants whose status was independent of any man's caprice or favour. Each station and calling had its own standards of conduct, its own wisdom, and its own lapses from them.

Besides all this underlying uniformity there were lines of communication which bound this civilization together and sent impulses through it from end to end. Distance and remoteness impeded intercourse to a degree that we can scarcely imagine nowadays, and yet the paradox is true that the conditions of the time were more favourable to 'internationalism' and to mutual understanding between men from different countries than they are now. We often speak of a medieval 'internationalism' of which the most obvious expressions were the Catholic Church and the use of Latin by the educated classes, and we speak of it as if it resulted from the good dispositions of medieval men, and as if its disappearance was not merely a calamity but somehow reprehensible. This internationalism was, however, in another sense a symptom of weakness in civilization and not of strength. For the very reason that population was scanty, there were altogether very few men who pursued any of the more civilized and civilizing avocations. If these were to reach any high standard, indeed if they were to survive the dangers which beset them in a hostile or unconvinced society, their practitioners must not be solitary, but must to some degree draw together to share their knowledge and stand up for their common interests. Since they could not find enough of their own kind close about them to make such a community as they needed, they formed links with men like themselves in other places. We shall look in a moment from another point of view at the Church, in which the clergy of all Europe were organized for mutual support. We shall look at the universities; but for the present it will be best to take as an illustration one faculty of the universities, that of law, the next in seniority after theology, which stood first. Jurists in the universities were carrying on a great common enterprise of research and teaching. They were improving and transmitting an intellectual inheritance, of which the core was Roman law. Its study was very much alive, and it was proving itself increasingly useful in many countries, in spite of great differences of legal institutions and traditions. Law in general, and Roman law especially, formed an intellectual bond among the innumerable lawyers who practised in the courts or worked as officials for kings or lords or municipalities. The legal faculties of the universities communicated with one another. The lawyers had other, less visible, bonds, and so, although they had no single organization like the Church, they already formed a coherent profession over the whole area which that Church covered, a body which, as the price of its support, exacted from its members some degree of competent knowledge and conformity to a standard of professional honour.

Unity of this second kind, belonging not to the social founda-tions but to the superstructure of civilization, was transmitted mainly by definite routes. One town was linked with the next by a navigable river or coast, or by a road. The roads over a large part of Europe were chiefly the remains of the great system of military and administrative roads which the Romans had left behind them. They had fallen into disrepair because there was no longer a centralized empire that depended on them; but they still served the needs of the time, and they were sufficiently provided with inns and the other requirements of travellers. The influence of an artistic style or an idea may sometimes be traced along these routes. Building-stone was carried by water, and the map of local styles is often a network of irregular and narrow lines radiating along the rivers from the centres of quarrying. One of the characteristic religious movements of the time was that of the Brethren and Sisters of the Common Life in Germany and the Netherlands. It has been shown that all their houses were established in towns which traded with the annual fairs at Deventer, a few miles from the cloister which the great spiritual writer Thomas à Kempis made famous.

The unifying influence of the Church was the strongest of all, and it operated in many ways. At the highest levels there were conscious movements like this of the Common Life, intention-ally propagated through the channels of intercourse; and on the lower level of administrative activity there was no user of these channels to compare with the Church. Its organization was not only far larger than any other of any kind; it was also the oldest, the most experienced, the most regular and metho-dical in its operation. It preserved orthodoxy in belief by its inquisition; its hierarchy maintained something approaching uniformity of ritual and practice. In practical affairs the whole Church was centralized. Unions and divisions of parishes, dis-pensations to marry within the prohibited degrees, and innumer-able other matters of business were decided in Rome for the whole area which owned the papal supremacy. An ecclesiastical organization so vast and so complex came into daily contact at many points with every kind of authority outside the Church.

The landowner might fall out with the parson about tithe or a glebe-farm or a rent-charge; the king had few subjects more powerful than the bishops. In those countries which had been converted during the Dark Ages, ecclesiastics, even though they had no part in the government of towns or villages, sat in the 'estates' or parliaments and often ranked high among the great officers of state. In some places the bishop ruled as a prince; in others, where he had no such rights, his station and abilities might raise him to the highest offices. The clergy as a body were always able to keep some freedom from secular control. Long experience had shown that unmarried priests, even if many of them failed to live up to the ideal of celibacy, could remain free from the entanglements which marriage would have involved in a society founded on the family. They formed therefore, to a far higher degree than the lawyers or the doctors, a profession extending over the whole western world.

All this ecclesiastical structure rose from a common basis as deep and solid as the social groundwork of economic and political life, namely the religious needs of men and women. Apart from exceptions like those of the Jews, who were segregated, or the unconverted heathen of northern Sweden, Roman Catholic Christianity was not only the official religion but also the popular religion. Everyone except the people of the most inaccessible outlying farms could reach a church, and the churches were centres of worship. The parish clergy and the religious orders spread abroad, according to their lights, something of the many-sided devotional, ethical, and artistic inheritance. Every society, association, or institution had its religious observances, and no important transaction took place without the solemnity of an oath or a prayer. It was the Church which laid down and administered the law of marriage, the basis of the family, and so of the whole of society. In these and still other ways civilization was Christian.

No well-informed person supposed that all was well with the Church. There were many complaints of laxity among the clergy, and many writers criticized or satirized them. Europe was full of reformers, authorized or self-appointed, lay or clerical, orthodox or eccentric, local or universal, spiritual or practical, organizers or preachers, worthy or dangerous or merely futile. Some of them had done notable work. The Benedictine Order in the Netherlands and northern Germany had been reformed; high authorities had encouraged some, though not all, of the spontaneous movements of devotion, even when they assumed unaccustomed forms. But these achievements fell far short of what was needed. The Church lay in the shadow of the failure of the movement for reform by a general council; a failure which, after decades of negotiations and preparatory work, had extinguished all hope of a comprehensive and generally agreed reform of head and members. It was recognized that there were abuses in high, even in the highest, places which made it impossible to set matters right below; so that the Church could neither persuade nor compel its members to rise to the requirements of its own universality.

There was a failure of initiative which left the way open to other authorities less universal in their range. The conciliar movement had ended with concordats between the papacy and various kings, of which the general nature was that the central authority of the Church surrendered some of its control and allowed the kings to increase their share in the management of ecclesiastical business. Like most great and long-lasting transferences of authority, this was not merely an arrangement made from above; in some way it satisfied large numbers of the people whom it affected. For a long time national feeling had been growing up in various countries, and it grew most effectively where three factors contributed to it: a growth of vernacular language and literature, a tendency to dissidence or at least to administrative friction in religious matters, and the influence of a vigorous court. All these factors were present in France, and the French monarchy had won a certain degree of autonomy for the Gallican Church; but there were other countries, such as England, in which the gathering force of national consciousness, though perceptible in other ways, had not for a long time past disturbed the balance between the religious and the secular powers. Nowhere, however, were the forces entirely absent which might disturb that balance.

Next to that of the Church the greatest unifying achievement of this civilization was one derived from the Church and still dependent on it, that of organized knowledge and thought. At the middle of the fifteenth century there were more than sixty universities, from Coimbra in Portugal to Prague and Cracow and Buda; others were soon to be founded in north, south, east, and west. These universities were international in many senses. In their reading and teaching, and much of their everyday conversation, the scholars used Latin, the still living language of the Church, and so they were able to travel freely from one university to another, and to find everywhere at least some of the same great books and some of the same habits of mind. All the teaching was watched by ecclesiastical authorities, who had terrible powers of punishment in reserve, and this supervision, if it cramped the freedom of speculation, also promoted uniformity and made it easier for the educated men of different countries to understand one another.

The purpose of the universities was held to be the transmission of true beliefs about the various subjects of study. All the different subjects were held together in an elaborately articulated framework of doctrines. These doctrines had to conform to Christian principles, but there were different schools of philosophers, who disagreed profoundly about logical, metaphysical, and even ethical questions. The range of subjects was fairly wide, though in many of them the amount of actual knowledge was still very small. They included Latin grammar, logic, various literary studies, and not only theology but law, medicine, anatomy, astronomy, the theory of music, physics, and, at an elementary level, some other sciences. In the study of scientific subjects observation played some part, and the testing of hypotheses by experiment was not unknown; but, in general, science was learnt and taught in much the same way as the other subjects. In these there were two main methods. The first was made necessary by the scarcity and high cost of books in the days when they were all written out by hand: it was the exposition of standard textbooks. The second method was discussion. This was carried on in various ways, especially in formal disputations conducted according to set rules. It too was natural in communities of men and boys with few books but with many opportunities for meeting together. These two methods of teaching fostered certain special qualities of mind. Learning and acuteness were highly respected; a good memory, readiness in debate, and skill in constructing systematic arguments were the powers which brought reputation.

For a variety of reasons, some of which we shall notice later, the region in which thought was most active and original, both in the universities and outside them, was the study of classical antiquity. The Greek and Latin classics had always formed an inexhaustible reservoir of thought and imagination. Some of

their writers, such as Virgil, were specially esteemed because
they were believed to have had a place in the preparation for
Christianity; others, such as Aristotle, because Christian philosophers had built on their foundations. But, side by side with
these allies of the Christian tradition, there were others who
were absolute strangers to it. There were materialists, sceptics,
immoralists, and mockers. No censorship concealed them from
those who were learned enough to read them; and the scribes of
the monasteries and the university towns faithfully transmitted
everything in them, even if it was atheistic or obscene. For a
long time past the study of this inherited literature had been
growing deeper, more comprehensive, and more exact. Forgotten Latin books had been rediscovered; Italian and other
scholars had learnt Greek and had begun to collect Greek
manuscripts. In 1450 Pope Nicholas V, a friend to these studies,
founded the Vatican Library, and by that time there were many
active workers both in Italy and beyond the Alps who were
investigating not only the languages and literary methods of
the Greeks and Romans but also their antiquities in general.

Educated men were coming to believe that ancient literature
could teach much-needed lessons in many practical matters. In
philosophy and law, and in anatomy and other sciences, indeed,
Europe had already been learning from these masters for two
centuries, and the only great change now was that the Greek
writers were read in their original language, and in this and
other ways were better understood. But the field in which the
classics seemed to offer a new revelation was widening, and it
continued to expand for more than a century longer, until it included all the arts of government and war and many branches
of technology. At this time the fine arts were brought into it in
Italy, and there followed the greatest breach in the continuity
of artistic tradition in Europe since the fall of Rome. Before this
change architecture, sculpture, and painting, with their minor
accompaniments such as jewellery and embroidery, were very
rich, mature, and varied, providing outward decoration for
every phase of social life, expressing many moods, from the
heights of mystical religion to the quiet levels of family affection.
Whenever there was a respite from the toil of supplying immediate necessities, the craftsman or the needlewoman set to work.
There was no clear line between popular and aristocratic art,
nor did any distaste for incongruity keep the refined and the

delicate apart from the coarse and the grotesque. There had been schools of realistic painting in Italy and outside it for a considerable time, in which the method, though not the purpose, was to paint things and people as they were. Now Italians studied and imitated the classical remains of architecture and sculpture in the buildings and ruins about them. When new fragments were dug up intentionally or by chance they taught new lessons. In 1450 the Florentine Donatello was at work on the equestrian statue of Gattamelata at Padua, more splendid and technically more expert than any work of sculpture that had been made for a thousand years. Fifteen years earlier a writer, Leon Battista Alberti, soaked in the classics and familiar with the paintings of Florence and other north Italian cities, had written a prophetic treatise on painting which drew inspiration —since few ancient paintings survived—from classical sculpture. These two were among the leaders of a great movement of change which brought new skill and new ideals.

This movement of change was in part a revival of classical forms. In architecture the new men imitated Roman buildings so successfully that few people can see any essential difference between the models and the copies. They conceived a building as one whole, and threw away the old traditions of aisle beyond aisle, of pointed arch and crocketed gable, to build flat entablatures and low pediments above their Ionic or Corinthian pillars. In other arts they had not enough of the antique to make a new creative art merely by following the old; they took over this and that, but their antiquarian knowledge was confused and limited, and they did not retreat from the fields of artistic expression which had been opened up in the Christian centuries. They found a new sense of harmony and proportion, of simplicity and directness. They preferred ornaments in low relief to the deep shadows and sharp angles of Gothic carving; but they retained many of the traditional habits of eye and hand in form and colour, so that their revival was not merely learned but was able to live and create.

In their innovations there was a strong intellectual element. In architecture they calculated stresses and measured proportions. In painting they set themselves the scientific problem of representing material objects in relief like the relief of sculpture, straining to see them as they knew them to be in their measurable nature. Thus the higher forms of art began to draw away

from popular craftsmanship, and began to be comparatively
'abstract', that is specialized, distinguishing ornament from
structure. This intellectual tendency was intimately connected
with the classical studies of the scholars. These scholars were
not merely discovering what had happened in the past; they
stood for intellectual honesty in the search for truth, and they
were often critical and sometimes sceptical of the doctrines that
were generally received. They began to form 'academies',
voluntary societies of courtiers and scholars, who exchanged
ideas and literary productions, in a freedom altogether unlike
the regulated intercourse of the universities. They felt that they
were breaking away from the immediate past and resuming an
interrupted continuity with the ancient world. In 1483 Flavio
Biondo, a careful student of the monuments of ancient Rome,
blocked out the main lines of the history of the world from
A.D. 410 to A.D. 1410, as a period different from the preceding
and the following ages. He was not the first inventor of this
notion. Early in the fifteenth century the great German thinker
and ecclesiastic Nicholas of Cues had already referred to this
period as *media tempestas*, the Middle Age.

So far only a few exceptional men were conscious of this
transition, but as time went on awareness of it spread, partly
for reasons which we shall notice later, until it came to be
generally believed that there had been great changes in or soon
after the late fifteenth century in all the mutable parts of human
nature. A great historian completed the idea by inventing
the name 'the Renaissance', the rebirth, under which he tried
to group together, as aspects of the revival of antiquity,
all the revolutionary changes of those days, not only those
which we have mentioned, but also others to which we have
still to come. This idea, like the idea of the Middle Ages, did
good service, if only in reminding historians how every department of human life is influenced by every other; but it also did
harm by leading to fanciful comparisons between the naïve,
superstitious men of the ages of faith, whose universe seemed to
them familiar and friendly, or at least accessible to conciliation
by means of the Church; and the men of the Renaissance, fear-
less and free, asserting the rights of the individual, pouring out
a defiant literature of which Man was the hero, or substituting
the cold certainties of science for the comforts of religion. Such
interpretations of history try to compress into a phrase and

discern in a short stretch of years changes which are never alike in any two men, which are never complete in any one man, which draw their sinuous course through many generations. Continuities are never wholly broken. Many medieval habits and beliefs and institutions persisted until much later; some of them survive, but little altered, in our own time. The Renaissance was gathering force in the twelfth century, and it is still being continued by archaeologists, by grammarians, by artists, and by thinkers.

There is, however, another good reason for taking the middle of the fifteenth century as the beginning of a new age in western civilization. Except in one direction, the importance of which was not yet widely understood, and to which we shall pay attention in later chapters, the west was as good as cut off from the outer world. This one direction was the farthest south-west, where the Spanish kingdoms were on the brink of a new greatness of their own and whence the Portuguese were making their explorations in Africa. Portugal, the first in time of the seafaring states of the Atlantic coast, had a virtual monopoly of trade with West Africa and the Atlantic islands, and this trade brought in not only sugar, gold, ivory, pepper, and other cargoes, but also experience and ideas which in due course were destined to work revolutions. But these still lay in the future. The explorers were not in contact with any foreign civilization worth the name; as yet they had encountered only barbarous tribes. Western Christendom had learnt precious lessons in former centuries from one civilization outside its own borders, namely from Islam. Directly or through Jewish mediation western scholars were still acquiring something from Arabic learning and science, but little of importance that was new came from these sources now. A few missionaries and an occasional shipload of pilgrims to the Holy Places penetrated into the Islamic world; with the Christians outside Europe there was practically no contact. No other part of the world depended on Europe for its necessaries or its luxuries, and Europe did not derive its necessaries from any other part of the world. Asiatic and African ships were hardly ever to be seen in European ports, and the Italian traders, who brought gums and silks and spices from the ports of the Levant, supplied for the most part only the demands of luxury and display. Even in commerce Latin Christendom almost formed a closed world of its own. This isolation helps to explain the intensity of the preoccupation of the west with its own classical past.

Not only was western civilization isolated; there was a great and evident danger that Islam, which held southern Spain, all the North African shore and the Middle East, might overrun central and western Europe as well. The religion of Mahomet is the nearest to Christianity of all the major religions, so near that no Muslim people has ever become Christian and no Christian people has ever become Muslim; but in relation to their social setting the two religions were utterly unlike. The two institutions of polygamy and slavery made the ethical development of Islam differ from that of Christianity, while, on the other hand, they gave it an advantage in making converts. Arabic, the language of the Koran, which had never been translated by Muslims into any other, was the language not only of learning but of commerce; there was no priesthood and no distinction between religious and secular law, so that the merchant was a missionary, as effective in winning proselytes as a priest or a conqueror. To primitive peoples in Asia and Africa Islam brought literacy and the civilizing influence of the belief in one God. The Muslims held the simplest possible views of political authority. They recognized no nobility and no distinctions of rank: the authority of rulers was unlimited in both the religious and the secular spheres. They offered complete equality to all who accepted Islam; and even those, Christians, Jews, or heathens, who refused to change their religious allegiance were allowed to live and were not denied employment. These infidels were indeed subjected to capricious and sometimes cruel exactions and oppressions; but the advantages offered by Islam even to these classes of its subjects had helped it to spread, as it was still spreading, over a great part of the world. Pilgrims assembled every year in Mecca from southern Spain, from Nigeria, from Java, and from Turkistan. Over the world as a whole the Muslims far outnumbered the Christians. They were indeed divided by religious schisms and political frontiers; but the dynasty which faced Christendom in the east, that of the Ottoman Turks, was a formidable military power. More than a century before, a Byzantine emperor had called in its aid in a civil war, and so had given it a foothold in Europe. Ever since that time it had pushed its frontiers forward, step by step.

Half-way through the fifteenth century the Turks held all western and northern Asia Minor, and in Europe all Bulgaria, Thessaly, and Thrace except Constantinople and a mere patch of land about it. Virtually nothing was left to the eastern emperors except their capital, and this was cut off from the possibility of Christian help by sea or land. One Turkish army had been repelled from its walls a generation earlier, but in 1453 another appeared before them with the most powerful train of siege-artillery that had ever been assembled. The emperor made convulsive efforts to summon help. He offered even the supreme price of ecclesiastical conformity with Rome, but it was too late. The city was stormed and sacked. Under a pile of corpses someone saw eagles embroidered in gold on a pair of shoes, and so identified the body of the last direct successor of Constantine and Augustus.

This was the end of what had once been the most imposing of all Christian states. It gave the Turks the most populous city of Europe, and it made the patriarch of the east, the head of Orthodox Christianity, a subject of the sultan. It did not give great additional resources to the conquerors, and, from the strategic point of view, it merely removed an obstacle; but its moral significance was immense. It led to no answering blow. In the west there was indignant and vociferous emotion, but it was out of the question to organize common military action. There was no crusade.

It was from the south-east that western civilization was threatened; farther to the north its eastern boundary was neither dangerous nor abrupt. The endless plains between the Black Sea and the Baltic were sparsely populated by peoples whose life also was relatively self-contained. They imported manufactured goods from the west, especially textiles, metals, and munitions, exchanging them for primary products, the furs and wax of the forests, or corn, flax, and hemp from the cultivated lands. North of the Carpathians most of the inhabitants spoke Slavonic languages. This more northerly region was unlike any other in the world, because there two Christian civilizations had advanced across an intervening belt of heathendom and met. Poland was a fully western country, with the Roman Church, an educated class using the Latin language, universities, and Gothic art. Its kings, however, also held, in loose personal union with it, Lithuania. These two states had combined in successfully resisting the strong power of the Teutonic knights, a crusading military order which had become a territorial power and pressed southwards from its bases on the Baltic. Lithuania had become Christian centuries later than Poland, and its Christianity had come from the south-east; it followed the Orthodox rite, and its ritual language was Church Slavonic. In this, Lithuania was like the lands farther to the east, and in its ways of life it had little in common with Poland. It had no university; western ideas and practices were only slowly permeating it, and although politically joined to the west, economically and socially it had more in common with the east.

This eastern region was divided by vague and fluctuating frontiers, amongst which was one state stronger than the rest, the Russian state called Muscovy from its capital Moscow. There had recently been an ecclesiastical event in Moscow which was a sign of the times. Earlier in the century the Council of Florence had unsuccessfully attempted to reunite the Roman and Orthodox Churches. The Roman Catholics virtually refused to make any concessions to the Orthodox; but there remained a chance that the east, or parts of it, would so far admit western influences as to accept the decrees of the council. A metropolitan bishop of Moscow ventured on this step, but he was deposed. From that time his successors were always Russians, and they were no longer appointed by the patriarch in Constantinople. When Constantinople fell Moscow became the most important independent centre of the eastern Church, and it largely ceased to draw intellectual nourishment from the Greek-speaking world. It may almost be said that Muscovy remained a colonial country but no longer had a metropolis to look to. The grand dukes who reigned there had borrowed some of their methods of government from the warlike Tatar nomads to the east, on whose behalf they still collected tribute from their subjects, but in ceremonial and in the religious conception of monarchy their models were the Christian eastern emperors. Their state, unlike those of the west, had claims over the subject which were limited only by custom. The illiterate population enjoyed little personal or economic security; social life, with extreme contrasts of domination and servility, was completely strange to the few western visitors. Dress, the treatment of women, household furniture, and the ubiquitous eikons before which the people prayed, were all alien. There were no universities; there was no naturalistic art in painting or letters. Yet the Russians were neither Asiatic nor barbarians. They were civilized men, aware of their ethical difference from their Muslim neighbours to the south and their heathen neighbours to the east, and as consciously Christian as anyone in the west. Not only some of their monks and married priests but some of their laymen explored the recesses of the spiritual life. But their theologians had not passed through the intellectual discipline of scholasticism; their languages and practices almost isolated them from any exchanges with western thought, so that on this side too the west was communicating nothing and learning nothing from outside.

II

THE EUROPEAN STATE-SYSTEM

IN matters of government there was as much variety as in everything else. There were indeed limits to this variety. No state had two kings like ancient Sparta; no republic had kings as its vassals like ancient Rome. The prevailing types of kingship and lordship had come down from the barbarian conquerors of the ancient world, but institutions had grown up independently in many separate regions, and so had grown up differently. Sometimes a successful device was copied by one state from another; but there was no compelling reason for uniformity.

No clear line distinguished political from economic, especially agrarian, institutions. All property carried with it other rights and duties besides its merely economic rights and duties: the landowner was not merely entitled to the crops from his demesne and the rents or labour-services of tenants; he was, for some purposes, their judge, or their military leader and their representative, even perhaps an elected representative. The burgher not only had the right to keep shop in the town; he took his turn at watch and ward; he could be elected an alderman or mayor and so sit in a court of law. Conversely government was commingled with ownership, and there were not yet any supreme authorities which were charged with the duties of legislation, administration, and justice and with these alone. A king's realm was his estate. It might be elective, or it might descend by heredity and be combined with others by marriage, like any other feudal estate. The king had his rights over it, but his subjects as tenants had their rights too, not only in relation to their equals and inferiors, but in relation to their superiors and to the king himself. He had other estates besides his kingdom, and some of them he might hold of other kings. Europe was not divided up into exclusive sovereignties, but covered by overlapping and constantly shifting lordships. The kings, like all other owners, whether feudal lords or peasants, were apt to be hungry or greedy for land; either they added to their dominions or they lost them to stronger and more ambitious neighbours. So dynastic policy, especially in the matter of marriages and hereditary claims, played a great part in their fortunes; and, as it was a rough

world, with a headstrong military class, there was constant fighting, both on a small scale between neighbouring owners and on
a large scale between neighbouring kings.

Since political authority was proprietary its boundaries were
very loosely related to the communities over which it was
exercised. It was exceptional for a kingdom to lie all in a piece
with clearly-marked limits. Detached outlying provinces and
islands of foreign territory within the realm were common. The
subjects of a king did not usually consist of one national community. The only western kings in whose dominions only one
language was spoken seem to have been those of Portugal. At
the same time, as with all landed properties in all times, there
was a tendency to adjust their boundaries to those of real economic or geographical or social units. It suited the ambitious man
better to round off his estate or dominions than to acquire
some outlying land that would be harder to manage. It was
better for defence to have a definite frontier. It was better for
administration, from the subjects' point of view as well as the
ruler's, that one man should have the right to all the dues or
taxes within a compact dominion than that a number of rivals
should send their collectors, with armed escorts, to collect what
they could from ill-defined and intermingled areas. It was better
for justice and order that criminals should not always have
a sanctuary close at hand in some other jurisdiction. So, for a
hundred reasons of common sense and general advantage, there
was this tendency for kingdoms, like other estates, to become
consolidated.

The more consolidated were fitter to survive in the struggle
for existence, and they had a better chance of strengthening
and rationalizing their organization. Two types of organization
were now found almost everywhere side by side. On the one
hand was the central administration of the kings and the
greater lords. These employed educated and disciplined civil
servants, either clerics or laymen, who used such scientific
methods as were available, for instance mapping and elementary statistics, for ascertaining the resources of their dominions
and laying them out to the best advantage. They hired armies
of mercenary troops, more reliable than the feudal levies of
knights. They tightened up and systematized the collection of
taxes and the administration of justice, often with the aid of the
rules of Roman law, which were based on a simple conception

of authority and obedience. All this rested ultimately on finance and so on the growth of commercial wealth and of the business class. It had reached a far higher stage of development in the trading republic of Venice than anywhere else. Here an efficient aristocracy directed what was for those days a large international commerce, and ruled over extensive territories in Italy, on the Balkan coast, and in the Greek islands, using systematic statistical information as the groundwork of its policy.

In the simpler and poorer countries, those where town-life was less highly developed, the central authorities could not command such complex machinery. Instead of dealing directly with their individual subjects, they had to receive their information and pass down their decisions through intermediate authorities who were not their own servants but who owed their positions to their own rank or power, that is, usually to their positions as landowners or feudal lords. In Poland and Hungary, for instance, central machinery, for lack of a middle class, had made little headway, and the kings could do nothing except through their feudatories. On the other hand the assemblies of 'estates' had spread all over western and central Europe. In order to get the assent of those who would have to pay and obey, kings had always consulted some of their subjects, with more or less formality, and as time had gone on they had found it best to assemble together from time to time not merely the chief men but some of those below them who were coming to have such a mind and status of their own that the feudal magnates could no longer answer for them so satisfactorily as they had once done. The Church had a long experience of elective representative machinery and to some extent this served as an example. Thus most of the kingdoms had general or regional gatherings, more or less rigidly divided up into sections corresponding to the main divisions of the community and reflecting, in their functions and their degree of independence, the position of their members. In most of them there appeared the greater nobles, a select number of the lesser landowners, and representatives of the townsmen. In a good many countries, especially in times of crisis, the estates might venture on opposition to the civil servants, or to the feudal magnates, or to the kings themselves. They might try to enlarge their functions; they might become a factor in the general contest for power.

Although we can generalize to this extent about political

conditions, the picture was infinitely confused and irregular and there were exceptions to every rule. In the Holy Roman Empire there were two strata of monarchy, one above the other. The emperor had a very feebly developed central government, with an assembly of estates, called the diet, which came, roughly speaking, from Germany, Bohemia, and parts of the Netherlands. In it there was a house of seven 'electors', powerful princes who elected their emperor; then there was a house representing the less important members of the second stratum, and there were representatives of some of the greater towns. But there were other towns which were subject to the authorities of the second stratum, and these authorities were more than 300 in number, varying in rank and power from the kings of Bohemia through electors, dukes, margraves, and counts to 'free imperial knights' who were no more than small landed proprietors. Each of these, if his dominions were of any size, might have his own assembly of estates. Nominally the empire extended outside Germany, Bohemia, and the Low Countries, including northern and central Italy; but here the emperor had few powers left besides that of appointing to vacant fiefs. Here the strongest states were virtually independent principalities like Milan or republics like Venice. Beyond the nominal boundaries of the empire almost all Europe was monarchical. In the west and south the monarchies were hereditary; in Poland, Hungary, Denmark, and Sweden the crowns, like that of the empire itself, were elective.

Christianity stood, as it had always stood in some sense, for an ideal of peace; the word 'peace' sounded in changing contexts through its prayers and observances; but the Church did not command all Christian men never to fight against any of their fellow men. Ecclesiastics taught, as the jurists also taught, that some wars were just, and although they did something towards humanizing and restraining warfare, they did not try to abolish it altogether. Only superior strength could restrain the princes or the feudal lords or aggrieved individuals or even burghers and churchmen from using force to assert what they claimed as their rights. Every state was organized to fight against anarchy within and against enemies without, and men who looked about them with clear eyes regarded warfare as necessarily bound to recur whenever the conditions were ready for it.

The character of warfare, and the conditions in which it

comes about, are always changing, and at this time these changes had effects on the character of civilization. The consolidation of states was not merely a change in their internal structure; it was even more clearly seen in their mutual relations. The conflicts of states and their consolidation furthered one another reciprocally. A state tightened its organization in order to be strong against its rivals, and the strength which it acquired in the contest for power in turn strengthened its government at home. The organs which it developed for conducting foreign policy were specially fitted to act quickly, secretly, and according to unhampered calculations of interest, and so they reinforced the other tendencies which were bringing these qualities forward in social and political organization. The small states of Italy showed perhaps more of these qualities in the middle of the fifteenth century than any others, and it was among them that a new machinery of diplomacy developed. In the Middle Ages the only international assemblies were the ecclesiastical councils and the only well-developed system of diplomacy was that which linked the bishops, the religious orders, and other components of the Church with one another and with Rome. The mutual relations of states were carried on by intermittent negotiations through heralds, jurists, and ecclesiastics. These ambassadors performed occasional missions, but they were distrusted as a ceremonious kind of spies. From about 1448 Florence and Milan found that it suited them in their rivalry with Venice to maintain standing representatives at one another's courts. The Italian states soon multiplied their alliances, undertook greater obligations to one another, for longer periods of time and over a wider geographical area, and this system spread. By the middle of the sixteenth century there was a network of standing diplomacy which included everything west of Turkey, the exception that proved the rule.

With the machinery of diplomacy the forms of intercourse developed. There were rules of etiquette. The first manuals of diplomatic practice were compiled. The immunities of ambassadors were defined, such as freedom from arrest and from other kinds of obstruction, for the present without much success: in the sixteenth century they were violated with impunity. The more efficient governments devised intelligence services and received able reports on the affairs of other states. The language of diplomacy was Latin, but as early as 1508 French began to appear in some of the formal documents exchanged in negotiations. In 1504 the first official order of precedence among states was drawn up, a papal list of Christian kings, with a list of ruling dukes which followed it. The body of international law which dealt with larger matters grew more solid and won wider acceptance. The line of the classical writers on international law begins with the Spaniard Francisco de Victoria who was writing in the fifteen-thirties. There was no separate diplomatic profession until long after his time—missions were still given to ecclesiastics, jurists, noblemen, soldiers, or other men of position or ability—but there was a diplomatic tradition.

All this was symptomatic of the rise of an actual system of states. From about this time the states of Europe could be classified in war, and in the peaceful combinations which were entered into in anticipation of war, or to prevent it, into three groups. There were great powers; there were satellite allies; and there were neutrals. Much of the history of Europe turned on their action in these capacities or on their movements from one of these classes to another. In building up their strength the great powers availed themselves of support from within the frontiers of other states; they organized and helped their supporters. Thus the internal divisions of states, which had been mainly feudal or local or concerned with the relations between State and Church, now became more involved with international relations, and discontent very often turned into collaboration with the enemies of the state.

The richest, the most populous, and the most highly civilized of all European kingdoms was France. It had perhaps twelve million inhabitants. A great historic achievement had brought a new national consciousness into this feudal society. The expulsion of the English, begun by Joan of Arc, was completed a few weeks after the fall of Constantinople. It left, however, as a sequel a second great national task, that of checking the ambition of the dukes of Burgundy. This branch of the royal house of France had built up a new power on the northern and eastern frontiers of the kingdom. To their original duchy they had added other lands, some of them fiefs of the empire, besides the richest parts of the Netherlands, the greatest western centre of trade and manufactures. Their court at Bruges was unsurpassed for artistic and ceremonial display, and in it worked

PLATE 25

The Master of Mary of Burgundy: The Virgin and Child worshipped
(See p. xxiii)

as able a body of administrators as any in the world. They made conquests and alliances. After a long contest of craft and tenacity their great plans fell to pieces when the Duke Charles the Bold was killed in battle in 1477; but the heiress of Charles the Bold still ruled the Netherlands and Franche-Comté, and she took her inheritance in marriage to the Archduke Maximilian, the son of the emperor, who became emperor himself in 1493. France thus became the immediate neighbour of that ever-advancing Austrian house of Habsburg from which the emperors were elected in that age. The Burgundian problem was not ended, or the English problem either, for the English were still in Calais. Their economic interests were closely bound up with those of the Netherlands, and often enough they had found allies there in the Burgundian princes. Towards the end of the fifteenth century the French had a respite from these anxieties, but it was only a respite. In the meantime they were acquiring new lands, and in 1486 the acquisition of Provence gave them an important part of the Mediterranean seaboard.

Along the coast from Provence was Italy, splendid but politically chaotic. Its entire population was perhaps half that of France, but it was divided into a score of little states. The Venetian republic, the most stable, had substantially more than a million inhabitants in its Italian territories. West of it was the duchy of Milan, with nearly a million people, but with less to boast of in government or in the arts. Florence, smaller still, under its Medici rulers, was the most brilliant centre of art and intellect in all Europe. Round these were crowded the duchy of Savoy, with its Alpine passes, the maritime republic of Genoa, the financial and commercial states of Siena and Lucca, and little, fighting states ruled by *condottieri* who had troops for hire or, on occasion, for their own ambitious purposes. South of all these the papal states, the largest of all ecclesiastical principalities, ill governed and almost disintegrated among the nominally subordinate rulers of its towns, sprawled from sea to sea across the Apennines. The whole of the southern half of the peninsula belonged to the 'Kingdom', Naples, the only kingdom in Italy, sparsely peopled and numbering much less than a million inhabitants. Sicily belonged to the Spanish kingdom of Aragon, but had its own estates and administration.

The royal house of France had feudal claims to the inheritance of both Milan and Naples, not more frivolous than some of the other claims that kings and lords were constantly putting forward as pretexts for aggression. There were exiles who urged the young French King Charles VIII to assert his claims; there were reformers who hoped that he would take up their cause and depose the reigning Pope Alexander VI, the most disreputable of all the popes, the Spanish Borgia. Charles had an army of perhaps 30,000 men, the strongest in Europe. It was not a feudal army. The infantry were foreign mercenaries, largely Swiss, for military service was the chosen export industry of these mountaineers, an industry in which they excelled. The heavy cavalry or *gens-d'armes* were the younger sons of French landowners, first-rate in quality. The artillery and the engineers were the best in the world. In 1494 Charles led this army into Italy. No one could stop his advance, and by the next year he had settled the affairs of Milan and Florence to his liking and had been crowned king in Naples itself. But the struggle for supremacy in Italy which he began was to last until 1559 and during all that period to dominate the international relations of western Europe.

It was to be expected that even a victorious campaign would give an opportunity for rival powers and that successes in Italy would excite their jealousies. Charles had insured himself against them by a diplomatic preparation for the war. He had provided against any reopening of the Burgundian question by restoring some recently occupied territories to Maximilian, and on his other flank he had conceded a claim of the King of Aragon to two frontier provinces. In making his move into Italy he may indeed have intended to forestall a Spanish intervention there, and it was in no way surprising that Spain should have been one of the powers which drew together defensively when it looked as if Charles would master all Italy. Some of these powers did not matter seriously. Milan was divided by faction; Venice could be bought off with the Apulian ports, and this concession put Venice at odds with the pope. But the emperor, Maximilian's father, had his rights over the northern Italian states and he had his own ambitions there. And opposition from any of these powers would be dangerous if Spain were behind them.

The history of the Iberian peninsula in the fifteenth century was unlike that of any other part of Europe. For the most part it was barren land, much divided by natural barriers, and its population was smaller than that of France, perhaps eight millions in Spain and less than two in Portugal. But while Islam was sweeping forward in the east, the Christian kingdoms of this south-western peninsula were advancing and growing in power. The Portuguese were pushing forward by sea and the Spaniards were driving back the Moors on land. This movement was in some ways comparable with the expulsion of the English from France. It created special types of feudal powers, for instance, great military orders, and fiefs which were almost independent like that of Burgundy. It by no means prevented rivalries between the various Christian kingdoms. In 1462 the kingdom of Castile took a step forward, acquiring Gibraltar and other places, and the right to an annual tribute from the Moors. There was nothing left now of Muslim Spain except the small kingdom of Granada, encircled on the land side from sea to sea by Castile. Castile was feudal and military and had little sea-borne trade. It had more of the crusading spirit than either of its neighbours, Portugal and Aragon, and might look forward to great achievements if it could unite with either of them. Portugal, as we have seen, was the trading and crusading state of the Atlantic. It had been fully independent from the thirteenth century; in the fifteenth it normally enjoyed peace with Castile and an English alliance. It made conquests, and it had a foot-hold in Morocco and on the west coast of Africa and in the Atlantic islands. On the Mediterranean shore, drawing much of its civilization from France across the Pyrenees, was Aragon, with about a quarter the area of Castile, most of whose inhabit-ants spoke Catalan, Valencian, and Italian: Aragon looked east-wards. It owned the Balearics, Sardinia, and Sicily. It had close relations with Genoa and Naples.

Almost accidentally dynastic policy brought about a personal union of Castile with Aragon in 1474. It was not converted into an organic constitutional union until long afterwards, and Spanish nationality was far less solid and uniform than French. In Castile the monarchy had to contend with privileged nobles and municipalities, but the *cortes*, the assembly of estates, were relatively weak; in Aragon they were stronger, and the liberties of the four component parts of the kingdom were firmly rooted. But Ferdinand and Isabella built up a strong central admini-stration of the new professional type, which gradually streng-thened its hold over government at the expense of all the other authorities. The 'Catholic kings', as they were called, acquired a unique control over ecclesiastical affairs, an ecclesiastical despotism. The personal union immediately altered the whole political state of the peninsula. The Moors in Granada were foolish enough to refuse to pay their tribute and to seize a frontier fortress. There followed a war of ten years, from 1482 to 1492. Granada was divided by dynastic quarrels. The Castilian fleet cut it off from Africa and blockaded its ports. The Spanish army was mainly feudal, and it was poor in quality; but there was enthusiasm behind it. A new national force, the *hermandad*, was recruited; Switzers were hired and other foreigners volunteered. It was a war of sieges, and the Christian artillery and engineers, some of them foreigners, though crude were effective. Granada surrendered on liberal terms and the last Muslim kingdom in western Europe disappeared. The terms were violated; there were rebellions and punitive expeditions until 1508; but there has never been any revival of Moorish rule.

A new power was coming into existence. At the same time Spain displayed a new mastery in many of the arts of civilization. During the war Queen Isabella started the first modern field-hospital. In the year when it ended one of her subjects presented to her the first grammar of the Castilian language, which was the first grammar of any modern language. New universities were founded. Thought was active; organization, discipline, the assimilation of the newly conquered south moved forward together. The conquest of Granada naturally led to a further advance in the same direction. It was followed immediately by a reconnaissance of North Africa, to which the refugees from Granada had crossed. In 1509 the great minister Cardinal Ximenes accompanied an expedition which captured Oran.

The Spaniards held Oran for 200 years, and they followed up its conquest by taking Tripoli; but their pressure rallied the forces of Islam, and the conquest of Egypt by the Turks enabled them to come to the rescue of Tunis and Algiers. In alliance with the Turkish sultan these newly founded states were saved by sea-power, and the Spaniards, from about 1515, were checked by a new maritime resistance, a Holy War at sea. And the Spaniards had never turned their backs on Europe to concentrate their new energies on Africa. The western Mediterranean was a single theatre of trade, of politics and of war, and from the first successes of Charles VIII of France in Italy, Ferdinand and Isabella had been drawn into the Italian struggle.

The price which Charles had paid for their neutrality was high; but they watched every step of his advance with jealous apprehension, and the bribe was not rich enough to make them contemplate with equanimity the sight of a French king in Naples. The French were sometimes powerful and sometimes weak, but no other power took a strong initiative in Italy. The Italian states and the neighbours of Italy grouped themselves in short-lived alliances, chopping and changing as they hoped more from uniting against the French or from sharing in the spoils of French victories. Charles's rule in Naples lasted only from summer to autumn: when Ferdinand, the emperor, the Pope, Milan, and Venice combined against him he had to withdraw. Two years later the emperor and Venice had dropped out of the coalition; but the Spaniards and the Neapolitans drove the French forces out of south Italy. A second phase of the French adventure began when Charles's cousin Louis XII succeeded to the throne in 1498. He handed over a further instalment of frontier places to the Duke of Burgundy to keep him neutral, and he had both the Pope and Venice on his side. For a time it looked as if this would lead to a rearrangement of the map of Italy. The French established themselves in Milan and gratified the ambitions of Venice for an improved land-frontier. Caesar Borgia, the ruthless and able son of the Borgia pope, made the papal state into an efficient despotism. Ferdinand of Aragon thought it best to agree to a partition of Naples. But these events did not correspond with the realities of power. Venice lost a sea-battle against the Turks, and had no strength to maintain the new mainland possessions that she had rashly acquired. The Spanish army had been quietly growing in size and efficiency, especially its infantry. When Louis accepted the surrender of Naples from its king, he brought this force down upon him. The Spanish general, Gonsalvo de Cordova, 'the great captain', marched through the kingdom winning battles. The French failed miserably in a double invasion of Spain to the east and to the west across the Pyrenees. Naples was annexed to Aragon in 1504, and the dream of French power in southern Italy was ended.

For the remaining ten years of his life King Louis still counted for something in Italy, but his footing there depended on the vicissitudes of the constantly shifting alliances, and the French showed no greater common sense than the sharp-witted Italians

in distinguishing petty immediate gains from solid and permanent interests. Louis tried an offensive alliance with Burgundy,
but this time he tendered so great a price in territory that the
French states general made a stand for national interests, declaring that the provinces which he offered were inalienable and that
the princess whose dowry they were to be must marry Louis's
own heir. The last remaining ally was the Pope, the warlike
Julius II, and it was Julius who gained from this combination,
by turning the French against the Venetians and taking all he
needed from the republic. The Emperor Maximilian, who joined
in the attack on Venice, failed to win anything. Then the
French quarrelled with the Pope. They talked of a council, and
a council, hostile to the Pope, did meet at Pisa and afterwards at
Milan. Louis had victories, then defeats, then victories again in
north Italy. In 1515 he died, and his successor, Francis I, had to
face renewed war with Spain. He marched an army over the
Alps, won a battle, and broke the power of the Swiss in north
Italy. In 1516 there was a settlement. The French claim to
Milan was recognized and the Pope restored the disputed
border-places to it. The Concordat of Bologna regulated the
relations of Church and State in France. This diminished the
power and independence of the bishops and handed over much
of the control of ecclesiastical affairs to the king and the Pope.
As between these two it amounted almost to a grant of independence to the Gallican Church. Thus Francis, like Ferdinand,
though to a lesser degree, had added ecclesiastical to his temporal power.

There were indeed ideas in the air which denied the whole
way of thinking on which this settlement was founded. Two
books which were written in the year 1513 show how fundamental they were.[1] Niccolo Macchiavelli, a Florentine official
who was an historian, a playwright, and a master of Italian
prose, wrote his *Prince*, a handbook of the arts of political success.
It admits no place in these arts to justice or mercy, and its hero
is Caesar Borgia; but it calls up the vision of an Italy united and
free from foreign rule. The other masterpiece of 1513 was the
anonymous pamphlet *Julius Exclusus*, a dialogue on the shutting
out of the dead Pope Julius from the Heaven which he had not

---

[1] Machiavelli's *Prince* circulated freely in manuscript during his lifetime but was
first printed, with papal sanction, in 1532 after his death; the *Julius Exclusus* was
published in 1514 at Cambridge.

deserved. This denunciation of the worldly and victorious pon-
tiff was an expression of Christian ethics, but there was something revolutionary in it. It was written secretly by Erasmus, a
classical and Biblical scholar of the highest celebrity, born in
Holland but a restless wanderer over Europe, brought up as
a churchman but never satisfied with the life that the Church
could offer him. Like Macchiavelli's book it was not medieval:
it had a directness that derived something from the ancient
classics. And in their different ways these two books were signs
of fundamental changes in civilization then coming to fruition,
to which we must soon turn our attention. Before we do that,
however, we must look at eastern Europe and see how its relations
with the west were affected by the changes we have already
noticed.

Naturally both the intellectual movements and the changes
in political organization had their influence in that part of the
world. About the middle of the fifteenth century Italian architects went to work in Moscow, where Italian work still stands
in the Kremlin. But the fall of Constantinople came at a time
when Muscovy was growing stronger. The Tatars of the
Golden Horde were weakened by emigrations, and the Prince
Ivan III, called the Great (1462–1505), by allying himself with
the Khan of the Crimea, played off one set of Tatars against
another and freed himself from paying tribute. As the Turks
advanced in the Black Sea region the western powers turned
their eyes in that direction, seeking for allies. The Papacy and
Venice arranged a marriage between Ivan and a niece of the
last eastern emperor. As late as 1519 a papal legate was in
Moscow spinning plans. The Habsburgs also tried to draw Ivan
into their system of alliances. In 1486 a Silesian merchant
travelled across Lithuania to Moscow and reported to Vienna
what he had seen. He was sent back on a diplomatic mission:
the Emperor Maximilian offered to invest Ivan as king and to
bring him into the European system. Ivan replied that he
needed no investiture. He made the startling suggestion of an
offensive alliance to gain Hungary for Maximilian and Lithuania for himself. The exchanges of diplomatic missions with the
emperor led to no more results than those with the popes. From
the point of view of the west Muscovy was a new but an in-
tractable power. From the Russian point of view a western

question had arisen, the problem how to take advantage of
western technical skill without losing independence. At the
same time the west and the Baltic were the most inviting field for
using the state's new strength to make conquests. The Turks
were strong and there was every reason to trade with them and
to maintain friendly relations. Ivan III invaded Finland. The
trading republic of Novgorod was the centre of trade with the
league of north German cities called the Hanse, and it was a
centre of Russian civilization only less important than Muscovy.
Ivan turned against it and mastered it. He transferred some of
the inhabitants to the south, and terminated the trade of the
Hanse. Then he made war on Lithuania, and a few years after
his death the Russians took Pskov and Smolensk. In 1518 Ivan's
successor, Basil III, in official correspondence with the emperor,
used the title of tsar, the Russian form of Caesar. That was
as much as to say that there was a second state-system over
against that of the west and not to be absorbed into it, but a
system consisting of one state. Nevertheless, Russia was not yet
a great power like the consolidated states of the west. It could
not compare with them in military strength. It was ambitious,
but ambitious rather to extend its frontiers than to conquer
other states. It did not contemplate adventures at a distance.

No considerations of distance limited the ambitions of the
Turks, nor did they feel any doubt of their military superiority
to the west. That the west had special skill in certain arts and
industries they recognized; but the products could easily be
bought. Curiosity about western ways did not lead to imitation.
Mahomet II, the conqueror of Constantinople, sat for his portrait to the Venetian painter Vittorio Carpaccio, whose pictures
of St. George and St. Ursula are popular nowadays for the
naïve and childlike sentiment that is mistakenly read into them.
But he did not westernize his army or his state.

The social organization of the Turkish empire was utterly
unlike that of Europe and it was well fitted to turn military
victory into lasting conquest. There were no legally recognized
distinctions of status or class. The Turks themselves were a
minority, but they were not a governing class. Among the officials, who were entirely dependent on the sultan, were Slavs,
Greeks, Albanians, Georgians, and some Italians. The Greek
Church was as docile to the sultans as it had been to the Byzan-

PLATE 26

Vittore Carpaccio, St. Jerome in his Oratory. (See p. xxiii)

tine emperors. Many Christians kept their lands or gained promotion by renouncing their faith, but the remainder were contemptuously tolerated. Although there was no industry, and
the export trade in Syrian silks and Egyptian spices was in the
hands of Europeans, the state had the largest and most regular
revenues of any, and it was the only state in Europe with a
constant surplus. Taxation was light and diminished as the
empire grew, because there was no proportionate increase of
the army. The military equipment was inferior to that of the
west, but artillery was imported, and though the Turkish
artillery was inferior in quality, none of it was needed to preserve internal order and so the whole was available on the
frontier. In the same way the technical inferiority of the other
troops, who were drawn from relatively backward peoples, was
outweighed by their numbers and organization. They were not
mercenaries, like those of the west or those of the old eastern
empire; they were conscripts, raised by the 'tribute of children'
mainly from conquered Christian territories in Europe, especially Serbia and Albania. These janissaries, of whom there were
8,000, could not marry. They were the only standing army of the
time, the only army that remained on foot through the winter
from one campaign to another. In quality they were inferior
to the best western infantry, but their pay was regular; their
musters were full; commanders and men spoke one language.
They were the nucleus of an army in which the best troops were
the numerous light cavalry. This was the period in which infantry was taking the place of cavalry as the decisive arm; but
for the present the Turkish land forces as a whole were very
nearly invincible. At sea they had no such advantage. They had
many ships; but they were badly built and the crews were badly
trained.

The Ottoman empire was far more powerful than any European state, and it was growing. Between 1485 and 1559 its
area was trebled. In his reign of thirty years Mahomet II subjugated all the remaining Greek independent states, besides
Albania, and all the remaining Slav states in the Balkans except
for the region about Montenegro. He took the Genoese possessions in the Crimea and made the Crim Tatars his tribu-
taries. He did indeed fail before Rhodes, and the Venetians
held on to a few points on the eastern coast of the Adriatic
besides their islands, but at the end of his life he made the

formidable advance of establishing his power on the heel of Italy by capturing Otranto. A year later, after Mahomet's death, Otranto was retaken. Islam never again came so near to closing the Adriatic or to overrunning Italy; but farther east its advance was not checked. Moldavia, which had regained its independence in the latter part of the fifteenth century and even set out on a brief career of conquest, was overpowered early in the sixteenth. The defence of the Levant was improved when the Venetian republic accepted the cession of Cyprus from its last queen; but ten years later the Turks defeated the Venetian fleet, and Venice returned to her normally amicable relations.

Europe was preserved only because their European affairs were always less important to the Turks than those in Asia. From 1512 to 1520 the Sultan Selim the Grim made enormous advances there. He took wide provinces from Persia. Turning southwards he conquered Syria and Egypt. These events gave Europe a respite; but they portended danger.

If the western states had been capable of combination they could have taken advantage of the weaknesses of the Turks in armament, in infantry, and at sea; but they were incapable of it. They allowed the Turks to attack them one at a time. The Catholics did not help the Orthodox. The Venetians were hampered by the jealousies of their Italian neighbours, and by the Austrian Habsburgs who were increasing their territories at the head of the Adriatic. So, in the eighty years after the fall of Constantinople there was nothing resembling an alliance against the Turks. The growth of the western state-system was feeble in comparison with the mounting Turkish danger.

III

PRINTING

IN the year after the fall of Constantinople Pope Nicolas V proclaimed an indulgence, a remission of spiritual penalties for their sins, for all who would contribute money to the defence of Cyprus against the Turks. It happens that the announcement of this indulgence is the earliest piece of paper printed from movable type in Europe to which we can assign a definite date. We have no reason to suppose that anyone foresaw the full significance of this new technological contrivance. Certainly Mahomet II, if he ever heard of it, did not infer that the west had new reserves of strength and inventiveness which in time would reverse its relations with the east. Looking back on it now we can see, in spite of many obscurities in our defective records, that the invention of printing, as we commonly call it, was more than a signal that enormous changes were to come. It also proved that the way had already been prepared for them by a number of converging alterations in society.

Something of the same sort had been known in China long before this time, and we cannot be certain whether the Europeans learnt printing directly or indirectly from the Chinese or found it out for themselves. We do not even know exactly when or where it was first practised in Europe, but our ignorance of these matters reinforces the knowledge that the new art was not brought full-grown from outside to a western civilization wholly unprepared for it, as the telephone was brought to nineteenth-century Africa. There had been a series of preparatory stages on the technical side. As early as the thirteenth, or even the twelfth, century designs had been printed on textile fabrics from wood blocks cut in relief. Until the beginning of the fifteenth century writing had to be done on parchment and similar materials made from skins, of which the quantity was necessarily limited and the price comparatively high. From that time, however, there were ample supplies of rag-paper, and these made it possible for book-production and writing in general to expand indefinitely. Block-printing on paper came in: there were wood-cut pictures of saints and playing-cards. Then only a few adaptations of presses and block-making were necessary to perfect the art, and the final steps were taken most likely in Mainz, a rich trading town and a cultivated ecclesiastical capital.

The preparation had been not only on the technical side; it also sprang from changes in men's minds. So far as we can tell, the technical improvements could perfectly well have been made much earlier if anyone had wanted them, and there are two reasons for thinking that in some way a new desire for devices of this kind came into being. First, although most historians now reject the competing claims of places other than Mainz to call the invention their own, there is enough substance in them to prove that it was taken up very quickly in other places, particularly in that great centre of the arts and manufactures, the Netherlands. It may even have been worked out independently in more places than one at about the same time. Secondly, printing was not the only development from the wooden block-engravings. Men were, we may say, experimenting outwards from this in various directions. One was *intaglio* engraving, in which, instead of standing up like the black parts of type or of a woodcut, the engraved line is cut into the wood or metal, and the paper is pressed into it to take the ink. A whole group of methods of engraving are based on this principle, so that before the middle of the fifteenth century artists had at their disposal several methods of reproducing their works exactly in many copies.

This was something new, something which immediately began to change men's ways of seeing and working. There were some engravers who made their own drawings, others who engraved pictures drawn by other men for other purposes. Works of art became familiar which were not unique, or approximately like their originals, as hand-drawn copies may be, but so nearly identical that for ordinary purposes there was no difference. Many people could possess the same picture. That was a very great change, but there were others. By constantly seeing woodcuts and other engravings, people acquired a new habit or power of seeing not in colour but in black and white, which in some ways enriched and in other ways impoverished their mode of seeing. The world of sight and imagination altered. For nearly 400 years—until the beginnings of photography—there was no fresh development to compare with this, but throughout these centuries the modes of seeing continued to change, gaining new delicacies of perception or losing familiar satisfactions. Besides these changes in and from the visual arts there ran even greater and more frequent changes in the nature of reading and writing, and their uses in life, more pregnant because they affected all kinds of men and women in almost everything they did or thought.

No sooner was printing discovered than a great demand for printed books and papers made itself effective throughout all the Latin area. Within a generation there were presses at work in France, Italy, Spain, the Netherlands, England, and Denmark. Before the end of the century Portugal and Sweden had them, and even Montenegro, the Balkan outpost. Books, of course, could be exported to countries where there was no printing; in the sixteenth century a well-organized international book-trade grew up, serving most of the western countries. From the very first there were two kinds of copy for the printers, just as there were two kinds of originals for the engravers. On the one hand the printers made available editions of the books already existing in the world, every sort of books, from the Greek and Latin classics to the most recently popular romances. This task was so enormous that it has not yet been, and probably never will be, completed: there were so many books and documents in manuscript that it was necessary to select the most important, but, as the process went on, fresh claims were always coming forward, either from chance discoveries in old libraries or from the opening up of whole literatures, like those of the east, as the knowledge of languages extended. In both these ways the expansion of the known past in literature has always gone on with endless acceleration. On the other hand—and this is the main reason why the printers have not caught up with the printing of what was already written before printing was invented—they have always had to divide the use of their machinery between this task and the competing task of printing what was being newly written in their time. Along with the old, the first printers also disseminated the new, and very soon there were talented authors who wrote specially for the press. We have seen already that they lived in a time when the new, in literature and thought, was exceptionally different from the old, and exceptionally attractive. By putting it quickly into many people's hands, and by postponing the printing of much that had recently become old-fashioned, the early printers helped to cut off their contemporaries and their successors from the immediately preceding centuries.

Books could now be produced far more quickly, far more cheaply, and in far greater numbers. This was a revolution, a revolution continuing until, in our own time, the new inventions for reproducing sound have ended the age in which the printed word has been the main vehicle for spreading knowledge, information, ideas, and even emotions abroad. Beneath all the events of these centuries there has gone on the change from the first printers, who could put out a few hundred copies of a book in a few weeks, to the modern printers who can make a million copies of a newspaper in a few hours. The world has been filled with these uncountable printed sheets and volumes, large and small, cheap or costly, rare or universally familiar, durable or ephemeral, treasured or neglected, commonplace or exquisitely beautiful. Every one of them has left some result behind it, and the sum of these results is far beyond calculation.

It is easy to see that printing made the spread of literacy much easier; and the power to read and write is an instrument of authority if it belongs to a few, but a stepping-stone to equality if it belongs to many. As the number of readers increased, the influence of writers grew with it. In universities, in public affairs, and among general readers there were more books to be had, and so the more personal influence of the teacher or expositor gave way before the might of the book, of the unseen author. Literary reputations could be made and spread as quickly as ships and horses could carry packages of books. Erasmus had a European reputation, and every book he published was known from one end of the continent to the other as soon as it was ready. Every man who could read or be read to was accessible to persuasions, propaganda, from far and near, perhaps authorized, perhaps directed against established ideas and institutions. Governments and the Church, trying, in accordance with their traditions, to keep their control of men's minds, made rules of censorship and new institutions for enforcing them; but the simple machinery of government which they had at their disposal was often unable to dam the rising streams. From clandestine presses, through secret channels of distribution, writers could still appeal to their readers against the established order. Even when there was no conflict of opinions, the relation of the writer to his public altered. He worked now through the medium of an industry. From the beginning, by co-operating with the business man who owned and organized the printing-shop, an author could earn money which came from his readers and not from any patron or employer. As the industry grew it offered greater rewards, and so greater freedom, though sometimes it offered them on hard terms. The press, a new institution, with its own mixture of good and evil, stood between the writer and the reader.

Perhaps the greatest changes which printing brought with it were not these social changes, but the changes in language and literature themselves. Printed books set the standards of uniformity for languages, and so the multiplicity of dialects began to give way before a few great standard literary languages, centred on the political or academic or trading capitals. All Englishmen came to write the language of London; all Frenchmen that of Paris; most of the Spaniards that of Castile. This took time, and it happened more or less quickly according to circumstances. In Italy Dante had raised the language of Tuscany to primacy long before; but the country was so divided that there was a polished dialect literature in Venice as late as the eighteenth century. Wherever it did emerge the metropolitan language had a binding and inspiring force of its own, and strengthened the national feeling that was already growing.

In literature the changes were subtle, but radical. It was much easier than before to bring together many books in one place, and so masses of information could be assembled quickly, and the apparatus of learning was transformed. Great books of reference, dictionaries, encyclopaedias, histories, and collections of texts, put at the disposal of every student knowledge which once could not have been gathered in a lifetime. Knowledge of the present was deepened, but also complicated and hindered, by an ever-present consciousness of the past. At the same time standards of correctness became more exacting. With so many identical copies of books before them, not varied by the little touches of individuality which scribes and copyists always introduced intentionally or by accident, readers learnt a new strictness in verbal accuracy and grammatical correctness. The individual work of an author was distinguished more sharply from the inherited or borrowed elements. Copyright became a legal fact, while authorship and plagiarism, as literary and ethical conceptions, were more clearly defined. The Renaissance was helped on not only as an intellectual movement but as a movement in the art of letters as well. The commonest way of enjoying poetry had been to hear it recited; the commonest way of using a book had been to read it aloud. Now there was so much reading that more and more people read silently to themselves, and books came to be written so that they could best be taken in by the eye and not the ear. Prose gained at the expense of verse; sense gained at the expense of sound. Memory lost some of its value. The story that can be followed without a teller has to be told in a special way: the words themselves, without a voice to clothe them in expression, without accent or intonation, must create their own illusion. So printing set new problems for literature, and as skilful writers devised means of solving them, the range of literature increased until it became, for millions of human beings, almost a substitute for imagination. In the beginning of pre-history speech had given the power of communicating experience, of imagining oneself as a different being, in another time or place. Long afterwards writing had made imagination fixed and lasting and able to add one fancy to another beyond the range of memory, far away from the personal present. Printing set the works of imagination, along with those of thought and emotion, still more securely outside the chances of the present time and place.

THE REFORMATIONS

LIKE Judaism and Islam, Christianity had always been the religion of a book; it now became something which the world had never seen before, the religion of a printed book. This need not by itself have meant anything except the addition of a quick-firing weapon of precision to the armoury of the Church. In Spain Cardinal Ximenes, who was Grand Inquisitor as well as minister, saw to the production of a magnificent edition of the Bible in Latin, Hebrew, and Greek. But in countries where the Church was in difficulties with heretics who questioned its doctrines, or princes and laymen who encroached on its rights and its possessions, it was a disturbing factor that thousands of readers, even the most ignorant, could now read the Bible for themselves, drawing their own conclusions from its vast and, in many ways, mysterious contents. The authorized text of the western Church was an old and imperfect Latin translation. Within a century of the rise of printing there had been two enormous changes, closely intermingled at every stage. Vernacular translations had been printed in a number of European languages. The best linguistic and critical skill had been applied to the Hebrew and Greek originals, to establish the true text and, inevitably with far less success, its true meaning. Each of these processes was connected with fundamental controversies in which the participants and the audience were more numerous than in any previous discussions of religious and public matters.

We have seen that strong rulers everywhere, particularly in Spain and in France, strengthened themselves in relation to the Church, and that there were many attempts, on a greater or a smaller scale, to press forward, either by a council or otherwise, the lagging movement of reform. Whether the rulers were actuated by cupidity or by a public-spirited desire to support the reformers, the wealth and power of the existing ecclesiastical institutions were equally likely to suffer. Local and limited reforms might have much good in them, but they upset the existing state of possessions. Strong governments or strong bishops could prevent upheavals; but both at its centre and in its outlying parts the Church in the early sixteenth century was threatened by new tendencies, each of which sometimes checked but sometimes assisted the others. First, intellectual and moral innovations were troubling the uniformity of belief and loyalty to the authorities. The scholars, with their enthusiasm for truth and their formidable good sense, questioned much more than the mere wording of sacred texts. An Italian, Lorenzo Valla, exposed the falsity of a famous document (already called in question by Nicholas of Cues and others) by which the Emperor Constantine was supposed to have granted rights of secular rule to the Papacy. He also gave expression to an ethical theory, by no means novel, which may be called utilitarian: right meant no more than useful, in other words the results to individuals were to be its ultimate test. This doctrine, and even his more startling suggestion that the Pope was the Antichrist predicted in the Book of Revelation, did not prevent Valla from holding an office at the papal court until his death. An eminent Aristotelian scholar, Pietro Pomponazzi, preserving his ostensible orthodoxy by a transparent device, argued against the immortality of the soul; but he did not lose his professorial chair in the great university of Padua. This unsettling of the old beliefs made some men more indulgent, and others more censorious and alarmed, when they saw worldliness and laxity among the clergy, from the popes who lived like magnificent princes to the many priests whose housekeepers were their concubines. The lower the clergy sank, the less chance they had of defending their property. Landowners stole the glebe-lands and used their ecclesiastical patronage as a mere part of their wealth. The popes themselves sanctioned many schemes by which the endowments of canonries or monasteries were taken away and given to universities or colleges, which rulers or statesmen founded in the interests of education.

These far-reaching changes were rumbling throughout most of Europe, but the political circumstances of one country brought it about that there they led to a revolution which transformed the whole political and spiritual life of the continent. This country was Germany. The German language was spoken by more people than any other in Europe. The German part of the Holy Roman Empire was more populous than France: it had somewhere near twenty million inhabitants. Neither the empire nor the language came anywhere near to coinciding in its boundaries with a single race. East of the Elbe the peasantry, whose status still showed that they were conquered peoples, had once spoken Slavonic languages, of which some islands survived. There were also German settlements of landlords and traders, and in some parts peasants, not only here but also farther to the east, beyond the empire, as in the Baltic ports as far as Reval, and in the region of Livonia which was ruled, as we saw, by a German military order. For the history which we have to consider now, the racial distinctions within Germany are of little importance. The same is true of the distinction between the old civilization of western Germany, which went back continuously to the Roman empire, and the more recently imposed Christian civilization of the region to the east. The educated and responsible elements of Germany were sufficiently homogeneous to respond in much the same way to political and ecclesiastical emergencies, whether they belonged to one region or to the other.

Among the states into which the empire was divided, the most powerful was that of the Habsburg family, from which the emperors had been elected since 1438 and from which, in spite of some narrow escapes, they continued to be elected as long as the empire lasted. They had perhaps nearer two million subjects than one. The centre of their power was in the five duchies which ran down from Vienna to the Adriatic. Of these Austria was the chief, and so the Habsburgs are often called the house of Austria. The borderline between German and Slavonic speech ran irregularly through three of the other duchies. Besides these the Habsburgs had wide possessions in western Germany. As German princes they were not so powerful as to be safe from the jealousy of other princes. Like their predecessors as emperors, they had lost much of their constitutional leadership through the concessions which they had made to the electors, the most considerable of these princes, at one election after another. The Emperor Maximilian and his successor had before them a number of projects for constitutional reform; but none of them went through, and the machinery of the imperial government worked very badly. This was the more ominous because in the late fifteenth century the German hold over the frontier lands was becoming less secure. The Teutonic Order had to submit to the overlordship of Poland. The Habsburgs themselves lost their dominance over the lands to the east of the five duchies. They had held together in personal union the elective crowns of

Bohemia and Hungary; but this combination broke up, and Hungary became the centre of a new grouping of states. The fortunes of the Habsburg dynasty were not declining. An emperor could still at need become a rallying-point for old loyalties and for the common interest in law and order. The loss of influence in the east was more than compensated for by huge Habsburg acquisitions of territory elsewhere; but these were of such a kind that the Habsburgs ceased to be merely a German dynasty. They acquired territories all over Europe, which sometimes enabled them to bring strength from outside to bear upon German affairs, but more often led them to neglect these affairs in order to pursue their own ends abroad.

By an extraordinary result of their dynastic marriages, the most extraordinary result that the old dynastic system ever produced, and one which affected the main lines of European history until the French Revolution, the Habsburgs became an international power. We have seen that the Archduke Maximilian, before becoming emperor, married the heiress of Charles the Bold of Burgundy, so that their two agglomerations of states were merged. They pooled their strength; they improved their administration together; each furthered the ambitions of the other; but each also had to meet the other's liabilities. The princes who were opponents of the Habsburgs, especially those in western Germany, now looked for support to France, the old enemy of the Burgundians. Maximilian and Mary had an heir. He died too young to make a great name, but he married and in his turn had a son. At the time of her marriage the mother of this son was not an heiress; she had a brother and an elder sister, but they both died and she became the greatest heiress in the world, the heiress to Castile and Aragon with all their possessions overseas. So, without anyone's having planned or intended it, an unexampled personal union of states came to pass. Charles of Habsburg inherited the Burgundian assemblage of provinces from his short-lived father in 1506, Aragon and Castile from his maternal grandparents Ferdinand and Isabella in 1516, and the German territories of the Habsburgs from his other grandfather Maximilian in 1519, in which year he was duly elected emperor.

Many of his contemporaries believed that Charles aimed at converting this chain of monarchies into a domination over the whole western world. Actually he never entertained any such fantastic hope. Even if his character had been that of the aggressive conqueror, which it was not, he never would have found himself free to give it rein; but, in trying to maintain all that he had inherited, he found himself in perpetual conflicts on all his frontiers, and any one of his opponents might take up the cause of any other. When religious strife began in Germany he could not stand aside, but that meant that this strife would rouse all the antagonisms of his international position. He was an orthodox Catholic all through his life; but he understood the need for reform. He did not refrain from taking away powers and privileges from the Church. In 1528 he secularized the great ecclesiastical principality of Utrecht, in his Burgundian dominions, and in the following year the pope had to grant him the right of nominating the bishops there, although their authority was now purely spiritual. But he was essentially conservative and moderate. Government could not be carried on satisfactorily in any of his dominions unless he gave it his personal attention; in every part of them he had war or civil war or heresy on his hands, and as soon as one was quieted another called him away. In Germany, therefore, for a whole generation his ecclesiastical policy was a series of expedients which broke down one after another. In his other dominions, if he enforced religious uniformity he strengthened his government: in Germany, if he repressed heresy the opposition of the princes and others became so dangerous that it weakened him against the Turks or the French. On the other hand, if he conciliated the better elements of this opposition by furthering reforms he opened the way for social disturbances and encroachments on ecclesiastical property by princes or knights. Thus the political state of Germany made ecclesiastical changes cut deeper there than anywhere else.

Reform had begun in Germany before Charles's time, and had even been spreading outwards from Germany, for instance among the houses of the Benedictine order of monks. In German art and in German thought the new spirit which came in from Italy was fused with an indigenous ethical seriousness, so that there the Renaissance quickened the impatience of the reformers. Late in the fifteenth century and early in the sixteenth a German scholar, Reuchlin, won a great victory for the spirit of honest inquiry by reviving Hebrew studies. He began an age which has only lately ended, in which the most valuable studies of the Hebrew Scriptures have been carried on not by Jewish but by Christian scholars. In the course of his work he became involved in a fight against obscurantism. His immediate enemies were those who aimed at blotting out the learning of the Jews; but, in resisting them, he had able allies who opened a general attack on the wilful ignorance of the worst kind of ecclesiastical conservatism. They won their victory with educated opinion by using the printing-press, and so they dressed the arena for the great gladiator of reform, Martin Luther.

Luther was a prophet, a man with a great power of believing and converting. Some parts of the inherited religion were intensely real to him, but there were others of which he was unaware and yet others which he loathed and vilified. His mind had been trained in the medieval distinctions and methods of theological disputation, and he had lightning flashes of penetration into human nature and beyond it; but he never foresaw the consequences of his words and acts and he was forced along from one position to another. He looked for precedents for his opinions among the writings of the previous century, and he found them, as indeed he could have found adumbrations of almost any other opinions, if he had chanced to hold them; but in the complex processes of his mind the intellect never broke away from the emotions. He was no stranger to the Renaissance. He visited Rome and he learned Greek. But when the great Erasmus would write no more against the evils of the Church than could be written, with whatever pungency, within the limits of orthodox belief, Luther showed nothing but contemptuous anger. Yet he was infinitely inconsistent. He was conservative and medieval. He had none of the scientific spirit or the Hellenic directness. He was against the new astronomy, and if his common sense sometimes asserted itself against astrology and palmistry, he was none the less superstitious. He believed in witchcraft, as everyone else did, but his mind ran far more than many men's on fearful tales of ghosts and the devil.

Beginning as an Augustinian monk, he became professor of theology in the university of Wittenberg on the Elbe, newly founded by a highly orthodox elector of Saxony. This elector prohibited the raising of money for papal purposes within his dominions by the sale of indulgences. The particular purpose in question at the time, the sumptuous rebuilding of St. Peter's in

Rome, appealed far less to Germans than, say, defence against the Turks. Luther backed up the elector by making a contribution to a long-standing academic debate on the implications of indulgences in general. The discussion spread and ceased to be academic. If indulgences were as unjustifiable as Luther maintained, there was danger for the finances of the Church. If his underlying principles were sound, princes would have much to justify them if they took possession of church property. The Church, as we have said, was a highly centralized body; but it was centralized only for administration and not for defence. Rome could do no more than appoint or send representatives, first to argue, then to negotiate, but not to negotiate with Luther alone, for so many public and political issues were raised that they were discussed in the imperial diet.

Four years after the beginning of his first controversy, Luther had become the leader of a movement in which one of the motive forces was German national feeling. He had been driven step by step to take up the position which has ever since been the Protestant position. Since Luther was almost as difficult to deal with, either in practical affairs or in intellectual argument, as anyone who ever lived, this does not mean that any notable body of people ever exactly accepted any one of his varying formulations of his doctrines; but millions have followed him in fervently believing many things, especially that a man can be justified to God by faith but not by works; that all believers are priests, and so that the laity should receive the communion in both kinds; that priests should be allowed to marry; that private masses should be done away with; that the pope is Antichrist. These views he spread broadcast in pamphlets written with a mastery of German idiom which had never been equalled; and from his writings and the legends of his sayings his followers formed not only their creed but also their image of their leader—of his joviality, his love of music, his courage, his coarseness, his deep earnestness. He was condemned as a heretic, but he burnt the papal bulls. He was outlawed by the diet, but his elector, though he never became a Lutheran, hid and protected him. In his hiding-place he began to translate the Bible into German, and the prose of this translation set the standard by which German became a single literary language.

It was not only in language that Luther left legacies to all Germany; but his religious revolt at once led to conflict and disruption in social and political life. No sooner was he at the head of a movement than it became the reason or the pretext for disorders. A turbulent knight, who had a private war against one of the prince-bishops, took to theological controversy and gathered about him both armed bandits and venomous pamphleteers. The peasants of south-west Germany rose against their masters, burning and destroying. Luther fulminated against them, calling on the authorities to slay; but his own defiance had done something to liberate theirs. He had shaken some of the beliefs on which the social order rested. For him marriage was no longer a sacrament. That might mean much or it might mean little in practice. Luther himself condoned the bigamy of one Protestant prince. In western Germany there were fanatical extremists who did not stop short of holding their wives as well as their property in common. They seized the episcopal city of Münster and held it as a communist republic for sixteen months, until the stern punishment of the authorities overtook them. Meanwhile one prince after another was declaring himself a convert to the new opinions, seizing church property and demolishing ecclesiastical jurisdiction.

The Germany which shook with this earthquake was part of the European state-system shaped in the wars of Italy, and its crisis was a signal for the renewal of that mêlée. In the year when Luther was outlawed, a new king of France, the showy Francis I, had a second temptation to go to war in some disorders in Spain. The pope, again intending to acquire frontier towns, joined him, and so the questions of Milan, Naples, Burgundy, and other places were reopened. Altogether the Emperor Charles V had four wars with Francis I, and they were followed by a fifth against his successor, Henry II, during the course of which Charles, worn out with his labours, abdicated, leaving his successor Philip II of Spain to conclude that war. The French miscalculated in relying on the trouble in Spain, for Charles put these disorders down quickly, and the commonalty of Spain gave their rulers very little trouble until the early nineteenth century. The first war was like those that preceded it, but it ought to have served as a warning that the power of Spain was growing firmer at home, and making firmer links with its international system of allies. The pope changed sides; and he was succeeded by a pope from the Netherlands, a subject of Charles who had been his tutor. The war ended with a smashing victory by the Spaniards in north Italy, but if the French had not divided their forces they might not have been beaten, and so they were tempted to try again. A new pope took their side. They detached England from its traditional Burgundian alliance. This time Rome was sacked by Spanish, German, and Italian troops under a renegade French general. The Spaniards conquered all Italy; but in a third war the French did better. Charles had had failures in the Mediterranean, which we shall notice in a moment, and the European system was now so torn by dissension that when the French attacked again, it was with the Turks as their allies at sea. But England had reverted to its normal alliance, and the Spanish army was steadily improving. Its discipline was incomparable. Even in these two least successful wars the Spanish *tercios* of arquebusiers and pikemen in equal numbers were the best infantry in the world. The artillery was being modernized. The commanders, drawn like the men from Italy as well as Spain, were the leaders of their profession.

The last war of Charles V was almost a European war. It began badly for him, for Germany was by now so divided that the French had a group of Protestant allies there. This enabled the French to occupy the three ecclesiastical principalities of Metz, Toul, and Verdun which commanded the river-routes of the Meuse and the Moselle. The Spaniards invaded the papal states once more, but their general, the Duke of Alva, refrained from attacking Rome, and thus obtained not only the submission but the absolution of the pope. The French also ousted the English from Calais, and for the last time a pope sided with them against the Spaniards. The treaty of Le Cateau-Cambrésis in 1559 made a peace between France and Spain which lasted for a generation, and a settlement of Italy which lasted far longer. There was no new French intervention in Italy until 1597, and although France intervened often enough after that, the Spanish supremacy now established lasted until the duchy of Milan passed to the Austrian branch of the Habsburgs in 1701. The Spaniards now held Naples, Sicily, Milan, and the smaller ports of the Tuscan coast, and they had allies in Genoa and the duke of Savoy, 'the porter of the Alps'.

They gave Italy internal peace, but their predominance was

not merely political. Spanish ideas were acclimatized in Rome; Spanish dress and etiquette and ceremonial in the courts of the whole country. The city of Rome saw a new period of greatness in architecture and painting; it grew in size and in splendour. For these wonderful Spaniards were not mere conquerors; they were leaders in the arts and letters until far into the next century. But their power in southern Europe had not been established without sacrificing much of the more widely extended authority which Charles V inherited. It had suffered not only from the French wars and the encroachments of the German princes but, worst of all, from heavy Turkish pressure. In the year after Charles became emperor the Turks had a new sultan, the most successful of them all, Solomon the Magnificent. He it was who turned westwards at last, from the now subjugated Near East, and in that year he took Belgrade. He lived until 1566, and he brought the Ottoman empire to its highest point of power. The two great divisions of western Christendom both played into his hands. Protestants accepted his protection against Catholics, and after 1535 France was his ally against the emperor. He was diverted twice by wars against Persia; but he brought the Turkish danger nearer to the heart of Europe than it had ever been before. At sea he took Rhodes in 1522, and expelled the Knights of St. John, who had held it for two centuries. Then he backed up his North African allies in their sea-war against Spain by sending troops to their support. The viceroys who governed Algiers and Tunis in his name built up a strong power, aspiring to conquer Morocco. Charles V gave Malta to the homeless Knights of St. John as a fief, strategically a point of the first importance. He gave them Tripoli as well; but the chances of Spanish progress in North Africa were at an end. None of the Christian states rendered any help in the western Mediterranean; indeed a success of Charles at Tunis confirmed the French alliance with the Turks. After that Charles met with disaster in an expedition against Algiers. The Algerines threatened Rome and wintered in Toulon. The position in the western Mediterranean, however, was stabilized. The knights in Malta, in a heroic resistance to a long siege, put a stop to Turkish hopes of capturing the island. On the other side the Portuguese attacks on Morocco stimulated the tribesmen there to unite in the Sherifian empire, which withstood all attacks by land from the east. The ports of Tunis and Algiers, with reconquered

Tripoli after 1560, harassed the commerce of the Christians by
their privateering until the nineteenth century, and occasionally sent squadrons to support the sultan in the Levant; but,
in the latter years of Solomon the Magnificent, North Africa
dropped out of the main stream of history. The Christian powers
could never combine to attack it, but it could never muster
enough strength to be a danger, or indeed anything worse than
a nuisance, to them. Nor did Solomon win any great victory at
sea in the eastern Mediterranean. His one important gain there
after the fall of Rhodes, the capture of Chios in 1566, was made
not from any state but from a Genoese trading company.

On land it was very different. He annexed southern Bes-
sarabia. By capturing Belgrade he completed the conquest of
Serbia and then pushed forward in Hungary and Croatia.
The king of Hungary, twenty years of age, a brother-in-law of
Charles V, went to battle at Mohacs in 1526. He was defeated
and killed, with seven bishops who accompanied his army. The
Turkish conquests in the Balkans were now safe for three centu-
ries. Until our own time Hungary never stood alone as a separate
kingdom but was always in personal union with a neighbour.
At first the succession was disputed, the Turks supporting the
Magyar prince of Transylvania. He failed, however, to win the
Hungarian crown, which went to the late king's brother-in-law
Ferdinand of Austria, the emperor's brother, to whom Charles
had entrusted the defence of the duchies. In 1529 Solomon
carried his war against Ferdinand to the farthest point he ever
reached, the walls of Vienna. If Vienna had fallen then, with
Germany in a state of revolution behind it, there is no knowing
what the fate of Europe would have been; but Vienna stood.
Year after year the Turkish armies continued to attack. On his
eighth invasion Solomon died, at the age of 76. After his death
the position on the Danube too was stabilized, in an illogical
position which lasted for more than a century and a half.
Hungary was divided into three parts. In the centre was the
Turkish province, from the Banat of Temesvar to the Adriatic.
East of it was Transylvania, a Magyar state ruled by its own
elective princes, tributary to the Porte. In both of these there
was religious toleration, and in Transylvania the national
customs and the old estates-constitution of the ordinary European type survived. Royal Hungary, where Ferdinand ruled,
was a mere frontier-strip, almost a no-man's-land. It remained

independent of the Turks because the Habsburgs held it in personal union with their duchies and with the kingdom of Croatia; but this union inevitably did much to assimilate its institutions to those of Austria.

Islam controlled the Mediterranean east of the Sicilian narrows. It had established itself more than half-way from the Aegean to the Baltic. France was its ally. Yet this was its farthest advance, and the affairs of the west, in unexpected ways, were preparing forces which in time were to throw it back. Before Solomon died the Italian question had been settled. Politically Germany was settled too. It has often been said that Charles ought to have put himself at the head of the Lutheran movement and made himself a national leader of Germany; but even if Charles had not been a true Catholic, as he was, that would have availed him nothing. If he had declared himself a Lutheran, even if he had carried with him the conservative elements in the towns and universities and the countryside, his opponents among the princes could have chosen the other party. One diet after another tried to set bounds to the arbitrary reforms of the princes or to meet discontent half-way by inducing the Church itself to reform abuses. Every compromise broke down. The Protestant princes formed a league and Charles defeated it in battle. An unbeaten Protestant elector, who had not been a member of the league, took umbrage at the victorious emperor's proceedings, made war on the emperor, and won. Although their common sense and their respect for the imperial dignity and general interest held them back from some extremities, the princes got what they wanted. The peace of Augsburg, in 1555, gave Germany religious peace. In each of the 300 states the ruler was to decide which should be the one tolerated religion. Thus Protestantism was established in a number of states in all parts of Germany, while the Roman Church maintained itself in the Habsburg lands, in the ecclesiastical principalities, and in some other states, such as Bavaria. The death penalty was no longer inflicted for heresy[1] in Germany; religious dissidents henceforward were only to leave house and home and betake themselves to some territory where their own confession prevailed. So there began the miserable processions of refugees who, in the bad times from then until now, have left behind them the homes where they could no longer worship in accordance with their

---

[1] There were some exceptions, especially in cases of Anabaptists.

consciences. For nearly seventy years there was no further religious warfare in Germany. During those seventy years it was
the surrounding countries which suffered from persecution, rebellion, conspiracy, and civil war.

All this experience had plainly shown that the dominions of
Charles V could not be held together in a single personal union.
During his reign he had to hand over German affairs to his
brother Ferdinand, and when Charles abdicated, Ferdinand,
already king of Hungary, was elected as his successor in the
empire. His son Philip succeeded him in Spain. The house of
Habsburg was thus divided into two branches. In spite of
occasional estrangements they worked together as long as they
both lasted, and they followed a policy of intermarriage of
which the principle was that if either line were to die out, a
successor should be forthcoming from the other. Charles had
a choice as to the division of his dominions between these two
lines. He might have handed over to Ferdinand not only his
German possessions but also the Netherlands. Instead of this he
took a decision which enabled the Spanish power to come to the
aid of the Austrian Habsburgs by using the Netherlands as a
base for waging war against France or for sending reinforcements into Germany: he resigned the Netherlands, along with
Spain and the Italian possessions, to his son Philip. With them
he passed on to Philip and to Spain the dormant Burgundian
question, which was to come to life again a few years later.

It was a necessary consequence of the old unity of western
civilization that, from its beginning, Lutheranism attracted adherents outside Germany. National churches, more or less on
the Lutheran model, were established in Sweden and Denmark.
In other countries there were Lutherans, but they were only one
sect among others, for the Lutheran crisis had revealed and
released a number of divergent types of anti-Roman belief.
Among these the most important, if only because it alone became the official religion of sizeable states, was Calvinism. John
Calvin was almost as different from Luther in disposition and
upbringing as it was possible for a highly educated man to be.
He was a Frenchman, a classical scholar, trained to the law.
He organized the Church in the little city-state of Geneva as a
model of what the Church in his view should be; it exercised undisputed power over the civil government of that republic, and

it was widely imitated abroad. The great instrument of Calvin's power was his book *Institutio Christianae Religionis* (Instruction in the Christian Religion), which he published in 1539. There was nothing fundamentally new in this book. Protestantism was already formed before Calvin wrote. His work was to define and systematize where there was so much confusion, and to work out a plan for church government and for the Church's place in the world. His method was intellectual; he used argument and invective, writing excellent Latin with a classical simplicity, dropping all the jargon and formalities of the schoolmen. There is nothing occasional or ephemeral in his book, and nothing mean or scurrilous. He relied on the Scriptures, which, he held, are known by faith, and not by argument, to be the word of God. Thus the printing-press made possible a new authoritarianism, and, except in a polemic against the bold heretics who had already challenged the doctrine of the Trinity, Calvin scarcely applied his critical powers to the Bible. To the history of Christianity he applied it to some purpose. He held that the test of the true Church was not continuity through tradition handed on by persons, but purity of doctrine. In the 'medium saeculum' of Pope Leo I, of Gregory the Great, and St. Bernard, that is from the fifth century to the twelfth, he saw a corrupted faith,[1] and so, from a new point of view, he strengthened the tendency to regard the Middle Ages as a period of darkness. His view of the relations between the religion of Jesus Christ and apostolic Christianity and the Christianity of the early Fathers, his account of creeds and dogmas, his judgements on papal claims and Roman practices, were all worked out by acute historical criticism; but in another field his doctrine was anti-historical, for he held that doctrine as contained in the Scriptures was fixed and final, overriding all previous knowledge and all knowledge from other sources. He had no patience with idle curiosity, nor much with scientific curiosity. He did indeed admit that scientific knowledge must be respected, as when he wrote that, although God gave the rainbow to Noah for a sign, there were rainbows before Noah, since the rainbow is only a reflection of the solar rays on the opposite clouds. But such excep-

[1] *Institutio*, Bk. IV, vii. 22. This passage does not appear to be mentioned by the historians who have investigated the origin of these ideas; but it seems to be a link without which it is impossible to account for their general prevalence among Protestant divines in the subsequent period.

tions did not trouble his conviction that he was teaching religious
certainties. He condemned what the Lutherans condemned. In
intellectual matters he simplified and straightened out what
they had put forward tentatively and obscurely. The central
belief of his followers was predestination, the idea that each
man was predestined to salvation or to eternal punishment. If
this belief narrowed their sympathies, it also fortified their will.
They submitted to a severe system of discipline. Calvin's programme for church government gave them a fighting organization in which the ministers, who were not priests but primarily
teachers of the Word, were supported by assemblies of believing
laymen.

The tendency to define, and to fight for the principles once
defined, appeared on the Catholic side almost simultaneously
with its appearance in Calvinism. In the days of the German
negotiations and expedients about Lutheranism, there were
ambiguities and uncertainties in some of the Catholic doctrines
that Luther impugned. There were openings for concessions
from the Catholic side which did not certainly involve a depar-
ture from the orthodox tradition. In Austria the cup was offered
to the laity with papal approval; perhaps priests might marry;
at any rate the papacy might agree to the demands of the
German princes and burghers, which the emperor supported,
for a council to discuss the whole matter of reform. Reform indeed had, as we have seen, begun in Germany before the revolution, and in the fifteen-twenties it began in Italy. There too
religious orders were reformed; new orders were founded, and
also new charitable institutions. Influential ecclesiastics worked
for religious renewal in a spirit of enlightenment if not of
compromise. Appropriately enough the spirit of militant and
uncompromisingly orthodox reform came from Spain.

Among Calvin's contemporaries at the university of Paris was
a disabled Spanish officer, Ignatius Loyola, who had been born
a gentleman of one of the Basque provinces adjoining France
on the Bay of Biscay. After his wound he had gone through
an experience of religious conversion, and now he brought the
disciplined zeal of the Spanish army to the aid of the Church in
its danger. At the age of thirty-seven or thereabouts he sat among
the boys and youths of the Paris lecture-rooms, taking a course
in theology. He made the pilgrimage to Jerusalem. He had

visions, but they were not of the kind that brings illumination
to others. Ignatius did not excel as a writer or a thinker; but he
was a great leader of men. In his book of *Spiritual Exercises*
he provided a manual not to convince men's intellects but to
subdue their whole personalities to obedience and endurance.
Eight times he was charged with heresy; but he defeated his
accusers. He inspired first one disciple and then another with
the will to convert the heathen and to confute the heretic. With
his soldier's eye he saw that the way to reorganize the Catholic
front was to strengthen the papacy. Before Calvin went to
Geneva, Ignatius founded the Society of Jesus. There were years
of conflict before the Jesuits, with Ignatius as their general, received their final autocratic constitution under papal auspices;
but their historic influence was immediate. In 1545 the general
council was at last assembled at the town of Trent in the Tyrol,
conveniently between Germany and Italy. The emperor wished
it to begin with the reform of the abuses of the Church; but
the pope decided that it should first clear up the uncertainties
of doctrine. In the next year, the year of Luther's death, the
Jesuits were given the commission of providing the theologians
who were to advise the papal representatives in the council.
The work of the council was impeded for years by long inter-
ruptions and much resistance from other schools of thought and
from governments; but it was already certain that, both in
Germany and outside, religious militancy would not be found
only on the Protestant side. The Roman Church was not yet
centralized for defence; but it had gained efficient mobile
forces.

The council, before it finally separated in 1563, did two things.
It defined belief in such a way that there was no loophole for
misunderstanding or concession in the matters where Lutherans
or Calvinists or other innovators had taken up new positions.
It regulated the outward and practical affairs of the Church in
such a way that the inveterate abuses were gradually overcome.
The full programme of reform could not be enforced without
the consent and help of the states, and some of them resisted.
France never accepted the decrees of the council officially
before the Revolution. But, however the states hung back, there
were ardent reformers among the bishops and clergy, and before
long the Roman Church had a good right to consider itself
reformed.

From this time until the present day western Christendom has been divided among churches and sects. The religious settlement that was made in Germany by the peace of Augsburg is commonly summed up in the formula *cuius regio, eius religio*— 'whose the region is, his also shall be the religion' or 'he who rules the region may dictate its religion'. This formula may be given a far wider application: it describes the state of things all over Europe throughout the sixteenth century and in most parts of it until well on in the eighteenth. Every strong government, whether Catholic or Protestant, tried to enforce religious uniformity. Where there was no strong government there was religious dissidence; but where there were strong powers at a lower level than that of the territorial state, they determined the religion of those whom they controlled. In many places, from France to Poland and Transylvania, landowners set up a local 'seigniorial protestantism', whether of a Lutheran or a Calvinistic tinge.

In a sense there was nothing new in this. Christianity had been spread long before by missionaries who converted emperors or kings with the certainty that their subjects would conform. The Church had been reluctant to countenance forced conversions, and it never admitted any right of the state to interfere between the individual and his God; but, where men were not free, this could have only a doubtful meaning. The break-up of ecclesiastical unity in conflict, and the mutual estrangement of consciences, led many men to think of belief as the individual concern of the believer; but even so the new Churches, and even the smallest and most eccentric sects, were held together by other ties besides those of creed and practice. Each of them appealed most to some special psychological type of person—Calvinism, for instance, to men with something of Calvin in them; but few individuals had the chance of gravitating to the body that would best have fitted their idiosyncracies. After the first missionary phase, membership was mainly inherited. Like the society in which they originated, the confessions were based on the family: they were clans, making a wider or narrower use of adoption. Every religious group has, besides its creed and its church order, boundaries which are related to the boundaries of some other social group. Its place in the world, especially its position below or beside or against the state, must affect those boundaries. Its common life creates common *mores*, manners, and even mannerisms in other matters outside the religious sphere. Its own members will see more clearly than anyone else the religious element in its life; others will see more clearly than they the social and the external. Religious organizations are not more closely intertwined with social groupings than religious with secular motives; and so every religious movement has some economic or social, as well as some intellectual, antecedents and accompaniments, all of which are more easily visible from outside than from within. In recent times it has been shown in much detail that Protestantism developed readily among those who were impatient of the old economic order, like some of the commercial men in town and country, or economically at a disadvantage, like the craftsmen of towns during industrial depressions, and that Catholic conservatism meant the preservation of church lands as well as orthodox beliefs. So it was bound to be; but it remains none the less true that the glories and miseries of religious strife in the sixteenth century drew their intensity from spiritual good and spiritual evil.

Persuasion and compulsion divided Christianity; the divisions, intensified by robbery and bloodshed, were perpetuated by habits and loyalties. There were always conversions from one confession to another. The converts sometimes modified the beliefs of their new associates; but many of them, in their loneliness, were more exclusive in their new beliefs than those whom they joined, and their secession was apt to harden the rigidity of those whom they deserted. There were always men of wide sympathy and imagination who hoped and schemed for the reunion of some greater or smaller number of the divided Churches. Most of these irenic endeavours were limited to the unpromising fields of intellectual tenets or constitutional machinery, and throughout the period with which we are concerned they yielded no positive results. There were changes in religious allegiances through the conversions of princes, or the local failures or successes of policy; but in their main lines the divisions which began in the sixteenth century have lasted down to the present time and have been complicated by fresh disagreements.

Nevertheless the unity which they disrupted was never entirely destroyed. The innumerable Protestant Churches and sects had much in common in spite of their dissensions, and in spite of their different relations to political power, which some of them controlled, while others submitted to it or hid from its vigilance. They thought that many Roman practices, instead of giving access to an invisible world, interposed between it and the believer another world of visible or tangible or audible symbols. None of them had a celibate priesthood or monastic communities, or used Latin as the language of worship. Few of them retained episcopacy or made use of the visual arts or of an elaborate ritual in worship. All these were carried on by the Roman Church, which was thus unique in its outward appearances as in its internal structure. Yet there were great things which even Protestants and Roman Catholics had in common. Even the determination to define doctrine in strict theological terms, though it led to apparently irreconcilable conclusions, was common to all except a few small groups of intellectually anarchistic *illuminés*. It was an expression of intellectual integrity: it implied that, whether he did it for himself or allowed the experts to do it for him, without strict thinking a man's ultimate beliefs were not on the right foundation. The dogmas accepted by absolutely all who called themselves Christians were very few; there were some who kept nothing of the old religion except shreds and tatters; but in the sixteenth century there was still no organized religion, nor any religious literature, except what was or purported to be Christian. There was still religion everywhere: there were still millions whose virtues all depended on their belief in a spiritual order of the universe, in the Kingdom of God; and the secular government, of whatever persuasion, still relied on religion as the guarantee of law and justice.

To minimize the differences between the confessions, or their consequences in every department of life, would be to push out of sight the explanations of much of the later course of history. One illustration may perhaps make this clear. Luther and Calvin, and a number of others who were associated with them, or lived similar lives in other places, were unlike the great historic or legendary persons who had been admired and imitated in the past. These had belonged to many types: the just ruler, the learned doctor, the knight without fear and without reproach, the saint or holy man. Here were men, looked up to by whole peoples and by some men and women almost everywhere, whose claim to greatness had something new in it. Unlike the founders of new movements in the Middle Ages, some of whom had their troubles with authority, they had never been reconciled to the powers that they had challenged. To find others of whom this might be said it was necessary to go back to the heroes of freedom in antiquity, but their inspiration had been merely secular or human, while these were men who professed to be serving God. Thus a new type was added to the gallery of the men on whom popular leaders modelled their lives, the type of the reformer. Resistance and private judgement acquired a kind of sanctity. A reforming tradition spread through political, social, and intellectual life, slowly calling into being a less conscious answering conservatism, and at last engendering a belief that revolution in itself, whatever its aims or methods or results, might be a social good.

Within the sphere of religion, however, there remained, precisely because religion is something essentially different from everything else, an identity beneath the conflicts. The deeper we look into the records of religious life, the more clearly it appears. In varying proportions, and with various alloys, the same elements entered into the experience of all the sects and churches. Prayers, hymns, devotional books, the language and substance of worship passed through the frontiers of formulae and regulations, and, unawares, men contended for the same cause under opposing colours.

The richly developed art of the Renaissance was nourished by so many channels from the whole life of the community that it could not live unaltered through this epoch of disturbances. The glorious outburst of creativeness in Italy was at its brightest, and was kindling the arts of other European countries, at the time when the troubles began. Botticelli and Mantegna died during Luther's boyhood. Michelangelo and Titian were his older contemporaries, and they both outlived him. All these painters added wonderful adornments to churches, and each of them had his own individual vision of the splendours of line and colour, of design and of the human form. Michelangelo was a poet and an architect as well as a painter, and he was one of those whom the antique had liberated from the narrowness of the present. There were some, like the Dutchman Jerome Bosch, whose greatness lay in their rendering of the most terrible intimacies of the soul; others, like Giorgione, whose glowing tones

PLATE 27

Albrecht Dürer, St. Jerome. (See p. xxiv)

and velvet shadows conjured up a delightful world where neither thought nor deity could be born. Among them all perhaps the most typical, or the most impressive in his versatility and his power of will, was Leonardo da Vinci. The subjects of some of his most admired pictures were religious, of others mythological, of others, the most profound of all, only human; but in all of them he treated pictorial representation as a problem, to be solved by bringing together everything that research could discover about light, perspective, and anatomy. He wrote, in a secret shorthand, hundreds upon hundreds of sheets of notes, with hasty or careful drawings among them, working and questioning as the scientist, shrinking from no discovery, however strange, about the nature of substances, or the laws of mechanics, or the nature of living things.

A heavy curtain fell. The wars of Charles V almost put a stop to building and painting in Italy. Poverty, destruction, and danger were not more sobering than the admonitions of the churchmen. There had always been a puritan strain in Christianity; now it asserted itself and men shrank back from headlong enjoyment. Some great artists, the greatest of them being Albrecht Dürer, the German painter and engraver, were converted to the Lutheran beliefs, and brought a new gravity into their creative work. The Calvinists and many of the sectaries were enemies not only to religious art, with its graven images, but to all visible beauty. The Jesuits had their own austerity. The Italian renaissance, though it can never end, was no more than one theme in the music of the past.

THE WIDER WORLD

ALMOST every year from the early fifteenth century to the middle of the seventeenth brought news of geographical discoveries outside Europe in the south or west or east. From year to year these discoveries were amongst the most momentous of current events, not only for their intrinsic interest and their material results but for less tangible and even greater reasons. They freed European life from two cramping limitations: its seclusion from the wider world, and the scale on which men thought of distances. Lands which had been immensely remote, or even unknown and unguessed at, became accessible, and consequently what had seemed distant now seemed relatively near. We shall have to trace some of the many meanings of this change, and also of another which the discoveries implied. Regarded in detail, they were made by an immense number of travellers by sea and land, whose enterprise and endurance took them, one by one, over the ocean-horizons and over the mountain watersheds, through the fatigues and dangers of one day after another, but, taken as a whole, they amounted to a co-operative enterprise to which not only the personal courage and energy of the explorers were essential, but also the organizing abilities of statesmen and financiers, the technical skill of industrial workers, and the hard thinking of scientists. In comparison with the planned undertakings of our own time it must seem simple, small, and almost casual; but in comparison with what had gone before such a joint enterprise was entirely novel, and it was evidence of something new in the civilization which achieved it. The first signs had been visible long before, but until the movement was far advanced it seemed to be only an excrescence from the life of Europe. From the late sixteenth century expansion overseas was seen to be an integral, indeed a major, part of European history.

We have seen that in the fifteenth century Castile and Portugal were the two Christian kingdoms which not only held their own against Islam but made headway, and we have seen how the Spaniards turned their forces against their European neighbours and were checked in North Africa. Portugal was separated from the rest of Europe by this strong Castile, and it is a curious fact that, although the two kingdoms have never been far apart either in language or in religion, the eastern boundary of Portugal has been less modified by the gaining and losing of frontier-provinces than any other in Europe. After 1479 the Portuguese never yielded to the temptation to nibble at the mountainous barrier which separated them from their neighbours; but they too had the crusading tradition and sought wealth from conquests. They gained a foothold on the Moroccan shore, and they extended it until the Sheriffian empire checked them about the same time as the Spaniards were checked. But, unlike the Spaniards, they ventured, from about 1415, into the Atlantic. They took Madeira and the Azores, and then they went southward along the African coast.

Not only the success but the distinctive character of the Portuguese explorations was largely due to Henry the Navigator, a Portuguese prince born of an English mother, who died in 1460 after more than forty years of activity. Voyages were made under his auspices, not under those of the state. He made himself acquainted with everything that books and experts could teach him about the needs of travel, and he used his wealth and position to set up what may be called a geographical research-station. A new type of ships, the light, manœuvrable three-masted caravels, carrying a complement of about sixty men, was designed especially for this work. Voyage followed voyage; it began to seem possible that there might be a sea-route to Asia. Pope Nicholas V granted bulls in which he authorized the Portuguese to make war on the Moors and pagans.

Among the privileges granted by these bulls was that of making slaves of Africans, or, in effect, of taking advantage for the economy of Europe of the slave-trade which already existed in Africa. When the Guinea Coast was reached some hundreds of slaves were brought thence each year to the Portuguese territories. The trade never grew to any importance in Europe, where Africans could be of little use, but it was destined to supply great labour-forces in some of the new environments in which Europeans came to work later on, and to present them with immense moral and economic problems. For the present this was not foreseen, nor indeed were most of the problems of the future, but before the death of Henry the Navigator the Portuguese had already a rich experience of trade and government overseas. In Madeira and the Azores they had established colonies of settlers; they had taught their own religion and ways of life to the inhabitants they found there, and they had set up feudal estates on the European model. In the Cape Verde Islands and San Thomé they had slave-labour colonies under military governors. Within a few years after Prince Henry's death this experience was multiplied many times in extent and variety. The Portuguese rendered to the rest of Europe the immense service of making the first great experiments in colonization, and paid the inevitable penalty of making the first great mistakes.

It was not intentionally that they handed on these benefits to other nations. In the Middle Ages no form of enterprise was safe from interfering rivals unless it could be protected, and the normal way of protecting a trader was to give him a share in a monopoly. The Portuguese derived from the papal bulls a title to exclude others from their trade and settlements, and they did what they could to keep all information about their routes and methods secret. But soon they were so active, and over so wide an area, that secrecy was impossible. Within twenty-five years of Prince Henry's death they were in a much stronger position than during his lifetime. Except for one temporary experiment in leasing it to a company, the business of expansion was now carried on by the state itself, and the kings, having overcome the nobles and prelates, were now absolute monarchs. In Africa new sources of wealth were reached, and a fort was established on the Gold Coast at Elmina, 'the Mine'.

In the same year, 1482, an expedition reached the Congo, and this expedition was in two ways more remarkable than any of those that went before. It brought scientific invention directly into play on the spot. The navigators of ships depended on the stars for knowing their positions, and there had been good instruments for centuries by which they could ascertain latitudes. But the estuary of the Congo is south of the equator, under a different sky. A German geographer, Martin Behaim, was retained to invent a new instrument for use in the southern seas. He sailed with the expedition to test it in practice himself. And the Congo, when it was reached, was the gateway to more surprises. Here, instead of a multitude of petty tribes, there was a paramount chief who ruled over territories as broad and populous as some of the European kingdoms. For the next hundred years the history of this region was strange and wonderful. From 1509 to 1540 it was ruled by an African Christian, with the name Alfonso and the title 'Highness'. His eldest son became a bishop, and there were dukes, marquises, and counts among his subjects. When he exchanged diplomatic missions with Portugal, the Portuguese ships brought priests and soldiers, masons and carpenters to build churches and government offices, and lawyers with six folio volumes of law-books for use in this very inappropriate tropical environment. All the hopes which these things typified foundered ultimately in disastrous military adventures. The Congo became tributary to Portugal, and Angola, farther south, was founded by military force and ruled directly by the right of conquest.

Long before these last events, however, the Portuguese had gone so far that the Congo seemed small and poor. Only four years after it was discovered, Bartholomew Diaz rounded the Cape of Good Hope. Now all the east lay open to the Portuguese, for the seas are one. Chinese junks had already found out the ports of East Africa, and the Arabs had traded along them since the days before Mahomet. The Portuguese knew the way to India from Egypt by the Red Sea and they quickly found pilots who could take them across the Indian Ocean. Before the fifteenth century ended, in a voyage of twenty-one months, one of Magellan's four ships made the first voyage round the world.

Wherever the Portuguese went they were traders as well as explorers, and, in order to establish trade, they had to protect it by settled power. To trade at a profit it was not enough to land a cargo and buy eastern goods with the proceeds. The Asiatic merchants knew well enough how to take advantage of visitors who could not indefinitely stay away from home. They combined to buy cheap and sell dear. So the Portuguese had to lease warehouses on shore, and store their merchandise to wait for opportunities of selling. These 'factories' were tempting to robbers of every rank and description, and so they had to be protected by forts. Portuguese trade, as it expanded, deposited round the coasts of Africa and Asia the elements of an empire. In 1505 this empire had its first viceroy, and four years later he won a memorable sea-battle against the Arabs and Egyptians in Indian waters, which may be regarded fairly enough as the beginning of the long age in which, until the rise of modern Japan, European fleets were the masters of all the eastern seas.

The second viceroy, the great Albuquerque, was a strong man

who paid little regard to restraints of law. He had his failures, but he conquered some of the greatest strategical points of Asia. We must pass over the events by which the empire was completed and, merely noting its full extent, which it reached about 1557, consider briefly what it meant to the world. There was the long chain of posts along western and eastern Africa, then opulent Goa on the Indian coast, the viceroy's capital. All trade with Europe had to pass through Goa, by regular routes which have left behind them the names of Algoa ('to Goa') and Delagoa Bay ('from Goa) in Africa. The most important trades were royal monopolies. On the flank of the routes to Europe the Portuguese held Ormuz, a naval station which protected them from the Turkish power. To the east they held Ceylon, and the trade of the richest tropical area of the world, the Malay Archipelago. They had settlements in Malacca, through whose straits all this trade passed, and in the Moluccas, the greatest source of spices, very profitable commodities which were then almost necessaries to a Europe which lived through the winter on autumn-slaughtered meat. In China they had their own trading-station at Macao. Far away in America they held Brazil; but we have not referred to America yet, and we must defer that for a little longer.

Up to a point the circumstances in which European traders arrived in these new places dictated their policy. If they were to stay at all, they must set up factories, forts, and naval bases; they must be ready to resist local aggression by arms and by seeking allies; they must set up a system of administration to manage these responsibilities. In these tasks, none of which was simple, the Portuguese learnt and inadvertently taught many lessons; but there were others, of even greater moment, in which they had far less guidance from the obvious necessities of the situation. First was the question of religion. It was assumed from the first that one of the objects of expansion was to convert the heathen to Christianity, and, since Christianity was known exclusively, or as good as exclusively, in the context of that European civilization of which it had for so long been an inseparable element, it was supposed that conversion would be equivalent to making these peoples resemble Europeans for all social purposes. In the early days the profession of Christianity and knowledge of the Portuguese language qualified an African to be treated legally and socially as a European. There was no feeling against intermarriage, which seemed to be a means to the effective manning of the ever-widening undertakings overseas. Men of mixed blood commanded ships, were ordained as priests, or rose to affluence as business men.

It was only gradually understood that assimilation was not so easy as this. Just as the conversion of the Congo fell far short of the first hopes, the policy of miscegenation created great masses of people in Africa and Asia, and even in Portugal itself, who were not completely European in character and could not build new societies comparable with that of Portugal, but formed a third element uneasily suspended between the inharmonious worlds from which they derived. Within the great problem of assimilation there were many subordinate differences of opinion. Some of the missionaries were content to work within the limits which seemed desirable to the indigenous rulers; others alarmed or offended them by founding schools and instructing women. Some held that missionary work could not succeed without the help of traders; others blamed the evil example of the traders for missionary failures. Missionaries of various orders were amongst the bravest of the travellers, and before the middle of the sixteenth century the Portuguese had taken St. Francis Xavier, one of the companions of St. Ignatius Loyola, to the Japanese island of Hirado, where he died; but not even the missionary work was free from the conflicts of practical aims and the intellectual perplexities which made the reality of empire fall far short of the earliest hopes.

Before the disillusion came, the Portuguese were no longer alone in the wider world. Another kingdom had added to its possessions an empire of the same order of magnitude as theirs. Although on the surface it seems to have been a mere chance that this kingdom was Castile, in fact no other state was so likely to imitate the Portuguese example. They had much in common. The Atlantic ports of Spain were close to those of Portugal, and the two states had both maintained their resistance to Islam. There were other countries, such as England, which had early opportunities but did not follow them up until the Spanish empire was full-grown. The persistence of Spain in the new endeavour is the best evidence that she did not merely blunder into it. Appearances were indeed to the contrary. As the Portuguese moved forward from one finger-post to another, an Italian sea-captain conceived the bolder idea of sailing blind into the Atlantic. Much is uncertain about Columbus. It is uncertain how much he knew about the existence of America. Anyone might know of legends about a lost continent or undiscovered islands. It may or may not have been possible in those days to read of the Norsemen's voyages to North America in the tenth and eleventh centuries. There was certainly enough conjecture about what lay beyond the Atlantic to justify the merchants of Bristol, some years before the voyage of Columbus, in sending an expedition which came back empty-handed to Ireland. Columbus may have thought that he would find the East Indies; but he may have intended to find a new continent. He asked for Portuguese ships and money, but compared with the certainties on which the Portuguese were already engaged his plans were not convincing. It was Queen Isabella of Castile who became his patron, and it was under her flag that he landed in the Bahamas in 1492.

The first American landfall of Columbus was one of the greatest moments in the history of the human race, but after it one disappointment followed another. Columbus found gold, but no mines. For more than twenty years the Spaniards searched this way and that, but they reached the Pacific across the isthmus and explored more than 7,000 miles of American coast before they brought back any proportionate reward. Then Cortez marched up with a handful of followers from the coast to the high plateau of Mexico and discovered something the like of which none of the European explorers had seen. Hitherto they had found new tribes and even kingdoms, but these had all been primitive, and there was little or nothing in their arts or their ways that the Portuguese or Spaniards could regard with admiration, or even with respect. Now they saw a state with many inhabitants and, in some respects, a high degree of organization. Its king lived in a palace of dazzling magnificence. The cunning workmanship of the wood, stone, metals, fabrics, and feathers astonished them as much as the profusion of gold. This was a civilization of which not the faintest rumour had ever penetrated to Europe; and, although it was so rich in these enviable things, it lacked half of the prerequisites for rising out of barbarism. The Mexicans seemed diabolically cruel and immoral. They were cannibals, and their mightiest monuments were devoted to human sacrifice. They had no domestic animals; they did not know the use of iron or of the wheel; they built on a gigantic scale, and yet they could not build a keystone-arch. They had achieved luxury without emerging from the stone age. Fortunately for the Spaniards the Mexican confederacy was torn at this moment by intestine divisions. The new-comers were welcomed as allies by one party. Cortez was a gallant soldier and a born diplomatist. He made himself first indispensable, then powerful, then master. In three years he conquered the country.

After an interval of no more than two years, high up in the Andean range in South America, another Spanish conqueror, with none of the romantic attractiveness of Cortez, the brutal Pizarro, visited a second, and totally different, new civilization, that of Peru. Here was a highly organized, indeed a planned, economy, with engineering works of irrigation and a systematic regulation of man-power. Pizarro's way was made easier by the lessons which Cortez had learnt, but this was a slower conquest, and when the Peruvian resistance was overcome it was followed by civil wars within the new Spanish province. But the two conquests of Mexico and Peru fixed the character of the Spanish dominions in America. Portuguese and Spanish explorers have left their traces in geographical names from the cold Tierra del Labrador in the north to the volcanic Tierra del Fuego, the land of fire, in the south; but the empire which the Spaniards left behind them had its centre of gravity in the Isthmus of Panama, with its richest provinces in Mexico, Peru, and the Caribbean islands.

The chief new elements in the colonial problems of the Spaniards came from their having overcome alien civilizations; though they also acquired large areas where the peoples were more primitive. Like the Portuguese they set up a feudal system, and they controlled it by administrative and judicial machinery on their European model, with Roman law, financial accountability, and royal supervision. They had more difficulty than the Portuguese in maintaining control over their officials and their European subjects in general; chiefly because they had so much to do with the settlement and cultivation of large land areas. In their aims and methods, however, the two nations differed no more than might be expected from the differences of the places which they occupied. The Spaniards did not try, any more than the Portuguese, to preserve their racial separateness. Spain had a larger population at home, and so could spare more officials and settlers. On the average there were probably between one and two thousand Spanish emigrants to America every year throughout the sixteenth century. But the Spaniards also needed negro slaves in the islands, and they granted privileges to companies which acquired them from the Portuguese. Generally speaking they regulated American trade on lines similar to those of the Portuguese trade in the east, though the element of royal monopoly was smaller and the corporations of traders played a greater part.

As Spain was the larger country, and the second comer, it was to be expected that there would be a more thorough theoretical discussion in its universities and government offices of the ethical and political and juridical problems of empire. There were divergent opinions. Some maintained that the heathen had no rights against their conquerors; but the highest authorities on the whole accepted the liberal view of the great Victoria, whose conception of justice rested on a recognition of duty to all men. The religious motive among the Spaniards was strong and sincere. It resulted at times in severities to which we should now give the name of persecution, and the Spanish kings set up in America an even more complete royal control over ecclesiastical affairs than they exercised in Spain; but the more central and populous of the Spanish colonies acquired a Christian civilization. There were soon great cities which almost had the appearance of European towns. There were not only cathedrals and monasteries; there was also a printing-press in Lima from 1584 and in Mexico from about 1535. In the second quarter of the nineteenth century an English administrator wrote with truth that until his time Spanish government had done more for the welfare of the indigenous inhabitants of colonial territories than that of any other European nation. The foundations of this imperishable work were laid in the first fifty years of Spanish dominion overseas.

For this we must ascribe much of the credit to the Christianity of those days, and we may doubt whether so good a result would have followed if these conquests had been made under other auspices. Again, the Church did much to mitigate and postpone the friction which colonization created between European states. In one form or another, conflicts of interests were bound to arise as soon as the subjects of different states appeared as rivals in the same waters and harbours. In Europe their trade

was parcelled out in national monopolies, and their masters
were perpetually embroiled over conflicting territorial claims.
If the merchants of Asia and Africa made one European nation
bid against another for their wares, there would be no chance of
establishing the regulated and monopolistic trade which alone
could bring profit from these hazardous and distant voyages. If
two flags were run up on one patch of American ground, the
territorial rivalries of the old world would extend to the new.
When Columbus came back from America the Spaniards and
the Portuguese alike were aware of these dangers; but they were
able to apply to the same authority which had granted the bulls
to Henry the Navigator. In the name of Pope Alexander VI a
bull was granted which divided the globe by a great circle into
two hemispheres, one for Portuguese and the other for Spanish
navigation. This first bull of 1493 came too early in the unfold-
ing of the new geographical knowledge. Fresh voyages soon
showed that the line did not accurately separate the areas in
which two states had made their respective discoveries. They
negotiated a new agreement, and in 1506 the papacy sanctioned
the new line on which they had agreed, a line running, to use
our modern notation, about 50° west of Greenwich.

Generally speaking this line gave America to the Spaniards,
Africa and Asia to the Portuguese; but there were exceptions
both in the east and in the west. The Philippine Islands fell to
Spain, and Portugal was allowed to develop Brazil. Here the
Spaniards offered no opposition, and at first the colony was not
much valued, but it was the first colony established in America
for the purpose of agriculture. By the middle of the sixteenth
century the sugar-cane had been introduced there from Madeira
and the export of tobacco had begun or was about to begin.
Brazil attracted more immigrants from Portugal than all the
other colonies together. It had its bishopric and its governor-
general, and it yielded gold.

The resort of Spain and Portugal to papal a djudication
their claims impressively illustrated the international primacy
of the Papacy, but even then it was primacy, not supremacy,
and there were limits to its extent. Other seafaring men along
the Atlantic coasts besides the Spaniards and Portuguese had
made discoveries, and other kings were not content to be shut
out from all the new opportunities. They did not regard the
bulls as binding, and legal doctrines were soon formulated

which denied some of the monopolistic Portuguese and Spanish pretensions. There was, for instance, the English doctrine of effective occupation, according to which a claim to territory was invalid unless the discoverer had not merely set foot there but actually taken possession. As it happened, however, neither the Spaniards nor the Portuguese had to reckon with serious European attacks on their colonies before the treaty of Le Cateau-Cambrésis in 1559. Various Frenchmen, Germans, and Englishmen had been active in America and Africa. The English had begun their regular long-distance voyages, and hoped to find a new passage to the Far East by the northern coasts of Russia, but this had brought them no farther than Archangel, far away from the Indies of the east or west, and their still small resources were absorbed by the Russian trade. Something more like 'a threat had come from France. The French had made notable discoveries in North America; and, during the wars against Charles V, they had attacked his American trade. A body of Huguenots, French Calvinists, had attacked Brazil, but in 1557 their one fort was captured and destroyed. When the European settlement came with the end of the war, the two empires of Portugal and Spain still stood alone and, to all appearances, stood firm.

The most wonderful feature of these two empires, as of the other European empires which have followed them, down to our own day, is that in spite of the immensity of the distances and the bewildering variety of entirely novel conditions their civilization held together. During many of their advances the explorers had a technical superiority which gave them easy victories over those who stood in their way. No one fired a gun at the Portuguese until they had rounded the Cape and worked their way up the east coast as far as Mombasa. The Aztecs of Mexico were not only without firearms, they were without iron, and at first sight the horses of the Spaniards struck terror into them. But in Mexico and everywhere else the numbers of the Europeans were so small that their technical advantages would have been useless without two greater things, discipline among themselves and judgement in dealing with others. Where, as in India and China, the established monarchies were too powerful to be overthrown or even shaken, these qualities enabled the Europeans to set up their factories and to settle orderly relations with the rulers and the merchants. It was not merely that among the adventurers there were a sufficient number of individuals who were suited to take the lead because they happened each to be happily endowed. These qualities were not the private possessions of one man and another; they were not distinguishing idiosyncrasies; they grew from the living European tradition, and they were nourished from the organized life of the European communities. The little clusters of settlers and traders were not lost to Europe. They did not, for the most part and in the long run, adopt the dress, the manners, the morals, or the religion of the populations among whom they made their homes. In time it became clear that their destiny was not to be assimilated but to assimilate. Of course there were deserters, and of course the colonists took over here one custom and there another from their new neighbours; but, even where there was free intermarriage and where the original inhabitants became Christians, it was still to Europe that they looked for their examples.

Materially the colonists depended on their homelands. The long arm of sea-power, which had placed them where they were, could still reach them, to support and to control. They could prosper best if they kept up their intercourse with Europe, sending home the raw materials of the tropics and the manufactured goods of the east in exchange for weapons, or slaves, or tools and machines. But stronger than this material dependence was the hold of their own civilization over their hearts and minds. Among the conquerors there were brutes and cynics, but there were many men who carried their loyalties with them, and so it came about that in these new far-flung communities the kings of Portugal and Spain were acknowledged and, in the long run, obeyed. Methods of government which they had lately developed in the full energy of their rising states were successfully adapted to the new and unprecedented tasks. The administrators paid attention to ideas which were hammered into shape in the universities. Just as the builders introduced the European architectural styles, the colonists in general brought their own way of life and invited their new subjects to adopt it.

In sketching the relations of the European states it will be necessary, from the point which we have now reached, to keep these colonial affairs constantly before us; but before we go on with the course of events, we may look forward and see how the expansion of Europe altered the tenor of life in Europe itself. It had great, immediate, and ever-growing effects in the region of the mind. Civilization was already in transition, gaining new powers and new aspirations, turning aside from some of its accustomed paths, when it was suddenly enlarged by this lifting of enclosing barriers. Thousands of men partook of new and thrilling experiences. Every thinker was confronted by new facts and new mysteries. For geographers and astronomers the new knowledge not only completed the old but transformed it. Physicians discovered new diseases and potent drugs. Theologians examined new religions, and judged the social systems peculiar to the newly discovered races or engendered by contact with them. Lawyers elaborated and codified the principles of property and contract appropriate to the new relationships. These great revisions of science and belief began in Portugal and Spain, and were taken up successively by the other nations of Europe, to continue down to the present time. With them there came a new consciousness of success and power. Conquest on a scale never dreamed of before had brought fabulous wealth and opportunities. For an enchanted hour real life had become romance.

Literature soon gained new themes and new moods, both in prose and poetry; for a similar enrichment the other arts waited longer, but in the sixteenth century Indian silks or choice pieces of Chinese porcelain were already prized by the rich or fortunate. And the economic result of expansion changed the conditions of life not only of the few but, sometimes for better and sometimes for worse, of whole peoples. Even the simplest economic system can never subsist for long together without change, and in the late fifteenth century economic life was as much stirred as political or intellectual life by currents of change, some of them swift and some slow, some deep and some superficial. Among the slower and deeper was an increase of population. We cannot give even approximate dates and figures for particular areas; but, about this time, in Europe generally population, after declining or remaining stationary for more than a century, began to grow. There is little that we can say about the reasons for this change. To say that epidemics were mitigated is not so much to answer the question as to restate it in part. We can, however, connect the change with some important changes in economic life to which it must have stood in the relation both of cause and consequence. We may presume that production was on the whole increasing, since a larger population found the means of subsistence and, in all probability, acquired them for the most part by doing productive work. This accords with what we know from other sources. The clearing of land and bringing it into cultivation can be traced in many places at this time; in others, changes in organization had similar effects. Some of the industrial regions were producing more goods, employing more men, becoming more populous. There seem also to have been more hands available for tasks outside agriculture and industry.

The size of armies seems to have begun to increase: the rise of infantry is a sign of it. Armies were not national. States which had money at their command hired troops from abroad, especially from the poorer countries like Switzerland, where a surplus of sturdy men could not find work on the land. Again, the emigration to far lands indicates that there were, for whatever reason, men available. Taking it all round, and allowing for decline in industry and agriculture in a number of regions, it appears that in Europe generally the population began to recover after its decline. The greatest rise was probably in the industrialized regions of western Europe, and in the lands immediately connected with them as sources of supply for food and raw materials. The increase, at first moderate, probably continued, with some acceleration, until the early seventeenth century, gradually slowing down about the middle of that century, and then continuing only in some favoured places.

The growth of numbers was favourable to the growth of production; the continent grew richer. This implies that its economic organization altered, or rather that certain methods which had been followed only in special branches of business and in special places became more widely diffused. These were methods which are commonly called 'capitalistic', and the period of their diffusion, from somewhere about the twelfth century until somewhere about the late eighteenth, is often called the period of early capitalism. The terms are not the best that could be devised, but they are so familiar that they can hardly be dispensed with. Capitalism means a system in which economic activities are under the direction of the owners of capital or of managers who are employed, actually or nominally, by these owners. Capital has been defined in many ways, but in this connexion it means wealth, whether money or physical objects, in use for the purposes of production. Thus it includes the buildings and wharves, the cranes and tools of a shipyard, the ships under construction and the cash in the pay-chest; but it does not include the owner's private house, or his pleasure-boats, except that we have to include some proportion of their value if his private house is in the yard and is used partly as an office, and if he uses the pleasure-boats occasionally for sending messages about the port or for entertaining business friends. The capitalistic system exists in its simplest form when the owner has the capital completely at his own disposal, when he can shut or open the business, engage labour or pay it off, decide what to make and where to sell it, without consulting anybody else. It does not exist at all where these matters are in the hands of all the workers in the concern, acting co-operatively, or where everyone is under the orders of some authority entirely outside the industry. Almost everywhere in recorded history the ownership of capital has carried with it some degree or semblance of controlling power, and economic life has been organized on innumerable plans in each of which there has been some element of capitalism.

The difference between the historical types of organization which are specially called capitalistic and the other types lies mainly in the degree of freedom which the owner has in his work of direction. A medieval peasant might be rich, and yet he might have no right to sell his land and invest the proceeds in some other piece of land or in industry, no right to choose what market he would sell his crops in, no right to decide what crops to grow, and no right to set up his son in business as a dealer to work in with the farm. There have often been conditions in which it suited peasants or industrial workers well enough to work in such bondage to custom or traditional rules, and a rigid system of this sort has the merit that it prevents both the incompetent man and the unscrupulously greedy man from upsetting the affairs of their neighbours as much as they might if they were free all round. But where there was specialization there had to be freedom. A printer might set up an expensive machine, buy paper and pay wages to compositors, so that he had spent a considerable sum before he had a book to sell. Unless he was rich he must have recourse to a capitalist who was free to advance money when and where he judged it best. In the south of France and in one German district the farmers grew rich by concentrating on growing woad, a plant which gave a famous blue dye. It was bought by dyers all over Europe, and this trade

in woad could not have arisen without merchants to carry it to
the places where it would sell to advantage, without a trade in
foodstuffs that freed the woad-growers from growing their own
food, in short without a system of free markets and calculations
of prices by various people who were free to sell where the best
prices ruled. The rise of capitalism meant the division of labour,
the prevalence of calculation, the growth of commerce, and the
development of subsidiary institutions which facilitated all these,
especially by providing money as and when it was needed.

Other demands besides those of industry furthered the same
results. If a king wanted money quickly to hire troops and could
only raise it slowly by taxation, a banker, or more probably a
banking family, would come to his rescue. The kings dealt in
larger sums than anyone else, but noblemen who were contrac-
tors for troops, clerics, and even popes who built cathedrals, all
helped to build up the network of financial institutions. At first
Italy was its home. The Renaissance made its contribution: the
first treatise on book-keeping by double entry was written by a
friar who was a friend of Leonardo da Vinci. It was printed and
versions of it soon appeared in French, Flemish, and English.
This shows that the new methods were spreading widely. As the
relations of individual men and of communities came to depend
more and more on bargaining in the markets and on agreements
for money, new needs arose. Above all there was a need for
money. Paper money, in the form of bills of exchange, was
familiar among business men, and had an international circulation; but for a thousand everyday purposes metallic money was
needed, and Europe grew hungry for gold and silver. In the late
fifteenth century the richest man in Europe was the south
German banker Jacob Fugger of Augsburg, and what made him
so was his control over silver-mines in Germany, Bohemia, and
Hungary.

These were some of the economic changes of the age of the
discoveries, and the discoveries gave a fresh impulse to them all.
In those days it was a great undertaking to fit out a ship, to
victual it, to provide a cargo and to pay the crew. There were
many different ways of spreading the costs and the risks between
different owners and merchants; but the far trades needed
finance of a new order. The ships were costly; the crews were
large; the dangers were so great that it was foolish to send one ship
alone, but a voyage might last for years before anything came back

to sell, and from two voyages out of three no ship might return. The discoveries therefore helped on capitalism in the maritime countries. They also transformed the map of European commerce. The Mediterranean ceased to be the one highway to the east and became a secondary route, almost a blind alley. When they heard that the Cape had been rounded, the wise Venetians thought of a canal through the Isthmus of Suez, but that would not have saved their commerce. Even in competition with the Cape route, the 'overland' routes by the Red Sea and the Persian Gulf might still have been frequented if economic factors alone had been at work; but the Portuguese did not allow free play to the economic factors. Their naval squadrons based on Ormuz stopped the trade. At a much later date, in the late seventeenth century, the Turks resisted the attempts of the French and others to reopen it, and historians, reading back this obstructiveness into the earlier age, imagined that it was the Turkish conquest which diverted the life-giving stream of traffic from the ports of the Levant. We know now that it was not only to the disadvantage of the Turks but in their despite that this came about. At the very time when they were sweeping forward in eastern Europe, western Europe was growing richer and more efficient and was cutting off one of the springs of their wealth. Egypt and Syria were impoverished, and this may have been the beginning of the decline which, much later, was to afflict the Ottoman power itself.

The Venetians, who had been the chief intermediaries in eastern trade, were now short-circuited. As Venice sank, the south German cities, stages on the Venetian trade-routes, suffered; though they still gained wealth from the mines. Trade now flowed from the ocean seaboard up the great rivers; Lisbon and Antwerp rose. With Antwerp the prosperity of the Netherlands and England was bound up; and their textile industries also gained at the expense of south Germany.

Perhaps the total quantities of spices and textiles imported from the east did not increase notably for some long time; but the American cargoes soon released great economic forces. There were entirely new commodities, like tobacco and potatoes, which were beginning to alter social life in the late sixteenth century. There were large supplies of commodities which had been scarce: it is supposed that by 1600 half the world's supply of sugar was coming from Brazil. Above all there were the com-

modities which made the most direct impression on the economic structure, the precious metals. First the Portuguese brought
gold from the Gold Coast; then the Spaniards found gold and
silver in America. In 1545 they discovered the silver-mine at
Potosí in Upper Peru (now in Bolivia). There they applied a
new method of extracting the metal from its ore, and in a few
years they were bringing silver into Europe in quantities that had
never been imagined before.

This might in other conditions have affected silversmiths and
ladies more than anyone else; but coming at this time it played
a part, and perhaps a very great part, in changing the hunger
for the precious metals as money into a surfeit of them. All over
Europe metallic money became easier to get; in other words
there was a great rise in prices, which is called 'the price-
revolution'. It came first in Spain, where the silver was landed;
then it spread through all the countries west of Russia and the
Turkish empire, more rapidly in some and less rapidly in others,
as they were able to get their share of American treasure by
exchanging goods for silver. Price-levels, the purchasing-power
of money, the relative wealth of different economic groups were
upset, and it was a time of economic disturbance. Some men
were ruined and others found business difficult, while others
became suddenly rich. All those who were entitled to fixed
sums, whether as rents or as taxes or dues, could buy less with
these sums than before; all those who were free to demand what
prices they could exact had new and rising opportunities. So,
broadly speaking, the old world of landlords and peasants
found it harder to carry on; the traders and bankers found it
easier, and capitalism advanced.

All these changes combined, as they persisted more or less in
the same directions far into the seventeenth century, to accen-
tuate some of the social contrasts between different parts of
Europe, and so they modified the foundations and the power
of the states. One great contrast was between a western area
where the cultivators of the soil kept a fair degree of personal
freedom and an eastern area where their status was steadily
depressed into subjection. There was great diversity within the
western area. In France and England large estates were growing
up, while in parts of the Netherlands and of Switzerland the
countryside came more and more under the control of the towns
and their merchants. It is, however, roughly true that in the

west there was much free ownership and much freedom of contract between landlords and tenants, while in Poland, Germany east of the Elbe, and Denmark, agriculture, especially corn-growing, was an export industry, working for the populous and commercial west, and managed by great landowners, with powers over the peasantry which they often used oppressively.

Until the middle of the sixteenth century the chief political result of economic change was that, in unison with the military and ecclesiastical events which we have noticed, it established Spain as the strongest Christian power.

VI

WARS OF RELIGION

FOR almost exactly a century there followed wars and revolutions in which there was never a genuine and general peace. In the political sphere their greatest result was that Spain lost its ascendancy both in Europe and overseas. Mercifully for the survival of western civilization, the pressure of the Turk was relaxed. The peace of Le Cateau-Cambrésis put an end to the active alliance with France which had almost brought them into the European system, and there were signs that all was not well with their empire. One sultan was deposed and another was murdered; the others, and their viziers, were mediocrities or worse; the court became more and more corrupt; the outlying pashas disregarded the central power. The discipline of the army was impaired, and the janissaries became a hereditary caste with other interests outside their proper military business. Before long the French, by means of their commerce and through acting as protectors of its Christian subjects, began to acquire influence within the empire itself. For the present, however, the main fabric was unshaken. The dynasty maintained itself; Constantinople was unapproachable and safe; no territory worth mentioning was lost in the wars.

There was indeed one very famous encounter, the battle of Lepanto. In 1570 the Turks planned an attack on Cyprus, and, to save it, the pope and Spain made an alliance with the Venetians. In 1571 the attack began. The principal fortress of the island surrendered and its garrison was treacherously massacred. Then the allied fleet put out from Messina, with contingents from Malta and nine Italian states. At Lepanto they destroyed the Turkish fleet, and won the most unqualified victory of the Christian arms for nearly 600 years. It proved that, once they could combine, the Christian states were a match for the Turks, at least by sea. That was a great thing; but that was all. The victory was not followed up. The alliance fell apart. Cyprus was lost. In 1580 the Spaniards made a truce of long duration with the Turks. The position in the Mediterranean remained for more than a century substantially what it had been before, with the Christians predominant to the west of the Sicilian narrows, and the Turks to the east, where by degrees they tightened their hold.

On land there were frontier wars, but nothing decisive happened in Europe. In the late sixteenth century the fighting was on the whole favourable to the Habsburgs, who took advantage of a diversion in the Turkish rear brought about by the revival of Persia under its great ruler Shah Abbas. In 1606 the Turks made a treaty of peace with the emperor, and for the first time they negotiated the terms instead of dictating them. For more than half a century the emperors had paid tribute to the Turks, and now they bought it off with a lump sum; but they won back no territory, and it was another fifty years before they had enough quiet at home to conduct any serious military operations on their eastern frontier. In 1620–1 the Turks were at war with Poland, but this was a mere episode, and for more than twenty years after that they had no trouble from any of their Christian neighbours. They were left at liberty to extinguish the Persian revival.

In the quarrels which prevented the European states from combining against the Turks, religion and politics were more closely connected than at any other time, both in the internal affairs of the states and in their mutual relations. It was, indeed, impossible to distinguish domestic from international affairs, for the religious parties were bound together by loyalties which transcended national boundaries. They took sides in political and constitutional conflicts, and tried to succour their friends in other countries with the resources of their states. So intense was this militancy that it threatened to undo the consolidation of some of the strongest states. It broke out as soon as the peace of 1559 set Frenchmen and Spaniards free from their absorption in the struggle for Italy. The great survivors from the crises of the early sixteenth century died within a few years of one another, Ignatius Loyola in 1556, Calvin and the Emperor Ferdinand in 1564. The men who were now in office and in power had grown up after the religious schism began; they no longer tried to restore the old unity by compromises, but took their positions on one side or other of the dividing lines for granted. Having inherited the new religious enmities along with the old dynastic and constitutional feuds, they sharpened contention wherever they found it.

The year of the treaty of Le Cateau-Cambrésis saw the foundation of the academy at Geneva, a university on a new model, to which ministers and laymen came from all over Europe to learn the fighting faith of Calvin. When the men who were trained at Geneva returned to their homes they nowhere set up institutions exactly on the Genevan plan; but everywhere they did set up organizations of their own, and throughout Europe Calvinism became a unified political and intellectual force. The final sessions of the Council of Trent marked the same stage on the Catholic side. It was natural that the Catholics, once the first confusion of their losses was over, should win some of them back. In Germany they regained here a building, there a convent; there were legal decisions by which property or privileges were restored. It was often necessary to apply or interpret the peace of Augsburg, for there were still princes, including prince-bishops, who turned Protestant; but the peace was meant to keep things as they were in 1559, and therefore it forbade any further secularizations of ecclesiastical property. In Germany the Catholics lost no more ground, either literally or metaphorically. The conquests of Lutheranism ended with the first generation. The Jesuits, who gained control of the university of Ingolstadt in 1563, began to make themselves useful to the Catholic princes and to make use of them. Soon there was an open Catholic counter-offensive; but it lacked leaders. For many years none of the emperors took a decided line and none of them was willing to use force for the recovery of ecclesiastical rights. The Habsburg possessions were for the time being divided, since two younger branches had been provided with appanages after the death of Ferdinand; this and the feeble character of his successors made the imperial authority less effective than it had been during his lifetime. Thus, although the Catholics organized, converted, restated their claims, the religious peace of Augsburg, which satisfied neither sort of extremists, was stable enough to prevent a renewal of general bloodshed and confusion in Germany for more than sixty years.

During this period of two generations the full force of the great antagonisms was not felt in Germany, or to the eastward. Now and again an emperor or a German prince would take a hand in the ecclesiastical and political strife of a neighbouring country, perhaps as a mediator, perhaps even by sending or leading troops to the help of some belligerent; but not as a

principal fully committed to the contest. For Germany it was a
long period of neutrality, and incubation. The theatres of war
were in the west. In France and the Netherlands the religious
strife blazed up and rekindled both old constitutional disputes
and the old rivalry of the French and Spanish crowns. During
the wars between them each had repressed' the heretics in its
own dominions. In the Netherlands many of the people, especially the townspeople, had been disgusted by the severity of this
persecution, some from mere humankindness, some because
they were impressed by the doctrines of the sufferers, or by their
patience. The government had not, however, stayed its hand
for any reason of policy. In France, on occasion, the persecution
had been suspended in order to preserve unity for the purposes
of the war. No sooner was the war over than the French Calvinists held their first national synod. As it happened the French
monarchy, under a succession of unprincipled and incapable
kings, did more to divide the nation than to unite it. Calvinism
passed from the seigneurial to the political level. The great lords
who took it up, some of them in all sincerity, alternated between
factious intrigue and a national policy. National policy meant
an aristocratic constitutional programme of government in co-
operation with the estates.

Across the frontier to the north there were dissatisfied magnates who wanted to increase their own influence in affairs by a
similar programme, and some of them wanted to put an end to
religious persecution. They looked for foreign allies against their
master Philip II of Spain. From Germany they got some little
help from time to time; but to Frenchmen, of one religion or
the other, in power or aspiring to it, they could offer an inducement that might purchase more powerful aid. The only point
where France could hope to damage Spain strategically was in
the Netherlands, so threateningly near to Paris that it seemed a
French national need to push back the frontier there. There was
no chance of setting up a French party in Spain itself; Spain
was so united that France could gain no leverage by playing on
religious or constitutional opposition. King Philip II indeed did
away with the last remnants of constitutional liberties in Castile
and the more considerable liberal elements in Aragon, making
both his crowns absolute monarchies; but his opponents, or
rather victims, there had no body of friends abroad. In France,
on the other hand, Spain was able, in the name of Catholic

militancy, to collect a party and divide the nation. The first leader in this collaboration with the strongest and most Catholic of all states was the Duke of Guise, the lucky general who had captured Metz and Calais. He was a person of no small international consequence: the family of which he was the head had connexions ramifying as far as Scotland. These were some of the elements of the situation in which there began a series of civil wars, simultaneous and inextricably involved together, in France and the Netherlands, in all of which, directly or indirectly, Spain took part.

These wars were cruel and destructive. One after another the leaders on both sides were assassinated. In the Netherlands the Duke of Alva enforced military rule with a severity that had never been known before in a rich and highly civilized country. In France Guise touched a new depth of savagery in the massacre of St. Bartholomew. After years of misery the chaos changed into coherent warfare, in which the states kept order at home and waged orderly hostilities against one another: the civil wars became international wars, and in 1598, when France and Spain again made peace, the political, social, and economic map of the region between the Pyrenees and the German frontiers had been redrawn.

In France the constitutional results were decisive. The aristocratic programme of limited monarchy and reliance on the states general had failed, and so had the alliance of the Guises with the democracies of Paris and other cities. For the future nothing was possible except a strong and centralized monarchy. After 1614 the states general never met again until the French Revolution began in 1789. The royal officials overcame, one by one, all the local, regional, feudal institutions which had hampered their activities. The only check came from the lawcourts, which were manned by a largely hereditary body, with a corporate feeling and not lacking in professional ability.

The religious settlement was a combination of absolute monarchy with toleration protected by special guarantees. France was mainly Catholic, and there could be no future for a régime which did not recognize this fact. The final victor in the civil wars, King Henry IV, began life as a Huguenot, but he was the embodiment of the national spirit which survived the ruin of the two extreme religious parties. He became a Catholic, and sincerely, and he bought off his opponents at whatever price was necessary. Although they had no chance of fulfilling their original hopes of imposing their belief, the Huguenots were still strong enough to ask a high price. In the year when he made peace with Spain, Henry granted them the Edict of Nantes. By this he gave them freedom of conscience, that is freedom from inquisition, and the right to maintain churches in all places where they had them already. They were to be admitted to all offices and to all schools and colleges. They were to be given political control over many towns, one of which was the strongly fortified trading port of La Rochelle; but they had to give up their provincial assemblies and all alliances or negotiations with foreign powers.

In spite of all the confusion, this was one of the great periods of French literature. In the first half of the sixteenth century the most original French writer was Rabelais, a doctor and a priest, a contemporary of Calvin and Loyola at the university of Paris, who fought some of the battles of the Renaissance with an overwhelming uproariousness, and left behind him stores of vitality which writers have drawn upon ever since. During the worst of the warfare there came the poetry of Ronsard, a Catholic soldier and a companion of the tragic Mary Queen of Scots, a poet of roses and nightingales and of French country scenes. Literature in general became more polished, and this is true of political literature. The civil wars turned on questions of authority and resistance, of constitutional right and the relations of Church and State. The main arguments had been stated in the Middle Ages and restated in the early days of the Protestant Reformation; but some of the French pamphlets and treatises gave them classical expression. Catholics and Calvinists in turn, when they were in opposition, claimed the right to resist on religious grounds and so maintained that government ought to rest on the consent, or at least respect the rights, of the governed. The book which in the end held the field, as Henry IV did in action, was a new statement of the case for authority. It was written by Jean Bodin, a lawyer who, like the king, had once been a Huguenot,[1] but who now formulated the doctrine of sovereignty, the doctrine that there ought to be one supreme will in every state, to which all other wills are subject. France, like

[1] This seems to be proved by N. Weiss in *Bulletin de la Société de l'histoire du protestantisme français*, vol. lxxii (1923).

Spain, had now become a state to which this doctrine seemed
obviously appropriate, and neither of them now fitted the older
interpretation of the nature of the state, according to which no
authority was unlimited, and due subjection to one authority
was compatible with some subjection to others.

In the Netherlands the dissatisfaction of the magnates proved
to be the prelude to a revolution in which Calvinism and con-
stitutionalism were intertwined with a nationalist element.
From time to time the revolutionary party were helped in their
civil war by the French and also by the English, who were
jealous lest the French might become dangerously strong in
that quarter. There was a brief period in which all the Netherlands were united in resistance : a great leader, William the
Silent, persuaded them to combine for constitutional government and religious toleration. In the end, however, a dexterous
governor regained a foothold from which he renewed the war.
The end of it was that the Spaniards retained their hold only on
the ten southerly provinces, corresponding very roughly to the
modern Belgium, including what had been the richest and
most populous parts. Here the Spaniards had to renounce their
schemes of modernized and centralized administration. The old
prosperity of this region was gone, for many reasons, but most
of all because their opponents shut up the port of Antwerp.
None the less, although this truncated state, which remained
Spanish all through the seventeenth century, was repeatedly a
theatre of war, the court of the governors, the palaces of the
nobility, and the public and private buildings of the rich bur-
gesses had a characteristic art of their own. It combined the
old Flemish warmth and vitality with the proud display of the
reformed Catholic Church. Its greatest figure was the painter
Rubens.

The other seven provinces, of which the chief was the maritime trading province of Holland, the western centre of shipping
and of the Baltic corn-trade, became a new state, a federal
republic. This was not the first new unit to be added to the
European system, for in the time of Charles the Bold the Swiss
cantons had thrown off their old allegiances; but Switzerland
was content with safety behind its mountains, and the Dutch
republic was the first new state to play an active part in international politics. Although its population can scarcely have

numbered more than two and a half millions, its commercial wealth enabled it to build up a navy and to hire substantial numbers of foreign troops. After the struggle for independence had gone on for more than thirty years with the aid of allies, at last none of these was willing to fight on, but the republic was strong enough to stand alone. It began to attack the Spaniards where they were most vulnerable, in their colonies and sea-communications. The Spaniards saw that only a respite could save them from disaster, and in 1609 they agreed to a Twelve Years Truce mediated by the French. They meant to resume hostilities when they were ready, and so they neither recognized the republic as *de jure* independent nor explicitly conceded its right to trade in the East Indies. The truce gave the new state its opportunity. Its East India Company, imitating the Portuguese methods and improving on them, did business all over the east, and especially in the Malay Archipelago. A few years after the truce they had the nucleus of an empire, with a capital, Batavia in Java, and a governor-general. They excluded other European nations from these waters. The trading families, growing in wealth, became a gifted and cultivated governing class, and during the truce the republic immediately established itself as a model of cleanliness and welfare. Classical learning, science, poetry, and architecture flourished there, and above all painting.

The republic shut out the Catholics and some of the Protestant dissenters from full citizenship. They might not hold office. The letter of the law denied them freedom of worship, but they were allowed to buy off the magistrates, so that this was the first populous and developed western state where the sects enjoyed a large measure of toleration, and its example offered Europe an important lesson. These unprivileged religious minorities had little or no share in political power and responsibility, and only imperfect contact with the main streams of education and social life. They had their limitations and their eccentricities; but their freedom to experiment in religious ideas and practices enabled them to awaken receptive minds outside them, and they stimulated creative thought. The municipalities admitted, or sometimes even welcomed, religious refugees from all over Europe: Jews from Spain and Portugal, independents from England, French Huguenots, and, later, Czechs. They helped to stimulate the inquiring, inventive, adaptable spirit of

enterprise. In economic affairs both the native and the immi-
grant dissenters were prominent. While the great monarchies
tried to organize their resources in uniformity and system, this
federal republic drew its strength from variety and intellectual
freedom.

Another European power came into the arena at the same
time as the Dutch and partly for the same reasons. Except for
brief intervals of friendship with France, England had oscillated
between isolation from continental affairs and alliance with
the Habsburgs, whose Netherlands were the great market for
English wool and cloth. Twice the English royal family, the
Tudors, had come into the Habsburg marriage-combinations.
On the second occasion the queen, Mary, was married to
Philip II of Spain himself, and he reigned jointly with her for
four years. This personal union was ended by Mary's death, and
her successor Queen Elizabeth would not renew it. She was indeed, at times in spite of herself, the representative of new and
revolutionary elements in England which could not exist in the
old intimacy with the Habsburgs. During the price-revolution
England grew in wealth and population, and in spite of upheavals of popular unrest the governing class grew stronger.
The Tudors worked with it by means of parliamentary legislation and aristocratic local administration; through this co-
operation King Henry VIII, and the ministers of his young son
Edward VI, carried out great ecclesiastical changes. They confiscated much church property; they assumed even greater
authority over church-government than the kings of France and
Spain; they closed the monasteries and the chantries. Each
stage of these changes was linked by attraction or repulsion with
continental Protestantism and war and diplomacy. The reign of
Philip and Mary brought a partial reaction, but Elizabeth
established a national Church which the papacy could not
countenance. The religious settlement was ambiguous, but it
was definitive. Continental Protestantism of every colour was
kept at arm's length; dissent was punished; but a new nationalism was founded on hostility to Rome.

The same dynasty made great advances towards ending the
gravest weakness of England, the Scottish problem. The smaller,
poorer, and less settled kingdom of Scotland had naturally been
for centuries a potential or actual ally of England's continental

enemies and therefore had an old tradition of alliance with
France. As it chanced a Scottish king contracted a French marriage during the brief period of the ascendancy of the house of
Guise, and so it was that when Queen Elizabeth drew away
from friendship with the Habsburgs the Scottish crown was held
by Mary, the daughter of a Guise princess, a member of the
family which rose and fell with international Catholic militancy
under the aegis of Spain. She was faced by rebellious nobles
and Calvinistic reformers, and, when she fled from them to
England the hopes of the English Catholic peers could not but
be centred on her. Conspiracy followed conspiracy, and at last
she was executed. This brought open war between England and
Spain. The English had been sending aid to the Dutch for
fifteen years already, at first informally and then by assuming
an open protectorate over the nascent state. They were no more
willing to see the French as masters there than the Spaniards.
With the Dutch as allies they withstood the first shock of
Spanish attack, and the defeat of the Spanish armada in 1588
was one of the proudest feats in English history. For the remaining years of Queen Elizabeth's reign the fortunes of the war, in
alliance with the other enemies of Spain all over the world,
swayed to and fro, but the glory of that deliverance was never
forgotten. It was not followed by a revival of all the arts. In
painting and architecture the Reformation had destroyed so
much that it took long to repair the damage, but English literature broke into full flower. The instruments had been tuned by
courtly and learned poets of the previous generations; now the
supreme players took them up. Shakespeare came to London
in the year before the Armada. All through the orchestration of
his versatility there sounds his pride and joy in the greatness of
England.

This greatness lay not only in glory but in common sense.
The Elizabethan statesmen kept in sight the need to settle their
problems, and in nothing were they more sagacious than in the
matter of Scotland. Mary Queen of Scots had Tudor blood, and
they handled the thorny Scottish problem so well that when
Queen Elizabeth died she was peacefully succeeded by Mary's
son, James. For the first time one king ruled from the Shetlands
to the Channel. To be sure, it was only a personal union. James
failed to complete it by a union of states, because it was still a
union only of heads and not of hearts; but Great Britain, with

a population of more than five millions and another million in turbulent Ireland, was now one unit in international affairs. Five years before the Dutch Twelve Years Truce, James made peace with Spain, and his peoples were able to thrive and to quarrel among themselves in full security.

When the French, the English, and the Dutch had successively made their peace, Spain was still the strongest power in Europe. All through the reign of Philip II, who died in 1598, she was so strong that he was believed, with more justice than his father, to be aiming at a 'universal monarchy'. It was only because his many preoccupations in all the continents made it impossible for him to meet them one at a time that each of these three powers had grown in strength. The Dutch made good their first patch of territory in the year after Lepanto; eighteen years later Philip lost his last chance of mastering them by dispatching an army to intervene in the French civil wars. And in spite of all his losses he had made enormous acquisitions. In 1578 the young king of Portugal was fighting in North Africa against the Moors. At the battle of Alkazar-el-Kebir he was defeated and killed. His successor was his great-uncle, an aged and infirm ecclesiastic, during whose reign of two years half a dozen claimants had their eyes on the succession. One of them was Philip II, and the army, under Alva, which enforced his claim won him two dazzling prizes at a stroke. For the first and only time since the Roman empire, the Iberian peninsula was united, and this personal union, greater in itself than the union of Great Britain, carried with it the union of all the European possessions in Africa, Asia, and America. Spanish civilization rose to its summits. Cervantes, who was wounded at Lepanto, wrote *Don Quixote* to be read in every country of the world. El Greco's genius fused together the solemnity of Byzantium, the pictorial glow of Venice, and the vision of the Spanish mystics. After him came Velasquez, the painters' painter, to commemorate the dignity and courtesy of courtiers and campaigners. There was no decadence in these fields until far on in the seventeenth century; but in social and economic matters there were ominous deficiencies. Spain was rich from the treasure of the Indies, but she had no sufficient industry of her own. She depended on foreign manufactures, shipping, and commerce. While the perpetual drain of warfare overstrained her finances, population began to decline and,

especially in the south, lands went out of cultivation for lack of
hands. Peace with France, England, and the Netherlands gave
an opportunity for reform, and it was well understood that the
need was pressing.

It was at best an uneasy peace; the old forces of disunity still
heaved below the surface; but the next great outbreak left all
these countries outside its range at first, and brought war in the
region which had for so long been immune, Germany and some
of the lands to the eastward. A good many German princes had
been improving their administration by imitating French or
Burgundian or Austrian arrangements. Each of the religious
parties had become more capable of fighting and more determined to press its claims. At the end of the sixteenth century and
in the early seventeenth the two junior Habsburg lines died out,
and the inheritance was reunited. The emperor of the moment
was out of his mind, and his successor was both elderly and ineffective, but behind the two stood their heir, Ferdinand, a pupil
of the Ingolstadt Jesuits. Another of their pupils, a capable
military organizer, succeeded to the duchy of Bavaria, Austria's
western neighbour. On the Protestant side down to this time all
the leading princes had been Lutherans, and so content with the
peace of Augsburg which gave a place in the world to Lutheranism but not to any other Protestant creed. Now the Elector
Palatine[1] became a Calvinist, so that a leader was available who,
like all Calvinists, brought religion into politics, and who was
in a position great enough to raise his German quarrels to the
level of international affairs.

At the time of the Dutch Twelve Years Truce and for some
years after, it looked as if there would be a European war over a
German question, because Protestant and Catholic claimants
disputed the inheritance of the Catholic Duke of Jülich and
Cleves. His possessions about the lower Rhine were as important
strategically as they are in our own day, but Henry IV of France,
when he was about to begin hostilities, was assassinated. All the
parties accepted a compromise by partition, so that the crisis
came in 1618 in another storm-centre.

[1] The other electors had territorial titles, 'Elector of Saxony' and so on; the
Elector Palatine was so called because his remote predecessors had held a court
office (*Palatium* being the Latin for a palace), and his dominions were named from
his office, the Upper Palatinate, the Lower Palatinate, &c.

PLATE 28

El Greco, St. Jerome as penitent. (See p. xxiv)

North-west from Vienna and open on that side, but shut off from Germany and Poland by its mountains, was the kingdom of Bohemia, the country of the Czechs, to which Silesia and Lusatia, across the mountains, also belonged. According to the more or less accepted constitutional law it was an elective kingdom, and, after the battle of Mohacs, Ferdinand I had been elected there, as in Hungary. In Bohemia the religious position was even more confused than in Germany: there were not only Lutherans but also considerable remnants of older national sects, strong in seigniorial support, which traced back their origin to the schism of John Hus in the early fifteenth century. Here the Habsburgs tried to preserve the Roman authority by generous concessions; but heresy spread continually and at last the attempts of Ferdinand II to enforce ecclesiastical rights led to a revolution. The leaders of the opposition tried to murder his representatives in Prague, and this was the signal for a rising not only all over Bohemia but in Austria as well.

Ferdinand was almost without an army. The rebels got troops together and appeared before Vienna. They hoped for foreign aid, and they offered their crown to the Calvinist Elector Palatine, Frederick. He, among various high connexions, counted King James I of England as his father-in-law; but James was not to be drawn into this ill-considered adventure. The only foreign prince who intervened was the Calvinist Gabriel Bethlen, prince of Transylvania, who in the end gained nothing for his allies but added some Hungarian counties to his own dominions. Ferdinand did not take long to recover his position. He made sure of Maximilian of Bavaria and the other Catholic princes, and he bought off the Lutherans by surrendering Lusatia to their leader, the elector of Saxony. Then his general, the Netherlander Tilly, routed Frederick at the White Mountain before Prague.

The Bohemian episode lasted a bare three years. Afterwards, at his leisure, Ferdinand extinguished the political liberties of the country, and stamped out all forms of belief except the Catholic. During the next 200 years Czech culture was put down; German landowners and officials depressed the Czechs to the status of a subject nationality whose language and traditions sank into obscurity. In Germany, however, the Bohemian episode left a legacy of strife. Ferdinand, who had become emperor, caused Frederick's electoral rank to be transferred to the younger branch of his family in the person of Maximilian of Bavaria. This drastic action made many of the princes apprehensive for their 'German liberties'. They feared that the Habsburgs would use their growing power to turn the imperial dignity into a real monarchy. The fugitive Frederick was a symbol, and from time to time one enemy of the Habsburgs or another took up his cause. All this was the more dangerous because in 1621 the Twelve Years Truce ran out, and the Dutch and Spaniards fought again on sea and land.

The fears and ambitions of some of the princes of north-west Germany led them to invite King Christian IV of Denmark, a warlike prince who had German possessions, to invade north Germany. The emperor defeated them by the help of a new man, Wallenstein, who used a great fortune, made from the confiscated estates of the Bohemian rebels, to collect a cosmopolitan mercenary army stronger than any that any German prince or emperor had ever commanded. Wallenstein established the emperor's power on the shores of the Baltic, or rather his own power, for political allegiance meant little to him. Even before the Danes had withdrawn from the war, Ferdinand rashly revoked his guarantee of the *status quo* to the Protestants. This, and his new strength on the Baltic, brought a very formidable antagonist against him. We shall see later how it was that Sweden had recently gained great power round the Baltic coasts. Her king, Gustavus Adolphus, was a great soldier, a reformer of armament and tactics; he was also a Protestant leader, and a statesman, well served by able ministers. Some of the German princes, including the electors of Saxony and Brandenburg, found him an uncomfortable ally. His schemes might well be inimical to their liberties, and they had, after all, a genuine regard for the empire so long as it left them at ease. Gustavus won a succession of lightning victories: then he was killed in battle. The dubious electors drew away from the Swedes; but there were still minor princes who kept the field with them. The emperor detected Wallenstein in treasonable designs and had him murdered; but his army was loyal and it became the standing army of Habsburg Austria, a new great power. The Spanish ally gave effective military help. In 1635 the emperor abandoned his attempt to recover the Catholic losses, and so conciliated most of his German opponents. He had reached an unquestionable primacy in Germany. Only two minor German states were still in arms against him. But it was still thirteen years before Germany was pacified, and they were years of still greater destruction and suffering.

The reason was that the Danish and Swedish episodes had given time for the most persistent of all the enemies of the Habsburgs to collect its strength and to choose its ground to attack. France in the early seventeenth century was gaining energy as quickly as Spain was losing it. Henry IV had begun the erection of an efficient monarchy. His death caused an interruption, but the work was taken up again with relentless determination by a minister, the Cardinal de Richelieu. Richelieu found the French nobility dissatisfied and unmanageable, from the magnates who were almost the equals of kings down to the country landowners whom the price-revolution had ruined. Some of them still cherished the militant faith of Calvin, and when France fought a short war against Charles I of England, the son of James, it called out the old combination of Huguenot nobles with a foreign enemy. Richelieu ended this. He deprived the Huguenots of their guarantees, leaving them their toleration but without the means to defend it. He tamed the whole nobility, making them into obedient subjects, some of them ornamental and others useful, especially in the army. All this was not achieved without many acts little fitting the character of a churchman; but Richelieu was not entirely out of touch with a strong religious movement which began under Henry IV and continued throughout his own time. It owed much to the founders of new orders in Italy, and to the Spanish mystics; but it bore the stamp of the French mind. St. Francis de Sales, the most cultivated of devotional writers, and St. Vincent de Paul, the most effective of philanthropic organizers, were both essentially French. They had a confident touch like that of the new French literature, the silken verse and the rapier prose, which gathered European influence in those years. The movement in literature was consciously national. The men of letters were gathered under the cardinal's protection in the French Academy: every polite accomplishment advanced the prestige of France.

It was only slowly and gradually that this strength became effective in international relations, but the way was made ready for it by well-informed and rationally-conducted diplomacy. First France mediated between Sweden and Poland in the peace-negotiations which set Gustavus Adolphus free for his German enterprise. After his death French subsidies kept the Swedish army in pay. Then Richelieu made a fresh alliance with the Dutch and declared war against Spain. By this time the German princes were so much weakened that Germany became a theatre of international war, as Italy and France had been in their turns in the sixteenth century. The rivalry between the two strongest powers in Europe overshadowed and absorbed the lesser conflicts, and the German questions were only settled when the power of Spain was brought low. Before Richelieu died in 1642 the French had conquered Alsace and the Portuguese had begun a long war to recover their independence at home and in the colonies. In the year after he died a French general won a decisive victory over the once invincible Spanish army. This battle of Rocroi proved to all the world that the ascendancy of Spain was ending. She had failed to take her chance of recuperating after the wars of Philip II. Five years later she withdrew from the German fighting and Germany had peace.

Looking back on all this German fighting since the Bohemian revolution of 1618 historians gave it the name of the Thirty Years War,[1] a by-word in after-times for cruelty and misery. Two things have fixed attention on the recorded horrors of this time. Firstly there was the feeling that much of the misery had been inflicted on Germany by foreign invaders, and this feeling grew stronger in the nineteenth century when a united German nation, strong in military power, was able to wage its wars abroad and to keep the German soil inviolate. But it is an anachronism to allot praise or blame to the soldiers and statesmen of the seventeenth century in proportion as they furthered or hindered the rise of a national spirit and national cohesion in Germany. There was indeed, as we have seen, loyalty to the emperor and the empire; but loyalty in those days was as authentic when its object was dynastic or religious as when it was national, and no one thought it morally reprehensible to call in foreign aid for his church or his dynasty. The second reason which has blackened the name of the Thirty Years War is that

---

[1] This name seems to have become generally current from the publication of Schiller's *Geschichte des dreissigjährigen Kriegs* in 1792; but it appears in the title of the *Kurtze Chronica von dem dreyssigjahrigen Krieg*, published in 1650, of which there is a copy in the Acton collection in the Cambridge University Library. In the following year it occurs in a more prominent place, the dedication, to John George of Saxony, of *Musladini Sadi Rosarium Politicum* (Amsterdam, 1651).

its total effects are thought to have been injurious to Germany and advantageous to almost all the neighbouring states. Here again it was the abstract Germany of subsequent national sentiment which suffered more than actual groupings of Germans; if this abstract element is omitted, and if exaggerations are pruned away, the Thirty Years War will be seen not as unique but as typical of the wars of the sixteenth and seventeenth centuries.

Considerable German provinces, though remaining constitutionally within the empire, passed to sovereigns whose main territories were outside it. France was confirmed in the possession of Metz, Toul, Verdun, and Alsace. In all these places her lordships fell short of sovereignty, and in Alsace they were so ill-defined that they left obvious openings for future disputes. Sweden took some ports and some strips of territory along the Baltic coasts, and two bishoprics on the estuary of the Weser, though not the great port of Bremen. Thus the kings of Sweden and France now became, like the kings of Denmark and Spain, nominally members of the empire. The Austrian Habsburgs already had possessions outside it in Hungary; the elector of Brandenburg had recently become Duke of Prussia, in Poland; the Bavarian house had supplied prince-bishops to Liége since 1581, so that most of the leading states of Germany had interests outside it. In due course this process went still farther when the electors of Saxony became kings of Poland, and the electors of Hanover became kings of England. The emperors, having lost so much in the west, naturally paid more attention to their affairs in Hungary and Bohemia, the more so since in that quarter they had gained so much that they were on balance stronger than before. Theirs was the only one among the greater German dynasties which lost any of its lands. Saxony, Bavaria, Brandenburg all gained. The German liberties were now secure, and if this meant that the empire as such could never become a strong and consolidated state, it also meant that the religious settlement of 1555 was reaffirmed and its benefits were extended to Calvinist princes. The emperors had to reckon with a group of strong neighbours, each with his territorial aspirations; but, although these might lawfully make alliances with foreign powers, they did not aspire to be more than states within the empire. Their rise had simplified the map of Germany and removed some of the impediments to good government.

The political fragmentation of Germany stood in the way of economic unity, but the absorption of some small territories by the greater states made this somewhat less irksome. No noticeable economic loss ensued from the Swedish occupation of the mouths of the Oder and the banks of the Weser. The mouth of a still greater German river, the Rhine, had never been German; but it belonged to men who made their livelihood by trading with Germany. No scientific estimate has ever been made of the economic ravages of the war. Some places were devastated and some were depopulated for a time; but the people were not all slaughtered; some of them merely shifted to safer places. The war may perhaps justly be blamed for the failure of such tardy efforts as German princes made to join in the colonial trade; but Sweden and Denmark also fared badly in that field. It is hard to separate the economic results of the war from the other changes of the time. The shifting of the trade-routes had already drawn trade away from the south German cities; the rise of the Dutch republic and of Sweden had done the same for those of the north; but the shifting of routes, while it depressed some parts of Germany, brought prosperity to others. The great days of Hamburg began.

The sphere in which the war certainly left deep wounds behind it was that of the mind. The Protestant universities lost many of their foreign students and much of their excellence. Literature had no great names to show; and from the early years of the war there were complaints of the infiltration of French literary influences. But even in the sphere of the mind it was more in national feeling than in absolute merit that decline could be noticed. There were gains to set against the losses. The great musical history of Saxony began, and the first German opera was performed when Wallenstein was operating towards the Baltic. Within a generation of the end of the war there were men in the German courts and cities who were famous all over Europe as scholars and thinkers. The name of Magdeburg is remembered for its sack when Tilly took it in 1631; but in 1652 its burgomaster was one of the most distinguished living physicists. At the episcopal court of Mainz Leibniz was soon to display his almost universal genius. In one respect indeed the war cleared the way for developments which, while they were beneficial in some ways and harmful in others, at least fostered the specifically German types of government and character. Except in some minor states the towns declined and the assemblies of estates declined with them. The populace, including the educated townsmen, subsided, so Leibniz complained, into indifference to questions of creed, politics, and morals. But the rulers came to a *modus vivendi* with the nobility. There were no more robber-barons. In the great corn-producing area, for instance, the landlords gave up their political rights and their voice in taxation in virtual exchange for greater rights over the serfs on their farms. The princes were thus able to finance larger and better armies, and to promote a policy of economic welfare by means of an authoritarian bureaucracy. The universities became training-schools for administrators.

Many of the evils which afflicted Germany during the Thirty Years War were as great or greater in other countries. Bohemia and the Spanish Netherlands were perhaps those which suffered altogether the most. Probably the only country in which the universities did not to some extent decline was the Dutch republic, which was not a theatre of war, and whose tolerance attracted students and men of letters from every quarter. In Great Britain there were twenty years of civil war and revolution which, although they kept the country out of European embroilments, were connected with the German war both by diplomacy and by 'ideologies'. The union of England and Scotland sharpened the antagonisms within each country, as such unions sometimes do. In this case the most obstinate antagonisms were religious, and the Calvinist opposition in England now had Scottish allies, just as the episcopalian minority in Scotland, which included the king, now had strong English backing. This issue became fused with a constitutional struggle between the Crown and some elements of the English governing classes. King Charles I was defeated, deposed, and executed. The victorious parties formed a united republic of England, Scotland, and Ireland; but it was troubled by sporadic risings of democratic elements hitherto outside the governing classes and not concerned with public affairs. This whirl of ideas and action ended with a restored but constitutional monarchy, holding England and Scotland once more only in personal union, and leaving each to its own separate religious tenor. In the end the crisis cleared the way, as in Germany, for new methods of government well suited to the island peoples; but the arts and letters had been badly injured, and their recovery after the restoration was curiously parallel to the German recovery: science and music flourished especially; in literature and manners there was a strong French influence. This French leaven, indeed, was working in every country from Poland to Sicily.

In after years the Congress of Westphalia came to be reckoned as the first in the series of European diplomatic congresses and conferences in which the peace-settlements and other great international agreements were negotiated. For the first time there was an assemblage of ambassadors and ministers comparable in power and dignity with the ecclesiastical councils, but its members were representatives of states. It showed how far the sovereign states had consolidated their system. One sign was the insignificance of the ecclesiastical diplomacy. Although ecclesiastical principalities were annexed or dismembered by the secular states, the pope, whose predecessors had claimed supremacy over kings and republics, could only protest. Another sign was the maturity and completeness of the international law embodied in the treaties. During the previous hundred years international lawyers, working on the basis of Roman jurisprudence, had made notable progress. The most famous of them, Hugo Grotius, published his masterpiece, a treatise on the law of war and peace, in 1625. He was a poet, a very learned scholar, a theologian, a historian, a practising lawyer, and a diplomatist. His active career was unhappy: he was a prominent member of a party in his native country, Holland, which tried to press religious tolerance and provincial autonomy further than the more Calvinistic and anti-Spanish military leaders would allow. When his party fell he had to spend many years in exile. He wrote this great book in Paris in Richelieu's day, and afterwards he served the Swedes as an ambassador. Thus, though he wrote it to point out ways of ending what seemed to him the growing inhumanity of wars, he wrote with the hard facts of the times before his eyes. He accepted the sovereign independence of each state as the initial postulate from which international organization must start. He treated the law of war, the reasonable regulation of its conduct, and the rights and wrongs of resorting to it, as part of a wider law which also covers the peaceful relations of states, their contracts with one another and with their subjects, their rights to territory, and all their other activities which can be brought within a legal framework.

He died while the Westphalian Congress was sitting, and his book still gives us a programme and an inspiration in the light of which that Congress, in spite of all its shortcomings and failures, is seen to have done something for justice and for peace.

It was, however, only to Germany, Sweden, and the Dutch republic that the Congress gave peace. France and Spain still fought on for eleven bloody years. When Spain, isolated and doomed as a great power, at last gave in to the French demands for frontier provinces in the Netherlands and along the Pyrenees, she gained no respite. The Portuguese still waged their war of independence with French support; and there was no interval of stability for Europe between the end of Spanish ascendancy and the beginning of the exorbitant power of France. Although they were continuous, however, the wars which raged round these two dominations were different in so many ways, and were fought in such different atmospheres, that it is not absurd to regard the humbling of Spain as the end of an age. Fundamentally it had come about because the rest of western Europe had grown in wealth and energy so as to over-take the lead which Spain had gained in the conquering days of colonial discovery and Catholic revival. As the price-revolution and the growth of population continued, her rivals had estab-lished their own colonial empires. The French now had Canada and its fur-trade; the English had settled on the eastern shore of North America and in the West Indies; the Dutch were their neighbours in both these regions, and were fighting the Portu-guese in Brazil. Spanish trade was harassed and interrupted; indeed the economy of the New World was passing into the control of the smugglers and buccaneers of the new colonizing nations. But about the middle of the seventeenth century all this began to change. The price-revolution slowed down and ended: in most of Europe the general level of prices stood still or began to fall. The flow of emigrants ran more thinly. Instead of expansion there was soon more of organization within the limits which had been reached. And these changes corresponded in some way to great changes in men's minds. Religion and poli-tics were no longer locked together so that every incident in one had its counterpart in the other. A new page of history was being written; but before we turn it, we must again take up the story of eastern and northern Europe.

The Protestant Reformation and its sequel of wars and revolutions altered the relations of east and west. To begin with it gave Sweden a hegemony in the Baltic. Gustavus Vasa, the most businesslike and least romantic of all founding fathers, built a national state round a Lutheran Church, a unified economy, and a monarchy strong enough to keep at arm's length the two powers to which late medieval Sweden had been subordinate, the Danish Crown, which had dictated its policy, and the Hanse, which had dominated its trade. The country was poor in everything except iron and copper; but Gustavus enriched the Crown and the nobility from the lands of the Church. He and his successors called in the capital, the shipping, and the organizing ability of the Dutch to develop the mines. Denmark, to which Norway and what is now southern Sweden were subject, also became Lutheran. Its kings had assured revenues from the tolls they raised at the Sound and they made more of a figure in relations with the western states; but before the end of the sixteenth century Sweden had more compact and efficient naval and military forces than any other power on the Baltic. In Russia the Reformation made no impression. Its doctrines were irrelevant to the Orthodox habits of mind, and since the time of Ivan the Great the Russians had walled themselves in inaccessibility. But in the whole region between this Russian mass and the newly solidified Sweden and Denmark, from the Baltic southwards to the Turkish dominions, political institutions, less strongly rooted than in the west, were shaken and disrupted when Protestantism broke in.

Most of this region, sparsely settled by perhaps three million people, belonged to Poland–Lithuania. Here was a dual state, a personal union, in which the hereditary dukes of Lithuania were elective kings of Poland much as the hereditary dukes of Austria were elective emperors. They ruled over, or rather with, some thousands of families of landowners, some of them very poor, among whom the magnates stood out even more prominently than in the west. Protestantism came to Poland in all its forms, including even anti-Trinitarian teachings which no western country tolerated, and by 1563 a diet granted to all the Protestants, and to the Orthodox, rights equal to those of the Catholics: that is to say there was full toleration in the towns and for each lord on his estates. The Knights of the Teutonic Order, whose power on the neighbouring Baltic shore had been curbed in

1466, adopted the new doctrines, in which crusading orders had no place, and so they became a body of German landlords, and they had to conform to the existing types of secular political organization. The grand master of the Order became Duke of Prussia, as a vassal of the Polish Crown. He happened to be a member of the house of Hohenzollern, to which the electors of Brandenburg belonged, and about a century later his inheritance fell in to that branch of the family, so that in the later stages of the Thirty Years War yet another personal union created the dual state of Brandenburg-Prussia. Until then Prussia was merely a Polish province, and, though it was different historically and socially from the others, its history was of no more than local importance.

About the middle of the century there were great changes in Russia. In 1547 Ivan IV, a bloodthirsty tyrant well called the Terrible, began his reign of thirty-seven years. He was crowned with antique Byzantine imperial ceremony, but he was the first great westernizer of his country. His task was to make conquests by using western skill. He made himself agreeable to the Englishmen who appeared at Archangel and traded up the rivers, but he gave no monopoly to them or to the merchants of any other nation. He bought weapons and munitions from the west; he employed German, Scottish, and other western technicians; he set up a bureaucracy. Thus he gained strength to press outwards in every direction in turn; but his great advances were to the east. He broke the strongest barrier in his way by capturing Kazan, on the Volga, the stronghold of the Golden Horde. Three years later he had worked his way down the Volga to its mouth, and seized Astrakhan on the Caspian. Before he died the Russians held the Caspian coast as far as the River Terek, below the Caucasus. From the middle Volga their traders and settlers had moved eastwards across the Urals. Resisted only by scattered tribesmen who had no firearms, they were pushing across the fertile Siberian plain.

Although it was so unlike the western states, Russia had equal success in keeping control over its pioneers. The river communications through the forests and over the steppe were as difficult and as dangerous as the sea communications with America; but the Russians, like the Spaniards, made one empire. They made good each large advance with fortified lines, and where they sat down at a frontier, as they did before the Turks, they manned it, in that instance by organizing the Cossacks, a kind of feudal cavalry. This is one half of the main theme of European history in that time, for that theme was a double movement to east and to west, in which two great forces, not obstructing each other but back to back, were pushing out, the one by sea and the other by land, along lines of least resistance. But eastward expansion changed the face of Russia's western problems. It increased her need of the west, and it increased her sense of danger from the west. Events on the Baltic coast-line took a turn which threatened to close the trade-routes, so Ivan turned his armies to the north.

Finland had long been subject to the Swedish Crown, and there were Swedes there as landlords and townsmen, in positions similar to those of the Germans of the other Baltic provinces. Round the gulfs immediately to the south of it were other settlements of the Teutonic Order like those in Prussia. In this region the Finnish-speaking inhabitants of Estonia, the Letts with their Indo-European language, and the ports of Narva, Reval, and Riga, were governed by Germans, the Prince-Archbishop of Riga and the grand master of the Order, with, under him, the knights whose descendants were afterwards known as the Baltic barons. The territorial advance of Poland had cut off this region from Germany by land, and Albert of Hohenzollern, before he turned Protestant, had granted independence to the provincial grand master. The Reformation took away the cohesion of this state. When Ivan attacked it, the archbishop and the grand master sought help from Poland, their neighbour and a neighbour whose main trade was with their countries. They offered to submit to Polish suzerainty, as the Duke of Prussia had done, but the Poles were unwilling. The Swedes saw their opportunity and established themselves in Reval, which became the corner-stone of a new Baltic empire. The Danes, the Russians, rival Swedish princes, and the Poles all fought one another. In 1563 the Swedes made a short-lived neutrality treaty with the Russians, and addressed themselves to the northern Seven Years War against Denmark, and at times also against Poland and Hanseatic Lübeck. The need for defence against Russia in this war induced the Poles to turn their personal union with Lithuania into an organic union. In 1569 the diet of Lublin made the new constitutional union. Each state kept its own army, administration, and laws; but there was a common senate, a common diet at Warsaw, a common currency, and a common system of land-tenure. The common institutions did not cover up all the strains and stresses between the two countries; but they brought Poland to its greatest territorial extent, and they served the immediate purpose of checking the dangers from without. Unfortunately the union also tempted the Poles into a wasteful and over-ambitious policy of expansion. They took over ill-defined Lithuanian claims to the Ukraine, where they organized the Cossacks of the Dnieper. Until 1648 they dreamed of partitioning Russia and, as a secondary aim, of winning land from the Turks. While the wars were sometimes successful and sometimes disastrous, the constitutional machinery fell into disorder. The monarchy became purely elective, the field being open to almost all comers, and all the nobles having votes. The royal power dwindled. The kings were uniformly successful only in one thing, namely in pressing on the characteristic measures of the Catholic Reformation.

The result of the warfare in the Baltic region (1558–83) was that Russia remained cut off from the sea. Estonia was Swedish, and Protestant. Livonia proper, although Polish, was also made Protestant by the landowners, and in both the gentry kept their privileges and their German language. Courland was a virtually independent province of Poland. But there was no rest for the Poles or the Swedes. In 1587 the Poles elected as their king a Swedish prince, the son of a Polish princess, and like his mother a Catholic, who succeeded five years later to the Swedish crown. He tried to introduce the Catholic Reformation in Sweden. To keep out the Inquisition the Swedes threw themselves again into the quarrels on the farther shore of the Baltic. They succeeded against their king, whose only success for his religion was in his other kingdom of Poland. Here, at the Synod of Brest-Litovsk in 1595, a new Uniate Church was set up for Lithuania, obedient to Rome but following the Orthodox rites. Most of the bishops and nobles, with some of the clergy, adhered to it, but not the towns or the mass of the peasantry, so that it deepened the social divisions and indirectly weakened the kingdom.

Both the Swedes and the Poles took advantage of the 'Troubled Times' in Russia in the early seventeenth century. The Swedes took Novgorod and from 1610 to 1612 the Poles had a garrison in the Kremlin. Gustavus Adolphus of Sweden succeeded to the throne when they were there. His position as a national hero was established before he landed in Germany, and, although it was not until after his time that Swedish names were famous in European thought and letters, he led a national movement of far more than merely political scope. He made peace with Russia, handing back Novgorod but keeping Carelia and Ingria, thus holding the keys of Finland and Livonia and barring Russia's way to the Baltic. The Poles too kept some of their advanced posts on the road to Moscow for a time; but they were about to lose ground in all directions. They had war with the Turks and another, much more serious, with Sweden, which deprived them of Livonia and a number of places on the Baltic. Fortunately for them Gustavus Adolphus was called off at this stage to his German enterprise; but they still had troubles on their hands. They began to have wars with the Cossacks. Their prospects of maintaining their positions were poor. The kings had little jurisdiction, little revenue, little executive authority. The army, though sometimes well led, relied mainly on ill-disciplined feudal cavalry. The national policy was one of romantic military adventure rather than calculation. Poland had, as it proved, nothing more to fear from Swedish imperialism; but in Russia these western wars had left behind them enduring hatreds.

In Asia the Russian progress had never halted. Even during the 'Troubled Times' wide territories had been brought under control in the remote northern tundra and in the Siberian plain. When the vigorous little German states composed their differences in the Peace of Westphalia, the Russians had founded one of the great historic empires of mankind. The king of Georgia paid them tribute. They stood on the shore of Lake Baikal. They looked across the Iena and the Aldan rivers at the confines of China. They held the coast of the Sea of Okhotsk, to the north of Japan. And they had abated nothing of their separateness from the west. While they traded actively with the western states, and while they imparted and received a modicum of information, their arts and thought and social structure remained substantially as they had been. The two spheres of European civilization were growing more unlike, and, as the experience of each became more complex, it became harder for the other to understand.

VII

SCIENCE AND THOUGHT

A T the present time the great majority of those people, all over the world, who think about such matters, believe that among our different kinds of knowledge and ideas about ourselves and the universe we live in the most reliable are those which we derive from science. There are so many shades and varieties of this belief that it may be understood in a hundred different ways, but most thinking people, and many unthinking people, agree that science is exact, impersonal, and positive, not distorted by bias, not speculative, in short as authentic and as nearly certain as any acquisition of the human mind can be. If they were asked to define what they mean by science they would not agree on every point; but they think of it as following the method and spirit that are most familiar in the 'natural' or 'physical' sciences, that is, as based on observation, on experiment, and on the testing of hypotheses by strict reasoning, very often of a mathematical character. They think of it as progressing from discovery to discovery; as using, so far as it can, all relevant data; as capable of being planned ahead, and as resulting in power to control material objects and living beings, in a conquest of nature.

This state of mind is so familiar that millions of people have grown up in it and take it for granted; but it has not always been so. In the Middle Ages there was not only a great recovery of ancient knowledge that had been lost; there were also new discoveries, fruitful criticisms of principles in natural science, and applications of physics and chemistry to technology, as in the mariner's compass and in explosives. The spirit of scientific inquiry was alive and active; but it was of subordinate importance in the general scheme of thought. Discovery as such was not valued as it is valued now. Many of the scientists mixed up their experiments with mystifications and tried to control nature by magic, invoking occult spiritual powers. Novelty in ideas was distrusted, and the general opinion was that the main outlines of truth laid down in theology and philosophy were permanently fixed, and provided adequate explanations of the nature of existing things. The standard of scrupulously methodical thought was set by the great theologians, philosophers, and jurists. The astrologer and the alchemist had something of the charlatan in them, or at least a more than normal dose of eccentricity and credulity. The orientation of the human mind was altered through the working of many causes over a long stretch of time; but the decisive period was the period with which we are here concerned. Somewhere between the late fifteenth century and the late seventeenth another spirit took possession of many leading minds in western and central Europe, but only there.

We have seen that the Renaissance had an intellectual aspect. The artists investigated optics and anatomy; the closer and deeper study of ancient Greek writers not only equipped Europe with better textbooks of mathematics, physics, medicine, and zoology, but it sharpened method in every kind of research. We have seen that the widening experience of men of action brought masses of new knowledge about the world, and also set new problems which the men of action could not solve for themselves. The new facts would not have been assimilated and the new problems would not have been tackled if there had not already been in existence a magnificent organization of thought and education. It was the traditional work of the universities to keep themselves at the height of the best knowledge of the time. There was constant emulation between them and it was in the universities that the first striking advances of modern science were made. In 1543, in a book which he was permitted to dedicate to the Pope, a Polish astronomer, Copernicus, overthrew the accepted system which regarded the earth as the centre of the universe. In the same year Vesalius, who was born in Brussels and lectured in Italy, published the first modern standard work on anatomy. The new interests did not indeed appeal equally to all the leaders of thought in universities; they never can. There are always some, and there was a greater proportion then than there is now, whose cast of mind is conservative and authoritarian. We have seen that both Luther and Calvin, who had many disciples in universities, looked askance at scientific curiosity, and the Protestant reformation diverted many teachers on both sides into theological controversy; but the original *point d'appui* from which modern science was able to set out to make converts in every other sphere of life was the medieval university. This is true not only on the social and personal side but on the intellectual side as well; the universities not only found the men, they

also equipped them with mental tools. Many of the essential
ideas of modern science were quietly prepared beforehand by
medieval thinkers, including even the idea that the 'absolute'
and spiritual are not the only realities, but the material and
'contingent' also are in some sense real.

There were an infinite number of motives which led men to
engage in scientific work and to clear the scientific point of view
from encumbrances; but we may group together some of the
most important under general headings, always remembering
that in actual life each of them was compounded with the
others. There were economic motives. The Portuguese explorers
wanted their new instrument for navigation; the German mine-
owners asked questions about metallurgy and about machines
for lifting and carrying heavy loads; Italian engineers improved
their canals and locks and harbours by applying the principles
of hydrostatics; English trading companies employed experts
who used new methods of drawing charts. Not far removed from
the economic motives were those of the physicians and surgeons,
who revolutionized anatomy and physiology, and did much
more good than harm with their new medicines and new operations, though some of them now seem absurd. Like the doctors,
the soldiers called science to their aid in designing and aiming
artillery or in planning fortifications. But there were other
motives far removed from the economic sphere. Musicians
learnt the mathematics of harmony; painters and architects
studied light and colour, substances and proportions, not only
as craftsmen but as artists. For a number of reasons religion
impelled men to scientific study. The most definite and old-
established was the desire to reach absolute correctness in calculating the dates for the annual fixed and movable festivals of
the Church: it was a pope who presided over the astronomical
researches by which the calendar was reformed in the sixteenth
century. Deeper and stronger was the desire to study the wonders
of science, and the order which it unravelled in the universe, as
manifestations of the Creator's will. This was closer than any of
the other motives to the central impulse which actuated them
all, the disinterested desire to know.

Well before the end of the seventeenth century natural
science had made such advances in positive achievement, in
practical applications, in organization, and in public repute
that many able men esteemed it more highly than any other

branch of knowledge. There was a definite movement for promoting 'the new philosophy'. Its chief seats were some of the universities: Padua, Leiden, Oxford, and Cambridge housed and fed and applauded some of the greatest experimenters and thinkers; but it also had other means of propagation which sprang from the new conditions of the time. It was helped by improvements of printing, transport, and postal services as Europe grew in prosperity. Its special vehicle of diffusion was not the book but the scientific periodical, which carried the news of the latest experiments and calculations, with tables and diagrams, to a new international public. It also had a new form of organization in the scientific academies, the best of which published their own periodicals. Of these the Royal Society of London, chartered in 1662, may serve as the type. The main body of its most active and useful members were, from the first, men trained in the universities, and a number of them made their careers in universities; but the Royal Society was unlike a university in two ways. It had nothing to do with teaching, and in it the scientists were associated with men of action and men in power. These men, some of whom were themselves more than mere amateurs, kept the scientists in touch with the needs of government, agriculture, transport, and industry, and in return they provided prizes for inventors, a few paid posts for research-workers, honours and rewards for intellectual eminence.

This movement, together with the work of scattered scientists who were more or less independent of it, brought about a great positive advance in practically every branch of science. The greatest triumphs were in astronomy. With the telescope men literally saw new worlds. The work of Copernicus was completed and his hypothesis won general acceptance. A steady advance of mathematics culminated in the comprehensive explanation of the mechanism of the heavens by Sir Isaac Newton, of Cambridge, in the light of his principle of gravitation. This surpassed anything that had ever been done before in any field to bring together a multiplicity of facts as manifestations of a single law. It was, however, only the supreme example of a process which was at work in every branch of physics. Outside that realm there was nothing that appealed so forcibly to the contemporary imagination; but chemistry and its allied sciences were set on sound foundations; in anatomy and physiology a new era began with research into the circulation of the blood and the detection

by the microscope of living organisms so small that their existence had been unknown. In botany, zoology, geology there were
no revolutions yet, but there was steady preparatory work, and
there were puzzling new questions.

As population, wealth, and enterprise grew, and as the scale
of economic organization grew with them, there were many
opportunities for applying the new knowledge in practice, and
it was associated with many improvements in technology.
Technology gained most where it could make use of the new
dynamics. Clocks were greatly improved. The introduction of
the pendulum into clocks in the late seventeenth century is the
first important example of an industrial invention made not by
a craftsman, or a person directly concerned with manufacture,
but by a scientist whose interest was primarily not practical at
all. Pocket-watches which kept tolerably good time were made
possible in the same generation and soon became common.
Before the end of the seventeenth century the results of a long
series of investigations into atmospheric pressure, carried on
over a long period of time in various European countries, were
brought together in the first steam-engine. For many years
steam-engines were few in number; there were none outside
England, and they were not used for any purpose except pumping the water out of mines. But in due course steam-power was
to become the great instrument of transforming economic life.
It was the greatest single product of a general improvement in
technology. Not only were quicker, cheaper, and more effective
practices devised for agriculture and many industries. So much
was done to provide instruction by textbooks and articles in periodicals that the general level of efficiency was slowly raised.

Scientific method was applied in every direction where it
yielded results, and the limits of its usefulness, at the stage which
it had then reached, were found by trespassing beyond them. In
administration better methods of surveying and map-making
were useful for many kinds of business connected with property
and taxation. They were extended to the delimiting of political
frontiers, and in 1718, perhaps for the first time, an engraved
map was annexed to a treaty. From surveying it was an easy
step to collecting statistics of the resources of a country, and in
the late seventeenth century there were high hopes of what
might be done by means of 'political arithmetic', as the rudi-
mentary statistical science of the time was called. A beginning

was indeed made in the study of population and its relation to birth-rates and death-rates. The idea of a scientific survey of the resources of a country was congenial to the economic ideas of the time, which were largely directed to exploiting such resources to the full. It was used to good purpose, especially in some of the smaller and simpler countries, like the West Indian islands. The Royal Society drew up a questionnaire for travellers, and the method of the questionnaire was typical of the times: it was also used in English poor-law administration, and by inquirers into education and antiquities. There was a new sense of the relevance of systematic and comprehensive information to the organizing of states; but it made no noticeable mark on policy, and the influence of statistics on practice did not extend much farther than to make some difference to the theories of commerce and some improvements in insurance and finance. Further progress had to wait until the greater states were able to command much fuller and more accurate information about the numbers of people, their births, marriages, deaths, and occupations, and about imports, exports, and production.

As on the practical, so on the theoretical side, the limits of the usefulness of scientific methods were found by trial and error. Some of Newton's most distinguished contemporaries tried, like the old alchemists, to transmute base metals into gold; and Newton himself at least took the trouble to examine their recipes and consider the problem. It is not very long since scientists wrote of this condescendingly as an example of the fallibility of great minds; but research has changed their notions of the permanence of chemical substances, and a few years ago one of the pioneers of nuclear physics wrote: 'the future . . . holds out prospects of still larger-scale activity, and perhaps the practical achievement of the philosopher's stone'.[1] If scientists have withdrawn their disapproval of Newton's glances in this direction, there were, however, others which they would still regard as aberrations. They are indeed often mentioned in conjunction with the fact that at one time his wonderful powers of mind were darkened by a nervous breakdown. He spent much time in applying himself closely to the study of the fulfilment and nature of biblical prophecies. Since he did not publish his results it may be presumed that they did not satisfy him, but neither he

[1] J. D. Cockroft in a broadcast printed in *Science Lifts the Veil* (1942).

nor some of the ablest of his acquaintances thought the effort ridiculous in itself. With his encouragement they tried to demonstrate propositions in theology by the use, as far as possible, of methods akin to those of mathematics.

We can scarcely help regarding those factors in the thought of the sixteenth and seventeenth centuries as the most significant which have left their traces behind in the modern ascendancy of science, but the scientific movement was one wing of a wider transformation which coloured every kind of mental activity, and, if it did distinguish natural science from theology and the arts, did not, for all that, regard any subject as less amenable to scientific treatment than any other. This may be illustrated from one small instance which is typical of many. Until the early seventeenth century deaf-mutes were amongst the hardest to help of all mankind. No one knew how to give them access to the possession of speech, let alone to reading and writing. No one could know it until human sympathy for them was reinforced by three kinds of knowledge. There must be knowledge of the nature of language. The grammar of the classical languages was a long established study, but the grammar of modern languages lagged behind, and it is not a pure coincidence that Spain was the first country to have a grammar of its vernacular language and also the first country to have, in 1620, a book on the teaching of deaf-mutes. But in this book the knowledge of the logic of language was joined to scientific knowledge of the organs of speech and knowledge of the art and science of teaching. More than one of the great scientists of the seventeenth century worked at the problem of teaching the dumb on all its three sides, and we may reckon it as an integral part of their movement that this problem was solved.

When we consider the wider consequences of the intellectual movement, we see that the influence of science in any narrow sense cannot be disentangled from other influences which worked through all the studies of the history, languages, beliefs, and social life of mankind. The classical scholars went forward from the printing of texts to a general study of ancient times, and in this they applied a new and specialized technique of chronology which involved an understanding of the astronomical basis of reckoning time. There were other ways besides this in which historical and social studies became more 'scientific'. Nevertheless the most important fact about the intellectual life of the

seventeenth century is a fact about natural science, a main fact
so well established, indeed so obvious, that it is often forgotten
because it has become too familiar to be noticed. The main fact
about this intellectual movement is not that it led to improvements in technology, and so assisted the rise of capitalism
and the wealth of nations; or even that it made the first great
strategic advances in man's conquest of nature. It is a fact on a
different plane from these, on the plane of thought and not on
the plane where thought and action interpenetrate. Yet many
of those who contemplate the intellectual movement on its own
plane deny or misrepresent this overwhelmingly important fact.
Comparing the multiplicity and the contradictions of beliefs in
the following centuries with the immature but simple and sym-
metrical systems of earlier times, they regard the scientific
movement as a disintegrating force. They recognize that men
came to know many things of which they had been ignorant,
but they see that the new bodies of information, and the scientific laws under which they were ranged, were no longer subordinated to the principles of philosophy and theology which had
formerly satisfied the desire for intellectual stability and coher-
ence, and that, while the information continued to grow, these
scientific laws were subject to unresting revision. Without denying that the advance of knowledge was real, they regret that it
broke the old moorings of the European mind, so that, instead
of remaining satisfied with what had passed for certainties, men
vacillated between conflicting probabilities. In this way preoccupation with the unifying of human life, like preoccupation
with its practical and economic aspects, diverts attention from
the central reality of the scientific movement.

    This central reality is that the scientific movement was a
great illumination of the human mind. Knowledge is a good,
and ignorance is an evil. There is, of course, a great deal to be
said about the relation of knowledge to other values; not all
knowledge is equally good, and so on. But, whatever our scale
of values may be, it must give knowledge its due place, and it
must accord to natural science the full value which belongs
to knowledge as such. Among the nine muses of the ancients
there was one, Urania, like the others a daughter of Zeus and
Memory, whose special province was astronomy and who had
mathematical instruments among her symbols. In the sixteenth
and seventeenth centuries she widened her domain. After a

PLATE 29

Rembrandt, Faust in his study. (See p. xxiv)

long interruption there were now leaders of thought who felt, if we may adapt a telling phrase which has been used of another kind of study: 'There is poetry in science; its poetry consists in being true.'

So great an accession to the data about the universe was bound to influence philosophy, and in this there were many new departures. Some of them were false starts, but, for many reasons, those which were initiated by René Descartes gave such a new turn to the course of philosophy that it almost began afresh, and many learned men, down to our own time, have thought it possible to understand his doctrines and those of his successors without looking into those of medieval and Renaissance writers. Descartes did indeed incorporate, as was inevitable, many things which he had learnt from his teachers or read in books, and he was a Catholic who never quarrelled with the official custodians of religious tradition; but he was in many ways the type of the new generations which were putting the Middle Ages behind them. He wrote some of his books in Latin, but he wrote others in French, for a wide circle of educated but not academic readers, and he wrote them all in an easy manner, without the formalism of scholastic argument. He was not a university teacher but a retired French officer who, after fighting in the later stages of the Thirty Years War, lived in the congenial environment of tolerant Holland. He was an important figure in the scientific movement. He inaugurated co-ordinate geometry, the now familiar method of defining positions by their relation to two fixed straight lines. He worked out a system of physics, in which he attempted to explain the structure and motions of all material bodies by purely scientific laws. Then he went on to the ultimate questions of thought and being. These also he tried to answer with proofs as clear and self-evident as those of mathematics. He believed that he had demonstrated the existence of God and of the external world, and explained the interaction between the spiritual and the material, both in the universe at large and in the individual man.

Among the Catholics there were powerful bodies of students and teachers who never entered on these lines of speculation. The Jesuits and the Dominicans were by no means inactive as thinkers; but in their writings, and in their schools and colleges, they maintained many of the forms of medieval thought until, in the later nineteenth century, respect for these revived, and there was a reaction against the innovations which Descartes had brought in. Nor were these innovations anywhere exempt from criticism. There were flaws in the Cartesian physics. In his philosophy there were discrepancies, and arguments in which he had only been able to reach consistency by forcing the facts : he held, for instance, that animals have neither intelligence nor feeling but are automata. In the universities there was much controversy about more fundamental points. Thinkers of different schools tried to find alternatives to his separation of mind and matter. Few accepted all his conclusions; but many followed them in the main, and some met the criticisms with ingenious improvements, while others made allowances for realities which had been embarrassments for Descartes. Among these the greatest was Leibniz. He lived from the seventeenth century into the eighteenth, and he knew the science and learning of his day from every side in a way that perhaps no later thinker has ever equalled. He was a politician, historian, theologian, and scientist. In mathematics he stood very high as one of the inventors of the differential calculus. In philosophy he applied the conception of quantity on which the calculus is based, the conception that any quantity is a function of something variable. Thus he thought that the ultimately real was not an unchanging substance beneath all changes and differences, but the principle of change and difference which was itself a force. In this he was a forerunner of ideas which have arisen from the scientific discoveries of the twentieth century.

Henceforward there was a separation between philosophy and science. On the one hand philosophy dealt with the mind of man, the nature of his thought, and the ends of his action. Science, on the other hand, made no use of the conception of purpose, but sought for causal laws which should explain the world of matter. This separation was completed by the triumphant success of mathematical method in the work of Newton. Where calculation could be applied, in those spheres where it was possible to count or weigh or measure, general laws were formulated, and these general laws were instruments for the subjection of nature to man. They gave him his telescopes and clocks and steam-engines. No such laws were detected in the sphere of life, the sphere of biology and psychology, and here neither were calculations made from which such laws might be derived, nor were practical benefits expected from applying them. Some bold spirits indeed attempted to account for character and social behaviour by determinist systems modelled more or less closely on the natural science of the time. There were penetrating thinkers among them, who have since come to be esteemed as belonging to the highest rank; but in their own day they were suspect. The general tendency of opinion was to give up the attempt to synthesize the material and the animate worlds, or to investigate both by one method. In 1686 Edmund Halley, the newly elected secretary of the Royal Society, received a letter from one of its distinguished fellows, who told him derisively about a party which had been forming within the society. They were for rejecting all kinds of useful knowledge except 'ranking and filing of shells, fishes, insects, birds, &c.', which they termed natural history. They merely investigated nature, never attending to the uses and properties of these things for helping mankind, and reckoning chemistry, astronomy, mathematics, and mechanics as 'rubs'. Halley and his correspondent were on the winning side. The party they laughed at went quietly on with its work; but the science which captivated the educated world had nothing to teach about life or mind or will.

It was partly for this reason that the conflict between science and religion, which might easily have arisen, was softened and postponed. In the sixteenth century the Churches, Catholic and Protestant alike, believed that it was their duty to prevent or to punish wrong beliefs in matters of faith and morals, and therefore they did not allow complete freedom of opinion. In the Middle Ages science had given them little trouble, if only because there was so little of it; but now that a great bulk of its ascertained results had to be integrated with theology, the heavy-handed guardians of orthodoxy were presented with an exacting intellectual task. They committed one famous injustice. One of the greatest authorities on mechanics, astronomy, and scientific method in general, in the first half of the seventeenth century, was the Florentine Galileo Galilei. It was he more than anyone else who persuaded the educated world to accept the Copernican system. The Inquisition, perhaps in part for other, if equally discreditable, reasons, but certainly in part because they were stupid enough to reject the Copernican astronomy on theological grounds, condemned a book in which

Galileo supported it, imprisoned him for three days, and sentenced him to recite the seven penitential psalms once a week for three years. This gave Galileo and Copernicus fame which they could never have gained without it, and it made the inquisitors a permanent laughing-stock, to the advantage of all heretics. There was no other case in which the heresies were so purely scientific. Science had its martyrs in the sixteenth century, but most, if not all, of them meddled with theology. Science as such was not strongly discountenanced. Both in Catholic and in Protestant countries there were ecclesiastics among the scientists, and their scientific work helped some of them to preferment. There was, however, a general agreement to let science and religion occupy separate spheres of influence. It was usually a tacit agreement, but there were writers who justified it, and this could be done most convincingly if science was conceived as using mechanical and determinist methods which had no relevance to the subject-matter of religion. Most of the churchmen were satisfied with their share of this partition, and it was exceptional for anyone to take the view of Pascal, an eminent scientist and mathematician and an apologist of Christianity, who wisely wrote that he could not forgive Descartes, because after bringing in God to set the world in motion by a twist of His finger and thumb, he had no further use for Him in his philosophy.

Although no one succeeded in fusing scientific with theological opinions, it was impossible to keep them altogether apart. The belief in miracles was shaken. During the controversies of the Reformation many Protestant writers had criticized the miracles of the Church, that is all the miracles from the end of the Apostolic age. Although they still accepted the miracles of the Bible as facts, and as evidence of revelation, they had turned two kinds of criticism against later miracles which might be applied elsewhere. They had disputed the evidence for some of them as facts, and they had doubted others on grounds of inherent improbability. Bit by bit a long chain of writers proved that all the phenomena of witchcraft could be accounted for without belief in the evil powers which it professed to invoke. There was no lack of theologians and lawyers to argue on the other side, and there were outbreaks of ferocious witch-hunting in the seventeenth century in the Protestant countries of Europe other than Holland and in America; but the first quarter of the eighteenth saw the practice virtually ended so far as lay and ecclesiastical courts of law were concerned, and the last recorded judicial execution for sorcery came in 1782, in Switzerland. In the meantime science directed a third battering-ram against some of the supposed irruptions of the miraculous into daily life. This was the belief in laws of nature which were incompatible with the supernatural origin of certain events. During the seventeenth century astrology, a relic of what had once been the best available theory for explaining the course of human life, was deprived of the last vestiges of its astronomical groundwork and sank to the status of a superstition. Even then there still remained signs and wonders in the heavens, and wise men still justifiably expected pestilence or public calamities when a comet appeared. That was ended when Halley calculated the orbit of the comet of 1682, which now bears his name, and so proved that these appearances could be predicted, and were as natural as eclipses, which had once been equally terrible.

Thus the frontiers of the miraculous and the mysterious seemed to be driven back, but even at the end of the seventeenth century it was not safe to express unrestricted scepticism. In Holland, most liberal of the western countries, the philosopher Spinoza published a book in 1670, interpreting the Old Testament entirely in terms of natural laws; but there were threatening protests, and no one in that generation ventured to write about the New Testament in that way. In 1696 the English parliament, of which Sir Isaac Newton had been and was again to be a member, passed an Act which made it a penal offence to deny the divinity of Christ. After Newton's death it was found from his unpublished papers that he himself did not believe in the doctrine of the Trinity as he understood it; but this fact was not clearly published until the twentieth century.

We know that many men were more unorthodox in private than they dared or cared to be in public. This was one of the reasons for the emergence of religious toleration. There were others, varying with times and places. We have seen how different kinds and degrees of toleration appeared in France, the Dutch republic, the eastern European countries, and England. Freedom of conscience was the most generally admitted; freedom of worship seldom; freedom of speech exceptionally and incompletely. The Dutch and the English were the only nations among whom they were firmly rooted. But, except in the countries where one stern creed was dominant, like Catholic Spain and Lutheran Sweden, they made some headway everywhere. The sects cried out for them and the churches acquiesced when they were granted by the states. Some men were disgusted by the uncharitableness of theological disputants; others, including men of strong religious feeling, were indifferent to the points at issue. It was in the seventeenth century that the phrase was coined: 'In essentials unity, in non-essentials liberty, in all things charity.'

Since toleration and open-mindedness were growing, the way was open at last for new influences from the world outside to work on western civilization, and they came in full flood when the wider world came to be known and at the same time ceased to be feared. There was now no part of the world from which the west was not able and eager to learn. The wealth and antiquity of the great eastern monarchies, and the marvels of oriental art, seemed to surpass anything in Europe. One of Newton's most admired contemporaries wrote of 'the most civilized nations of the world (such as anciently the Greeks and Romans and now the Chineses and East Indians)'. During his lifetime eastern designs were imitated in European textiles and china and silver; Rembrandt copied Moghul drawings; delicate new crafts were introduced from Japan. But these influences on the arts were superficial and trivial in comparison with the influences on literature and thought. The whole of the east was not merely observed but studied. Among the languages Arabic was studied most thoroughly, partly because, as a Semitic language, it was akin to Hebrew, which was already studied in universities; partly because Arabic learning in general was related to biblical studies. Altogether many Asiatic languages were learnt, as were those of Africa and America, first for the purposes of Christian missions, and in the second place for those of business and administration. Not only were they learnt: type was cast for a number of them, and books were printed. These were momentous innovations in the countries where Christian missionaries worked, and they stand for something of the greatest importance for the history of the world. Even when they investigated ancient civilizations like those of Asia, which were rich in records and in a learned literature of their own, the western scholars were able to learn many things about them which no one had been able to learn before. They brought to bear not only the printing-press but the whole of their developed skill in research, their knowledge of language, of chronology, of natural science, of everything which could interpret the new material. They were able to compare the civilizations of the east as no oriental had ever compared them, and they were able to do it the better for their own newly-won objectivity and openness of mind.

The rise of oriental studies made its first great impressions on the European mind in the spheres of theology and what we now call comparative religion. In the same year in which Copernicus and Vesalius published their books there appeared the first printed Latin translation of the Koran. Before the end of the seventeenth century at least one of the Islamic mystical and philosophical books was very widely known in translations in the west. So were the Analects of Confucius. It had always been conceded by Catholic theologians, and by at least some Protestants, that religion did not consist solely in what was revealed, but that there was natural religion and natural theology. On its theological side the tendency towards toleration was closely related to a tendency to lay stress on the beliefs which the various kinds of Christians had in common rather than on those in which they differed. The discovery of unsuspected wisdom and spiritual depth in the alien religions gave this tendency a wider extension, and this came about at a time when the unaided human mind was asserting for itself a higher place than ever before in the discovery of truth. Thus many men came to hold that the surest and most valuable truths were those which formed the highest common factor of the religions of the great civilizations. In other words they were guaranteed by the faculty which worked equally in all of these and in secular science and learning as well, the faculty which was known as reason.

Different people understood 'reason' and 'reasonableness' in many different senses; but to a greater or less degree they were contrasted not only with passion and absurdity, but also with mystery and revelation. A reasonable faith was apt to mean a consistent and beneficent but moderate, intelligible, and unemphatic creed accommodating itself easily to the fashionable intellectual and practical requirements of the age. As the seventeenth century melted into the eighteenth all the underground opinions came out into the open. Unitarianism gained ground, and alongside of it deism, which retained the god of the scientists as an object of worship, but no longer accorded any primacy or uniqueness to Christianity among the religions. There were also many who openly professed themselves atheists, and many sermons were preached against them; but irreligion was still generally identified with immorality, and atheism was rather a negation by individual rebels than a combined movement against religion itself. In the first quarter of the eighteenth century it was still generally assumed by the governing classes that religion was the cement of society, and there was no interference with the religious ceremonies and oaths by which that assumption was made effective. In one respect, however, the scepticism and criticism of this period brought about a new kind of division in western civilization: Christian beliefs and institutions as such were challenged in the name of religion.

Besides the isolated rebels and blasphemers who defied authority at every point and for every sort of reason, there had always been heretics who claimed to stand for a purer Christianity than that which they saw about them. There had also been quasi-religions, fantastic or distorted anti-Christian practices. Now, however, there were many serious and high-minded men among the educated classes who rejected the dogmas of Christianity and found a religious value in beliefs drawn from various other sources which they tended to work together into a coherent body. A number of streams of thought were converging. Some of them ran off into backwaters, some were dammed back and sent down only a trickle, some were swift and others slow; they were different in colour after they joined; they swept along wreckage with them which made it hard to distinguish one from another; the main channel was tortuous and overflowed its banks, but it was a river. Like all new movements of thought it carried over much from the old. It carried on from Christianity the humanitarianism, the will to diminish suffering, which had been growing more articulate in charitable and educational enterprises. Some of the beliefs which it reaffirmed had been carried down from pre-Christian thought by Christian thinkers, such as the belief of the Stoics that the human race was one and that all men had their rights. But in other ways it turned away from Christianity. It repudiated the doctrine of original sin, and preferred an optimistic view of human nature.

Such a view can be traced far back; Erasmus sometimes leaned towards it; but now, in spite of the evidence, primitive man was idealized, and a glow of sentiment lit the ages 'when wild in woods the noble savage ran'.

Strangely enough this illusion joined hands with the other illusory confidence in human nature which was engendered by the successes of natural science. The literary men of most of the western countries carried on a long controversy on the respective merits of the ancients and the moderns. There was no denying that the moderns had surpassed the ancient Greeks and Romans in knowledge, and the general opinion gained ground that they were superior all round. Thus the belief in progress arose. The general course of history, considered more broadly than in the days when the Middle Ages had appeared to be a thousand years of retrogression, seemed on the whole to be a process of improvement. This process seemed to express the nature of a divine principle working in it, and it seemed the highest duty to help it forward. The most famous of the Dutch scientists took as his motto: 'The world is my country; to promote science my religion.'

If it was a religion, it was no substitute for the historic religions. It was not concerned with the same needs of individual men and women. It had no Church, no organization, and no buildings, for it had not captured the scientific academies and made them its conventicles. It had no liturgy, no ritual, no art or ornaments, and no hierarchy. It was not a society. It had not yet extended beyond the circles of highly educated men, and for the most part it was expressed in their peculiar language. Its adepts made no attempt to convert the masses or to sponsor their discontents, still less to rouse them against their masters, among whom were these adepts themselves. At the same time it was at many points in opposition, if not to the existing order, still to the ruling beliefs. It provided grounds for criticizing mystical visions and ascetic practices, ecclesiastical repression, whether by the Catholic inquisition or by the Calvinist consistories, and the whole fabric of authority in matters of belief. It professed to appeal against the imperfections of Christianity, or the deceits of churchmen, to a higher truth, and when its votaries suffered, as many of them did, from social disapproval or official censure or even worse, they were fortified by moral indignation. The time was not long distant when they would find allies and followers among other opponents of things as they were.

For the present this tendency was aristocratic, and so was the whole intellectual movement from which it arose. It made its contribution to polite literature. Some excellent writers, especially in France, wrote treatises on science for gentlemen and ladies, and there were some schools, though they were exceptional, where boys were taught some of the new subjects; but in education the movement had only a limited effect. In the maritime countries schools of navigation were founded; but, except in these, technological instruction was still imparted by means of apprenticeship, and the new methods percolated downwards through the employers of labour. It was a consequence less of the advance of science than of the growing scale and complexity of commerce and industry that far more people in the busier countries, down to skilled craftsmen, learnt elementary mathematics. Shopkeepers did their sums on paper; the abacus and the casting-board were relegated to the nursery. Gunners ceased to call their pieces by picturesque names like 'cannons petro' and 'bastard cannons', and began to talk about 'twenty-four-pounders' and 'forty-two-pounders'. Until this time the only way of distinguishing the houses in a street was by carved or painted signs, such as we still have for inns and barbers' shops. It is said that as early as 1512 someone in Paris tried to do it by numbering the houses, but the attempt was a failure. In 1708 a London topographer wrote that 'in Prescott Street, Goodman's Fields, instead of signs the houses are distinguished by numbers, as the staircases in the Inns of Court and Chancery'. But popular education did not go far enough for the numbering of houses to become a general practice in any European city until the late eighteenth century.

In various countries, it is true, schools were opened for the children of artisans and labourers, and this development coincided roughly in time with the great intellectual movement, but there seems to be no reason for supposing that the two were closely connected. The contemporaneous increase of economic needs and opportunities explains some of the foundations of schools, and most of the others would not have been founded if it had not been for religious reasons. In the countries where Calvinism was strong, for instance in Scotland, attempts were

made to provide every parish with its school, in order that every
man and woman might learn to read the Bible. The same motive
operated, no doubt with an admixture of others, in other environments besides that of Calvinism and Bible-reading. In France
a newly founded religious order opened many schools for the
poor. In due time these institutions were to be linked up with
others which sprang from the intellectual movement; but for
the time being its influence was circumscribed, and so far from
doing anything to efface the differences of educational level which
separated the more fortunate from the unprivileged, it accentuated them and gave the privileged a still greater advantage.

VIII

THE WEALTH OF NATIONS AND THE POWER OF STATES

THROUGHOUT the sixteenth and seventeenth centuries, and on into the eighteenth, there continued the long-drawn processes of early capitalism, each sometimes helping the others forward but sometimes delaying them or masking them from view. Population grew. One rough estimate, as good as another in this poorly-lighted field, is that Europe, the whole continent west of the Ural Mountains, had about 95 million inhabitants in 1600 and about 130 millions in 1700, whereas in 1930 it had about 475 millions.

There was at the same time a steady, though not spectacular, improvement in transport. In all the more prosperous countries roads, with their appurtenances such as coaches, stage-wagons, and inns, were improved, as were the breeds of horses for riding, for hauling vehicles, and for carrying packs. There were ships with better rigging and better lines; there were more ships and larger ships. Harbours and docks were made more commodious. Rivers were cleared for navigation, and some of them were connected by canals. Every improvement in transport enabled a greater number of sellers to bring their wares to the same markets, and so it enabled those who could produce more cheaply and in larger quantities to undersell their competitors. It tended to concentrate the production of each commodity in those places which were best suited for it, whether by their situation or by their ready access to materials or by the cheapness or the exceptional skill of their labour. Thus it drew together large numbers of people employed in the same occupations or in occupations which dovetailed in with one another, draining them away from regions which could not produce for distant markets: it differentiated the regions. The manufacturing districts and the districts which exported agricultural produce became more specialized, and much of the increase of population was concentrated in them, while other places lost in numbers, and many people were unaware that the total population was rising.

Some great industries needed to be near wood and water, and so in many parts of Europe the industrial districts consisted not of towns but of scattered villages or settlements in the country-side. In the textile industries water-mills were used for fulling and other finishing processes; they were coming to be used for the elaborate and newly invented Italian machinery for 'throwing' silk. The metal industries used great quantities of wood for fuel and so they flourished where the mines were near the forests: it was only in a few places, especially in England, that coal was used as fuel in industry. Commerce, however, unlike industry, built up the towns everywhere: its nature is to bring goods together at points where they can be sorted, graded, and marketed, and from which they can be dispersed to the best advantage. Town life seems to have become healthier as the towns grew in size. This is hard to account for, because medical knowledge was growing only slowly, and there was nothing like the great movement of sanitation which arose in later times; but from about the middle of the seventeenth century there were more and better doctors and hospitals, and practically all of them were in the towns. Perhaps the cause was better diet. There seems to be evidence from English, French, German, and Swiss towns that death-rates fell between 1550 and 1720. They were still very high, especially the rate of infant mortality, and every country was still liable to periodical famines and fierce epidemics; but the new interest in the statistics of population arose, perhaps not accidentally, when human skill and fore-sight were beginning to influence the numbers of the people and the length of their lives.

Politicians thought much about these figures, and aspired to control them, indeed their ambition to do this outran what was possible in those days of loose organization. It was the general opinion that a dense population was conducive to wealth. There were phases of economic depression in which the contrary opinion was heard, as when enthusiasts for colonization advocated emigration as a means of relieving unemployment and overpopulation; but in the second half of the seventeenth century Europe needed men; the stream of emigrants to America ran much less strongly, and the general desire for dense population was justifiable. Politicians had another reason for favouring it besides the purely economic reason. A large population was the basis of military strength. As the continent grew richer and more populous, the scale of warfare increased. Armies became larger. It seems that for more than a century after the last years of Charles V no general commanded more than 50,000 men in the field; but during the great wars which began in the sixteen-sixties there was a rise in numbers, so that the French and the coalition opposed to them each had armies far exceeding 100,000. These were not national armies. They still consisted of mercenary troops recruited from every country where pay acted as an inducement to serve; but the national element was coming in. The stronger states, with their new mastery of administrative method, prevented their subjects from serving under any flag except their own. Of all the great powers France was the most unified, and her own large numbers were the basis of her power. Other states therefore had a reason for adding to their numbers, whether by annexing territory or by promoting economic welfare, and for unifying their peoples in every way that might produce well-knit armies.

Other considerations akin to these, but of even wider scope, affected policy and economic life. Man for man the armies made greater demands on the economy of their countries. When one of them improved its equipment the others had to do as well or better, at their peril. More artillery was needed, more small arms, more ammunition, more transport, greater stores of food, clothing, and boots, to say nothing of more pay and more regular payments. Along with the growth of armies went the rise of the navies. In the sixteenth century specialized ships of war were few in numbers outside the Mediterranean, where the warship was still, as in the times of the Homeric wars, an oared galley, a simple craft, comparatively easy to equip. Naval warfare was largely carried on by armed merchantmen collected from the ports. After Lepanto and the Spanish Armada there was an interval in which there were no large and costly navies anywhere. After that the new Atlantic maritime states began to build up their fleets. The sailing-ship with its broadside of guns dominated the Mediterranean. Merchantmen disappeared from the line of battle. Soon after the middle of the seventeenth century the Dutch and the English began to fight one another with great battle-fleets, and the French tried to emulate their naval standard, just as other powers were trying to reach the French military standard. These fleets could not be fitted out from the home resources of the Atlantic powers. They drew heavily on those resources: naval recruitment was parasitic on the merchant marine; guns, ammunition, clothing, and victualling were needed, as for the armies; but in addition timber was used in quantities which only the Baltic could supply, and along with it tar and pitch and materials for sailcloth and cordage. To buy and transport these necessaries new financial expedients were required.

Warfare gave the states these urgent reasons for concerning themselves with economic matters at a time when business men were happy to work with the statesmen. Although in well-conducted business a bargain leaves both the buyer and the seller better off than they were before, it was commonly said in those days that one nation's gain was another's loss. When the European traders crowded in to bid against one another as buyers or sellers in the markets of Europe and Asia and America, they often found that the ambassadors were there before them, negotiating for treaties which should give their own country-men a monopoly or a preference. From time out of mind the regular way of securing a profitable trade had been to buy a monopoly. In every little town there was some guild which enjoyed the sole right to make or to sell this article or that; in every port there were lawful quays where ships had to unload and pay their dues; every state had its trade-barriers, whether it merely laid special charges on foreigners in its own ports or tried to close whole seas, as the Venetians did in the Adriatic, the Danes in Iceland, or the Spaniards in the Pacific. In this again the middle of the seventeenth century seems to have seen a new phase. The ending of the great rise in prices was an ex-pression of the ending of the long phase of expansion. Produc-tion and transport had overtaken the widening of markets, and it was harder to find new outlets for trade. Competition was more intense. Something might be done by mechanization or by cutting down costs, but the quick way to get an advantage over a rival was to enlist the support of the state against him. Many of the characteristics of economic life at this time followed from the rendering of this support.

First there was protectionism, by which a state restricted certain economic opportunities to its own subjects. In principle it goes back to the beginning of the world, and old trading states like Venice had practised it with many refinements; but, until they attained a measure of internal unity and efficiency, large territorial states were able to use it only in crude and haphazard ways. Its typical instrument is the tariff. In the seventeenth century no state could set up a trade-barrier as impermeable as those of the nineteenth and twentieth. Their hold over society was still imperfect. They usually had to work either through officials who were easily corrupted or through tax-farmers whose interests might run contrary to those of both the state and the trading community. But there was a tendency towards stricter tariffs based on rational, if short-sighted, principles. The chief of these was the principle of the balance of trade. This was the idea that the trade of a country should be judged by means of an annual balance-sheet like that of a business. The merchant can tell from his ledger which of his ventures are profitable and which are not, and so the seventeenth-century economists regarded some branches of trade as advantageous and others as detrimental. They favoured most highly those which brought in such goods as they could not supply for themselves, especially the precious metals, in exchange for manufactured articles which employed their labour at home. The colonial traders fulfilled these requirements, while much of the trade within Europe did not. Each country therefore tried to draw up its tariff, and its other protective arrangements such as navigation laws, in such a way as to reserve colonial trade and the other paying trades for its own people, and to confine its own people to these selected channels.

The counterpart of state encouragement was state regulation. The more authoritarian a state was, and the more highly the administrators rated their own understanding of economic affairs, the more they were apt to lay down rules for the conduct of business. Here again they were only continuing, with greater powers and in a wider sphere, activities which had been handed down to them by their predecessors, but they now had the new aim and the new incentive of promoting the unity and strength of their realms. With the new facilities for movement and the new methods of surveying resources, they thought of the whole country as one great farm. The old feudal franchises and local immunities, which they were sweeping away, were objectionable primarily because they enabled rival powers to set themselves up against the state; but often they also impeded the production of wealth. When a nobleman or a municipality levied a toll on river traffic, they interrupted the free movement of goods, and slowed down the concentration of industry in the most promising centres. Governments tried to remove these impediments. The typical economic statesman of the age was the great French minister Colbert, who was in power from about 1660 to his death in 1683. His successive tariffs were landmarks in the hardening of European protectionism; but he had an even greater task in removing some of the internal tariffs surrounding the old provinces which had been combined to make the French kingdom as he found it. While he was engaged in this negative work of excluding foreign trade and removing domestic obstructions, it was natural that he should also throw his energies into the positive work of increasing industrial production. He issued many regulations which were intended to raise the quality of manufactures, and to provide capital for their expansion.

As it turned out the paternalism of Colbert had another negative side. Economic enterprise could not be turned into the channels which governments thought desirable except by closing the others, and many French business men would have preferred to take their own risks and make their own mistakes. The time was still far distant when state trading and state management in industry were possible alternatives to private enterprise. Even the manufacture of commodities such as explosives, of which the states were the only large consumers, was mainly in the hands of private firms, and so, when statesmen tried to encourage manufactures, they commonly acted as imperfectly informed outsiders. The typical form of large-scale enterprise was the joint-stock company to which the state granted a monopoly. It was not an entirely new form but one which had arisen in earlier times when the circumstances called for it; from about the middle of the sixteenth century it was used in the larger business affairs of the English, the Dutch, and the French. In a joint-stock company many shareholders contributed the capital, leaving the management to an inner circle. They brought together far greater accumulations of capital than even the richest merchant would have risked on a single venture, and it was possible for shareholders to come and go without disturbing the continuity of the company's business. There were, of course, special dangers from fraud and mismanagement; but the system took root. In England the aristocracy, and even the kings and queens, took advantage of it to invest in colonial and industrial undertakings. In Holland, where the business class almost coincided with the governing class, several great companies were formed for the purpose of that colonial commerce which was indistinguishable from war against Spain. The Dutch East India Company, the greatest trading concern of seventeenth-century Europe, became almost an imperial power. In France, where the royal authority was more pervasive than in either of these countries, joint-stock companies were created in pursuance of Colbert's policy; but it was their misfortune never to outgrow this tutelage.

Financial institutions changed in consonance with these and other changes of the times. The political decline of Spain was associated with the breakdown of the international finance by which war and diplomacy had been floated. The great banking families were unable to satisfy the demands of the states; the Spanish kings and some others fell far short of the reliability by which alone a borrower can keep his banker as an ally. Each stage in the military and political decline of Spain was signalized by a repudiation of public debts. At the end of the sixteenth century and in the early seventeenth none of the greater western European states was financially sound, and when a new system arose it was unlike the old. States borrowed from abroad even more heavily than before, but among the lenders there were now states and banks which were more or less directly upheld by states. Private finance was connected with public finance. The Dutch, who were pioneers in many fields of business, built up a sound banking system of their own, and Amsterdam became the great money-market of the seventeenth century. Towards the end of the century London originated methods suitable for English conditions, and the eighteenth century was not far advanced when London, although still a centre of borrowing while Amsterdam was the centre of lending, became a rival for the first place in the world of finance.

The theory and practice of economics in this age, of which Colbert gave the classical expression, are often summed up under the name of 'mercantilism' or 'the mercantile system', words which have been understood in many senses, but which almost always cover a close association of political and economic factors. The states aimed at increasing their power through economic prosperity. At home they tried to exorcize discontent and disunion by a policy of welfare. One means of doing this was to remove internal restraints and obstructions to trade, another to stimulate production; but foreign trade seemed to offer the greatest chances of enrichment and the greatest markets for home manufactures, so that a strong state moulded its own country by pressing against the resistance of the surrounding states. This has been well called the economic aspect of sovereignty. The rise of the sovereign states, through the two-sided process of overcoming rival authorities within their realms and eliminating the interference or jurisdiction of external powers, coincided at many points with paternal government and the jealousy of trade. These truths, however, are often overstated. In practice, policy always fell short of its professions, and the picture of western civilization in its economic aspects was still full of variety and confusion. Hardly any of the current generalizations about mercantilism hold good of the greatest trading nation of the time, the Dutch. Among them the commercial interest was so strong and the state so little centralized that almost any profitable opening for business could be followed without the sanction of any co-ordinating body. Again, in many countries there were forces at work in economic life which ran directly counter to the unifying tendencies.

The increase of wealth through commerce implied, or rather was, an increase of all those activities which were carried on by bargaining, by money-transactions, by exchange based on quantitative calculations of profit. It meant a diminution of all the activities which were regulated by custom, tradition, and authority, a movement from status to contract. In the fifteenth century a large proportion of the inhabitants of Europe hardly handled any money at all. A peasant, for instance, might hold his inherited house and farm without paying rent but by working on his lord's land; he might have the right to collect fuel in the lord's woods; he might pay the miller who ground his corn with a proportion of the corn; he would contribute to the Church by giving tithes of his produce. By the end of the seventeenth century a large proportion of the population, especially the urban population, of England, Holland, and France, was living by income-economy. The head of each household planned his work with the primary aim of making a money-income, and he spent most of this income as and when he pleased. His discretion in getting and spending had limits, for he had to pay taxes to the state in cash, and he had legal or moral responsibilities to his family, and perhaps to his employees, but, with some such exceptions as these, income-economy meant freedom. Where a large proportion of people in a prosperous community was free to choose whether to save or to spend, and what to invest in or to spend on, the aggregate result of their individual preferences was an independent determinant of economic life. It might build up trades or industries which the statesmen and economists had never thought about, or even disapproved and feared; it might suck away the nourishment from those they tried to promote. So the mercantile system, in so far as there was such a thing, could never make a national economy work like a well-drilled regiment with no will except the word of command.

In practice mercantilism was hampered all round by the traditional obstacles to which it was consciously opposed, and also by these new accompaniments of economic growth. There was no field in which it achieved so little as in the welfare of the peasants and wage-earners. Popular discontent became less alarming to governments in proportion as they got the better of the feudal or municipal powers which might make use of it in armed revolt. Whenever bad times or flagrant injustices caused intolerable poverty, or political confusion inflamed the eternal grievances of the oppressed, there were peasants' risings and journeymen's riots; but, on the whole, they were put down more easily in the seventeenth century than in the sixteenth and more easily in the later seventeenth century than in the earlier. There was a specially disturbed period round the middle of the seventeenth century in such widely different environments as those of England, Bohemia, and Switzerland; and it is to be accounted for on both political and economic, local and general grounds. For similarly complex reasons the late seventeenth century ushered in a more orderly period which lasted through most of the eighteenth. Governments, however, still had the fear of rebellion always in their minds, and, quite apart from that, they had enough sense to see that it was in every way best for the people to be healthy and satisfied. Humanitarian feeling was not impotent. Much was done in the richer countries by private and public charity for the unemployed, the sick, and the orphans. While there were occasionally bitter complaints against the established order of ranks and government it was neither shaken nor seriously criticized. When large numbers of industrial workers were congregated in towns there were tumultuous strikes, and among the more prosperous artisans there were beginnings of something like trade unionism; but they were only beginnings, and they cannot be said to have modified the general position of the workers. In no country was there anything resembling a national working-class movement. Manual workers in different trades had no consciousness of common interests and no network of communication among themselves. It was only in political or religious movements that they acted together over wide areas. Mercantilist thinkers, indeed, for the most part believed that national industry would thrive best if labour was cheap. If civil war and social unrest played a smaller part after the middle of the seventeenth century than before, this came about not as the reward of a policy of welfare, but partly because the states were stronger and better able to keep order, and partly because unguided economic processes carried some share of the new wealth to every stratum of society.

As in its other aspects, sovereignty in its economic aspect gathered, about a few great centres, power which had been dispersed among many that were smaller, and so simplified the scheme of European conflicts. Of this the most notable instance was that of the colonial conflicts. The Portuguese and the Spaniards, as we have seen, built up their trade and their empires under royal auspices and royal regulations; but the newer colonizing nations had far looser relations to their governments. The English Queen Elizabeth gave commissions authorizing her merchant captains to carry on hostilities; and she took shares in the companies which financed them. Her ministers and those of her successor watched their actions closely, and gave diplomatic support when they claimed the right to trade or colonize where the Spaniards had no effective occupation. They gave the highest diplomatic rank to representatives in Turkey and India who were appointed and paid by trading companies. But they regarded trade itself as a matter for companies or merchants and not a matter of state; they neither prescribed rules for its management nor took the initiative in clearing away the barriers set up against it by foreign governments. Some of the most successful of the English colonists owed scarcely anything to official support. New England was founded by religious refugees, whose royal charters in effect merely gave them permission to go their way unmolested. The French and Dutch governments stood in different relations to private enterprise, but their colonists also were far more free from supervision than their fellow subjects who remained at home. None of these three governments therefore espoused the quarrels of its merchants and settlers unless with cause shown. Their European affairs, which involved the issues of war and invasion, were much more important to them than colonial affairs, and colonial affairs soon generated a rivalry of all against all among the trading companies, which could not have been transferred to Europe without ending in anarchy.

Thus it was that in the first half of the seventeenth century there were informal wars in the colonial world which did not bring European wars in their train, because the European governments were not committed to them. When England and Spain were at peace, it was still a maxim of the English sea-rovers that there was no peace beyond the line. When the English attempted to trade with the Spice Islands the Dutch kept them out by violence. Dutch and English whale-fishers fought in the Arctic. There was fierce Anglo-Dutch rivalry wherever the English tried to trade, and the governments supplied their countrymen with munitions and much more. This rivalry led to a long series of diplomatic negotiations, but, all through the period of the Thirty Years War, friendship between the two states was a necessity, so that none of these negotiations ended with an ultimatum. When the Portuguese began their war of independence they almost automatically became allies of the French against the Spaniards; but this was no reason why the Dutch should discontinue their efforts to conquer Brazil, and they still fought against the Portuguese there, though indirectly, as allies of the French, they fought for them in Europe.

There were similar occurrences, though on a small scale and in out-of-the-way places, in later times. In the late seventeenth century, for instance, during a phase of friendship between France and England, the French officials in Canada did more than connive at the capture and destruction of the British trading posts on Hudson Bay. But this was now an exception, and the general rule had altered. About the middle of the century the new colonial states had gained so much in strength, their supervision of colonial trade was so much more strict and jealous, and the affairs of the world were so much more closely knit, that there could no longer be hostilities round the circumference and peace at the centre. First the quarrel of the Dutch and the English came to a head in a regular war in their home waters. This war had other contributing causes, but rivalry in the seas and the Indies was by far the chief. A few years later the Dutch and the Portuguese were openly at war. The French, who regretted this division among the old enemies of Spain, persuaded them to compose their differences; and in the same way, when Anglo-Dutch rivalry led to two more wars within a generation of the first, the quarrel was broken off before it was fought out, because a European danger, this time from France herself, appeared to both the combatants more alarming than anything they had to fear from one another. These nearer and greater dangers in Europe still outweighed all overseas affairs; but the political relations of Europe and the outer world were permanently altered. Henceforward European governments were fully committed to colonial quarrels, and these were a permanent element in the causes of European wars.

For this reason, and for others which necessarily followed from the conditions of the time and from mercantilist policy, each of the great wars in the second half of the century had an economic prelude. Plenipotentiaries were briefed with commercial statistics, and several of the great peace-settlements included treaties which stipulated for modifications of tariffs. There were also new formulae in diplomatic documents, which seemed to imply a more rational ordering of international affairs. The balance of power, or equilibrium of Europe, seemed as much a scientific conception as the balance of trade, and more conducive to the general interest. It was elaborated, by the Frenchman Sully who had stood in the first rank of statesmen, into a project for maintaining permanent peace between the European states. Their territories were to be so arranged that it could never be to the advantage of any to be an aggressor, and they were to form a federation which should make war on the enemies of Christendom, notably the Turks. The significance of this project, and of the few other proposals for perpetual peace to which the period gave birth, is only that they showed a desire for a better international order, and a belief, or perhaps only a hope or a wish, that policy could end the endemic warfare of Europe. In practice none of these plans had the smallest influence. Nor indeed did the idea of the balance of power provide more than a formula for common action which the states would in any event have taken when they were threatened with aggression, or when

they had to agree on some division of territory among themselves. Fundamentally international relations became neither
more co-operative nor more scientific.

Some historians have laid the blame for this on one man,
King Louis XIV, who ruled over France for more than fifty
years exactly at the time when the ascendancy of France over
the mind of Europe was at its highest. The French language
became not only the language of almost all diplomacy but also
the international language of the educated classes, and it began
to take the place of Latin as a medium of learned intercourse.
French literature reached a classical perfection. The tragedies
of Racine and the comedies of Molière became the possession
and the models of all Europe. Louis was a great master of
pageantry, and Versailles, which he created, became the pattern
of royal courts. France set the fashions in dress. The French
Academy, and the bodies of lower standing for the specialized
sciences, earned high prestige. Yet in many respects the France
of Louis XIV was old-fashioned and untouched by the dawning
enlightenment. There was a severe censorship of publications.
Not only was France outside the movement towards toleration;
the Huguenots were even deprived of the toleration which they
had enjoyed. They had given no offence and there was no
political danger from them; but Louis subjected them to pressure from the beginning of his personal rule. First propaganda
and then persecution were used to convert them; they began to
emigrate, to the great advantage of the Protestant countries
which received them; and finally the Edict of Nantes was re-
pealed. In all these oppressive measures Louis was immediately
concerned.

His personality counted for much. He was Spanish on his
mother's side, and his religious policy savoured of Spain not
only in relation to the Huguenots but in other ways as well. He
did not shrink from quarrelling with the Holy See on behalf of
the autonomy of the Gallican Church, in which he had so much
power. He threw his influence on the side of the Jesuits in a
bitter controversy against Jansenism, an evangelical movement
with something like a tang of Protestantism in it. In this he did
not carry all legal and ecclesiastical France with him, and the
controversy outlasted his lifetime. But, although he was more
than a figurehead, the character of the French state, his own

PLATE 30

Sébastien Leclerc, The Académie des Sciences in the Royal Library at Versailles in 1671. (See p. xxiv)

part in it, and its international action sprang from causes far deeper and wider than one man's mind. The events of Louis's early years confirmed the lessons which had already made France choose authoritarian government. During his minority there was anarchy. The old elements of disruption, the nobles and the law-courts, made a bid for power. They lacked the political experience and the social generosity which could have led to a liberal revolution, and an able minister, the Italian Cardinal Mazarin, restored his own authority and the king's by methods more adroit and less drastic than those of Richelieu. It was not until the defeats of Louis's later years that opposition again raised its head. Then some of its leaders used the true language of liberalism; but they had no programme except government by a narrow aristocratic class which was unfit for the burden. The nobility existed and could not be ignored, but as a body it was politically useless. Some of its members were content with the harmless occupations of courtiers, and many more took up the career which the French army, like the other professional armies of the time, afforded.

Despotism was the only method by which France could be kept in order and maintain her inherited international pretensions. More than that, it was a system of government which could boast genuine successes. It provided Colbert with the administrative machinery that he needed. One of his fellow ministers brought the army into a better state of discipline and into stricter subordination to the state than it had ever known before. The great departments which could do so much could only work in accordance with their own construction, and Louis could not arbitrarily change the interaction of their parts. As the state ceased to be feudal it became impersonal. The king did not read all the documents that he signed, let alone write them. He even used secretaries who were authorized to forge his autograph. He did not understand all the decisions that he announced, let alone form them. By his time France, and others of the larger states, were passing into the condition, known in our day as that of all states and of some great private organizations, in which few men in office have actual power as extensive as their nominal responsibility. In such a state of things to talk of a policy as that of one man is seldom more than a picturesque abbreviation.

IX

SIXTY YEARS OF WARFARE

WHEN Europe was half-pacified by the treaty of the Pyrenees in 1659 the two main facts of the situation were that Spain was declining apace and that France had become the strongest of the powers. France laid claim to the gratitude of states, such as the Dutch republic and those of the German Protestants, which she had saved from Spanish or Austrian Habsburg domination. She had ties of friendship with a ring of states, Sweden, Poland, and Hungary, which had helped her to encircle the Habsburgs. She had a party at her service in every capital, as the Spaniards had once had in the days of their greatness. While the economic and political drift was towards intensified international competition, she had all the assets which could be of use in warfare. France had already passed from defence to attack, and for nearly fifty years she was never at war except of her own choice. She had the political initiative, and her opponents could not choose whether or when or where to begin hostilities or how to end them. The king and his people revelled in their glory. A few men whose voices could be heard in high places stigmatized the wars as cruel and unjust. They were easily silenced, and, so long as the victories lasted, they were forgotten.

The greatest issue in all these wars was the future of the Spanish dominions. They were still by far the richest and most populous which were owned by any European state, but Spain would certainly not be able to hold them together. Soon after Louis began his personal rule, a prospect came in sight which made it apear a public duty for France to control the settlement of this issue. The Spanish throne fell to a pitiable weakling who had no heir and no prospect of an heir. His death would bring into operation the old insurance system of the Habsburgs, by which the Austrians were to inherit if the Spanish line came to an end. This would have renewed the danger to France from Habsburg encirclement. Forty years went by before this fateful death occurred, and during these forty years the stakes became steadily higher. International relations went through the changes we have noticed in the last chapter, and France, under Colbert, had the initiative here too. In Canada the settlers and traders became pioneers of empire; the city of St. Louis was founded on the Mississippi, and it was possible to travel in French territory from the mouth of the St. Lawrence to the Gulf of Mexico. In Europe Colbert created a navy which made France a third maritime power on the Atlantic. If such a France were victorious over Spain the whole western and colonial world might well be at her mercy.

There were nearly thirty years of French aggrandizement before the grouping of the European powers fell into conformity with these threatening realities. On his northern and eastern and southern frontiers Louis edged forwards, taking one province and one fortress after another from Spain or from the empire in open war, or in undeclared war, or by ostensibly legal processes which had the threat of war behind them. But during that generation there were other European states which half-consciously prepared for a struggle. Some of the German princes resented the dominance which France had acquired on the pretext of protecting them against the Habsburgs. There were Austrian diplomatists everywhere who exposed the fallacies of the Francophil arguments. The Dutch held out stubbornly for their rights in the Baltic, and took alarm at the French advance to the south of them in the Spanish Netherlands. For a time Dutch policy was perplexed by the continuing British rivalry. The English strengthened their Portuguese alliance. Portugal was able to save Brazil and, after handing over strategic or commercial bases to the English, she saved all the other parts of her empire which the Dutch had not already seized. In the second of the Anglo-Dutch wars the new French navy was on the English side, and the English made valuable colonial gains at the expense of the Dutch. They took New Netherland, renamed New York, so connecting New England with Virginia and their more recent settlements in Maryland and Carolina. They gave up, however, their hopes of ousting the Dutch from the richest parts of the Malay Archipelago, and, though there was another war, in which the British and French navies co-operated while the French invaded Holland, the very success of this French invasion caused the English and the Dutch to suspend their colonial strife. It seemed a miracle that the Dutch were able to summon Spanish, imperial and Protestant German help and to save their independence. For ten more years France still divided and browbeat her neighbours;

but at last another miracle happened. William III of Orange, the great-grandson of William the Silent, more than any other man, or any hundred other men, had saved his country in the hour of invasion. England had a revolutionary crisis in its religious and constitutional affairs, and the opponents of France, of Catholic emancipation, and of authoritarian government needed a leader. The irony of fate gave them their leader by the working of the ancient dynastic principle, for William and his wife had a place, though not the first place, in the line of succession to the English crown. The opposition summoned him to England and to the throne. He saved western Europe, as he had saved Holland, by bringing Spain, the emperor, German princes, and yet other allies into the field, while at last the Dutch and the British fleets held the seas in concert.

There was an indecisive war of nine years (1688–97). It was a European war, involving all the continent except the east and the Baltic; indeed it was a world war. It was followed by a peace of four years in which all parties sincerely tried to overcome their mutual suspicions and reach agreement on the specific questions, territorial and economic, over which war might arise; but it was not only disagreements about 'danger-spots' that divided them. The world was now so closely knit that every local question ran into every other, and the contest for power embraced them all. Finally the crisis of the Spanish inheritance broke. Well-intentioned statesmen in every country searched for some compromise which should satisfy all the parties. It seemed that this first world-empire could be liquidated by parti-tion. One accident after another dissipated all such hopes, and at last the Spaniards themselves made all compromise impossible by insisting that their empire should be kept together as a single whole. The method they chose was to offer it not, it is true, to France, but to a younger line of the French royal house. That decision brought the armies and the fleet of King Louis to their side, but in the new world war, which lasted for fourteen years, the victory was not theirs. The principle of partition was applied after all, and France was forced back from some of her advanced positions.

These fifty years of warfare changed the map of western and Mediterranean Europe. They left France territorially larger than she had been before, with fresh provinces on the Pyrenees and on the eastern frontier and with parts of provinces torn away from the Netherlands. She had become strategically not less but more compact. The wars left the Dutch republic financially exhausted, and politically checked. They left Spain a second-class power, still mistress of the Indies but no longer of the Netherlands, or Milan, or Sicily. It was now Austria which undertook the task of defending all these three, and they gave her a great accession of strength, though of strength outside Germany. The old combination of the Spanish and Austrian Habsburgs was ended after its two troubled centuries of validity and Spain became normally a client state of France. Germany had become a theatre of rival ambitions. Brandenburg-Prussia had come forward into the front rank of German states. Its electors of the house of Hohenzollern had been both crafty and lucky in earning payments for their alliance. They had imitated the military organization and the conscription of the Swedes to such purpose that they had beaten Swedish troops in the field. They had adopted French methods with equal success, and they had begun to build up their own capable and heavy-handed bureaucratic state. The emperor had raised them to royal rank. Two other German electors had reached the same elevation. An elector of Hanover had succeeded to the British Crown as the Protestant nominee, and the elector of Saxony had become a Catholic and had been elected by Austrian influence as King of Poland. Thus in Germany all was ready for future contests.

For Europe generally the problem of French power was not ended, but it had entered a new phase. Spain was no longer the chief antagonist. Opposition now looked to the threefold combination of Austria, Great Britain, and the Dutch, which had an experience of common action matching its common interests. Now that the stronger states were more consolidated, and had welded together their colonial and economic affairs with their home affairs, their mutual relations were more orderly. The successive coalitions against Louis XIV were based on compromise between the general interest in the balance of power and the cupidities of separate states; but they were less impudently rapacious than the alliances of the fifteenth and sixteenth centuries. They had some conception of a common good of Europe, and both sides accepted the principle of equilibrium as the nominal basis of treaties of peace. In conducting their wars, the states of the coalitions had gained great experience of international co-operation, experience from which the technique and the spirit of diplomacy ultimately benefited everywhere. They had worked together not only to win and divide the spoils of victory, but also to save their power of managing their own affairs, and this effort had made them move, some farther and others less far, some unconsciously and others to the accompaniment of economic and political theorizing, towards the conception of the state not as dynastic property but as the guardian of the welfare of the land.

As an effective force in affairs this conception still took for granted the social fabric of limited governing classes ruling over an unenfranchised population. In no western country, and not even in any of the colonial settlements, was there any true democracy, any manhood suffrage or even any serious demand for it. But, while this period saw the extinction of this revolutionary challenge, it saw what may be called aristocratic or oligarchic liberalism established in a new stronghold. Aristocratic liberalism was government in accordance with the agreed decisions of bodies which were drawn from a limited class but acted after free discussion and with some degree of tolerance and of consideration for the governed. Its germs were alive in the estates constitutions of the Middle Ages. They had survived in more places than one through the period when despotism carried all before it in most of the continental countries. Hungary, for instance, still had its parliament, and there were one or two minor German principalities where the estates counted for something. Only one of the greater powers, the Dutch republic, however, had always managed its business on these lines, and it was a fact of the greatest moment that, at the time when this first sponsor of modern freedom was losing its place in the front rank, another state, of which the prospects had for long seemed uncertain, stood forward indubitably as a great European power and a liberal state.

This was Great Britain. Before the accession of King William III she had never been free from ecclesiastical and constitutional divisions. Richelieu, Mazarin, and Louis XIV had each played on these divisions, which kept England out of the European field; but the island was never invaded. The governing class worked out its own solution for its problems, the solution of a constitutional monarchy, co-operating with Parliament and granting toleration, but not full civil rights, to religious dis-

sidents. William III was equally the representative of this settlement and of an active resistance to France in Europe and overseas. In his time Great Britain began to act as the equal of
Austria in the European coalitions. Her fleets were larger than
those of the Dutch. After William's time her land-armies were
directed by the genius of Marlborough, and in the peace-
settlement she gained colonial conquests in Newfoundland and
Nova Scotia, and also strategic positions in Gibraltar and
Minorca. It was her liberalism which enabled her to deploy so
much of her strength. She turned the personal union of England
and Scotland into a constitutional union on a parliamentary
basis. She modernized her finances by a close association between
Parliament and the business world. And this was the time in
which the steam-engine was invented and the fame of Newton
spread abroad. For the first time since the early sixteenth century there were English thinkers among the recognized leaders
of European thought. English imaginative literature in its great
days from Shakespeare to Milton had been the private and un-
translated possession of the islanders; but now Europe and even
France began to learn from English teachers. Newton's contemporary Locke wrote the classics of liberalism. He wrote as a
Christian and an Anglican, but he wrote in terms which exactly
suited the fashionable demand for reasonableness in all things.
He advocated toleration, within limits; he defended the blood-
less revolution which had brought in William III; he argued
that good government must be government by consent, and
that the ultimate guarantee against arbitrary rule was to preserve society by revolution in the state. He wrote much else,
about theology and philosophy and education and economics,
and he played his part in public affairs; but it was as a political
theorist that he made his mark on history. There were continental and American readers for a century after his time, some of
them sparing no attention for his ambiguities and reservations,
who followed him in believing that the powers of governments
ought to be limited by law, and that laws ought to be made by
bodies chosen by the citizens.

The measure of the growing strength of western civilization
in the time of Louis XIV is the reversal of the old relations
with the Turks. For the first twenty years of Louis's time
the divisions of the west still prevented any strong action

against them. There was even a renewal of Turkish vigour and
efficiency. After they had crushed the Persian revival the Turks
turned westwards again and attacked the Venetians in Crete.
Then, indeed, there was an episode which promised great things
for the future. The emperor picked a quarrel with the Turks,
and in 1663, at the abbey of St. Gothard on the river Raab in
Hungary, he inflicted on them their first land-defeat in Europe.
But this promise, like the promise of Lepanto, was not fulfilled.
Louis XIV had sent a small contingent to share in the triumph;
but he did not take up the Turkish war in earnest. The emperor
had to make a truce, and French ambition in the west diverted
his energies so effectively that he kept it for eighteen years. The
Turks took Crete. They supported the rebellious Cossacks of the
Ukraine against the Poles and they took the fertile province of
Podolia for themselves. There was nothing to show that this
would be their last considerable gain of European land. There
was nothing to cause them apprehension in the advance of
the Russians, with Cossack aid, along the Dnieper. Austria, the
main enemy, was weakened by long wars against France; the
Turks attacked again in Hungary, and in 1681 once more, as
in 1529, they reached Vienna. This time they besieged it, and
for two months it was in peril. It was saved when John Sobieski,
the King of Poland, led his gallant cavalry charge.

    With the deliverance of Vienna a new era began in eastern
Europe. Louis could never command sufficient strength there
to turn the traditional friendship between them to the advantage of either France or the Turks: from Algiers to the
Aegean, as he weakened, the Turks were weakened too. At last
Austria, Poland, and Venice in alliance fought a long war, and
the results were marvellous. Although the emperor had to fight
on two fronts throughout the Nine Years War against France he
and his allies defeated the Turks again and again. In 1699, at
Carlowitz, peace was made. For the first time the Turks agreed
to a treaty in a conference where mediators, British and Dutch,
presided. Its terms registered the end of the Turkish danger.
Venice regained the Morea. The Poles recovered Podolia. The
Habsburgs took Transylvania and almost the whole plain of
Hungary. This was the first stage in the expulsion of the Turks
from Europe. It was still to take two centuries before they were
expelled from the rest of the continent; even now they are in
Istanbul; and it was long before Hungary was recolonized

and politically settled, but the Turkish occupation had left nothing behind it that could serve as a foundation for their return.

This first advance showed how great a material and moral superiority western civilization had wrung from its conflicts in the centuries since the invention of printing. It was followed by a few years in which the Habsburgs were drawn off into the last war against Louis XIV, while Hungary rose in a national rebellion behind them and other powers fought confusedly in the Ukraine; but once Louis was brought to terms, the Austrian armies again moved down the Danube, and the treaty of Passarowitz in 1718 marked the second stage in the Turkish evacuation. Venice, indeed, lost the Morea. Greece remained in subjection for a century more, and the career of the Venetian republic as a power was ended. But the dominions of the Habsburgs had reached their largest extent. Belgrade was once more a Christian town, and they ruled a great part of Serbia. From Vienna they set themselves to organize, to subject and, as far as might be, to unify peoples who spoke ten or a dozen languages and lived at every level of civilization from that of a polished capital to that of a devastated frontier. Neither in religious toleration nor in constitutional liberalism had they learnt anything whatever from the example of the western states or from the experience of their own new subjects.

Since the fifteenth century the western state-system had broadened to include all Europe from the Hebrides to the Dardanelles; but it was surrounded from Norway to the Caspian by states which moved in their own orbits and were absorbed in questions of little moment to the Atlantic and Mediterranean powers. England, France, and Holland, it is true, had their economic concern with the Baltic; the Turks and Austrians had to watch Russia and Poland, and none of these states could be indifferent to the affairs of the north and north-east; but in the middle of the seventeenth century observers in the west were accustomed to thinking of the Baltic states, Denmark, Sweden, and Poland, as forming, with some of their German neighbours and Russia, a separate northern system regulated by its own balance of power. The northern system was perpetually agitated by wars, but here the armies were smaller, there were few strongly-held lines of fortifications, and so the campaigns ranged over greater distances. In this period the wars led to several decisive results. One after another the three leading Baltic powers exhausted their energies until they fell back into the second rank, among the states which relied for their preservation not on their own strength but on allies or patrons.

The Swedes had two more great soldier-kings after Gustavus Adolphus. The first of these, Charles Gustavus, had something of the same reputation as a Protestant hero; but his successes were gained at the expense of Protestant Denmark. He drove the Danes out of their remaining provinces on the Swedish side of the straits which separated the two kingdoms. Temporarily he conquered another province, which brought him to the sea-coast of Norway, but the permanent result of his wars was to give Sweden the boundaries which it has today. His successor combined with the peasantry against the nobles to establish an absolute monarchy. From his time, however, the Swedish empire was on the defensive. The Swedes had not only the Danes against them, but from time to time the Dutch, who feared for their Baltic trade, and the Brandenburgers, who feared for their access to the sea. The French, as of old, supported the Swedes, and so their empire held together for a time; but their resources were insufficient to defend the long land perimeter and their sea-power was insufficient to maintain their communications. In 1699 the fourth great king of the house of Vasa, Charles XII, had to face a coalition of aggressors. For twenty-two years the Great Northern War, as it was called, rolled backwards and forwards from Copenhagen to Estonia and the Ukraine. Charles XII was a heroic figure, at once determined to maintain his country's territories and blind to its sufferings; but he was also a scientific soldier of great ability. He fought the Danes, the Poles, the Russians. He never surrendered; he never made a definitive peace; but it is also true that his terms, when he was victorious, were always moderate, and that he was never the aggressor. Three years after his death in action, Sweden made peace and paid a heavy price. Brandenburg-Prussia took one part of the Baltic coast, and Russia far more. In the eighteenth century there were Swedes who rose to European reputation in the arts and sciences, and the kings lived grandly, but, except for Sweden and Finland, their possessions, a few unimportant German districts, were held on sufferance.

Denmark gained nothing of moment from all this. There too

absolute monarchy was established; but Denmark remained
an agricultural country politically in the second rank. Poland
fell with Sweden. Charles Gustavus took Warsaw and Cracow,
and he planned a partition of Poland. The Danes and Austrians
prevented this; but the Poles had to renounce their claims on
Sweden and Livonia, and their overlordship over East Prussia.
Much greater losses soon followed. After a war of thirteen years
the Poles abandoned their ambitions in the direction of Russia,
leaving Smolensk for good. Kiev also they handed over: the
surrender was meant to be temporary, but it too was lasting.
The Ukrainian Cossacks on the left bank of the Dniester had
passed from Polish to Russian suzerainty. There followed a
period of peace with Russia in which the Poles did good service
against the Turks, service from which in the end not they but
the Austrians reaped the advantage. They recovered some lost
territory by the Treaty of Carlowitz; but they were weakening.
In the same year the elector of Brandenburg acquired their port
of Elbing. Above all the internal condition of Poland was going
from bad to worse. The elections of the kings were dominated by
foreign powers: French candidates were put up against Austrian
candidates. The authority of the crown sank lower than ever.
The gentry were still highly civilized, but neither they nor the
magnates showed political sense. The Jesuits completely controlled education and the old toleration was ended: in 1658 the
anti-Trinitarians were banished. Charles XII made short work
of the Polish armies. Like Charles Gustavus he occupied both
Warsaw and Cracow. When he was defeated by the Russians
at Pultawa in 1709 they, without making war on Poland, were
able to exert a preponderating influence in Polish affairs. The
king, Augustus the Strong, elector of Saxony, who was restored
after an interlude of a French-sponsored king of Polish stock,
had originally been put in by the Austrians; but now he reigned
as a Russian puppet. Poland, like the outlying Swedish provinces, survived on sufferance. The idea of partitioning it was
becoming familiar. At one time or another the Russians, the
Austrians, the Brandenburgers, and Augustus the Strong himself, all suggested it; the diplomatists of other powers speculated
anxiously as to whether they were in earnest.

The Baltic, the Ukraine, and Poland were now all dominated
by Russia from the east; but this was much more than a shifting
of the balance of power between the states of this system. It was

a revolution in the relations between the eastern and the western-central civilizations. The west had been transformed intellectually and materially; consequently the western question had been transformed for the Russians. As trade grew and diplomatic missions became more frequent, as one Scottish officer and one German physician after another came to seek his fortune, knowledge of the west accumulated. There had been printing in Moscow since the second half of the sixteenth century. It had scarcely been used except for ecclesiastical purposes; but some of the leading men of the country imported books of every kind. About the middle of the seventeenth century, however, it seems that foreign influence had done less to modify Russian ways than to excite repugnance. Even among reformers and innovators there were some whose inspiration was entirely home-bred. In 1649 the Tsar Alexis brought in a code of laws which is said to have taken something away from the powers of the monarchy, and so to have been contrary in spirit to the contemporary tendency of legislation in the western countries.

The first great changes in Russian life which resulted from contact with the west were in the ecclesiastical sphere. In 1650 two scholars of Kiev were called to Moscow to translate the Bible into Russian. This must be regarded as a following of western examples, though not of any one example in particular. The western influence was even less specific, though equally operative, in the innovations introduced, with far-reaching consequences for the future, by the patriarch Nikon. He asserted the independence of the Church from lay control and even claimed that it was superior to the royal authority. In this Tsar Alexis defeated him; but he introduced ecclesiastical reforms which showed, both in their own substance and in the reactions which they provoked, how utterly Russian Orthodoxy differed from either Roman Catholicism or Protestantism, and how utterly the Russian people differed from the peoples of the west.

The reforms themselves dealt with matters which were small, but to describe them as trivial is to betray ignorance both of history and of human nature. Nikon made some corrections in the text of the Bible and of service-books. He altered some points of ritual, such as the position of the fingers in giving the blessing. It would not be difficult to mention instances of even smaller changes which were bitterly contested in the west. Less than a century earlier, for instance, the Capuchin reform of the Franciscan Order had turned on a change in the cut of the friars' hoods. Small things are not trivial if they are symbolic, and many of the lower clergy regarded Nikon's innovations as symbols. He followed the best Greek manuscripts and practices; but in Constantinople the Church, besides being Greek, not Russian, was open to western influences. A generation earlier a patriarch there had corresponded with Anglican and Protestant divines, and his reforming dreams had ended with his murder. It is scarcely surprising that Nikon's opponents thought he was polluting Russian Christianity with Greek innovations and Romish heresies. Nor does its emotional intensity make their resistance different in kind from the schisms of the west. The difference is that in Russia there was a sectarian movement which owed nothing, even at a distant remove, to leaders of thought, but everything to instinctive dread of what was foreign and unfamiliar.

Those who refused to conform were persecuted. They persisted with fanatical determination, and they survived as sects under the name of Old Believers. These bodies, consisting mostly of peasants and traders, were strong among the colonists of the frontiers. They thought of the power of the state as a tyranny, an evil. Their schism, like the Lutheran Reformation in the west, was the signal for the rise of many other sects, evangelical, mystical, or extravagant, and Russia for the first time had its spiritual revolutionaries. On its side the Orthodox Church ceased to be equivalent to the people in its religious aspect; it became a body in alliance with the state and the educated class. Its leaders took sides for or against welcoming western influences; and when Russia pushed forward into the 'western lands' this division in high places became more momentous. Many of the new subjects of the tsar in the Ukraine were well acquainted with Polish manners and letters. For some forty years before Tsar Alexis annexed it, Kiev had been the most active intellectual centre of the Orthodox Church. It was no small matter that this tsar had three of his children taught the Polish and Latin languages.

Thus far the western question had unsettled Russia. By the end of the seventeenth century it came to a crisis. Russian expansion was going forward in the old, slow, many-headed way. In 1662 there were probably no more than 70,000 Russians in Siberia; in 1710 there were probably considerably more than

330,000, something like the same number as the British colonists
in North America. They had a stable frontier, fixed by a treaty
with China in 1689, along the Argun river. The advance in the
Ukraine brought the Russians into the front line of the war with
the Turks: as we have seen, they were in alliance with the
Austrians in their war on the Danube, and before the first cessa-
tion of that war they captured Azov. The Russians were not
parties to the treaty of Carlowitz, but their representatives took
part in the negotiations, and so won recognition as members
of the same state-system with the west. As their state grew in
strength, and as success nourished its territorial ambitions, the
Russians saw the technical and intellectual superiority of the
west at closer quarters. Then a direct western threat to their
safety brought the crisis. The Swedes and the Turks made
an alliance against them. The Russians went into the Great
Northern War with the hope of winning some of the Baltic
provinces from Sweden. Charles XII, who had needed the support of the Dutch fleet to get the better of the Danes, routed the
Russian army single-handed and easily. It was unequal to war
against western states. From that hour the whole future of their
country turned on the western question.

The tsar who had taken Azov and sent his ambassadors to
Carlowitz drew the moral. He was Peter the Great. He used all
the powers of his sovereignty, and all the furious strength of
his character, to force the western sciences and manners upon
Russia; but, although he opened her doors wide to western
influences, he did it in order to keep western power at arm's
length. He lived only fifty-three years, and his effective rule
lasted only from 1694 until his death in 1725. We have seen
already that in the end he worsted Sweden. He deprived her of
the Baltic provinces of Ingria, Carelia, Estonia, and Livonia. To
him this meant more than an addition of territory and more
than the control of the trade-route to the Baltic and the west. It
was the beginning of sea-power. He built a fleet on the Baltic,
fifty ships of the line, carrying 20,000 men. He built his new
capital Petersburg in the marshes of the River Neva in Ingria.
He did not actually use this new European outlet for any further
advance. He took some part in European politics, naturally
against the French because he was against the Turks and
Swedes, and consequently favouring the Austrians and the
maritime powers. But, like Charles XII, he refused to be drawn

into the western wars. Even against the Turks he made no headway. At the instigation of Sweden they renewed their war against him and they took Azov away again. After that he fought the Persians in alliance with the Turks, and extended his frontiers on that side. But he had taken the decision to join on equal terms in the contests of the great powers. He increased and modernized and westernized his army. In 1716 he issued a military code on the western model. He had a field army of perhaps 100,000 men, smaller than that of France but of the same order of magnitude as that of Austria, and far larger than those of Sweden or Prussia.

Although he was at war for twenty-eight years Peter carried out great plans of national reorganization. As a young man he learnt much from the German residents in Moscow and from the foreign officers in the army. He studied mathematics, navigation, fortification. He travelled incognito in Germany, Holland, and England, and learnt much of the crafts of shipbuilding, gunnery, anatomy, engraving; and he got an idea of western politics and ecclesiastical affairs. He recruited foreign technicians and officers. He did away with the prohibition on foreign travel for Russians and even compelled some of them to study abroad. He developed economic resources on foreign models, introducing the vine, the mulberry, and tobacco in his south-eastern provinces. He opened mines, and at the end of his time Russia was producing more iron than Great Britain. He projected great public works, to serve both economic and strategic ends: a canal from the Don to the Volga, another from the Volga by Lake Ladoga to the Neva. He transplanted what he could of the western enlightenment, and what he transplanted was in the new fashion of the time. He did something for education, especially for technical education. To printing he gave some little encouragement, and he established a newspaper. In 1724 he founded the Russian Academy of Sciences. It was not until three years after his death that a university was founded in Petersburg.

The line which he took in religion was determined by the confusion which had followed the schism. The conservatism of the clergy was an obstacle to his plans; their divisions were a danger. He therefore allowed the patriarchate to remain vacant and to lapse. He confiscated much monastic property. He did nothing to bring together the Orthodox and the western

Churches, but it was with the advice of a former Uniate, who had studied in Rome and in Lutheran Germany, that he frustrated the plan of the bishops for merging the Russian Church with the Orthodox of other lands and detaching it from the state. Instead of consenting to this, he set up the Holy Synod over it, which was virtually a government department. Thus he perpetuated the division of the Russian nation between the state-Church and the sects, and sharpened the division between the educated few and the suffering many.

Although he tried to westernize even the illiterate masses, for instance by prohibiting the old national dress, he did nothing to raise their status. Economically he even subjected the peasants still more to the landowners. In several ways he made land-tenure even more than in the past a function of service to the state. Although the social foundations remained the same, they were made to support a political structure of a new design. Finance was reformed by the introduction of a poll-tax. There was a rapid output of legislation, much of it varied and super-seded as soon as it was promulgated. The last check on auto-cratic power, the council of magnates, was done away with. A senate of nine members, later increased in numbers, was charged with legislation. Municipal institutions on a German model were introduced. Government departments were set up, with a board at the head of each, as in several western states of the time, according to a plan drawn up by Leibniz. The country was divided into twelve governorships, with areas which sur-vived as long as the Russian monarchy. Peter drew up a table of fourteen ranks, to one or other of which each of his subjects was assigned. In this wonderfully mechanical grading, birth and office each counted for something; but the interplay between the two was not lubricated, as it was in the west, by the inherent adaptability of the wealthy and the aristocrats, or interrupted as it was in Asia by the uncontrolled caprice of the despot. In Russia the service of the state was a middle term unknown else-where.

Many of Peter's reforms were projects rather than achieve-ments. Very likely he did not improve the economic condition of the country: it is thought that in his time the population de-clined. He did not make Russia a creative centre of the scien-tific movement: that, in any case, needed time. The western question in the sphere of the mind was still a question of admitting and receiving western ideas. Although by now the west was learning much from further Asia, Russia transmitted nothing. Peter could do nothing to fuse the spiritual inheritance of his people with that of the west, and scarcely anything to spread enlightenment except in the governing circles. During his reign thousands of pagans around Kazan and the Middle Volga were enticed or bullied into a real or nominal Christianity; but in his territories as a whole Islam made more converts than Christianity and made some from its professed adherents. With all its shortcomings, however, Peter's work helped to shape the lines of the European inheritance from his time to ours. He had let in so much from the west that much more was certain to follow; and he had let it in on such conditions that for a long time to come the Russian monarchy could govern the stream. Russia had become as much a member of the western state-system as Austria or France, and he had shown how western skill could be used to develop Russia without delivering her over to western power or western wealth or western ideas.

THE BAROQUE

TOWARDS the middle of the sixteenth century, when the impetus of the Renaissance was perhaps slackening already, the social condition of Italy deteriorated, as we saw, and became much less propitious for the arts; but we have also seen that before very long they recovered their vigour, not only in Italy, but in the Netherlands, in Spain, and indeed throughout Europe, wherever there was a breathing-space in this angry time. The arts of the late sixteenth century and the seventeenth did not, however, simply continue those of the Renaissance. The spirit of the Renaissance lived on, and not, like the Gothic, as a survival or a substratum, seen, for the most part, only in popular art. Here and there, as in English church-building, conservative feeling checked the degeneration of medieval forms and maintained them, as a more or less separate style, side by side with the classical; but, even where this was so, their principles were largely forgotten. The seventeenth century did not put the sixteenth behind it nearly so completely. The classical feeling for proportion and moderation, once it was recovered, never disappeared again, nor did the characteristics of classical style in architecture and decoration. This was partly because the classical revival was embodied in printed books and engravings, whereas Gothic art was left behind by the printers along with so much else that was medieval; but it was also partly because liberal education was based on the classical writers. Although taste often changed its favourites, the range of classical writers was so wide that, down to the time of Louis XIV, new literary movements could always attach themselves to Greek or Latin models. Both in literature and in the arts there were always elements which could not be assimilated into classical treatment; but there were always schools which kept classical purity before them as their standard. From somewhere about the middle of the sixteenth century, however, there formed beside this spirit another, which has also existed ever since, sometimes in new combinations with it, but sometimes in opposition.

This tendency is often called the baroque, a name which has the convenience of being a mere nonsense-word, not professing to imply any analysis of the thing to which it is affixed. The thing is not a period in the general history of the arts, for the baroque, however it may be defined, never became the universal fashion among artists, and in some countries, such as England and even France, it never predominated over the classical. There are indeed French châteaux of which the exterior shows nothing of the baroque and the contemporary interior decoration is entirely given over to it. Nor is it in any strict sense a style, for it constantly rebelled against the limitations and proprieties of conformity to settled style. It is a tendency, or if that is too quiet a word for something essentially robust and demonstrative, a force. One of its characteristics is the desire for effect. Baroque architects aimed at the superlative, at the appeal of mass and spaces, at grandeur. Mere size did not satisfy them; they used every device for magnifying its impressiveness by leading the eye to distances. They disguised the structure of their buildings under loads of ornament and improbable curves, playing with their materials almost as if they were designing scenery for the stage. They made their buildings exciting by contrasts. They lavished gilding and coloured marbles on sculptured pulpits and baldachinos, and they brought the spectacle close to the spectator by naturalistic realism in detail.

In painting Rubens has the same exuberance, and some of the Italian devotional painters are equally theatrical. They throw up the anguished or ecstatic features of their saints by melodramatic stage-lighting. Even Rembrandt, who has none of this emotionalism, is as baroque as they are. He kept a stock of gorgeous costumes for his models, and in his art he touched the extremes of close observation and of evoking the invisible. There was a change in the modes of seeing which found its fullest expression in some of Rembrandt's pictures, where the composition is disposed not vertically and horizontally but diagonally, where interest is concentrated in the centre, from which an incorporeal light glows outwards, merging objects together so as to show not determinate surfaces or lines, but space in depth. If such a change could ever be fully explained, no doubt a great part of the explanation would lie within the technical history of art; but another part of it would be drawn from all the other fields to which the conception of the baroque can be applied.

As it happens there is scarcely any field to which it has not been applied. It has been given the credit for every kind of ostentation or enjoyment that was popular in the seventeenth century, from periwigs to champagne. In literature it has been used to account for the measureless passions of Shakespeare's tragic heroes. When, however, we are told that the mathematics of the seventeenth century were baroque, we begin to suspect that such a conception can be misused. The argument is that mathematicians were much concerned with infinity, and that they have this in common with the artists who falsified perspective and led the eye beyond finite distances. There were architects who were also mathematicians. The greatest of them, Sir Christopher Wren, was an Englishman, and there were a number of restraints which kept him from exaggeration and from mere display or mere virtuosity; but it can hardly be doubted that his mathematical bent was one of them. Without pretending that the nature of the baroque can be expressed in any formula, we ought to keep our idea of it within bounds, not including anything merely on the evidence of a fortuitous or superficial resemblance.

So regarded, it is easily seen to be connected with some of the great movements of the time. In painting and architecture it began in Rome, and, although its seeds were sown earlier, it flowered as an expression of the Catholic reformation. The Jesuits had their own decided views about the planning and adornment of their churches. They wanted to make them impressive, and they wanted to drive a message home. The baroque did these things for them, and as religious and ecclesiastical revival spread outwards from Rome, they carried it with them to Spain and Portugal, to Austria, Bavaria, and Poland. Wherever there were artists who pressed beyond the bounds of the technique which they had learnt and wherever there were patrons who craved for the grand and the arresting, something of the baroque appeared; but it was in Catholic countries that it most completely captured ecclesiastical and secular art. The new influences from overseas provided it with decorative motifs, or stage-properties; it took on local forms in different climates and environments; but, all through the period with which we are concerned, in France and the Protestant countries it was more an overflow than a spring. The scientific and rational movement was unfavourable to it, and was closely connected, especially in literature, with a contrary tendency to clearness and simplicity. This tendency grew strong in both prose and poetry towards the end of the seventeenth century, for instance in the French drama and the English novel. It suited the tastes of the widening numbers of readers in the prosperous western countries. It made the 'enlightenment' of the eighteenth century comparatively restrained and sober, and it had its counterpart in the arts in lightness, daintiness, and the preference for the pretty to the ponderous.

Here we may glance at some of the great changes which western civilization had undergone since the fifteenth century. The map of the baroque gives another proof that the medieval unity had partly broken down, but it also shows that the result was not a mere splitting into Catholic and Protestant fragments, but something far more complex. Besides religion other factors of the Middle Ages had lost some of their unifying effect. The universities had increased in number with the growth of population, and served at least as many social needs as before, but they were no longer international to the same degree. Latin was still much used in learned writing and in lecturing, but the vernacular languages were gaining ground. The wandering scholars, teachers, and students were now the exception rather than the rule. States had set up national universities, or put obstacles in the way of attending universities abroad, and some of them had fostered or permitted schools of other types, following a more modern curriculum, and not organized as corporations. In spite of the development of international law and of international intercourse, the legal profession was less international than it had been. In England, for instance, the Roman canon law had been suppressed, and the Roman civil lawyers had been hemmed in to a position of very limited influence by the practitioners of a national system of law.

In these and other ways states and nations had loosened the old unities, and, as we saw, their action had much to do with the religious disruption. There were still states which were not national, and nations which were not under states of their own; but in many places and for many reasons state and nation were drawing together. The dynastic and proprietary system was substantially unshaken, and there was no visible weakening in the social foundation of states in the family and the hierarchy of ranks; but the interminable wars had steadily raised the demands which armaments and the rest of the apparatus of power made on social organization. One new state, the Dutch republic, had been born. Some states of the second stratum in the empire, especially ecclesiastical principalities, had ceased to exist. There had been personal unions of states for better defence, and personal union had been converted by Poland and Great Britain into organic union. Every one of these changes brought nearer the system under which the state was the common organization of all the people living in some region, a possession which they were able to maintain because they had other things in common besides this machinery for police and defence and taxation. Their common feelings of feudal, military, dynastic, or merely official loyalty melted into common devotion to religious beliefs, or customs and ways of life. In some of the strongest states, as amongst the English, French, and Dutch, although there were minorities who spoke different languages, a dominant language was one of the binding links.

Thus the state and the nation each grew in strength and consciousness, or rather each was made stronger and more aware of itself by its own action and that of the other. A great part of the activity of statesmen was directed to bringing recalcitrant elements under control: we have seen it in their dealings with churches, armies, universities, feudal jurisdictions, and foreign infringements of their sovereignty. We have seen in their economic policy how the community came more thoroughly under control as it became more truly a community, and this was so not only in economic affairs but in every activity. In the seventeenth century there were places where governments deliberately degraded a language and its literature, as the Austrians did those of the Czechs, or encouraged them, as the French ministers did their own. On the other hand such measures of encouragement, in language and in everything else which tended towards national spirit, were not only imposed from above but welcomed and asked for from below. There were scholars and scientists who gloried in the official status of their academies, merchants who begged for higher tariffs, priests who were enthusiasts for the Gallican liberties. The rise of sovereignty was one aspect of the emergence of political communities which were also economic communities and communities of sentiment and civilization, some of them with a national groundwork.

The more liberal states, especially the Dutch republic and

Great Britain, give us a warning that these developments were by no means everywhere alike, and we may draw another warning from the map of the baroque. It is true that the states were in some measure, and increasingly, the guardians of civilization. They had preserved the western way of life from the Turkish danger, and they had planted it over the world. It was their daily work to maintain the order and prosperity on which it always depended. But they were not its only guardians, and the communities which were forming under their auspices were not the only groupings on which civilization was based. Although the old European unity had been impaired, it still existed. Except for the changed relation to Russia, the state-system still kept its boundaries, and the common consciousness of similarity among Europeans and difference from the other continents grew stronger as these came to be better known. It was not, however, as definite as national feeling, and it was not maturing so rapidly. But there were other unities which transcended the frontiers of the states. The unity of the Catholic Church, which the baroque reflected, was different in quality from the Christian unity of the Middle Ages. It was disciplined by the constant presence of danger. Although the circumstances of different countries, and especially the different relations of states to Catholicism, gave various colourings to Catholic thought and practice, they were more uniform than they had been, and perhaps less tinged by nationality. On the Protestant side few of the many churches and sects had much communication across national frontiers, and even the Calvinists never succeeded in bringing together an assembly representing all their members dispersed among the nations; but, as we have seen, there was some common Protestant consciousness and it contained much more than opposition to Rome.

In another way the baroque showed that the course of the arts might run contrary to that of political affairs. Usually the power of the state, the wealth of the community, and the brilliance of literature and the arts all rose and sank together. We have seen that this was so in Spain, France, England, and the Netherlands. If we cannot say exactly this about the Italian Renaissance, at least we can bring it under the wider statement that civilization was most alive when political life was not languid or uneventful but lively. Some of the most extravagant successes of the baroque, however, belonged to countries which were politically unsuccessful or declining, as were Spain and Portugal and Poland. They were commissioned by noblemen or ecclesiastics whose wealth and consequence were not affected by the miscarriages of the states; indeed baroque magnificence, with its disregard of structure and function, seems specially appropriate to an aristocracy which has no intimate contact with the other orders of society. In the seventeenth century there were countries where the aristocracies grew prouder and stronger; and, even where they were depressed by the rising monarchies, there was a growing separation between the aristocratic life and the life about it. Something of this kind happened even in the liberal and commercial countries. Dutch art in the middle of the century was patronized and appreciated by farmers and shopkeepers, as well as by the rich; but, for whatever reason, this ceased to be so at the time when French influence reached its height. In Holland, as in England, the scale and expense of life in great houses seems to have risen. Not only the scientific movement, but the Renaissance before it, deepened the division between cultivated minorities and the people in general. Popular art became more separate from the refined and expensive arts which served the powerful and the rich. The artist became more distinct from the craftsman, and, with his wider view of the arts of many places and periods, he became cosmopolitan, like the scientists.

Everywhere, however, there were still healthy popular arts, and modern collectors hunt for objects which were made in those days for the everyday use of ordinary people, not only because time has made them rarities, but for their beauty. Changes in transport had done little to free those who built small dwelling-houses from their dependence on local materials, and so long as the craftsman grew up in a tradition of working on stone or wood, or using colours, which belonged to his own immediate environment, he kept his creative vitality. And this popular art, none the less a part of European civilization for being local, had its parallels in industrial skill, in traditional religion and morality, and in proverbial wisdom, even if they shaded off into superstition and conservative obstinacy.

During the centuries which we have been surveying, popular civilization had not been stationary. The whole face of Europe had been altered by the economic changes and the political

PLATE 31

Gian Lorenzo Bernini, The Cathedra in the Basilica of St. Peter, Rome.
(See p. xxv)

conflicts, which affected men in their masses, and by the articulate movements of ideas, which had worked upon these masses,
for the most part, by teaching or example from above. In this
brief outline it has been necessary to follow the thoughts and
acts of the leaders, just as it may be necessary, in a brief history
of a campaign, to trace the decisions of the commanders, but
to omit the movements of companies or battalions or perhaps
even of divisions. We should have mistold the history of these
centuries if we had laid more stress on the preparatory steps
which eventually resulted in universal education, manhood
suffrage, or democracy in any of its forms. There had been more
actual progress towards these than there had been towards a
definitive map of Europe or the peaceful settlement of international disputes; but it was progress in preparing the conditions
for them, intentionally or unintentionally, and not in bringing
them into operation in institutions or even in making men's
minds look forward to them. We break off in the early eighteenth century at a point where civilization was still thought of,
almost universally, not indeed as existing for the sole benefit of
the few, but as upheld by exceptional men whose rank or
abilities made them responsible for it, and there was truth
in this view. Nevertheless, it was also true that the rulers
and leaders could not have done their work unless the peoples
had responded to them: there can be no leaders unless they
are followed. Some of the changes penetrated more and
others less deeply into the compacted whole of society. A
thousand men were influenced by Luther for one who was
influenced by Rembrandt. There was endless violence, corruption, ignorance, ugliness, waste, and misery; but there
was a civilization, marvellously rich and fertile, and it was
sustained by society as a whole. Therefore, even then, there
was scarcely a man or woman who might not, at some moment
and in some small way, be charged with the custody of this
European inheritance.

THE EARLY MODERN PERIOD
DOCUMENTS
1. *Erasmus: Praise of Folly*

Encomium Moriae (1511). Translation of John Wilson (1688);
reprinted Oxford (1913), pp. 63–67

SCIENCES therefore crept into the world with other the pests of mankind, from the same head from whence all other mischiefs spring; wee'l suppose it devils, for so the name imports when you call them dæmons, that is to say, knowing.[1] For that simple people of the golden age, being wholly ignorant of every thing call'd learning, liv'd only by the guidance and dictates of nature; for what use of grammar, where every man spoke the same language and had no further design than to understand one another? What use of logick, where there was no bickering about the double-meaning words? What need of rhetorick, where there were no law-suits? Or to what purpose laws, where there were no ill manners? from which without doubt good laws first came. Besides, they were more religious than with an impious curiosity to dive into the secrets of nature, the dimension of starrs, the motions, effects, and hidden causes of things; as believing it a crime for any man to attempt to be wise beyond his condition. And as to the inquiry of what was beyond heaven, that madness never came into their heads. But the purity of the golden age declining by degrees, first, as I said before, arts were invented by the evil genii; and yet but few, and those too receiv'd by fewer. After that the Chaldean superstition and Greek newfangledness, that had little to do, added I know not how many more; meer torments of wit, and that so great that even grammar alone is work enough for any man for his whole life.

Though yet amongst these sciences those only are in esteem that come nearest to common sense, that is to say, folly. Divines are half starv'd, naturalists out of heart, astrologers laught at, and logicians slighted; onely the physician is worth all the rest. And amongst them too, the more unlearned, impudent, or unadvised he is, the more he is esteem'd, even among princes. For physick, especially as it is now profest by most men, is nothing but a branch of flattery, no less than rhetorick. Next them, the second place is given to our law-drivers, if not the first; whose profession, though I say it myself, most men laugh at as the ass of philosophy; yet there's scarce any business, either so great or small, but is manag'd by these asses. These purchase their great lordships, while in the mean time the divine, having run through the whole body of divinity, sits gnawing a

[1] This is a play on another Greek word, *daēmōn*, which means 'knowing'.

raddish, and is in continual warfare with lice and fleas. As therefore those arts are best that have the nearest affinity with folly, so
are they most happy of all others that have least commerce with
sciences, and follow the guidance of nature, who is in no wise imperfect, unless perhaps we endeavor to leap over those bounds she has
appointed to us. Nature hates all false-colouring, and is ever best
where she is least adulterated with art.

Go to then, don't ye find among the several kinds of living
creatures, that they thrive best that understand no more than what
nature taught them? What is more prosperous or wonderful than
the bee? And though they have not the same judgement of sense as
other bodies have, yet wherein hath architecture gone beyond their
building of houses? What philosopher ever founded the like repub-
lique? Whereas the horse, that comes so near man in understanding and is therefore so familiar with him, is also partaker of his
misery. For while he thinks it a shame to lose the race, it often
happens that he cracks his wind; and in the battel, while he con-
tends for victory, he's cut down himself, and, together with his
rider, 'lies biting the earth': not to mention those strong bits, sharp
spurs, close stables, arms, blows, rider, and briefly, all that slavery
he willingly submits to, while, imitating those men of valour, he so
eagerly strives to be reveng'd of the enemy. Than which how much
more were the life of flies or birds to be wish'd for, who living by the
instinct of nature look no further than the present, if yet man would
let 'em alone in 't. And if at any time they chance to be taken, and
being shut up in cages endeavour to imitate our speaking, 'tis strange
how they degenerate from their native gaiety. So much better in
every respect are the works of nature than the adulteries of art.

II. *Machiavelli: 'Prince'*

Chapters xvii–xviii. Translation of Luigi Ricci, revised by
E. R. P. Vincent ('The World's Classics')

PROCEEDING to the other qualities before named, I say that every
prince must desire to be considered merciful and not cruel. He must,
however, take care not to misuse this mercifulness. Cesare Borgia
was considered cruel, but his cruelty had brought order to the
Romagna, united it, and reduced it to peace and fealty. If this is
considered well, it will be seen that he was really much more merciful
than the Florentine people, who, to avoid the name of cruelty,
allowed Pistoia to be destroyed. A prince, therefore, must not mind
incurring the charge of cruelty for the purpose of keeping his subjects
united and faithful; for, with a very few examples, he will be more
merciful than those who, from excess of tenderness, allow disorders

to arise, from whence spring bloodshed and rapine; for these as a rule injure the whole community, while the executions carried out by the prince injure only individuals. And of all princes, it is impossible for a new prince to escape the reputation of cruelty, new states being always full of dangers. Wherefore Virgil through the mouth of Dido says:

> Res dura, et regni novitas me talia cogunt
> Moliri, et late fines custode tueri.

Nevertheless, he must be cautious in believing and acting, and must not be afraid of his own shadow, and must proceed in a temperate manner with prudence and humanity, so that too much confidence does not render him incautious, and too much diffidence does not render him intolerant.

From this arises the question whether it is better to be loved more than feared, or feared more than loved. The reply is, that one ought to be both feared and loved, but as it is difficult for the two to go together, it is much safer to be feared than loved, if one of the two has to be wanting. For it may be said of men in general that they are ungrateful, voluble, dissemblers, anxious to avoid danger, and covetous of gain; as long as you benefit them, they are entirely yours; they offer you their blood, their goods, their life, and their children, as I have before said, when the necessity is remote; but when it approaches, they revolt. And the prince who has relied solely on their words, without making other preparations, is ruined; for the friendship which is gained by purchase and not through grandeur and nobility of spirit is bought but not secured, and at a pinch is not to be expended in your service. And men have less scruple in offending one who makes himself loved than one who makes himself feared; for love is held by a chain of obligation which, men being selfish, is broken whenever it serves their purpose; but fear is maintained by a dread of punishment which never fails.

Still, a prince should make himself feared in such a way that if he does not gain love, he at any rate avoids hatred; for fear and the absence of hatred may well go together, and will be always attained by one who abstains from interfering with the property of his citizens and subjects or with their women. And when he is obliged to take the life of any one, let him do so when there is a proper justification and manifest reason for it; but above all he must abstain from taking the property of others, for men forget more easily the death of their father than the loss of their patrimony. Then also pretexts for seizing property are never wanting, and one who begins to live by rapine will always find some reason for taking the goods of others, whereas causes for taking life are rarer and more fleeting.

But when the prince is with his army and has a large number of soldiers under his control, then it is extremely necessary that he should not mind being thought cruel; for without this reputation he could not keep an army united or disposed to any duty. Among the noteworthy actions of Hannibal is numbered this, that although he had an enormous army, composed of men of all nations and fighting in foreign countries, there never arose any dissension either among them or against the prince, either in good fortune or in bad. This could not be due to anything but his inhuman cruelty, which together with his infinite other virtues made him always venerated and terrible in the sight of his soldiers, and without it his other virtues would not have sufficed to produce that effect. Thoughtless writers admire on the one hand his actions, and on the other blame the principal cause of them.

And that it is true that his other virtues would not have sufficed may be seen from the case of Scipio (famous not only in regard to his own times, but all times of which memory remains), whose armies rebelled against him in Spain, which arose from nothing but his excessive kindness, which allowed more licence to the soldiers than was consonant with military discipline. He was reproached with this in the senate by Fabius Maximus, who called him a corrupter of the Roman militia. Locri having been destroyed by one of Scipio's officers was not revenged by him, nor was the insolence of that officer punished, simply by reason of his easy nature; so much so, that someone wishing to excuse him in the senate, said that there were many men who knew rather how not to err, than how to correct the errors of others. This disposition would in time have tarnished the fame and glory of Scipio had he persevered in it under the empire, but living under the rule of the senate this harmful quality was not only concealed but became a glory to him.

I conclude, therefore, with regard to being feared and loved, that men love at their own free will, but fear at the will of the prince, and that a wise prince must rely on what is in his power and not on what is in the power of others, and he must not contrive to avoid incurring hatred, as has been explained.

How laudable it is for a prince to keep good faith and live with integrity, and not with astuteness, everyone knows. Still the experience of our times shows those princes to have done great things who have had little regard for good faith, and have been able by astuteness to confuse men's brains, and who have ultimately overcome those who have made loyalty their foundation.

You must know, then, that there are two methods of fighting, the one by law, the other by force: the first method is that of men, the second of beasts; but as the first method is often insufficient, one must have recourse to the second. It is therefore necessary for a prince to know well how to use both the beast and the man. This was covertly taught to rulers by ancient writers, who relate how Achilles and many others of those ancient princes were given to Chiron the centaur to be brought up and educated under his discipline. The parable of this semi-animal, semi-human teacher is meant to indicate that a prince must know how to use both natures, and that the one without the other is not durable.

A prince being thus obliged to know well how to act as a beast must imitate the fox and the lion, for the lion cannot protect himself from traps, and the fox cannot defend himself from wolves. One must therefore be a fox to recognize traps, and a lion to frighten wolves. Those that wish to be only lions do not understand this. Therefore, a prudent ruler ought not to keep faith when by so doing it would be against his interest, and when the reasons which made him bind himself no longer exist. If men were all good, this precept would not be a good one; but as they are bad, and would not observe their faith with you, so you are not bound to keep faith with them. Nor have legitimate grounds ever failed a prince who wished to show colourable excuse for the non-fulfilment of his promise. Of this one could furnish an infinite number of modern examples, and show how many times peace has been broken, and how many promises rendered worthless, by the faithlessness of princes, and those that have been best able to imitate the fox have succeeded best. But it is necessary to be able to disguise this character well, and to be a great feigner and dissembler; and men are so simple and so ready to obey present necessities, that one who deceives will always find those who allow themselves to be deceived.

I will only mention one modern instance. Alexander VI did nothing else but deceive men, he thought of nothing else, and found the occasion for it; no man was ever more able to give assurances, or affirmed things with stronger oaths, and no man observed them less; however, he always succeeded in his deceptions, as he well knew this aspect of things.

It is not, therefore, necessary for a prince to have all the above-named qualities, but it is very necessary to seem to have them. I would even be bold to say that to possess them and always to observe them is dangerous, but to appear to possess them is useful. Thus it is well to seem merciful, faithful, humane, sincere, religious, and also to be so; but you must have the mind so disposed that when it is needful to be otherwise you may be able to change to the opposite qualities. And it must be understood that a prince, and especially a new prince, cannot observe all those things which are considered good in men, being often obliged, in order to maintain the state, to act against faith, against charity, against humanity, and against religion. And, therefore, he must have a mind disposed to adapt itself according to the wind, and as the variations of fortune dictate, and, as I said before, not deviate from what is good, if possible, but be able to do evil if constrained.

A prince must take great care that nothing goes out of his mouth which is not full of the above-named five qualities, and, to see and hear him, he should seem to be all mercy, faith, integrity, humanity, and religion. And nothing is more necessary than to seem to have this last quality, for men in general judge more by the eyes than by the hands, for everyone can see, but very few have to feel. Everybody sees what you appear to be, few feel what you are, and those few will not dare to oppose themselves to the many, who have the majesty of the state to defend them; and in the actions of men, and especially of princes, from which there is no appeal, the end justifies the means. Let a prince therefore aim at conquering and maintaining the state, and the means will always be judged honourable and praised by everyone, for the vulgar is always taken by appearances and the issue of the event; and the world consists only of the vulgar, and the few who are not vulgar are isolated when the many have a rallying point in the prince. A certain prince of the present time, whom it is well not to name, never does anything but preach peace and good faith, but he is really a great enemy to both, and either of them, had he observed them, would have lost him state or reputation on many occasions.

III. *Luther: To the Christian Nobility of the German Nation*

Extract from the tract of 1520 as translated by Wace and Buchheim,
Luther's Primary Works

THE Romanists have, with great adroitness, drawn three walls round themselves, with which they have hitherto protected themselves, so that no one could reform them, whereby all Christendom has fallen terribly.

First, if pressed by the temporal power, they have affirmed and maintained that the temporal power has no jurisdiction over them, but, on the contrary, that the spiritual power is above the temporal.

Secondly, if it were proposed to admonish them with the Scriptures, they objected that no one may interpret the Scriptures but the Pope.

Thirdly, if they are threatened with a council, they pretend that no one may call a council but the Pope . . .

Now may God help us, and give us one of those trumpets that overthrew the walls of Jericho, so that we may blow down these walls of straw and paper, and that we may set free our Christian rods for the chastisement of sin, and expose the craft and deceit of the devil, so that we may amend ourselves by punishment and again obtain God's favour.

Let us, in the first place, attack the first wall.

It has been devised that the Pope, bishops, priests, and monks are called the spiritual estate; princes, lords, artificers, and peasants, are the temporal estate. This is an artful lie and hypocritical device, but let no one be made afraid by it, and that for this reason: that all Christians are truly of the spiritual estate, and there is no difference among them, save of office alone. As St. Paul says (1 Cor. xii), we are all one body, though each member does its own work, to serve the others. This is because we have one baptism, one Gospel, one faith, and are all Christians alike; for baptism, Gospel, and faith, these alone make spiritual and Christian people.

As for the unction by a pope or a bishop, tonsure, ordination, consecration, and clothes differing from those of laymen—all this may make a hypocrite or an anointed puppet, but never a Christian or a spiritual man. Thus we are all consecrated as priests by baptism, as St. Peter says: 'Ye are a royal priesthood, a holy nation' (1 Pet. ii. 9); and in the book of Revelation: 'and hast made us unto our God (by Thy blood) kings and priests' (Rev. v. 10). For, if we had not a higher consecration in us than pope or bishop can give, no priest could ever be made by the consecration of pope or bishop, nor could he say the mass or preach or absolve. Therefore the bishop's consecration is just as if in the name of the whole congregation he took one person out of the community, each member of which has equal power, and commanded him to exercise this power for the rest; in the same way as if ten brothers, co-heirs as king's sons, were to choose one from among them to rule over their inheritance, they would all of them still remain kings and have equal power, although one is ordered to govern.

And to put the matter more plainly, if a little company of pious Christian laymen were taken prisoners and carried away to a desert, and had not among them a priest consecrated by a bishop, and were there to agree to elect one of them . . . and were to order him to baptize, to celebrate the mass, to absolve and to preach, this man would as truly be a priest, as if all the bishops and all the popes had consecrated him. That is why, in cases of necessity, every man can baptize and absolve, which would not be possible if we were not all priests. This great grace and virtue of baptism and of the Christian estate they have quite destroyed and made us forget by their ecclesiastical law . . .

Since then the temporal power is baptized as we are, and has the same faith and Gospel, we must allow it to be priest and bishop, and account its office an office that is proper and useful to the Christian community. For whatever issues from baptism may boast that it has been consecrated priest, bishop, and pope, although it does not be-seem everyone to exercise these offices. For, since we are all priests alike, no man may put himself forward or take upon himself without our consent and election, to do that which we have all alike power to do. For if a thing is common to all, no man may take it to himself without the wish and command of the community. And if it should happen that a man were appointed to one of these offices and de-posed for abuses, he would be just what he was before. Therefore a priest should be nothing in Christendom but a functionary; as long as he holds his office, he has precedence of others; if he is deprived of it, he is a peasant or a citizen like the rest. Therefore a priest is verily no longer a priest after deposition. But now they have invented *characteres indelibiles*, and pretend that a priest after deprivation still differs from a simple layman. They even imagine that a priest can never be anything but a priest—that is, that he can never become a layman. All this is nothing but mere talk and ordinance of human invention.

It follows, then, that between laymen and priests, princes and bishops, or, as they call it, between spiritual and temporal persons, the only real difference is one of office and function, and not of estate. . . .

. . . Therefore I say, Forasmuch as the temporal power has been ordained by God for the punishment of the bad and the protection of the good, we must let it do its duty throughout the whole Christian body, without respect of persons, whether it strike popes, bishops, priests, monks, nuns, or whoever it may be. . . .

Whatever the ecclesiastical law has said in opposition to this is merely the invention of Romanist arrogance. . . .

Now, I imagine the first paper wall is overthrown, inasmuch as the temporal power has become a member of the Christian body; although its work relates to the body, yet does it belong to the spiri-tual estate. . . .

The second wall is even more tottering and weak: that they alone pretend to be considered masters of the Scriptures. . . . If the article of our faith is right, 'I believe in the holy Christian Church', the Pope cannot alone be right; else we must say, 'I believe in the Pope of Rome', and reduce the Christian Church to one man, which is a devilish and damnable heresy. Besides that, we are all priests, as I have said, and have all one faith, one Gospel, one Sacrament; how then should we not have the power of discerning and judging what is right or wrong in matters of faith? . . .

The third wall falls of itself, as soon as the first two have fallen; for
if the Pope acts contrary to the Scriptures, we are bound to stand by
the Scriptures to punish and to constrain him, according to Christ's
commandment . . . 'tell it unto the Church' (Matt. xviii. 15–17). . . .
If then I am to accuse him before the Church, I must collect the
Church together. . . . Therefore when need requires, and the Pope
is a cause of offence to Christendom, in these cases whoever can best
do so, as a faithful member of the whole body, must do what he can
to procure a true free council. This no one can do so well as the temporal authorities, especially since they are fellow Christians, fellow
priests. . . .

IV. *Speech of Cardinal Pole to Parliament*

27 November 1554; text corrected from the reprint in Cobbett,
Parliamentary History, i. 622

OF all princes in Europe the emperor hath travailed most in the
cause of religion, as it appeareth by his acts in Germany; yet happily
by some secret judgment of God he hath not achieved the end.
With whom in my journey hitherwards I had conference touching
my legation; whereof when we had understanding, he shewed a
great appearance of most earnest joy and gladness, saying, that it
rejoiced him no less of the reconcilement of this realm unto christian
unity, than that his son was placed by marriage in the kingdom; and
most glad he was of all, that the occasion thereof should come by me
being an Englishman born; which is (as it were) to call home ourselves. I can well compare him to David, who though he were a man
elect of God, yet, for that he was contaminate with blood and war,
he could not build the temple of Jerusalem, but left the finishing
thereof to Solomon, which was 'rex pacificus'. So may it be thought,
that the appeasing of controversies of religion in Christianity is not
appointed to this emperor, but rather to his son, who shall perform
the building that his father had begun. Which church cannot be
perfectly builded, unless universally in all realms we adhere to one
head, and do acknowledge him to be the vicar of God, and to have
power from above. For all power is of God, according to the saying,
'non est potestas, nisi a Deo'. And therefore I consider that all power
being in God, yet, for the conservation of quiet and godly life in the
world, he hath derived that power from above into the parts here on
earth, which is into the power imperial and ecclesiastical. And these
two powers, as they be several and distinct, so have they two several
effects and operations. For secular princes, to whom the temporal
sword is committed, be ministers of God to execute vengeance upon

transgressors and evil-livers, and to preserve the well-doers and innocents from injury and violence. Which power is represented in these two most excellent persons, the king and queen's majesty here present, who have this power committed to them immediately from God, without any superior in that behalf. The other power is of ministration, which is the power of the keys, and order in the ecclesiastical state, which is, by the authority of God's word, and examples of the apostles, and of all old holy fathers from Christ hitherto, attributed and given to the apostolic see of Rome, by special prerogative. From which see I am here deputed legate and ambassador, having full and ample commission from thence, and have the keys committed to my hands; I confess to you I have the keys, not as mine own keys, but as the keys of him that sent me, and yet cannot open; not for want of power in me to give, but for certain impediments in you to receive, which must be taken away before my commission can take effect. This I protest before you, my commission is not of prejudice to any person. I come not to destroy, but to build; I come to reconcile, not to condemn; I am not come to compel, but to call again; I am not come to call any thing in question already done, but my commission is of grace and clemency, to such as will receive it. For touching all matters that be past, they shall be as things cast into the sea of forgetfulness. But the mean, whereby you shall receive this benefit, is to revoke and repeal those laws and statutes, which be impediments, blocks, and bars to the execution of my commission.

v. *Descartes: Discours de la méthode*

Part 4, paragraphs i–iv (1637): Translation of Haldane and Ross
(Cambridge, 1911)

I DO not know that I ought to tell you of the first meditations there made by me, for they are so metaphysical and so unusual that they may perhaps not be acceptable to everyone. And yet at the same time, in order that one may judge whether the foundations which I have laid are sufficiently secure, I find myself constrained in some measure to refer to them. For a long time I had remarked that it is sometimes requisite in common life to follow opinions which one knows to be most uncertain, exactly as though they were indisputable, as has been said above. But because in this case I wished to give myself entirely to the search after Truth, I thought that it was necessary for me to take an entirely opposite course, and to reject as absolutely false everything as to which I could imagine the least ground of doubt, in order to see if afterwards there remained anything in my belief that was entirely certain. Thus, because our senses sometimes deceive us, I wished to suppose that nothing is just as they cause us to imagine it to be; and because there are men who deceive themselves in their reasoning and fall into paralogisms, even concerning the simplest matters of geometry, and judging that I was as subject to error as was any other, I rejected as false all the reasons formerly accepted by me as demonstrations. And since all the same thoughts and conceptions which we have while awake may also come to us in sleep, without any of them being at that time true, I resolved to assume that everything that ever entered into my mind was no more true than the illusion of my dreams. But immediately afterwards I noticed that whilst I thus wished to think all things false, it was absolutely essential that that 'I' who thought this should be somewhat, and remarking that this truth '*I think, therefore I am*' was so certain and so assured that all the most extravagant suppositions brought forward by the sceptics were incapable of shaking it, I came to the conclusion that I could receive it without scruple as the first principle of the Philosophy for which I was seeking.

And then, examining attentively that which I was, I saw that I could conceive that I had no body, and that there was no world nor place where I might be; but yet that I could not for all that conceive that I was not. On the contrary, I saw from the very fact that I thought of doubting the truth of other things, it very evidently and certainly followed that I was; on the other hand if I had only ceased from thinking, even if all the rest of what I had ever imagined had really existed, I should have no reason for thinking that I had existed. From that I knew that I was a substance the whole essence or nature of which is to think, and that for its existence there is no need of any place, nor does it depend on any material things; so that this 'me', that is to say, the soul by which I am what I am, is entirely distinct from body and is even more easy to know than is the latter; and even if body were not, the soul would not cease to be what it is.

After this I considered generally what in a proposition is requisite in order to be true and certain; for since I had just discovered one which I knew to be such, I thought that I ought also to know in what this certainty consisted. And having remarked that there was nothing at all in the statement '*I think, therefore I am*' which assures me of having thereby made a true assertion, excepting that I see very clearly that to think it is necessary to be, I came to the conclusion that I might assume, as a general rule, that the things which we conceive very clearly and distinctly are all true—remembering, however, that there is some difficulty in ascertaining which are those that we distinctly conceive.

Following upon this, and reflecting on the fact that I doubted, and that consequently my existence was not quite perfect (for I saw clearly that it was a greater perfection to know that to doubt), I resolved to inquire whence I had learnt to think of anything more perfect than I myself was; and I recognised very clearly that this conception must proceed from some nature which was really more perfect. As to the thoughts which I had of many other things outside of me, like the heavens, the earth, light, heat, and a thousand others, I had not so much difficulty in knowing whence they came, because, remarking nothing in them which seemed to render them superior to me, I could believe that, if they were true, they were dependencies upon my nature, in so far as it possessed some perfection; and if they were not true, that I held them from naught, that is to say, that they were in me because I had something lacking in my nature. But this could not apply to the idea of a Being more perfect than my own, for to hold it from naught would be manifestly impossible; and because it is no less contradictory to say of the more perfect that it is what results from and depends on the less perfect, than to say that there is something which proceeds from nothing, it was equally impossible that I should hold it from myself. In this way it could but follow that it had been placed in me by a Nature which was really more perfect than mine could be, and which even had within itself all the perfections of which I could form any idea—that is to say, to put it in a word, which was God. To which I added that since I knew some perfections which I did not possess, I was not the only being in existence (I shall here use freely, if you will allow, the terms of the School); but that there was necessarily some other more perfect Being on which I depended, or from which I acquired all that I had. For if I had existed alone and independent of any others, so that I should have had from myself all that perfection of being in which I participated to however small an extent, I should have been able for the same reason to have had all the remainder which I knew that I lacked; and thus I myself should have been infinite, eternal, immutable, omniscient, all-powerful, and, finally, I should have all the perfections which I could discern in God. For, in pursuance of the reasonings which I have just carried on, in order to know the nature of God as far as my nature is capable of knowing it, I had only to consider in reference to all these things of which I found some idea in myself, whether it was a perfection to possess them or not. And I was assured that none of those which indicated some imperfection were in Him, but that all else was present; and I saw that doubt, inconstancy, sadness, and such things, could not be in Him considering that I myself should have been glad to be without them. In addition to this, I had ideas of many things which are sensible and corporeal, for although I might suppose that I was dreaming, and that all that I saw or imagined was false, I could not at the same time deny that the ideas were really in my thoughts. But because I had already recognised very clearly in myself that the nature of the intelligence is distinct from that of the body, and observing that all composition gives evidence of dependency, and that dependency is manifestly an imperfection; I came to the conclusion that it could not be a perfection in God to be composed of these two natures, and that consequently He was not so composed. I judge, however, that if there were any bodies in the world, or even any intelligence or other natures which were not wholly perfect, their existence must depend on His power in such a way that they could not subsist without Him for a single moment.

VI. *Richelieu on the Nobility*

Part I, chapter iii, section 1. Translated from the Amsterdam edition of 1686 by Vera Miller

HAVING laid before you those things which I consider absolutely necessary for the re-establishment of the first Order of your kingdom, I pass to the second, and declare that the nobility must be regarded as one of the principal nerves of the State capable of contributing much to its preservation and stability. For some little time the nobles have been so oppressed by the great number of officials that this unhappy time has raised up to their disadvantage that they are in great need of protection from the encroachments of such people. The wealth and arrogance of the latter crushes the former in their need, for they are rich only in courage, which leads them to devote their lives willingly to the service of that State from which the officials suck the life-blood.

As they need to be upheld against their oppressors so must particular care be taken lest they treat those who are beneath them as they are themselves treated by others.

It is a failing somewhat common among those born in this Order to employ violence against the People, to whom God seems to have given hands to maintain life, rather than to defend it.

It is very important to check the course of such lawlessness by a sustained firmness, to ensure that the weakest of your subjects, although unarmed, will have, in the shadow of your laws, as much security as those who bear arms.

The nobles, having, in the war to which the Peace has happily put an end, shown themselves inheritors of that valour which caused Caesar to prefer their forefathers above all others, must now be disciplined so that they may renew and maintain their former repute, and so that the State may be usefully served.

Those who are of no use to it being harmful to the public, it is certain that the nobles who do not serve her in war are not only useless to, but a charge upon, the State, which may in this case be compared to a body which holds up a paralysed arm, a burden which weighs it down instead of assisting it.

As noblemen deserve to be well treated when they behave well, so they merit harshness if they fail in those duties which their birth requires of them. And I have no hesitation in saying that those who, falling away from the valour of their ancestors, fail to serve the Crown with their swords and their lives in that firmness and constancy which the laws of the State demand, will deserve to be deprived of the privileges of their birth and reduced to bearing some part of the burdens of the people.

Since honour ought to be dearer to them than life, it would be far better to punish them by depriving them of the one, than of the other.

To take life from persons who hazard it daily for a pure figment called 'honour' is much less than to take that honour from them, and leave them with life, which in that state is a perpetual torture to them.

If nothing is to be overlooked in order to maintain the nobles in the true valour of their fathers, then neither should anything be omitted which would tend to confirm them in possession of the goods which these have left to them, and enable them to acquire more.

Even as it is impossible to find a remedy for all evils; so is it very difficult to put forward a single expedient for all the ends which I propose.

The various marriages, which take place in every family in this realm, unlike others in which often only the eldest son marries, are a potent cause of the ruin of the greatest houses in a short time. But if this custom impoverishes individual families, it so enriches the State, whose strength lies in the multitude of her fighting men, that instead of bewailing it we should rejoice, and instead of changing it should only endeavour to give to those whom it brings into the world the means of existing in that uprightness of life which they derive from their birth.

Concerning this means of existence, we must distinguish between the nobles who live at Court, and those who live in the country.

Those who live at Court would be notably relieved if there were some retrenchment of luxury, and of the unbearable expenses which have gradually crept in there, for it is certain that such an ordinance would be quite as useful to them as all the pensions they could be given.

As for those in the country, although they might not receive so much benefit from such an ordinance, because their extreme poverty does not allow them to spend unnecessarily, they could not fail to feel the effect of this remedy, which is so necessary to the whole State, that to fail to adopt it is to court ruin.

If Your Majesty adds to the regulation which it may please him to bring to this disorder, the establishment of fifty companies of Life-guards and an equal number of Light Horse, to be paid by the provincial governments, upon the conditions hereinafter specified, he will afford no small means of subsistence to that part of the nobility which needs it most.

If, further, you suppress the sale of governorships of the kingdom, and of all military ranks, for which this Order pays a high enough price in blood.

If you carry out the same policy regarding positions in your household; if you ensure, that whereas now all kinds of people are received there by the sordid commerce of their purse, entry shall in future be closed to all who have not the good fortune to be of noble birth. If even entry should in future no longer be open even to those who have this advantage, except in so far as Your Majesty shall distinguish them for their merit, the whole nobility would receive both honour and profit from so wise a ruling.

Instead of being, as now, unable to rise to positions and dignities, except at the price of ruin, the nobles will in future be the more confirmed in their fidelity because, the more they are favoured, the less will they feel indebted to their purse for the honours they receive; or to the purses of their creditors, who never remind them of what they owe, but they feel some distaste at having been raised by this way.

If, moreover, your graciousness were to go so far as to be at some pains to benefit their children (as many as prove to have the requisite piety and learning) with a proportion of the benefices which are in your gift; then this Order will be the more obliged to you in that, relieving them of a part of the burden which weighs them down, you will give them a true means of maintaining their houses, since the maintenance and converse of some of the best houses depends often on those who espouse the ecclesiastical condition, and willingly look upon their nephews as though they were their own children, and find no greater happiness than in providing for the elevation of some of these to knowledge and virtue, in order that, if they show themselves worthy, they may be provided with some of the advantages which they themselves enjoy.

I might put forward many other measures for the relief of the nobility; but I suppress all thought of it, having reflected that

although it might be very easy to write them, it would be very difficult, and perhaps impossible, to put them into effect.

VII. *Locke: First Letter concerning Toleration*

Fourth to tenth paragraphs of the English editon of 1689

THE toleration of those that differ from others in matters of religion,
is so agreeable to the Gospel of Jesus Christ, and to the genuine
reason of mankind, that it seems monstrous for men to be so blind, as
not to perceive the necessity and advantage of it, in so clear a light. I
will not here tax the pride and ambition of some, the passion and
uncharitable zeal of others. These are faults from which human affairs
can perhaps scarce ever be perfectly freed; but yet such as nobody
will bear the plain imputation of, without covering them with some
specious colour; and so pretend to commendation, whilst they are
carried away by their own irregular passions. But, however, that
some may not colour their spirit of persecution and unchristian
cruelty with a pretence of care of the public weal, and observation of
the laws, and that others, under pretence of religion, may not seek
impunity for their libertinism and licentiousness; in a word, that
none may impose either upon himself or others, by the pretences of
loyalty and obedience to the prince, or of tenderness and sincerity in
the worship of God; I esteem it above all things necessary to distinguish exactly the business of civil government from that of religion,
and to settle the just bounds that lie between the one and the other.
If this be not done, there can be no end put to the controversies that
will be always arising between those that have, or at least pretend to
have, on the one side, a concernment for the interest of men's souls,
and, on the other side, a care of the commonwealth.

The commonwealth seems to me to be a society of men constituted
only for the procuring, preserving, and advancing their own civil
interests.

Civil interests I call life, liberty, health, and indolency of body;
and the possession of outward things, such as money, lands, houses,
furniture, and the like.

It is the duty of the civil magistrate, by the impartial execution of
equal laws, to secure unto all the people in general, and to every one
of his subjects in particular, the just possession of these things belonging to this life. If any one presume to violate the laws of public
justice and equity, established for the preservation of these things,
his presumption is to be checked by the fear of punishment, consisting in the deprivation or diminution of those civil interests, or goods,
which otherwise he might and ought to enjoy. But seeing no man

does willingly suffer himself to be punished by the deprivation of any part of his goods, and much less of his liberty or life, therefore is the magistrate armed with the force and strength of all his subjects, in order to the punishment of those that violate any other man's rights.

Now that the whole jurisdiction of the magistrate reaches only to these civil concernments; and that all civil power, right, and dominion, is bounded and confined to the only care of promoting these things; and that it neither can nor ought in any manner to be extended to the salvation of souls; these following considerations seem unto me abundantly to demonstrate.

First, Because the care of souls is not committed to the civil magistrate, any more than to other men. It is not committed unto him, I say, by God; because it appears not that God has ever given any such authority to one man over another, as to compel any one to his religion. Nor can any such power be vested in the magistrate by the consent of the people; because no man can so far abandon the care of his own salvation as blindly to leave it to the choice of any other, whether prince or subject, to prescribe to him what faith or worship he shall embrace. For no man can, if he would, conform his faith to the dictates of another. All the life and power of true religion consists in the inward and full persuasion of the mind; and faith is not faith without believing. Whatever profession we make, to whatever outward worship we conform, if we are not fully satisfied in our own mind that the one is true, and the other well-pleasing unto God, such profession and such practice, far from being any furtherance, are indeed great obstacles to our salvation. For in this manner, instead of expiating other sins by the exercise of religion, I say, in offering thus unto God Almighty such a worship as we esteem to be displeasing unto him, we add unto the number of our other sins, those also of hypocrisy, and contempt of his Divine Majesty.

In the second place. The care of souls cannot belong to the civil magistrate, because his power consists only in outward force: but true and saving religion consists in the inward persuasion of the mind, without which nothing can be acceptable to God. And such is the nature of the understanding, that it cannot be compelled to the belief of any thing by outward force. Confiscation of estate, imprisonment, torments, nothing of that nature can have any such efficacy as to make men change the inward judgment that they have framed of things.

V. 1

POLITICAL, ECONOMIC, AND SOCIAL DEVELOPMENT IN THE EIGHTEENTH CENTURY

By PROFESSOR PAUL VAUCHER

INTRODUCTION

THE contribution of the eighteenth century, or more precisely of the hundred years between 1715 and 1815, to the formation of the European inheritance, is most evident in the movement of ideas which makes this period great and significant. European thought at this time evolved new conceptions of man, of society, and of the universe. Their various currents are traced in the second section of this part. It is tempting to conclude that this intellectual movement shone with the greatest brilliance in France, because French writers inherited the prestige of classical literature, and because the French language was at that time the principal medium for the expression of ideas. But the contribution of other nations to European thought, if it was not as great, was at least as fruitful and perhaps even more original. England at the beginning of the century, and Germany at the end, were in the forefront of the movement of European thought.

Similarly the French Revolution might be considered as the culmination of this movement, and even, in a sense, of the whole development of the century. But that is only true if one takes into account the reactions which the Revolution caused in other countries, the ways in which England defended itself against the influence of the Revolution, and the survival, in most of the continent, of economic and social conditions which were opposed to the ideas of the Revolution and entailed the partition of Europe into two opposing camps.

The meaning and the trend of the movement of thought can only be understood within the framework of the political, economic, and social changes which gave rise to it. The movement reflects the modification of political institutions, the revolutionary development of economics, and the profound changes in the relations between social classes, which characterize the period.

It is necessary to consider separately the eighteenth century proper, down to 1789, and the period of the European crisis which started with the French Revolution and was continued by the conquests of Napoleon. It is also important not to include the whole of the eighteenth century proper in a single survey, for the wars which belong to its middle period, although they are of

comparatively little military interest, mark a significant stage.
They created new states, which shared henceforward in deter-
mining the course of political and social life in Europe. They
presented the English with unforeseen political, social, and
imperial problems; and on the other hand they entailed the
compulsory abdication of the French monarchy, which missed
its opportunity to reform, and perhaps to save, the *ancien
régime*.

I

THE BEGINNING OF THE CENTURY

§ 1. *European Affairs*

The first half of the century was, as French historians themselves admit, a period in which English influence predominated.
The English were in effect the principal beneficiaries of the
treaty of Utrecht. In spite of the bitter conflict which had divided
Whigs and Tories, both had contributed to the great victory,
the first by their conduct of war and the second by their conclusion of peace. England could safely leave a Bourbon on the
throne in Madrid, since France was now confined within her
frontiers, checked in the Low Countries by the emperor and the
Dutch, and cut off from Italy by the King of Sardinia and the
Habsburgs. English naval supremacy was uncontested. The
conquest of Newfoundland and Nova Scotia gave her mastery
of the North Atlantic. Firmly based on Gibraltar, she could
leave Italy to allies who had no powerful navies; and the commercial privileges which she had won from Madrid left her free
to exploit the riches of the Spanish empire. The decline of the
United Provinces freed her from fear of their competition. Her
financial and commercial system made possible a commercial
expansion which might find large openings even in Europe.

Louis XIV, at the end of his reign, had grasped the significance of a victory which made England henceforward more
formidable to France than the house of Austria; and he was
already seeking an alliance with Vienna. But his death enabled
England to disarm even French hostility. The regent, Philip of
Orleans, needed English support in order to resist the claims of
Philip V and to succeed to the throne of France if Louis XV,
then a weakly infant, should die. The Whig minister, Stanhope,
who took charge of foreign affairs under George I, was glad to
welcome the regent's confidential agent, Dubois, when he came
to The Hague to propose an alliance. The alliance was concluded at Hanover, and with the inclusion of the United
Provinces it became the Triple Alliance of 1717; later still,
when it was afterwards joined by the emperor, it became the
Quadruple Alliance of 1718. Thus, with the help of France,
England succeeded in renewing the links with her former allies
which she herself had broken by signing the treaty of Utrecht

without them. She was now able to maintain peace in Europe to her own advantage.

The peace, however, was precarious. It was threatened by the policy of Philip V of Spain, who was incited by his wife Elizabeth Farnese and his minister Alberoni to dispute the Spanish inheritance in Italy with the Emperor Charles VI. It was also threatened in the north, where Charles XII, King of Sweden, had to face a coalition of all the rulers who had territories on the Baltic, a coalition joined by the elector of Hanover, King George I of England, who cherished designs on Bremen. But with French help Stanhope was able to force Philip V to dismiss Alberoni and to abandon his warlike policy. After the death of Charles XII the diplomatic and financial help of France also enabled him to bring to an end the war in the north, and to satisfy both the ambitions of Hanover and the demands of English trade in the Baltic.

The Anglo-French alliance appeared still to hold good during the prolonged administration of Walpole in England and Fleury in France. In reality it did not prevent their rivalry. Fleury managed to escape from the bonds of the English alliance without breaking it. By insincere protestations of friendship he cleverly turned Walpole's obstinate pacifism to his own advantage. He not only renewed the Franco-Spanish alliance, but as Walpole refused to support the house of Austria in the war of the Polish succession he was also able to bring about an unexpected understanding with Vienna, which isolated England and made France, in the words of Frederic II, 'the arbiter of Europe'.

At the same time the English hopes of trade with the Spanish empire proved deceptive. English merchants saw their ships held up, and their crews captured, by the Spanish coastguards. The anger of the traders, and the public sense of a humiliating loss of prestige, forced Walpole to declare war on Spain in 1739. England was now in a dangerous position, involved in a war at sea in which France could not fail to support Spain, and deprived by Fleury's astuteness of any ally on the continent.

European politics were dominated at this period by Anglo-French alliance and rivalry. In the same way, the evolution of European civilization was dominated by new developments in the governments, the economic systems, and the social conditions of these two countries.

PLATE 32

THE TROELFTH CAKE. | LE GÂTEAU DES ROIS.

The Kings' Cake (the Partition of Poland), after N. Le Mire

PLATE 33

An interior in the time of Louis XV. From the painting 'Le Déjeuner', by
François Boucher, in the Louvre

§ 2. France

In 1715 France was still the most important state in Europe, and the one which seemed destined to make the greatest contribution to the development of the European inheritance. Her population, almost four times as great as England's, provided a labour force which was capable of making good use of her enormous resources. The Bourbons had at their disposal revenues at least twice as great as those of the Habsburgs. Their defeat in the War of the Spanish Succession had not greatly diminished their prestige. The sovereigns of the eighteenth century continued to model themselves upon the Great King and their palaces upon Versailles; while the great French classical tradition was still strong among writers of other nations. Yet the last years of the reign of Louis XIV had succeeded in exposing the worst evils of the *ancien régime*. It had drained the life-blood of France; and far-reaching reforms were necessary to enable her to recover her strength.

The death of Louis XIV seemed to provide an opportunity for the necessary reforms. The nobles thought that they might now shake off the idleness and impotence to which he had reduced them. The regent introduced governmental reforms, replacing the ministers by councils which were supposed to be controlled by the nobles. But this attempt at 'polysynodism' was only a flash in the pan. The *secrétaires d'état* were reinstalled in 1718, and the government reverted to the system of Louis XIV. Since Louis XV was not interested in governing, he allowed a prime minister to take his place. Thus his tutor, Fleury, was able to prolong his lengthy term of office into extreme old age.

Bold action could not be expected of such a government. Fleury was as cautious and timid as he was jealous of his authority. He succeeded by his adroitness, as we have already seen, in bringing about a remarkable diplomatic recovery, and at home he appointed able administrators: Orry for finance, and Maurepas for the navy. But he used them as mere clerks, and although he seemed to understand that a peaceful France could recover her prosperity by putting into practice the policy unsuccessfully attempted by Colbert, he dared not risk the far-reaching reforms necessary for such a programme. His was an authoritarian government which dared not use its authority.

France's difficulties were largely financial. For a short time, under the regency, it seemed as if a remedy had been found in the attractive 'system' of Law. A bank was set up, in imitation of the Bank of England, but it immediately fell into the hands of a great financial company. The unwise use of paper money and scandalous speculation hastened its downfall. The French, suspicious of monetary experiments for a long time to come, returned to the clumsy traditional method of financial expedients.

No effort at fiscal reform was made in order to compel the privileged classes to contribute their share. The *taille*, whose crushing burden was so unfairly distributed, and indirect taxes (such as the *aide* and *gabelle*) collected for the government by 'farmers' and only in part paid to it, were incompatible with a healthy financial system.

In the moral world Louis XV's government, unlike the government of Louis XIV, did not try to impose its wishes in the struggle which continued to rage between Jesuits and Jansenists, Ultramontanes and Gallicans. First Dubois and then Fleury tried hard to discover a compromise acceptable both to the clergy who had accepted the decision of the bull *Unigenitus* condemning Jansenism, and to those who appealed from it to a future council. But their only object was to keep matters quiet and to gain a temporary respite from the bitter quarrels which troubled men's minds and consciences. The government hoped to achieve this object by slow pressure and the increased use of *lettres de cachet* against those who refused to sign a 'formula' of acceptance of the bull. Finally Noailles, the aged archbishop of Paris and the head of the Jansenist clergy, yielded, and after 1730 there were scarcely any more Jansenist bishops. Jansenism, however, remained active among the lower ranks of the clergy, and Gallicanism had formidable advocates in the *Parlements*, which were always hostile to Rome.

In 1715 the regent had encouraged the spirit of independence in the *Parlements* by seeking their help to quash the will of Louis XIV and acquire power. Since then they had waged energetic war against the government's financial measures and religious policy. They considered that they ought to be associated with the government in the exercise of power. The banishment of the *Parlement* of Paris to the provinces, and the arrest of the most ardent agitators among its members, had not broken its resistance; the only result was repeated crises, and each time it was the government which really gave way in the end.

But social conditions in France, no longer controlled by the feeble government, were undergoing a transformation. The class barriers erected by the privileged groups had begun to totter and give way before a strong movement of challenge. This movement began as a consequence of the sale of offices, a system which since the seventeenth century had allowed anyone who could pay for a post to make himself a career; it allowed the bourgeois to join the *noblesse de robe*, and gave the latter entry to the old aristocracy. But the movement became increasingly the result of purely economic developments. Financial crises had enabled financiers to make fortunes and occupy an important place both in the state and in society. A man such as Paris-Duverney became an indispensable person whose will was law at court and in the ministries. The expansion of industry created a class of merchant capitalists, who employed some of the labour of the working class and that of the many peasants who wanted to add some additional gain to the profits they made by agriculture. Their competition upset the rules and regulations of the old corporations. Rapid commercial expansion trebled exports in the first half of the century, and gave rise to a class of rich shipowners. Finally, after 1730, the development of the economic situation began a period of higher prices which was to last for fifty years. It did not benefit the whole population. The majority of the working class, whose wages did not keep pace with the rise in prices, were penalized, and there was great distress among agricultural workers. But the rise in the rent of land favoured landowners, and all peasants who owned their own fields or cultivated them as hereditary farmers saw a great increase in their resources.

These events disconcerted the government. Officially it remained faithful to the principles of Colbert, increasing, for instance, the number of inspectors of manufacture. But the action of the administration was growing weak. The *intendants* tried to use persuasive methods and hesitated to enforce their decisions. The municipal authorities tried to throw off their control. The *Conseil de Commerce* allowed itself to be ruled by the representatives of commerce elected by the trading classes. Fleury, whose chief motto was patience, seemed to think he had only to wait and let the country recover of its own accord.

However, in his last years of office, it alarmed him to see Louis XV escaping from his control. The era of favourites was in fact beginning. The court watched the successive rise to favour of the four de Nesle sisters, followed by the long reign of Madame de Pompadour. The emergence of the problem of the Austrian succession in 1740 provoked an irresistible attack by those who favoured the age-long war against the Habsburgs, and the influence of the favourites thwarted the aged cardinal. The results of all Fleury's diplomacy were swept away, and peace, which was essential to his régime, came to an end. France embarked on disastrous wars. She returned to her traditional diplomacy and an even worse form of her old method of internal government.

What lesson was there for Europe in the spectacle of a country where the government was so weak and the king so indifferent to and forgetful of his duties? The influence of France, still great, depended entirely on the talent of her writers, on the still living memory of Louis XIV, and also on the development of a new code of manners. If the death of the Great King did not bring about a transformation of French institutions, it gave the signal for a new freedom of ideas and manners. After the years of licentiousness which marked the years of the regency, there grew up in France a cultured and charming social life which was universally admired throughout Europe.

§ 3. *England*

The important part played by England in the intellectual life of Europe at the beginning of the eighteenth century will be described later; but this was not her only contribution to the European heritage, which was also enriched by her political experience. The régime set up by the Revolution of 1688 had hitherto been little understood abroad, and the English themselves felt that it was precarious. In the first half of the eighteenth century it established itself on firmer foundations. Europe began to understand its originality and to appreciate its value.

The succession of the Hanoverian dynasty after the death of Queen Anne had eliminated a great danger. England had narrowly escaped the return of the Stuarts, which would have threatened and perhaps ruined the achievements of the Glorious Revolution, and it is well known how much this had weakened the Tories. The accession of George I, and the coming to power of the Whigs, who were to retain it for almost half a century, provided the conditions needed for the proper working of the parliamentary system.

A dynasty which was at the outset completely foreign took root in the country and gradually became a national monarchy. It is true that the majority of the English, and still more of the Scots, were not happy to see it established and confirmed in power by the support of the Whigs. They favoured the 'old party', that is to say the Tories, who had the double advantage of representing the country districts and embodying the cause of the Anglican Church. There were too many nonconformists and business men among the Whigs to please the squires and clergymen. But the Tory party was discredited by the conduct of its leaders during the last years of the previous reign. They had quarrelled bitterly among themselves for position, and they had tried to reconcile Queen Anne with her half-brother, the Pretender, James Stuart. Bolingbroke, that reckless and irresponsible gambler, was reluctant to admit that the Stuarts would refuse to give up Catholicism in order to recover the throne. Although they were without their leaders, who were accused of treason, arrested, or in flight, the Tories nevertheless rallied to their cause a large section of the population which still cherished the hope that the rightful king would one day be able to return. About a hundred members of Parliament still represented this opinion and this hope. But in the world of politics Toryism had no programme and no real vision of the future. Nevertheless it was always formidable, and in 1715 and 1745, when the Stuarts landed in Scotland and attempted to regain the throne, the ardour of their supporters endangered the house of Hanover.

Stanhope, the principal member of the first ministry of George I, succeeded in bringing about a *rapprochement* with the France of the regency and thus depriving the Stuarts of the support of the Bourbons. But it was during Walpole's long tenure of office (1721–42) that numbers of Englishmen rallied to the cause of the new dynasty. He set himself to win the support of the rural areas by seeing to it that the land tax was not raised as the country's wealth increased, but on the contrary was even lowered. The earlier English hostility to the Whigs had been partly due to the fact that, during the preceding wars, they had allowed a national debt to accumulate, which many feared that the country would not be able to meet; but the establishment of a sinking fund showed that the government was now alive to the danger. At the same time Walpole gave assistance to the business world. In England, as in France, the peace of Utrecht was followed by feverish speculation; and the shares of the South Sea Company, founded for the anticipated trade with the Spanish empire, soared to fantastic heights, like those of Law's Company in France. Both companies failed with a resounding crash. But this gave Walpole an opportunity to show his masterly ability. The South Sea Company was refloated with the aid of the Bank of England, and for a long time to come Walpole was assured of the support of the City of London and its prosperous and powerful houses.

Walpole's economic policy was not solely directed towards strengthening the position of the Whigs and the reigning dynasty, nor was this its only achievement. It opened up a promising future of commercial expansion for the nation. During this period England, like France, believed in mercantilism. Her trade was canalized by a system of customs barriers, rebates on re-exported articles, and export subsidies.

Walpole does not appear to have considered the possibility of a general reform, which he would not have been able to carry into effect; but at any rate he realized clearly that so ambitious and complicated a system encouraged an increase of smuggling which defeated its object. He made a determined effort to simplify customs duties. He proposed to take off certain duties levied at the port of London, which he hoped to turn into a free port; excises, or taxes on home consumption, were to replace them. The violent opposition aroused by this project forced him to abandon it. His attitude was founded on a great confidence in the ability of the country to achieve prosperity, and on a deep distrust of the results of excessive governmental interference. Even the burden of the debt would seem less heavy to a country with more strength to carry the burden. But the English could not understand his calm audacity; and they had also, as we have seen, some reason for being annoyed that England had not expanded her trade with America, and was without allies in Europe. Walpole was forced to declare war on Spain, and to resign soon afterwards.

But his work remained. The dynasty was more firmly established. The nation had built up its resources and was able to hold its own in the war which was just beginning. Commercial expansion resulted inevitably in industrial development. Hence-forth England presented to Europe the unique example of a country whose finances were sound and whose economic strength was making her one of the most powerful of nations.

She also offered the example of a country where a régime of liberty had been established within the framework of parlia-mentary institutions. The English themselves, it is true, did not fully realize what had been done. They loudly denounced Walpole as a dictator who maintained himself in power by means of a cynical system of corruption which gave him a servile majority in Parliament, enabled him to keep out of office all those who would not defer to his wishes, and allowed him to dominate the king himself. This was also the reputation he had earned in Europe.

England's political evolution was really quite different. The Whigs, who alone filled almost the whole political stage, were sadly divided among themselves and split into rival cliques and factions; Walpole succeeded in keeping his own group in power for more than twenty years, and in welding it into a disciplined majority against which the attacks of his enemies, even when they were helped by staunch Tory members, were ineffectual. He had removed from office his more able and am-bitious colleagues, retaining a cabinet which followed his views and was supported by the king. But had he achieved these results solely by corrupt methods?

The word 'corruption' was used at that time without any definition of its meaning. The secret funds which could buy support were too limited to enable Walpole to govern with their help alone. But every minister had at his disposal a number of posts at court and in the administration which were often simply sinecures but very remunerative. Walpole was particularly clever in his use of these posts to repay supporters or win over enemies. When George II, who detested him, came to the throne, Walpole had disarmed his hostility by persuading Parliament to grant him a considerable increase in the Civil List, and in this way he had retained control of the immense resources of the 'patronage' exercised by the crown.

But the explanation and justification of his authority lie elsewhere. The king had been taught by experience to recognize his exceptional qualities, which the queen with her quick intelli-gence had at once perceived and pointed out to him. Both in

Parliament and in the Cabinet Walpole took care not to impose his policies without first justifying his proposals by good reasons in their favour. The distribution of favours, whether in honours or money, was only used to consolidate what had already been largely won by the reasoned defence of a sagacious policy.

Walpole rejected the title of Prime Minister given to him by his opponents, because at this time it conjured up the picture of a favourite usurping his master's place. But he was, on his own admission, conscious of being a statesman who had won, and deserved, the complete confidence of his sovereign, because he was able to assure him of the support of a disciplined majority.

His most dangerous enemy, Bolingbroke, took up the defence of English liberties in his brilliant pamphlets *The State of Parties* and *The Patriot King*. He compared the parties to factions, putting their own interests before those of the nation and formed by ambitious politicians whom the king should remove from office to safeguard his own position. This was an unfair caricature of Walpole's régime. In reality Walpole, half unconsciously, taught his country the practice of the parliamentary system. He showed what could be achieved by a minister capable of leading a united cabinet and a disciplined parliamentary majority while still respecting the privileges of the crown and responsible to parliament for his actions. But the criticisms of his opponents were also instructive, since they showed the price which Englishmen had to pay for the preservation of their liberties.

§ 4. *Other European States*

Events in the other European states in this first half of the eighteenth century had few repercussions outside their frontiers. In Spain the house of Bourbon gave little support to a far-sighted minister, Patino, in his attempts to revive the country's economy. The Bourbons were preoccupied with the defence of their empire against the cupidity of English merchants, and with the recovery of the Italian territories lost to them by the treaty of Utrecht. But they could not recover them without the consent of the English and French courts. The policies of these two courts also decided the fate of the numerous states which were still to be found in the Italian peninsula. The old house of Austria had only strength enough to carry on the war against the Turks under the leadership of Prince Eugene; it stood waiting for the collapse which the death of Charles VI would bring. The emperor's chief concern was to ensure in advance the eventual succession to his dominions of his daughter Maria Theresa. Meanwhile, in the interval before her accession, the Habsburgs could make no attempt to solve the grave problems raised for them by the extent, the diversity, and the dispersion of their territories.

In Prussia Frederic William I, the *Roi Sergent*, was creating the instrument which Frederic II was later to use. His administration and his army were then to become a formidable power in Europe; but his timid and vacillating diplomacy was still weak and ineffectual. Poland, on the death of King Augustus II in 1733, became the stake in a European war; but the countries involved in the war had little interest in her fate. France found in it an opportunity to gain possession of Lorraine; Austria and Russia found an opportunity for drawing together in an alliance which already formed a grave menace to the independence of Poland.

At the end of the reign of Peter the Great in 1725 Russia seemed to hesitate about continuing his work. The Russian advance in the Balkans continued; and by the middle of the century the metal industry which he had established in the Urals became one of the most important centres of European production. But a succession of court revolutions involved the Russian nobles in a struggle with foreign favourites; and the weakness and vacillation of the successors of Peter the Great gave men of the time the impression that Russia was again isolating herself from Europe.

After the exhausting reign of Charles XII Sweden became a prey to domestic intrigues which were exploited by her neighbours. The peace of Utrecht failed to restore the United Provinces to the important position which they had held in Europe in the seventeenth century. It is true that, as we shall see later, they remained the centre of a great intellectual movement, and served as a sanctuary for writers who had no freedom of expression in their own countries. It seemed, however, that the work of their great artists and thinkers was over. Although Holland was still a first-class economic power, and could hold in check her neighbours in the Austrian Low Countries, she no longer exercised the same influence in London, Versailles, or Vienna, and no longer spoke with the same authority in the European world of politics.

The deciding factors in the common history of the European states during this period were, on the one hand, France's inability to instil new life and vigour into the *ancien régime* or maintain its power; and, on the other, the measures taken by the English to adjust themselves to a greatly altered political system and a remarkable economic expansion.

II

THE MIDDLE OF THE CENTURY

PEACE was maintained in Europe as a whole until 1740; but between 1740 and 1763 two wars, separated only by an insecure and often interrupted truce, set all the great nations in conflict. What was the influence of these wars on European history?

On the relations between England and France, the two great countries of western Europe, they had effects which are still felt even today. It was not their first conflict; the long series of Anglo-French struggles in modern times had begun in 1689. But though the wars of the reign of Louis XIV had led the English people and their government to regard the ambitions and institutions of the French monarchy as a permanent menace, they had not affected French opinion of England in the same way; and it was the Seven Years War which first awoke in France a feeling of permanent hostility to England.

The English attack in 1755, and the seizure of French ships at sea without a declaration of war, angered the French; and their resentment was increased by defeat. The court of Versailles, and even 'enlightened' persons, watched the loss of French colonies with a strange indifference; they felt keenly, however, the humiliation of defeat. Even Louis XV was roused from his apathy, and the whole of France longed for revenge, which it was the object of Choiseul's foreign policy to prepare. England, at that moment entering on a period of domestic crises, was constantly haunted by the feeling that her victory was threatened. Henceforth the conflict between the two countries was one of the principal factors of the European problem.

From another point of view these wars also marked the appearance in Europe of new states which were now in a position to play an important part.

The rise of the Prussian state was the most astonishing of all, and the brilliant achievements of Frederic the Great stirred the imagination. It was he who precipitated the struggle on the continent, at the beginning of these two wars, by attacking first Silesia and then Saxony; but he was not judged harshly for these acts of aggression, or for the easy way in which he had twice abandoned his allies in the course of the first war. Maria

Theresa, who was his victim, alone remained his enemy. The achievements of Frederic II had far-reaching results. They were largely responsible for the 'reversal of alliances' which put an end to the long rivalry between Bourbons and Habsburgs and thus transformed European diplomacy. Above all, Frederic gained a moral ascendancy over most of Europe by his extraordinary ability. By escaping from the stranglehold of his enemies he won enormous prestige, and placed Prussia among the great powers.

He also emerged as the creator of a new conception of the state and of the role which the sovereign should play, the role of 'the enlightened despot'. The philosophers complacently believed that they had themselves inspired it. He had, at all events, a number of illustrious imitators among his contemporaries. His example relegated the memory of Louis XIV into the distant past. Europe did not foresee that this new form of despotism was to be far more dangerous to the peace of the continent than the ambitions of the old monarchies had ever been, and that the despots would pursue the aggrandizement of their states without any scruple. Frederic showed more insight in learning the lessons of the disaster to which he had so nearly succumbed. During the Seven Years War the Russian armies laid Prussia waste and even reached Berlin. Henceforward the Hohenzollerns were never again to enter into conflict with a Russian sovereign. In order to conciliate Russia and to appease the enmity of the Habsburg monarchy, the kings of Prussia must for the future make proposals of common conquests in which they could all share. This was the policy of partition.

These wars were also important in the history of Europe for their repercussions on social life and institutions in England and France. 'The miraculous year', 1759, when she wrested victory, was a decisive year in the evolution of modern England. The victory was the work of William Pitt, who bore alone the whole burden of the conduct of the war from his town house in St. James's Square. He dominated his colleagues in office; he had complete control in Parliament, where he silenced all opposition. With superb self-confidence and burning patriotism he directed the navy, which kept vigilant watch round the shores of Great Britain; he sent great expeditions across the Atlantic, which was now closed to French reinforcements. He put in command of these expeditions young leaders fired with his own enthusiasm, and while Versailles failed to see the brilliance of the prospects which Dupleix offered to France in India, Pitt encouraged Robert Clive, who began to build there the empire which had been conceived by Dupleix.

In these wars, as in all others in her history, England was slow to understand the extent of the effort required of her. She had fought badly in the war of the Austrian Succession, and when the folly and indifference of Louis XV enabled her to end it as a draw, she allowed herself, without considering the consequences, to be dragged into a new struggle which began very badly for her. After the fall of Walpole the Whigs were divided into rival factions, and what counted in Parliament was not so much a man's own qualities as the number of his followers. The king's personal desires, and even more his personal dislikes, were perpetually embarrassing to his ministers. But when the loss of Minorca roused England to an understanding of her danger, she succeeded in giving herself a strong government. In spite of the repugnance of George II Pitt became its head, revealing himself to his country as the only man who could save it. His power and his success were not only founded on a popularity which was justified by his character; they were also due to the support of his colleagues, and particularly Newcastle, who used the vast resources of his patronage in his favour. The dictatorial powers which he wielded did not destroy, and hardly even interrupted, the normal working of parliamentary institutions. Discipline was accepted without any loss of freedom, and the public, feeling no threat to its liberties, rejoiced that a free country could also be strong.

After that it mattered little that the accession in 1760 of George III, who wished to conduct affairs himself, finally brought about Pitt's resignation before he had concluded the peace for which he thought the time was not yet ripe. His successors proved themselves incapable of solving the great political and imperial problems which were raised by the policy of the king and the results of victory itself. But Europe did not feel the consequences until later. What she immediately discovered was the unsuspected power of English institutions.

France presented a different picture, from which totally different conclusions could be drawn. She had squandered her strength in these wars. In the first place the French felt keenly the folly of the peace of Aix-la-Chapelle, which had brought them no advantage from the victories won by their armies under the command of Maurice de Saxe. Secondly, France had sacrificed the best of her forces in a continental war in which she had little interest, and had thus deprived herself of the means of resisting the English outside Europe. Even in this continental war, her armies had allowed themselves to be beaten, or had been unable to hold their own, because of the rivalry or inefficiency of their generals. In the words of Bernis, she had played an 'extravagant and shameful' part. Most of the blame was laid at the door of the Marquise de Pompadour, whose reign lasted from 1745 to 1764. In spite of her sincere patriotism, the criticism was justified by her constant efforts to assert her influence and her utter failure to understand the political and military affairs in which she persistently meddled. But what could be said of the king, who with a much greater grasp of affairs could not make the effort to assert himself?

It was at this precise moment that he was offered the greatest, and perhaps the last, opportunity of reforming the *ancien régime*. Louis XV fully understood the significance of the reform which his controller general, Machault D'Arnouville, wished to introduce. The tax (*impôt du vingtième*) which he proposed in 1749—a tax which would at last have touched the privileged classes, and the burden of which could have been fairly distributed by competent officials—would have provided the Crown with ample revenue, sufficient to meet its expenses and restore its financial credit. But the king did not defend his minister against the attacks of his enemies; and instead he yielded quickly to the demands of the clergy. Instead of attempting a decisive reform he allowed himself to be confronted by a most serious domestic crisis, provoked by a mixture of religious disputes and financial exigencies.

At the same time as the clergy rejected the proposed tax, the *Parlements* were attacking dignitaries of the Church who were attempting to suppress Jansenism by refusing to admit to the sacraments all who had not expressly renounced its principles. Even with the obliging help of the Holy See the government did not succeed in restoring religious peace. Jansenism survived in the form of 'Richerisme', which was the more dangerous to the state as it set the aspirations and unrest of the lower ranks of the clergy in opposition to the bishops, who were drawn only from the nobility. Jansenism also made use of the political aspect of

Gallicanism, which was supported by the *Parlements*. Eventually the *Parlements* took the offensive, and forced the king to suppress the Jesuit Order in France.

Louis XV could not avoid a measure of which he disapproved, because, being in financial distress, he was obliged to make concessions to the *Parlements*. After Machault's defeat the cost of the war had brought the government to bankruptcy, and when the peace was signed it was necessary to continue war-time taxes, and even to impose new ones. The projected reforms of the Controller General Bertin were immediately abandoned when the *Parlements* rose up in arms. The protests of the *Parlements* became more insistent. The *Parlements* of the provinces made a united front with the *Parlement* of Paris: together they attempted to form a body of counsellors of the monarchy, who were to act as an organ of the nation and to be associated for the future in the financial administration of the kingdom.

Magistrates, intended only to administer justice, and holding an office which they had bought in order to enjoy its profits, were in no way qualified to fill this role. They could not represent the nation, and apart from that they never forgot to put the defence of their own interests first.

But the opposition of the *Parlements* presented public opinion with a political problem closely connected with the future of the whole régime. Writers, who were themselves extremely hostile to the *Parlements*, sought to explain the issues involved. Voltaire was the first to defend Machault's proposals. It is worth noticing that the most important works of the 'philosophers' were almost all published during these critical years, from *L'Esprit des Lois* of 1748 to the *Contrat Social* of 1762, including the first volume of the *Encyclopédie*, Voltaire's *Siècle de Louis XIV* and his *Essai sur les Mœurs*, and Rousseau's *Discours sur l'Origine de l'Inégalité*.

In this way new political and social ideas were put before France and all the countries of Europe where these works were read. The 'philosophers', of course, were far from agreeing amongst themselves, and they did not produce a coherent plan for the reform of political institutions and society. But at a time when the French monarchy was astonishing Europe by its errors and its weakness their criticisms and their warnings emphasized the need to oppose the forces of prejudice, superstition, and self-interest with the power of reason. They called for a strong government, and at the same time opened men's eyes to the

value of political and intellectual liberty. Their contribution
to the European inheritance thus represented contrary trends.
Those trends became clearer in the period of paramount importance which lies between the end of the Seven Years War
and the beginning of the French Revolution.

III

FROM THE END OF THE SEVEN YEARS WAR TO THE FRENCH REVOLUTION

§ 1. *International Relations*

The years 1763–89 demand a fuller treatment. They mark an era of wider and more rapid changes in the economic and social conditions of the peoples of Europe on the eve of the Revolution; and a general survey of their history is necessary to an understanding of the causes which made France the scene of a revolutionary conflagration. To begin with, these years have the character of a period of reconstruction, such as men of our generation are peculiarly able to appreciate. The destruction caused by the Seven Years War may appear comparatively insignificant to us. Yet in certain areas in Prussia, in part of the Habsburg states, and in Poland, the passage of armies had left terrible ravages in its train. A total reconstruction was needed, and Frederic II was the first to give the signal when he entered his capital again upon the conclusion of peace.

This peace was different from those which Europe had known hitherto. It was what men of the next century were to call an 'armed peace'. Rulers remained armed for new battles. In this Prussia set the example. The presence of the Prussian army in Europe changed the whole atmosphere.

Frederic II had inherited from his father an army which was already 80,000 strong, equal to the emperor's forces, and in effective strength only slightly inferior to the French army but much more highly trained. This force did not satisfy him; and, even though it had saved his kingdom for him by 1763, he wanted a permanent army of 200,000 men. Nor was it enough for him to devote a very large part of his revenue to its upkeep. He maintained a war reserve, which he increased from the 10 million thalers of 1740 to 55 million. He thus held a sum which was equal to the proceeds of three years' taxes to meet the risk of a future war. This effort was completely disproportionate to the size of his kingdom, whose population was scarcely more than 2 million inhabitants at the time of his accession, and had not reached 6 million when he died. In addition to voluntary recruitment there was also a compulsory conscription of 'cantonists', in the districts or 'cantons', equal in number to the recruits, and earmarked for the needs of each regiment. The officer class, recruited solely from the aristocracy, gave this army a feudal character; many of the soldiers were under the command of their own squires, and although the king imposed the most rigorous discipline on his officers, he took no measures in the interests of the peasants which might have displeased the aristocracy.

It is easy to see the effect which was bound to be produced in Europe by the existence of such a force, very fully equipped and thus constantly ready for action under the command of the greatest soldier of the age. The neighbours of the King of Prussia were both envious and alarmed. They longed to imitate him. Joseph II introduced the system of 'cantonists' into the Austrian states, and reformed and strengthened his own army.

This military strength was used as the weapon of a diplomacy which aimed not at peace but aggrandizement achieved by means of aggression. It is true that the only principle followed by European diplomacy, at least since the beginning of the seventeenth century, had been that of *raison d'état*, and Montesquieu had already observed that 'the ruling spirit of monarchy is war and aggrandisement'. But the men of the end of the eighteenth century felt that 'enlightened despotism', which was the new conception of monarchy, went even farther and found new reasons for a policy of aggression. Frederic had in fact put these reasons in writing himself, arguing that a contract is only valid so long as it is in the interest of the state to keep it, and that a treaty which is no longer useful is no longer binding on the signatories. A sovereign whose power rests not on divine right, but on the mission given him by his people to be their ruler, should be able to repudiate his engagements for any compelling reason. If such a reason arises he must sacrifice himself, in spite of his repugnance, to the service of his state.

Frederic also invented a new method of conquest, the method of partition, which reconciled each country's need of expansion with the exigencies of the balance of power in Europe. A famous example was the first partition of Poland in 1772, which he began to plan immediately after the 1763 treaties. It amazed and horrified Europe. Men tried to ignore its implications by making Poland's mistakes responsible for Polish misfortunes. But preparations for a partition of Sweden, proposals for the annexation of Bavaria by Austria, and above all else the vast prospect

of a partition of the Balkans, soon compelled them to acknowledge that they were faced by a formidable innovation. The
French minister Vergennes protested against this 'political
gangsterism' and declared to Louis XVI: 'If might is right,
and expediency is law, on what can national security rest?'

These fears roused the countries of Europe to oppose any new
partition. But the partition of Poland remained; and henceforth it was a permanent feature in the evolution of European
diplomacy, and a permanent element in the conscience of
Europe. It laid the foundations of an *entente* which became a
necessity for the partitioning powers, as the nineteenth century
was to show.

§ 2. *Enlightened Despotism in Germany*

Nevertheless the achievements of enlightened despotism
provoked all over the continent a widespread movement of sympathy and admiration, which was justified by their rich contribution to the European heritage. According to the epitaph which
he composed for himself, Joseph II 'failed in all his undertakings';
and his efforts, which set his own subjects against him, were criticized as severely abroad. But Frederic and Catherine the Great
were European heroes. Voltaire was the first to honour the
coming of a prince 'who thinks like a man and is a philosopher
prince who will make men happy'. In spite of his disappoint-
ments, and in spite of his bitter quarrel with the king, the patriarch of Ferney still wrote to him from his retreat: 'You are the
one thing lacking to my happiness; you are the most fascinating
creature I have ever met.' D'Alembert was filled with boundless
enthusiasm for Frederic, and declared to him in 1770: 'Sire,
you were the leader and model of writers and thinkers; you are
now the god who gives them reward and punishment.' Diderot
was equally full of praises for Catherine II, whom he had
visited, and with whom he had discussed her projects of reform
in informal interviews. Although flattery and illusion played
a large part in all this admiration, nevertheless 'Old Fritz'
and the 'Semiramis of the North' became almost legendary
figures, wielding a sort of moral sovereignty in Europe.

The 'philosophers' believed themselves to be the inspiration
and almost the originators of their reforms: at any rate they
wished to believe it, and refused to listen to any denial. Frederic
might in his writings pronounce them 'intolerably arrogant',

and declare that their idea of destroying religion was 'extravagant' and that their works seemed to him 'a mass of paradoxes and ideas thrown out without consideration'; but this did not damp their ardour.

This ardour was not inspired only by illusions. The prestige of the enlightened despots in European society was justified by their achievement, which impressed their contemporaries by its merits. How could they fail to be impressed by the energy and clear-sightedness of the work which these sovereigns did for the improvement of their states, in comparison with the timidity and egoism of the French monarchy?

Their first efforts were directed towards a process of administrative centralization, which amounted to a system of personal government. The king himself attended to the minutest details, and kept for himself all decisions. In the Hohenzollern territories the work had been begun a century earlier by Frederic's predecessors, who had founded the Prussian administrative system. They had patiently built it up stage by stage. First there was the 'Beamtentum', or the body of bailiffs which managed the extensive private domains of the sovereign. Then, at the provincial level, colleges of officials forming the 'Chambers of Domains' took in hand all the public services, which were financed by a land tax. But after the end of the Thirty Years War the great elector, by a reform which illustrates the dominant tendencies of the Prussian state, created provincial 'Commissions of War', separate bodies of officials who specialized in military administration. A tax on consumer goods, imposed on their entry into towns, was introduced to meet their requirements. On assuming the royal crown of Prussia, Frederic I had set over the provincial chambers a central chamber of domains, and similarly he had set over the provincial commissions of war a central commission sitting in Berlin. Finally, the 'Sergeant King', Frederic William I, to complete this necessary process of unification, had merged the chamber and the commission to form a single General Directory. Frederic II profited from these determined efforts, which seemed to have achieved their object at the time of his succession, the more so as the old provincial diets, whose powers had gradually been diminished, were now about to come to an end.

Frederic managed to enlarge still more the process of centralization and the power of the sovereign. During his reign the

General Directory, which seemed destined to develop into a council of ministers, was nothing but an administrative council. The king retained all political control himself, managing affairs with the help of his personal secretaries, without the aid and often without the knowledge of his ministers, who only had to carry out his orders. He only called them together once a year for a 'budget review', which he held as he would a military review. He kept in direct contact with local officials by means of a prolific correspondence and through tours of minute and rigorous inspection. Few understood at the time the danger to the country of a system of government which depended for its success solely on the personal character of the sovereign and his utter surrender of his tastes and his time to the public service. Frederic himself seemed oblivious of the danger. But the whole of Europe, which had only known the clumsy and complicated centralization of the French monarchy, admired the intensity of his effort, and was attracted by a state where the will of an intelligent prince seemed capable of achieving anything.

The Habsburgs tried to achieve the same result. Centralization seemed peculiarly desirable in the wide territories governed by the house of Austria. In the middle of the eighteenth century the Habsburgs felt the need not to increase but to consolidate those territories, in order to make a better use of their resources. The Habsburg lands consisted of provinces and kingdoms administered by diets, which contributed only a small part of their revenues to the central government. They were so scattered, and so diverse in population, institutions, religion, and nationality, that the exercise of a central authority was extremely difficult. Without counting the Milanese and the Low Countries, which were really foreign colonies, the Habsburgs governed under different titles and by various methods upper and lower Austria, with their other German provinces, and the two kingdoms of Wenceslas and St. Stephen. In Vienna, besides the Austrian chancellery, there was a chancellery for Bohemia and another for Hungary. The diet or estates of Bohemia not only voted but also received the taxes, the proceeds of which were used to defray the cost of a system of administration acting under a delegation of the estates. The Magyar nobles sought to manage their own affairs for themselves through their council at Pressburg and the governments of their local 'Comitats'. The lesser aristocracy controlled local government in the assemblies and tribunals of the 'Comitats'. The Catholic Church retained a large measure of independence everywhere. These illustrations are enough to show the obstacles which confronted a policy of centralization.

By her tact, her perspicacity, and her charm, Maria Theresa achieved important results without any show of force. The estates of Bohemia accepted a new system of heavy taxes administered by imperial officials. The union of the chancelleries of Austria and Bohemia after 1749 brought under a single control the group of territories which now became known as 'the German hereditary States', corresponding to the Austria or Cisleithania of the nineteenth century. With this group of territories on the one hand, and Hungary on the other, Maria Theresa thus created the dualist régime of Austria-Hungary. Her hand was also strengthened in Hungary by the loyalty of the magnates, whom she attracted more and more to Vienna, and who allowed her to put a German lieutenant-governor at their head.

Joseph II, however, wished to go much farther and much faster. He thought he could break down all resistance. He deprived the diets in the hereditary states of nearly all their functions, and he did not spare the susceptibilities of the Magyars. In the Low Countries, where his predecessors had been careful to respect the privileges and customs preserved in their ancient provincial constitutions, and had only tried to extend their authority by particular measures and through the individual action of Austrian agents, he sought to achieve the forcible suppression of local liberties by a general policy.

Following Frederic's example, but also obeying the dictates of his own temperament, Joseph II had visions of governing absolutely through a mechanical bureaucracy entirely obedient to his wishes. He exhausted his strength in a zealous effort of constant inspection and the practice of a system of police supervision, which had the contrary effect of paralysing officials too terrified to show any initiative.

How could he possibly have achieved success, when he had to build a whole system of bureaucracy from the bottom upwards? Joseph refused to see that his administrative reforms encountered social and economic difficulties which had been unknown to the King of Prussia.

In the economic field Frederic the Great had a free hand for action. The extent of the crown lands was so great that much of the economic life of his kingdom resembled the administration of a private estate. The ravages of war had also given it something of the character of a colony. Only the king could repair the ravages by giving subsidies, distributing grants in kind, bringing the land under crops by settling farmers and building them houses, and reclaiming new land by drainage schemes. Industrial development was also largely the work of the king, and it was again Frederic who had to open up commercial channels and build ships. When, in imitation of the English, he started a system of credit and discount banks, he had himself to subscribe almost all the capital.

This great effort could only be made on the basis of mercantilist principles, and Frederic maintained those principles. Although he acknowledged the fundamental importance of agricultural produce, on which the physiocrats laid so much stress, he did not allow himself to be carried away by their doctrines in the direction of free trade; nor did his desire to raise the productivity of the peasants lead him to take social measures which would have undermined the foundations of the state. After the Seven Years War he thought for a moment that he might seize a unique opportunity for improving conditions among the peasants and putting an end to serfdom. But he quickly abandoned the idea, and satisfied himself by giving the peasants some protection against the brutality of their masters, and some relief from the burden and injustice of the *corvée*. It was essential not to anger an aristocracy which had been successfully enlisted in the service of the state.

The economic and social problems which confronted the Habsburgs were much more difficult. Frederic's frugal policy always ensured him sufficient resources, and at the end of the Seven Years War, thanks to English subsidies, his treasury was still well lined; but the strict economy practised by Joseph was not enough to establish his finances on a sound basis. For a short period he was able to balance his budget, but the Turkish War left him with a large deficit.

His territories, industrially undeveloped, were not self-sufficient, and the prohibitive taxes on goods imported from abroad caused much distress and discontent. He was obliged to leave Tyrol outside his customs barriers, as its economy could not survive in the absence of foreign trade; and his insistence on including the Low Countries was one of the causes of their rebellion. Hungary continually complained that she was treated as a colony, and that Austria would not accept any products which competed with her own.

Yet Joseph II was less tied than Frederic to a policy of mercantilism, and it was physiocratic theories which inspired his project of a land-tax. This was to be the culmination of his economic and the crown of his social policy; it had the double aim of covering the greater part of his expenditure and of serving as an instrument of social justice. The land register which he had compiled with feverish haste enabled him to tax all income from land and at the same time to fix the rents payable to the landlords by the peasants, who were now freed from serfdom. His attempt failed owing to the opposition of the nobles and the impatience of the peasants; and his successor Leopold hastened to put an end to his policy. Europe had not fully understood its significance. The physiocrats refused to see it as the realization of their theories, and the 'philosophers' were not interested in the conditions of a peasant class which in central Europe was still in a state of serfdom. They did not seem to expect the despots to bring about profound social changes. Yet they considered them 'enlightened' because they opposed prejudice with the force of reason, and fanaticism with tolerance.

It was their policy of tolerance which was, if not the most important, at least the most spectacular contribution made to the European heritage by the enlightened despots. Contemporaries saw the government of Louis XV exclude Protestants from the protection of the law, and condemn the writings of the 'philosophers' or allow the Church to forbid them. In England they saw the press exposed to the attacks of George III's ministers and the obstinacy of a parliament which still refused to allow its debates to be published. On the other hand they saw Frederic announce that in his domains 'each man seeks his salvation according to his lights', and Joseph II issue an 'Edict of Tolerance' which allowed his subjects to leave the Catholic Church and even to found other confessions. Both these rulers abolished, or at least greatly restricted, the powers of the censorship.

It is true that these authoritarians were very little influenced by an ideal of liberty. They surrounded themselves with precautionary measures. Frederic still required writers to obtain permission to print their works, and thought it quite natural that an imprudent journalist should be made to understand his mistakes by means of a flogging. Joseph reserved to himself the right to suppress any criticisms considered by him to be defamatory. But they had both realized that a people who were able to give expression to their wishes would be easier to govern, and this was in itself an acknowledgement of the value of freedom. The policy of tolerance, moreover, was implemented by positive measures. It was accompanied by far-reaching judicial reforms. It is true that this programme of reform was not fully realized. After giving strong support to his minister Cocceji, who had initiated the programme, Frederic seemed later to abandon it, and the Prussian code was issued only after his death. Joseph's code remained incomplete. The greatest merit of both rulers consisted in speeding up and improving the administration of justice, by means of reforms of procedure, and by the appointment of competent judges. This in itself was enough to make the work of the enlightened despots beneficial to their subjects. Moreover, the legal reforms which they introduced (new laws of succession, the suppression of torture, and the abolition, in Austria, of the death penalty) were partly inspired by the principles of natural law expounded by writers on jurisprudence.

At the same time their governments put forward, and began to carry into effect, a programme of public education. In 1763 Frederic had made education compulsory for all children, by a bold decision which was, however, imperfectly put into execution. Joseph went farther, and compelled the nobles, towns, and villages to open schools. The problem of education presented itself in a different form in the states where the Church of Rome was dominant. In the Hohenzollern territories the Protestants did not deny the king the right to participate in the administrative action of their consistories. Joseph II, although he was a good Catholic, judged it essential that a clergy which was too independent in its ideas should be made to submit to the royal authority. It exasperated his reforming spirit to see so many of his subjects and so much wealth buried in the monasteries. He decided to suppress the contemplative orders, and he then allowed himself to be persuaded to close a third of the convents and to confiscate their goods. He also revised the boundaries of the dioceses, compelled the bishops to swear an oath of allegiance to him, and restricted them to an income fixed by the state.

Government control of the theological colleges ensured a loyal body of clergy. He even dared to forbid what an 'enlightened' mind could hold to be mere superstition in religious ritual. Pope Pius VI made a fruitless journey to Vienna in an attempt to hold him back.

This policy, which was called 'Josephism', and which was the only part of the emperor's ambitious reforms to survive him, roused horrified protests. But it could not fail to make an impression in Europe, where so many governments wanted to seize the possessions of the Church, and where battles were raging, in every Catholic country, against Church doctrines and institutions. The fundamental ideas of 'Josephism', as has recently been shown, came from Italy and the Low Countries. The boldness and energy of the enlightened despots already gained by the contrast which they offered to the weakness and decay of the French monarchy; but the peoples of Europe were even more attracted by the enlightened character of the policies which they pursued. They could not help admiring sovereigns whose conduct was dictated by the idea of tolerance, who sincerely wished to reform justice and law, and who took upon themselves the education of their subjects.

By the spread of 'light' and knowledge, the enlightened despots prepared the way for the age of reason. In Germany, where these experiments were made, the age of the *Aufklärung* began.

The *Aufklärung* was a movement of intellectual awakening, inspired by ideas and feelings which produced brilliant literary achievements at the end of the century in Germany. It is a theme which belongs to the second section of this part. At this stage it is enough to say that Germany became conscious of her own powers, and that her writers tried to shake off the foreign influence of France and England, which had hitherto been dominant. They not only succeeded in that aim: their works had also a European importance, and became in their turn a rich source of new inspiration.

The first generation of the *Aufklärung* appeared on the scene at the beginning of the reign of Frederic II, when Lessing, Mendelssohn, and Nicolai met in Berlin. A new revival came a quarter of a century later. Roused by Herder and Goethe, who met at Strassburg, writers turned from the rules of reason and the classical model to the appeal of feeling and the beauties of the

Middle Ages. This was the movement, called *Sturm und Drang*, which was the harbinger of the coming of romanticism. But the *Aufklärung* still continued to exercise its influence for some time, and still sought to dissipate prejudices by the light of reason. Goethe himself, after giving an outstanding example of romanticism in his *Werther*, began to turn to ancient Rome for sources of inspiration.

The confidence in the power of reason which was a fundamental characteristic of the *Aufklärung* inspired not only writers but also many officials and even many members of the clergy. Under the influence of Semler at the university of Halle, and of Spalding in Berlin, young pastors were freed from the bigotry of a narrow pietism; and instead of preaching strict doctrine they began to preach the principles of rational ethics. Rationalist writers and protestant pastors adopted the attitude of tolerance taught by Lessing in *Nathan the Wise* and practised by the enlightened despots.

Frederic the Great and Joseph II had imitators in Germany at the end of the eighteenth century. In Berlin, it is true, Frederic William II, a less than second-rate ruler, was the prey to a strange mixture of mysticism and sensuality which offended against all reason. But many petty sovereigns, in a number of principalities, played the part of enlightened despots. Charles Frederic, the duke of Baden, was the only one with the courage to put an end to serfdom; but some other princes, such as Ferdinand of Brunswick, the elector of Saxony, and the landgrave of Hesse-Darmstadt, attempted reforms and gave a welcome to new ideas. Some of the ecclesiastical princes followed similar policies. The archbishop of Cologne founded the university of Bonn; the archbishop of Mainz made Förster his librarian and appointed the Swiss Johannes von Müller a member of his council.

But the part played by rulers was less important than that of the writers who reminded them of their duties. Friedrich Karl Moser took this line in a book, *Der Herr und der Diener*, which protested against the reactionary policy of the Duke of Württemburg. Many newspapers called for reforms. Schlöser took advantage of the moderate liberalism shown by the King of England in Hanover to make his *Korrespondenz* a powerful weapon of propaganda. The *Deutsche Kronik*, published by Schubart in Swabia, was a counterpart. The *Deutsche Merkur*, produced by

Wieland in Weimar, and the *Allgemeine Deutsche Bibliothek*, edited by Nicolai in Berlin, circulated all over Germany. These writers, it is true, had no systematic programme of reforms to propose; they had no new theory of politics, and they still showed much timidity in dealing with political matters. But it is true to say that in the last thirty years of the century they taught Germany to read and to think.

Thus the movement of *Aufklärung* and the work of the enlightened despots went on simultaneously in Germany. It is not easy to define their connexion.

Historians are still divided over the problem of the origin of enlightened despotism. Some think that it originated in the philosophical movement of eighteenth-century France; others that it began in the ponderous work of the German Cameralists of the seventeenth century, whose influence still survived. In fact it was mainly from the example of Louis XIV and from Hohenzollern traditions that Frederic II drew the inspiration which made him the original creator of a new conception of the state and sovereignty.

Enlightened despotism did not set out to put into practice the ideas of the *Aufklärung*. Nor did it encourage the full development of these ideas. Joseph II had very little influence on writers, and the influence exercised by Frederic the Great was quite involuntary on his part. He spoke and wrote in French; he only used German, which he regarded as a 'stupid language', with reluctance; he was ill acquainted with the work of German writers and took very little interest in them. This was a great disappointment to them, for his achievements during the Seven Years War seemed to mark him out as a national hero. Gleim's *Songs of the Grenadier* and Lessing's *Minna von Barnhelm* attest the feelings of writers who would have liked to sing his praises. Even Goethe, at Frankfurt, rejoiced at his victories, which he called *our* victories. But it was outside Prussia that the intellectual movement found full scope. Klopstock wrote his *Messias* in Denmark. Lessing fought for the creation of an original German theatre in Hamburg. Herder fled from Prussia to Riga to write his *Fragments on German Literature*. It was at the little court of Weimar that the greatest writers, Wieland, Goethe, and Schiller, established themselves.

The *Aufklärung* movement achieved the intellectual independence of Germany; German literature became aware of its inherent powers, and found in the German language a medium for their expression.

It is surprising that the writers of this time had no desire to see the political unity of Germany achieved. German nationalism had not yet emerged at the end of the eighteenth century. The problem of German unity might conceivably have arisen when Frederic the Great formed a League of Princes to oppose the ambitions of Joseph II. But the Germans did not, as yet, take the problem into account. Nicolai declared that German nationalism was a 'political monstrosity'; Lessing saw patriotism as nothing but an 'heroic infirmity'; and Goethe cried, 'Heaven help us! we should have no chair for it to sit on, or bed for it to sleep in.' For Herder mankind alone was the 'true fatherland'.

The cosmopolitan ideas of these writers prepared them to play a great part in the Europe of their time. They were greatly influenced by Rousseau, much more than by Voltaire. In the words of Kant, he taught them to 'honour humanity' and to defend its 'rights'. Germany was unanimously in favour of American independence, and waited for the coming of revolution in Europe. She was enthusiastic about the earlier revolutionary dramas of Schiller. But her most precious contribution to European civilization at that time was perhaps the philosophy of Kant, who, after Descartes and Hume, shed new light on the great problem of human knowledge.

But it was not only in Germany that the progress of reason, the passion for reform, and the growth of national consciousness began to produce profound changes in government and in social life. The same was also true of the greater part of the continent.

§ 3. *Enlightened Despotism in the Mediterranean States and in Northern Europe*

Experiments in enlightened despotism were also being attempted in the states of the Iberian peninsula and of Italy. There sovereigns undertook reforms with the help of 'enlightened' ministers and of many of their subjects. They were influenced both by the example of the German rulers and by French ideas, and these foreign elements were the more readily assimilated owing to the rise of national consciousness.

Spain began to recover during the reign of Charles III. Apart from the riches of her empire, great sources of wealth lay ready to hand in the irrigation of the soil, the pasturage of sheep, the mines, and the ports. The new king used them to advantage. He found able allies; Florida Blanca and Campomanès were his energetic and devoted servants. But the bourgeoisie, from which they sprang, was the only class capable of giving them support. The ignorant aristocracy neglected their great estates and led a frivolous life at court. The clergy, owning more than a quarter of the land, took refuge from the king's authority in the protection of a Church in which some of the bishops were still appointed by the Pope, the Jesuits still formed an advance guard, and the Inquisition was still on the watch. Although the Northern Provinces had many free peasants, the peasants of Castile and Andalusia were still in a state of wretched serfdom; they were prevented from enclosing their land, by the rules of the system of seasonal hill-pasturing, and kept in constant fear of eviction. Royal policy had also to reckon with the lack of unity in the realm, formed as it was of ancient kingdoms which kept their original differences and defended their special privileges.

On the other hand the monarchy had the advantage that it had no resistance to fear from privileged bodies such as the 'intermediary powers' in France. There was no organized body of nobles, and there were no *Parlements*. Only the clergy was in a position to oppose the ruler. It enjoyed greater prestige than it did in France, for it was trusted by the reformers. In the bourgeois class there sprang up many 'patriotic' and 'economic' societies for the promotion of schemes of reform and technical progress. They had a zeal for the public welfare and a feeling for the national interest.

Charles III was thus able to embark on a policy of strengthening the state. He tightened the bonds of administrative centralization, with the help of 'intendants' working under the encouragement of a Council of Castile and ministers who were alive to the needs of the time. He began the construction of roads which linked the great ports with Madrid, and he completed the road to Cadiz. He protected the Castilian peasants from eviction and permitted peasants in Andalusia to enclose their fields. He encouraged the enterprise of the pioneers of industry who founded free undertakings, such as the cotton-factories of Barcelona, alongside the old traditionalist guilds.

The number of commercial companies increased; commerce found wider scope and gained an increasing momentum.

But this progress was not matched by an improvement in public finances. The king attempted some bold reforms: he brought taxes under official control, and sought to ensure their equal incidence. But his revenue, even so, was much lower than that of the King of France, and it still failed to meet the expenses of a government which remained extravagant. He issued notes which quickly depreciated, and then sought to cover them by the creation of a state bank. But he was unable to find the necessary capital and finally had to abandon the project.

In some other respects he remained conservative. The idea of winning the goodwill of his subjects did not lead him, as it led the other enlightened despots, to recognize the value of a policy of toleration. The educational reforms which he carried out neither showed that he wished to take over public education as an obligation of the state, nor that he was willing to leave free enterprise to develop. As long as the Inquisition served the monarchy it suited him to accept its vigilant protection.

This explains why Spain was neither very influential nor very powerful in Europe. Although her army was very large, it was badly trained; her navy was built abroad, and was manned by wretched crews; and instead of rejoicing at the prosperity of her colonies, she began to be afraid of their rapid development, which made them impatient of her authority.

Nevertheless Charles III won an international reputation for his energetic attempts to control the Church in Spain. In this respect his neighbour Portugal set the example. Governed by the Marquis of Pombal, Joseph I's all-powerful minister, this small kingdom had aroused the interest and admiration of enlightened public opinion in Europe. Pombal introduced many administrative and economic reforms, created an efficient army on the Prussian model, and opened many schools. Lisbon was admired for the speed with which she rose again from her ruins after the terrible earthquake which caused philosophers to review their too optimistic theories of human progress. Above all, Pombal declared war to the death on the Jesuits. He caused the Pope to deny them the right to preach or hear confessions. An attempt upon the king enabled him to involve them with the police on a charge of conspiracy, and to expel them from

Portugal. He even had recourse to the Inquisition to have one of them condemned and burned. His excesses, however, were not judged severely, and he was hailed throughout Europe as an 'enlightened' reformer. Charles III's attack on the Jesuits was still more devastating. He could not tolerate their Ultramontanism. A riot in Madrid provided him with a pretext to have them expelled by a decision of the Council of Castile. It was a surprise move. The Jesuit fathers throughout all Spain were arrested in a single day, and put on shipboard for Italy. The Pope protested; for a long time he refused to receive the exiles. But the Spanish clergy and even the Inquisition resigned themselves to the blow; and the Holy See had to abandon its right to appoint a proportion of the bishops.

It was again Charles III who induced the other Bourbons, in Versailles, Naples, and Parma, to put pressure on the Pope to condemn the Jesuit Order, and in 1773 a bull announced its suppression. The king's victory was both a decisive stage in the battle waged by the 'philosophers' against the Church, and an example for the enlightened despots which was followed by Joseph II.

In the Italian states also, in the second half of the century, a movement of ideas took shape and developed, partly under French influences but partly also under the inspiration of memories of the Renaissance, which paved the way for the Risorgimento and caused a revival of national feeling. The influence of the leaders of the movement spread beyond the borders of the peninsula, and that of Beccaria was felt both in France and in the Russia of Catherine II.

At that time the Italian peninsula was split up into several states, not all of which shared in this movement. Progressive ideas could not be expected of the papal states, or from Venice, where life was one long festival and high duties drove trade from the port, or again from Genoa, whose merchants tended to seek their fortune abroad. But everywhere else rulers sought to introduce reforms, and tried to throw off the yoke of the clergy, to levy taxes more fairly, to emancipate and assist the peasants, and to develop agricultural and industrial production.

Although they tackled the same problems in the same spirit the different rulers achieved different results because they were confronted by different obstacles. In the kingdom of Naples, including Sicily, the brilliant life of the court at Caserta was far too extravagant, and the system of *latifundia* prevented an able minister, Tanucci, from achieving any advances in agriculture. In the Milanese, which belonged to Joseph II, an improved agricultural technique increased production, and Milan prospered. The Church was forced to accept a *concordat* reducing its power, and the suppression of the system of farming the taxes was boldly carried through and brought in large additional resources. Leopold of Habsburg, who was Grand Duke of Tuscany before succeeding Joseph II on the throne, filled the role of enlightened despot much more tactfully than his brother. He was a determined and successful opponent of the clergy. He managed his finances efficiently. He decided to abolish the serfdom of the peasants and the system of mortmain, but he refrained from pressing on too rapidly with the liquidation of the feudal régime. He improved agriculture by means of drainage schemes and abolished the restrictions imposed on artificers by the guilds. Trade prospered, and his free port of Leghorn flourished.

The reforms carried out in the kingdom of Piedmont-Sardinia were still more important and enduring. The peasants were already free, and the growth of a system of rents, in place of the *métayer* system, improved their lot. A flourishing trade grew up, encouraged by the construction of roads across the Alps. With a population of only three millions—which was, however, increasing—the kingdom maintained an army of 30,000 men; and under its own national monarchy it was able to defend its independence against neighbouring Bourbons and Habsburgs. It was thus preparing itself to become the rallying-point for an Italy already swept by the wind of reform and the spirit of liberation.

The two Scandinavian kingdoms also adopted the aims and the methods of enlightened despotism, and showed their beneficent influence. In Denmark, during the long reign of the mad King Christian VII, his doctor Struensee, the queen's favourite, made a preliminary attempt at despotism which was merely a wild adventure. His hasty reforms, entirely modelled on Prussian examples, did not survive his fall, which was engineered by a court intrigue. This marked the beginning of a national reaction and a period of stability. Two great ministers, the elder Bernstorff and his son, both proved themselves more able, more honourable, and more fortunate. When the king's son became regent, the younger Bernstorff, wielding an influence which he retained until his death in 1797, achieved results which gave his country a high reputation in Europe. A large programme of reform was carried out: freedom of thought and of the press was secured by the abolition of the censorship, education was developed, and the penal law and prison system were reformed. Economic policy was inspired by the liberalism of the Physio- crats and resulted in free trade in corn and livestock; and a great programme of agrarian reform restricted feudal rights and liberated the peasants. But the country's position at the entrance to the Baltic exposed her to the ambitions of her neighbours. The diplomacy of the Bernstorffs succeeded in averting danger from abroad, and especially in establishing friendly relations with Russia. Denmark, which had kept its neutrality during the Seven Years War, continued to remain immune during the wars of the Revolution. The firm and intelligent rule of the Bernstorffs, and the peaceful despotism which they exercised, aroused the astonishment and admiration of Europe.

The King of Sweden, Gustavus III, also played an important part. The *coup d'état* which he carried out in 1772 saved his country's independence after a long period of anarchy in which rival factions, dependent upon foreign assistance, had reduced the diet and the monarchy to impotence. Russia, with the aid of Prussia, was already preparing a new 'partition' which was defeated by the king's enterprise. His success was hailed as a victory for French policy: Louis XV's weak govern- ment had taken this opportunity to avenge the loss of prestige inflicted upon her by the partition of Poland. Gustavus III was in fact very much under French influence; he had recently been the petted and honoured guest of Parisian 'salons'; the Versailles government had backed his venture with financial assistance, and French public opinion was on his side.

The constitution which he forced the diet to accept made him a real sovereign if not a despot; and he used the powers which it conferred upon him to carry out a wide programme of reform. Officials were submitted to closer supervision, the courts were kept strictly to their work of justice, and an energetic financial administration corrected inflation and balanced the budget. Internal customs duties were abolished. The freedom of the press was recognized and torture forbidden. At the same time a better trained and organized army and a navy capable of protecting the Baltic coasts defended Sweden from the ambitions of her neighbours.

But a new diet refused to grant the king the increases in taxation which he demanded and which were indispensable for his increasingly ambitious schemes. Seeing Russia involved in an arduous war with the Turks, he sought to recover from her the Finnish lands abandoned by his predecessors. In 1786 he accordingly changed his policy and the character of his government. He attempted to attack Russia and met with a humiliating defeat. He returned to his kingdom determined to break down all opposition, and he imposed on the diet a constitutional law which liberated him from all financial control. But in order to break the resistance of the nobles he had to promise the peasants the abolition of aristocratic privileges. Was the enlightened despot going to turn into a democrat? On the contrary, the French Revolution which broke out at that moment found in him its most bitter enemy. He made his peace with Russia in order to be free to attack it, and summoned all the sovereigns of Europe for a crusade against the revolutionaries. In this role he died by an assassin's hand in 1792.

His brilliant and stormy career illustrated both the advantages which might be derived from enlightened despotism and the dangers which it could bring. Europe was led to see clearly the fundamental division between despotism of this order and the ideals of the French Revolution.

§ 4. *Enlightened Despotism in Russia*

It was immediately after the Seven Years War that Russia, as it were, made her entry into European society. Peter the Great had made a great effort to achieve this result, but after his death in 1725 Russia seemed to hesitate between a policy of continuing his work and one of isolating herself again from Europe. During the reign of Elizabeth, the Russian armies played an important part in the wars of the middle of the century; Russia built many new factories, and her foreign trade, particularly with England, was greatly increased. The young nobles of the court imitated French manners and French elegance. The Academy of Sciences, founded by Peter the Great in the year of his death, stimulated intellectual curiosity, though only among a restricted public. But Europeans generally did not regard as a part of their community a country in which the clergy and ritual were so different from their churches, the population was so ignorant and the economic system so primitive, and the fate of the sovereigns and their favourites lay perpetually at the mercy of palace revolutions.

When, after the assassination of Peter III in 1762, his wife, Princess Catherine of Anhalt, came to the throne by a final *coup d'état*, no one could have foreseen the great transformation which she was destined to bring about in Russia. But this German princess,the heiress and the successor to the work of Peter the Great, was a woman of lively intelligence and wide culture; and it was in the guise of an enlightened despot that she presented herself to foreign opinion. It could not but produce a great impression in other countries when the tsarina summoned her 'Grand Commission', a great consultative assembly consisting of representatives elected by the nobility, the towns, and a section of the peasants. The empress herself drew up a set of 'instructions' for its labours, in which she reconciled the exigencies of autocracy with principles derived from Montesquieu and Beccaria. The debates of the commission showed the difficulty of accepting all the claims which they made. It was hardly surprising, therefore, when their discussions were interrupted and their meetings adjourned. Catherine was now engaged in fighting the Turks and defeating the Poles. The partition of Poland and the peace of Kainardji which she imposed on the Turks were two brilliant successes which augmented her prestige; and the serious revolt of the Cossacks under Pougatchev, which drew the serfs in its train, is sufficient to explain why Catherine was unable to carry out the domestic reforms which were expected from her reign. But her reputation, maintained by her able correspondence with the 'philosophers', was not diminished: indeed, it was now that Diderot came, in answer to her request, to discuss with her at length all the plans she had in mind.

She was as clever as Frederic the Great and anxious to create her own legend; but would it be right to condemn her as insincere in the part which she played? On the contrary, all the evidence shows that she was strongly attracted by new ideas, and that she ardently longed to modernize her state. But she would not sacrifice an iota of her power, and she had to adjust her desires to what was possible in Russian conditions. Her policy was one which encountered the gravest difficulties.

She had, in the first place, to reckon with a vast extent of territory, impossible to administer by reason of its size. The central government could not cover it, and the eight governments created by Peter the Great were still far too large for administrative efficiency. Moreover, Russian society did not lend itself easily to direction. Catherine was aware of the important part which the peasants played in the state, forming as they did the vast majority of the population. But the greater part of the peasant class belonged as serfs to the nobles, and her chief task was to enlist in the service of the state an aristocracy whose ambitions had continually increased since the death of Peter the Great.

The nobles desired to throw off the duties of public service which Peter the Great had forced upon them, and they had succeeded in gaining their desire under the weak rule of Peter III. They asked in the Senate for a share in the exercise of sovereign power, and when Catherine came to the throne she had difficulty in refusing their request. They wanted to govern their estates in complete independence of the government, and they had gained recognition of their right to imprison their serfs and even to deport them to Siberia. They resented the great possessions of the Church, and they had made Peter III decide to confiscate them. Finally, the rise of a class of merchants and industrialists in the towns ran counter to their desire to keep the ownership and control of all undertakings in their own hands.

The two great reforms carried out by the czarina—the administrative decree of 1775, and the Charter of the Nobles of 1785—were an answer to the political problems thus raised. She divided her country into forty regional governments, each sub-divided into a number of districts. The administration of these units was in the hands of the nobles, who chose the officials among themselves under a president who was a marshal of the nobility. But these officials were supervised and controlled by imperial lieutenants who received their orders directly from the czarina. This system was meant both to please the nobles and to bring them under the control of the autocracy. After the Pougatchev revolt they showed themselves more ready to accept the protection of the royal power.

But there were other reforms of a different character which Catherine still desired to achieve. She never, indeed, promulgated the Peasants' Charter which she had planned, nor did she improve conditions for the serfs: on the contrary, like her predecessors, she continued to strengthen the great nobles by a generous distribution of 'souls' to her favourites. But a charter for the towns established a system of municipal government by councils elected by the inhabitants. It was not her fault if the nobles, always hostile to the towns, refused to take part in it, or if the merchants, satisfied with managing their own business, took little interest in municipal affairs, which still, in fact, remained under the control of the central government. Her economic policy, at any rate, was partly inspired by the liberalism of the Physiocrats. She was satisfied with moderate tariffs, and she left her subjects free to undertake industrial and commercial enterprises. Russian historians have recently thrown light on the important advances made by Russian industry in the second half of the eighteenth century. In spite of the hostility of the nobles and the concessions made to them by the czarina, the merchants succeeded in raising Russian industry almost to the level of other European countries. It was not until the nineteenth century that Russia failed to keep pace with the industrial progress of western Europe, and the gulf separating her from the rest of the continent began to widen once more.

'Philosophic' ideas had a marked influence upon the organization of local government. The exercise of jurisdiction was separated from the administration, and entrusted to separate courts for the different social classes, which elected judges from their own members. A 'Court of Equity', on the English model, gave decisions which were based not on the text of the laws but on the principles of fair dealing. Local government was expressly charged with the duty of providing a service of education and a service of public assistance. Although the number of schools was still ludicrously small, Catherine cherished the ambition of forming a great network of public education.

She also tried to stimulate intellectual life. She allowed private persons to establish publishing houses, and she founded a review to which she herself contributed. She was soon offended by the lack of respect with which journalists treated the writings of 'Grandmother'. In the end she confiscated the works of Novikoff and closed the Masonic Lodge which he founded. She did not approve of writers demanding that the nobles should share in the conduct of government, or taking pains, like Prince Surbatov, to improve the condition of peasants, or going to the length, as Radiscev did, of demanding the abolition of serfdom. It was for the enlightened despot himself to deal with such matters. During her reign, however, Russia developed a taste for intellectual discussion; there was now a body of journalists and a theatre, and along with increasing numbers of translations of foreign works there was also the beginning of a national literature.

The European world was accordingly ready to welcome this new-comer, destined to offer so rich a contribution to its life. The strange oriental spectacle presented by the extravagances of Potemkin, the favourite of the czarina, astonished but fascinated Europe. Catherine II seemed the most original and the most daring of all the incarnations of enlightened despotism.

§ 5. *England*

While the continent was carrying out various experiments in enlightened despotism, England was making very different but equally instructive experiments. George III's desire to take over control of the government himself was the cause of a prolonged crisis; but English institutions finally emerged victorious during the ministry of the younger Pitt. The sudden extension of her empire presented England with new problems which she was at first unable to solve, and she was even compelled to recognize the independence of the United States. There was a strong surge of political and social demands in a new and developing society which was simultaneously stirred by a religious revival and by economic changes of exceptional magnitude.

The transformation in British economy after 1760 was so great and so sudden that historians have described it by the significant term 'the Industrial Revolution'. In fact this revolution was not confined to industry, nor was industrial development, as it was a century later, accompanied by a decline in agriculture. On the contrary, the growth of population made an increase in agricultural production necessary, and progress in technique made the increase possible. As early as 1731 Jethro Tull had taught new methods for the rotation of crops and recommended the extension of leys. At the same time Lord Townshend set an example by applying modern methods to the management of his estates. But the new agriculture involved fundamental changes in the system of landed property, since the existence of 'commons', and even more the presence of 'open fields' in which small-holders cultivated their strips side by side, prevented the use of the new techniques. Accordingly the big landowners forced their smaller neighbours to agree to the inclosure of these 'commons' in their own estates. Parliament voted private bills to enforce this policy, and the number of these bills rose from 100 in the first half of the century to nearly 3,000 during the second. The majority of the small yeomen farmers disappeared. The growing demand for industrial labour led to their being absorbed by the towns.

Side by side with the old woollen industry there was now developing a new industry of the manufacture of cotton goods, which the English had hitherto imported, but which they now began to make for themselves. Unhampered by the outworn traditions which weighed upon the old industry, the new cotton industry made use of a brilliant series of inventions. John Kay's flying shuttle of 1733, and Arkwright's water-frame, were followed by Cartwright's power-looms in 1785. By the use of rotating cylinders and mechanical shuttles, spinning and weaving could be carried on on a large scale. At the same time the metal industry began to make rapid progress owing to the discovery of processes which enabled coal to be used in foundries and for the manufacture of iron and steel. It was the age of the great iron-founders, of whom Wilkinson was the prototype. Finally, in 1769, Watt's steam-engine appeared, and after it had been adopted in Boulton's works gave iron-founders and spinners the motive power which they needed.

Large-scale modern industry was thus born in England. On the continent the old crafts had only to meet the competition of hand-workers and of the merchant capitalists who supplied the labour engaged in domestic industry with raw materials and sometimes with tools. In English industry, on the other hand, the coming of the machine age opened up immense possibilities for the future. But it also disturbed and revolutionized English social life. Labour, driven from the countryside by the inclosures, became concentrated in the towns of a new England of the 'Black Country' which was growing up beside the old England and was soon to outstrip it. After the end of the century the increase in population, brought about by industrial development, presented a serious problem to which Malthus's book drew attention. The labour proletariat and industrial capitalism assumed dimensions which were alarming to the state; for how could it now pretend to control or regulate economic life? By 1776 Adam Smith was already arguing for the necessity for economic liberty. On the other hand the question arose whether it was not the duty of the state to intervene and to introduce laws for the protection of labour which would prevent exploitation of the working classes. Courage failed it, and Parliament, on the contrary, decided to prohibit combinations or trade unions of workers. The state was content to salve its conscience by an alteration in the system of Poor Relief, which was for the future to give money assistance to compensate for inadequate wages.

The English, however, were helped to a better understanding of the obligations which social evolution imposed upon them by a religious revival which coincided with the Industrial Revolution. During the first half of the century the Anglican Church, influenced by the intellectual movement of the time, was less concerned with its religious mission than with preaching a moral code inspired by rationalist theories. It had lost its enthusiasm; and even Dissenters were only the pale descendants of the terrible Puritans of the seventeenth century. From 1740 onwards John Wesley and Whitefield troubled the apathy of their fellow countrymen; open-air preachers had enthusiastic audiences and made many converts. Methodism began as a movement within the Church of England, and it soon made many recruits among its members. The peculiar organization developed by the Methodists, which brought them firmly under central control, served as an example to the dissenting sects who were affected by its influence. Later, at a time when Methodism had lost its original impetus though still continuing to make new converts, the moral revolution which it had caused was still strong enough to produce other results. It was the inspiration, at the end of the century, of the Evangelical movement in the Church of England, with its urgent appeal to the conscience of England to alleviate the sufferings of the people. Since the state showed itself incapable of action, private individuals on every side demanded and attempted reforms. Howard protested against the harsh prison régime; Raikes turned his attention to children and founded the Sunday schools; above all, Wilberforce began his campaign for the abolition of slavery.

In a society which was in a state of transition, political life was

inevitably disturbed, the more as the policy of the king had provoked a serious crisis. It was not that George III, as has often
been said, sought to establish a dictatorship, or that putting himself at the head of the Tory party he had driven the Whigs out
of office. The truth is rather that in a political world divided into
personal cliques the exercise of the royal patronage was directed
to achieving a docile parliamentary majority and restoring the
direction of public affairs to the Crown. George III did not
achieve this aim until North, who was the instrument of his
policy, formed his ministry in 1770. He kept North in office for
thirteen years, until 1783, when his fall brought royal ambitions
definitely to an end. England not only had to submit to the
disastrous loss of the United States; royal intervention in political struggles now brought about an alinement of formidable
forces in opposition to the Crown. The Whig opponents of
George III were at last compelled by his action to form a real
party, supported by an aristocracy which was still in control of
Parliament. At the same time a democratic movement was
beginning. The dangerous agitator Wilkes was elected and re-
elected to the House of Commons where he was persistently
refused his seat. The press became a weapon whose power was
shown by the campaign of the letters of Junius. Parliament had
to resign itself to the publication of its debates; and it was in
vain that the courts attempted to limit the power of juries in
the trial of press cases. A new word appeared: 'Radicalism'
became a term for describing the agitation for democratic
reforms, which included the reform of the electoral system, that
is to say, of Parliament itself. Finally, a new generation of politicians arose, attracted by Fox's irresistible charm and the preco-
cious genius of the younger Pitt, who were not content to be the
obedient servants of the Crown. The crisis, begun by North's
retirement, ended in the rise of Pitt to power.

Pitt won a decisive electoral victory in 1784. He owed it to
the influence of the king, who acted in his cause in order to
checkmate the Whigs; but he also owed it to his own popularity.
The memory of his father, his own authority, which was already
great, and the very isolation to which he was reduced by the
abstention of all the titled and discredited politicians, all contributed to his success. In Parliament he formed a disciplined
party no longer dependent on the Crown. A friend of Wilberforce and a disciple of Adam Smith, he was the leader of the

'new Tory' programme of reform. He was forced, it is true, to abandon many of his projects. He did not achieve the electoral reform which he believed to be necessary in order to strengthen the authority of Parliament; and he had to give up the measures by which he sought to disarm the hostility of Ireland. But he succeeded in reorganizing the governments of India and Canada; and above all he achieved, with a masterly skill, great financial reforms which were notable for the establishment of a new sinking fund and for a sweeping simplification of the system of taxes. These reforms set England on the path of economic liberalism, and provided her with the resources which enabled her to withstand the strain of future wars. England thus set a notable example to the French monarchy, which was in the throes of a disastrous financial crisis, and also to the enlightened despots in the rest of Europe, who kept the economy of their states entirely under their own control.

Having taught itself to believe in the decline, and even the approaching ruin, of English parliamentary institutions and the British empire, Europe might well be astonished by this recovery. Blackstone's lucid analysis painted for its inspection a picture of a political system founded on liberty, while Bentham's early criticisms were beginning to give expression to the progressive tendencies which inspired the Radicals. Lastly the writings of Burke, and his reflections on the function of parties and on the evolution of the Whigs, showed Europe a political society capable of pursuing an ideal of freedom without disturbing the actual tenor of its life.

It was evident that this society, which had been the scene of bitter political struggles, must expect to meet violent democratic and social demands. But there were deep springs of moral strength in the religious faith which was strong in many of its members, and the great progress made in its economy gave the nation confidence. The aristocracy, who controlled the ministers and Parliament and managed local government through the justices of the peace, felt itself secure from danger. It knew nothing of the preoccupations and anxieties which harassed the ruling classes of the Victorian era in spite of their prosperity. It did not, as yet, see the growth of a new industrial aristocracy as the menace to itself which it was to become in the nineteenth century. On the contrary, it welcomed the first representatives of the new class who were called by Pitt to sit in the House of Lords. Unlike the continental nobility, the English aristocracy enjoyed no fiscal privileges, and having no privileges to defend they had no idea of opposing social progress.

They could take life easily, without reserves. It was a life of luxury, often dissolute but always brilliant, in which men could live well at very little cost, with innumerable servants at their beck and call in receipt of very low wages. In Marlborough's palace at Blenheim or Newcastle's at Stowe, and in the country houses of the squires, the gentry gave themselves up to the pleasures of fox-hunting and sport. The pleasures of the intellect also had their place. It was a very cultured aristocracy, which in its refinement and unerring good taste was again very different from that of the Victorian era. The architecture it liked had a classical style which corrected any defects of solidity; and it preferred furniture of a type which combined comfort with elegance. Its members encouraged the theatre, where Garrick was now at the height of his powers. They inspired the school of portrait-painters which made English painting famous; and the leaders of this school, Reynolds and Gainsborough, were at work till the beginning of the Revolution. But the most characteristic personality and the most shrewd observer in this society was certainly Doctor Johnson. His dictionary and his conversation give the best picture of an intelligent and self-confident England, determined to grow without allowing political or social troubles to interrupt the continuity of its life.

§ 6. *France*

France offered Europe the totally different spectacle of the decline and finally the fall of an absolute monarchy. Even the government's attempts at asserting its authority soon degenerated into the convulsive efforts of exhaustion and weakness. In spite of the praises lavished on it by the 'philosophers', the rulers of France did not adopt the system of enlightened despotism. It was no such idea that inspired Louis XV's sudden burst of energy at the end of his reign. In 1770 he dismissed Choiseul to avoid being involved in a fresh war against the English, and on the other hand he supported the vigorous measures of financial retrenchment adopted by the Abbé Terray; he also allowed the Chancellor Maupeou to crush the intolerable resistance offered by the *Parlements*. Their members were dismissed and replaced by new magistrates who confined themselves to administering justice without playing any part in politics. But the king did not change his own way of life; he did not put himself at the service of the state, as a true enlightened despot would have done. On the contrary, it was at this period that the French court paid without question for the costly extravagances of Madame du Barry.

Louis XV had only attempted by a violent effort to revive his failing finances for the moment, even if it were at the cost of bankruptcy. At his accession Louis XVI immediately put an end to Maupeou's effort to reform the magistrates. The old *Parlements* were recalled and again renewed their dangerous opposition. In the new reign there were, it is true, many members of the administration, particularly among the 'intendants', who held progressive ideas. They encouraged agriculture, tried to correct fiscal injustice, and increased the amount of welfare services. Their long periods of office enabled them to exert a beneficial influence, and their memory is kept green in the fine monuments which they erected in provincial towns, such as those of Tourny at Bordeaux. But their sporadic efforts could not achieve results without the backing of the royal will.

No firm support was given by Louis XVI to the progressive ministers he appointed, of whom Turgot was the first. Nor, again, were these ministers guided by the principles of enlightened despotism; they were moved by liberal ideas. Their political liberalism was expressed in Turgot's plan for 'provincial municipalities' and in the more timid project of 'provincial assemblies' which Necker began to put into practice in two provinces. Both of these were evidences of the desire to form a body of persons which would represent the people at a local level. But they failed in face of the hostility of the *Parlements*, which were determined to oppose the establishment of other bodies that might compete with them for control of the government or attack their own privileges.

Economic liberalism gained ground because the Physiocrats had proved its merits, and more particularly because the evolution of the French economic system favoured its growth. Immediately after the Seven Years War, clear-sighted administrators like Bertin and Trudain tried to secure the free movement of corn in the country, to abolish useless pastures, and to divide up commons. They wanted to encourage new agricultural techniques, as had been done in England; but they also wished to increase the number of small farms, which had already become a characteristic feature of French life. Turgot courageously supported the free movement of corn, as well as the abolition of *corvées* and of the corporations. This would have established a free régime in agriculture and industry. The boldness of his policy roused such fierce resistance that the king quickly abandoned it. His successor Necker was chary of continuing his policy; the goodwill he enjoyed both in the 'salons' and in the business world enabled him to borrow on a considerable scale, but at a costly rate of interest, and he confined himself to carrying out some administrative reforms. When Calonne reintroduced Turgot's policy in the Assembly of Notables, it was, or at any rate it appeared to be, the desperate gesture of a gambler who was at his wit's end.

Yet liberalism answered the needs of the social structure of France. France was conspicuous among other countries for the number of its small peasant proprietors, who farmed their land by hereditary title and were regarded as its owners. The old corporations were reduced to impotence by the competition of the merchant capitalists, who established, for instance, a free industrial centre at Roubaix in spite of the corporations of Lille. The development of trade was another factor which impelled the government towards a policy of freedom. It had already been obliged to allow the French West Indies to enter into trade relations with foreign colonies. Vergennes made the experiment of a trade treaty for the reduction of tariffs on English goods, and he also concluded other treaties with Russia and the Netherlands. Even the disorder of the finances and the multiplication of loans, which enriched the bankers, served to stimulate the 'money-managers' to encourage in their turn a crop of new undertakings.

But the monarchy paid no heed to this economic evolution. Louis XVI did not seem to understand that the national prosperity resulting from a policy of liberalism would enable him to meet his deficit without any increase of the taxes. It would have been enough if he had improved the system of tax-collection and consented to make economies; but he was incapable of coming to any decision. The government remained dependent on the court, which was a crushing burden on the budget with its useless and costly charges and its continually increasing mass of pensions. Neither Turgot nor Necker brought about any effective improvement.

The king was therefore reduced to meeting his expenses by incurring loans on terms which became increasingly onerous; and here again he was opposed by the *Parlements*, who rose in resistance to defend the nation. Their clamorous hostility finally ruined the credit of the government, and made it impossible for it to obtain any new resources. A financial crisis then precipitated the fall of the *ancien régime*.

But the bad financial policy of the government was not the only factor which brought about its fall. The catastrophe was hastened by the economic situation and the rise of prices which, as we have seen, had been in progress for half a century. The high price of corn, aggravated before 1789 by a series of bad harvests, only benefited those farmers who were able to sell their crops. This was only the case with a small number of peasants. The others, like the majority of the population, suffered severely from the rise in feudal charges and ecclesiastical tithes and from the rising cost of bread. The dwindling of their resources also brought about a crisis in the vineyards. Reduced sales of wine, which the people gave up buying in order to buy bread, reduced the vine-growers to poverty.

A land-tax falling on large estates and enabling the government to take advantage of the rise in rents would have been the only method of restoring financial equilibrium and relieving the masses. But after the fall of Machault the monarchy had no longer the vigour to impose such a tax. On the contrary it permitted, during the last years of the *ancien régime*, a feudal recrudescence, which benefited the privileged classes. Not only did they evade taxation and retain a monopoly of office (in the eighteenth century the higher ecclesiastical posts were held only by nobles, and Louis XVI still excluded commoners from the higher ranks of the army); they also wanted to keep for themselves all the profit from agricultural progress. They diverted a large part of the property of the communes to their own use: they introduced a revision of 'terriers' which increased the burden of feudal dues. The French aristocracy, excluded from the government by the monarchy, also isolated itself from the nation by its own selfishness.

They devoted all their leisure and their income to the pursuit of a polished social life; they created an enchanting background for their amusements, which not only charmed their contemporaries but continued even afterwards to exercise its spell on European society. They gave themselves up to a gay and brilliant play of wit, which found its home in houses of a classical style of architecture, made lighter, simpler, and purer by the genius of Gabriel, and which had for its scene salons whose very furniture, by the elegance of its form and the variety of its colour, seemed to set the stage for a joyous life exempt from every care. They were surrounded by the masterpieces of an uninterrupted series of great artists. The art of Watteau, with its melancholy suggestions, Boucher's nymphs, Nattier's portraits, La Tour's pastels, the domestic scenes of Chardin, the languorous paintings of Greuze, and the more piquant canvases of Fragonard—all these formed an unforgettable background to aristocratic life both in the small apartments at Versailles and in the salons of Paris. It was all reflected at Sans Souci, St. Petersburg, Schönbrunn, and Stockholm; it will never be effaced from the eyes and the memory of Europe.

But in its life of pleasure, and even in its intellectual audacity, this aristocratic society seemed to be trying, above everything else, to hide its head in the sand. Their air of assurance showed thoughtlessness rather than confidence. In this they differed from the English aristocracy, which took part in the evolution of its country's life. They also differed from the aristocratic classes of other countries in Europe, where aristocratic power and privileges were not seriously challenged.

France played a very different role from that of other nations in the European society of the end of the eighteenth century. The weakness and bankruptcy of her government were a striking contrast to the energy shown in the activities of the enlightened despots. Unlike them, the French government was unable to impose the duties of public service upon the classes of which French society was composed. It made almost no attempt to assume responsibility for public assistance or education, and it was only through fear that it became resigned to showing a little tolerance. It won no gratitude by allowing philosophical writings to be widely disseminated, or by restoring civil rights to Protestants in 1787. The whole intellectual movement, and all the ideas of reform, found expression, and made their way, outside the government and in opposition to it.

It was the bourgeois class which gave power to this movement and vogue to these ideas. The bourgeoisie played a much more important role in France than in the rest of Europe. The groups which composed it were so many and so varied that it is difficult to define its extent. But its progress was eased and its influence increased by economic developments, by the system of selling offices, and by the growth of intellectual life.

The peasant class also was more important in France than it was elsewhere. The wretchedness of its condition should not lead us to underestimate its strength. In central and eastern Europe the great enlightened despots were reluctant to take any steps in its favour which might break their alliance with the nobility. The only ruler who had the courage to attempt such a policy was Joseph II, and he failed completely. Serfdom therefore survived in these countries. It was a crushing burden in Russia: it was still very harsh in eastern Germany; it only became less severe in the Rhineland. France, on the contrary, had now only a very small number of serfs; a large part of the peasant class consisted of small landowners or farmers; in the north a third, and in certain regions of the south a half, of the area of cultivated land belonged to the peasants.

The frontier of serfdom, which almost follows the line of the Elbe, is one of the essential factors in the history of Europe. At a time when there was a tendency for currents of thought to spread over the whole of the continent, and the diffusion of ideas and tastes was beginning to create a uniform civilization in Europe, the cleavage of European society into two opposing worlds of different social structures still persisted, and was even accentuated. In the wars of the Revolution, two different Europes confronted one another.

France, too, was the only great continental country to develop into a nation. Neither the Prussian state nor (it goes without saying) the Habsburg possessions had any national unity; and the Germans were only bound to one another by intellectual links. In France, on the other hand, the bourgeoisie and the peasant class formed the constituent elements of a French nation. In the past it had been the monarchy which had given unity to the kingdom; now it was in opposition to it, or at any rate outside it, that a sense of national unity developed. The French people was drawing together against the privileged elements. The nation was in opposition to the court. At the time of the intense agitation in 1788 and 1789, which preceded the Assembly of the States General, those Frenchmen who wished to reform the monarchy began to call themselves 'patriots' and claimed that they formed a 'national party'. Thus it was France that began to act the drama of the Revolution before the watching eyes of Europe.

THE PERIOD OF THE FRENCH REVOLUTION AND NAPOLEON

§ 1. *Europe and the French Revolution*

We need not trace the succession of changes in the revolutionary crisis which disorganized France for a decade and created a new country out of the ruins of the old régime. What we have to note here is the effects of the crisis in shattering the foundations of European society and opening new horizons for the future.

What was the immediate significance of the events of 1789? The event which created the greatest sensation, and which even today epitomizes the Revolution, was the capture of the Bastille on 14 July. The fall of this old Parisian fortress announced the death of the old régime to the whole of Europe. To contemporaries the Bastille was a symbol of this régime. In reality, however, the importance and the significance of the fourteenth of July lay in the events by which it was accompanied.

The Parisians had taken up arms to support a national assembly engaged in a conflict with the court; and it would be true to say that France was already in a state of revolution from the time when Louis XVI decided to call the States General. Since the deputies of the Third Estate were elected by all tax-payers, and since under the fiscal system of the monarchy taxes were mainly paid by the people, the elections had been, in effect, a consultation of popular opinion. The lists of grievances (*cahiers*) put forward by the electors represented the nation's wishes.

When the States General assembled on 5 May the deputies of the Third Estate believed themselves to be qualified to speak for the country. They could not resign themselves to being the third order in the kingdom, by the side of the clergy and nobles. Forming half the numerical strength of the Assembly, they demanded a method of common debates and with it a system of voting by heads and not by orders. Convinced that they alone represented the vast majority of Frenchmen, and aware that the lower ranks of the clergy pinned their hopes on them and many of the nobles shared their desire for reform, they judged that practically the whole of the nation was ranged against the

privileged minority embodied in the court. They formed themselves of their own accord into a national assembly, and took
oaths to one another that they would not part until they had
created a new constitution. Louis XVI yielded, but the court
prepared to suppress the Assembly by the use of force. The
rising of the Parisians saved the deputies.

The 14th of July is also important for the immediate repercussions caused in the country by the Parisian revolt. It started
the strange panic, called 'the Great Terror', whose causes are
still baffling but whose results are clear. Peasants everywhere
took up arms to protect themselves against an unknown danger;
they marched on the castles of the nobles, demanding to be
freed from their serfdom. This liberation had already been
largely attained when the Assembly itself was induced to proclaim the abolition of feudal rights on the night of 4 August. This,
however, was not as easy to carry into effect as people thought at
the time. The Assembly itself, when it decided to abolish serfdom, proposed a system of compensation for the surrender of
certain feudal rights. That did not prevent the general revolt
which ensued from precipitating the rapid liberation of the
people.

The people, at the same time, attempted to set up a new
organization for themselves. It is notable that they felt at once
the need for this organization. Paris set the example. On the
evening of 14 July the bourgeois, seeing the insurgents in possession of the city, successfully set up a new municipal government
and formed a national guard to enforce its authority. Many
other towns followed suit, and also formed municipalities supported by national guards. But that was not enough. Towns
and country districts immediately began to form 'Federations',
which were quickly extended to a whole province and then to
groups of neighbouring provinces. The spontaneous movement
towards 'Federation', in which the government and the Assembly had no part, culminated after a year, on 14 July 1790, in the
proclamation of the National Federation in Paris by delegates
from all parts of the kingdom. The French people was now
sure of what it wished to do: it wished to avoid the anarchy
threatened by the fall of the monarchy, on which national unity
had hitherto been founded, and to proclaim the voluntary
agreement of the people still to remain united by the bonds of
mutual 'fraternity'. The oath of loyalty taken that day by the

PLATE 34

The Oath of the Tennis Court, June 1789. After David

members, and first of all by the king himself, 'to the nation, the law, and the king', expressed the significance of this crucial event. Monarchy *jure divino* gave place to a monarchy founded on the national will; but the victorious nation was to obey laws which it had itself laid down through its own representatives.

As early as August 1789 those representatives had already begun to prepare a constitution, and had at once decided to preface its terms by a Declaration of the Rights of Man. In that they followed the famous example of the United States. But they were concerned, even more, to express their belief that the principles which they followed were valid for all humanity, and that their Revolution had an international significance. The Declaration of the Rights of Man and the Citizen claimed to be universal. The constitution which followed was, it is true, based upon considerations which were peculiar to France. The introduction of an electoral qualification, which deprived more than half the population of the right to vote, showed the desire of the French bourgeoisie to control the government. A strict limitation of the power of the king showed the Assembly's deep mistrust of the monarchy. Many of the articles in the Declaration itself showed that the deputies were afraid to push their principles too far at this early stage, and that they were anxious to reserve the powers necessary to enforce the authority of the government and, even more, to defend the rights of property-owners against the claims of the people. Nevertheless, with amazing speed, the Assembly carried out far-reaching reforms —administrative, judicial, and fiscal—which established a new France governed and administered by the chosen representatives of the sovereign people. The Declaration itself proclaimed, on the basis of the sovereignty of the people, that liberty and equality must be an integral part of every human society.

At first the national character of the Revolution was not properly understood in Europe; but its international significance aroused emotion and enthusiasm in a very large public. The striking tribute of Fox, who exclaimed of the taking of the Bastille, 'How much the greatest event it is that ever happened in the world, and how much the best', is enough to show the hopes and the interest awakened by the news from France. The sudden appearance of a sort of liberal democracy fascinated those continental countries which were still under the yoke of despotism and the feudal system. It was also of particular interest to the English, whose institutions, still dominated by the aristocracy, were no longer in agreement with their social life, which had been rapidly transformed by economic developments.

In the Mediterranean countries the influence of the Revolution was at first scarcely perceptible. But in the Austrian Low Countries, where the harsh reforms of Joseph II had in June 1789 resulted in the revolt of Brabant, the Belgians, fighting to defend their ancient privileges, allied themselves with democrats who formed armed bands which drove the Austrian troops from the country. In the neighbouring bishopric of Liége the French example gave rise to disturbances which forced the bishop to flee. French ideas penetrated into Switzerland and the Rhineland through Alsace, which was ardently revolutionary from the beginning. In 1792 the Rhineland was invaded by French armies, which were eagerly welcomed by the 'Club of Mainz'. Its president was Förster, whose enthusiasm did not represent the general feelings of the people of the Rhineland. They were sympathetic, however, towards the Revolution and irritated by the reactionary policy of their petty sovereigns.

All the greatest German thinkers had a lively sense of the magnitude of events in France. Even Schiller's hostility and Goethe's reserve were evidence of the fears which they felt at the disturbance caused by the Revolution in the free development of their intellectual life. In Hamburg Klopstock sang its praises. Herder, and even more Wieland, in his paper the *German Mercury*, brought a sympathetic judgement to developments in France. The philosophy of Fichte was formed under the influence of the Revolution: so too, in its inception, was the moral theory of his master Kant. But it is difficult to estimate how far these writers were giving expression to the feelings of the German people itself. In the Prussian states the French example did not diminish appreciation of the reforms introduced by Frederic's enlightened despotism. On the whole, the principles of civic liberty and equality proclaimed by France had only value in German eyes in so far as they fitted the framework of social ethics which Germany herself could best supply. This explains why the excesses of the French Revolution soon alienated Germany.

In England the Revolution, in its first beginnings, attracted determined followers. Following Fox's lead, the Whigs saw in it a replica of their own revolution of 1688, of which they were at that moment celebrating the centenary. The Radicals, with a better understanding of its significance, saw in it encouragement for their campaign for electoral and parliamentary reform. Thomas Paine defended the French principles in his *Rights of Man*, which was warmly acclaimed. They were afterwards carried to their extremest conclusion, in fact to the point of anarchy, by the philosopher Godwin, the apostle of *Political Justice*; while Bentham, the future leader of the Radical movement, attempted to direct the policy of the French Assembly through the medium of Mirabeau. In 1791 a Corresponding Society was founded, which was able, in virtue of the very moderate subscription required of its members, to direct its propaganda to a much wider public than previous political societies.

But Burke, in his *Reflections*, had already made his famous protest, and proclaimed the menace of the French Revolution to all European communities. It was natural that an Englishman should have been the first to realize the menace. In the attempt to create a new state by the application of abstract principles, without reference to the traditions of its past, France had embarked on an enterprise which was contrary to the English conception of a political society as a concrete reality, a living organism, developing by its own natural process of growth and the continuity of its life. Burke was not familiar with the administrative work of the Constituent Assembly, and he had not grasped the strength of the spontaneous national movement which inspired the French people. But he pointed out the danger of an attempt made by theorists, in the pursuit of an imaginary ideal, which might also involve other countries in its risks.

The progress of the French Revolution, and especially the conflict between Louis XVI and his subjects, finally alarmed other sovereigns. They could no longer cherish the illusion that the disturbances in France furthered their own ends by weakening her position in Europe. On their side the French, alarmed by the intrigues between foreign sovereigns and Louis XVI, were eventually induced to decide that they must be ended by force; the war between Revolutionary France and Europe began in the spring of 1792. Could the Revolution have been victorious in France without spreading beyond her frontiers? The answer is that the events which preceded the rupture—particularly the incident which set the German princes who owned lands in Alsace, from which they drew feudal revenues, in opposition to a revolutionary France determined to liberate all her citizens from feudal dues—showed that the new French system of law was incompatible with the old law of Europe. The Revolution ended by adopting a policy first of expansion and then of conquest. In the autumn of 1792 the National Convention announced its determination to liberate the peoples of the neighbouring countries which it had invaded and to 'revolutionize' their territories. A little later, challenging a coalition of sovereigns which was joined by England in the beginning of 1793, it began the conquest of its 'natural frontiers'.

The France of 1793 seemed to Europe very different from the France of 1789. She had very few supporters. No country understood her or realized her strength. She was confronted by a formidable coalition, composed of all the great European powers with the one exception of Russia. Invaded from the north and the east, and faced by serious risings in the west and south, the Convention seemed bound to succumb. But it won the day. At the end of the year it had driven the enemy forces from its territory, and in the summer of 1794 its armies were again on the Rhine.

The Convention won the victory by means of a reign of terror. The terror was the work of a 'revolutionary government', imposing a ruthless dictatorship through a Committee of Public Safety that dominated the Convention from which it had itself sprung. The committee enforced a strict system of centralization through its agents, the *représentants en mission*, who were themselves guided and supported by the Jacobin Club.

The other countries of Europe saw only the excesses of this régime, and they were horrified by what they saw. They did not understand its power, because they did not realize that it was the expression of the national will. Historians have since shown that most of the institutions of the revolutionary government— the committees of superintendence, the political police, and the popular societies—arose spontaneously at a local level before being officially created by the Assembly. The chief acts of the government were in response to the demands of the people, who had achieved universal suffrage in August 1792. The distribution of the possessions of the clergy and the *émigrés* turned the peasants into ardent supporters of the Revolution. The enthusiasm of the 'volunteers' enabled the Convention to impose conscription, and even to introduce the civil and military 'requisition' of the whole population in the cause of national defence.

But the spectacle of factions savagely engaged in internal feuds concealed the unity of France from the eyes of foreign observers. They thought that they saw a caricature of political parties, while the vast majority of the population had no other party than that of the 'Patriots' who stood on guard against enemies both at home and abroad. Just as they had been slow to understand the national character of the 1789 movement, they also misunderstood Jacobinism, which, in spite of all its excesses, was the expression of a national feeling. How could they have understood its significance, when they saw it only as an incongruous combination of theoretical idealism and personal intrigues? Europe had not yet witnessed a revolutionary democracy, for the English and American Revolutions could give her no guidance there. She was present, without knowing it, at the birth of a new force, which was to form one of the essential elements of French political life down to the present day. She gradually learnt to understand it and to recognize its presence in future revolutions.

This also explains why Europe was so bewildered by the peculiarly difficult problem which always confronts contemporaries at the end of a revolution. She expected a bourgeois reaction after the Terror, and she was acute enough to have little belief in the restoration of monarchy. But she could not understand how France, now split by irreconcilable feuds, and in the throes of a severe financial crisis, could maintain her armies far beyond her frontiers, surround herself with conquered countries newly organized in her own image as 'Sister Republics', and gradually impose peace on her enemies. If Europe at that stage foresaw military dictatorship, she naturally failed to imagine the exceptional role which Bonaparte was to play.

§ 2. *Napoleon and Europe*

When Napoleon seized power by the *coup d'état* of Brumaire (Nov. 1799) he created a new kind of state in Europe. The domestic achievements of the consulate marked at once the end of the Revolution and the achievement of the reforms of the system of Enlightened Despotism. The constitution of the Year VIII gave the first consul absolute executive and administrative power, and enabled him to throw off parliamentary and

electoral control. The legislature was split by the creation of two
assemblies, the one responsible for discussing and the other for
making laws, and was thus reduced to impotence. The framing
of the laws by a council of state dependent on the first consul left
the representatives of the people no real part in the government.
Moreover, an electoral system which replaced the election of
deputies by the introduction of mere lists of candidates left the
country no means of expressing its opinions. It is true that the
country was asked to approve the new régime by means of a
plebiscite, and was afterwards to give its opinion on the establishment of the consulate as a life office and on the creation of the
empire. But these popular votes were illusory, since they were
taken at the height of Bonaparte's popularity when the opposition had no means of criticizing his action. Napoleon thus
showed Europe how a democracy could be induced to sacrifice
all its liberties. His example was to be remembered by dictators
of the future.

The creation of a centralized administration in a framework
of democracy taught Europe another lesson. Bonaparte rapidly
installed his agents—prefects, sub-prefects, and mayors—in the
districts (departments, arrondissements, and communes) which
had been prepared for him by the Revolution. Under his direction they took over the entire control of the administrative services, and the local councils which survived were not qualified,
either by their composition or by their functions, to enjoy any
power of sharing in the control. Bonaparte thus created bodies
of specialized officials obedient to his will. For finance, there
were treasurers, controllers, and tax-collectors; for justice, there
were courts of the first instance and appeal courts, with judges
who, although they were permanent, were bound to serve a
government which guaranteed their salary and determined
their promotion. Even the members of the clergy became civil
servants; for by the conclusion of a concordat with the Pope, to
end the quarrel between the Church and revolutionary France,
Bonaparte meant to obtain control over the nomination of
bishops and priests, and even over the instruction they gave.
French centralization was henceforth to become a model for
many European countries.

In this organization of the new France, Bonaparte turned to
his own advantage, and enlisted in his service, the achievements
and the staff which had been left to him by the Revolution. He

claimed that he was its heir and executor. This claim was partly justified. Frenchmen indeed were no longer free, but they were still equal. There was no restoration of the old privileges and no distinction of persons either before the law or in the field of taxation. The fiscal system which the Revolution had substituted for that of the *ancien régime* remained in force, with its land-tax and its taxes on buildings and on businesses falling on every occupant of premises. The Civil Code, which Bonaparte took pains to prepare, was above everything else an expression of the principles of natural law; and though it was inspired by old French customary rules and by Roman law, it recognized the civic equality of all individuals.

True, the Revolution came to an end without carrying out the social reforms for which Robespierre, by some of his measures, had merely prepared the way. Financial reorganization, undertaken with the help of private initiative which Bonaparte stimulated and concentrated by his creation of a Bank of France, encouraged the development of capitalism and the growth of the bourgeoisie. Bonaparte sanctioned the return of the *émigrés*, and when he became emperor he tried to weld them into a new nobility in order to create an aristocracy round his throne. France, however, remained an egalitarian democracy in which the peasant class predominated. Social equality and administrative uniformity facilitated the practice of dictatorship and made its effects more oppressive. Napoleon, instinctively adopting the policy of Frederic II, governed in isolation and treated his ministers as mere agents; and he realized thereby the ambitions of the enlightened despots.

Napoleonic France exercised a tremendous influence on the future of Europe. Not only did succeeding political régimes in France itself preserve the foundations and the framework which he had laid down; his conquests had a much wider and more definite influence on the continent at large than the Revolution had been able to exercise.

Without attempting to make even a summary list of these conquests it is enough to indicate their most important stages, in order to be able to trace their effects. From 1796 onwards we may trace in the action of General Bonaparte a personal policy, which creates a sort of Italian proconsulate beyond the natural frontiers which the directorate sought to acquire. The next stage comes when the first consul, after obtaining at Lunéville and

Amiens (first from the emperor and then from England) the recognition of these natural frontiers and this Italian procon-sulate, proceeds to make a sweeping change in the map of Germany by the 'Recess' of 1803. Next the emperor, as he has now become, is enabled by the victory of Austerlitz to dissolve the Holy Roman Empire, and to increase the territories of the German princes under his orders at the expense of the house of Austria. Finally, the Prussian defeat at Tilsit leaves him in con-trol of Germany, and it seems as if the Russian alliance would now enable him to bring about the submission of Europe. Historians have often, but unsuccessfully, attempted to define and delimit this giant enterprise, which, inspired as it was by a limitless ambition, inevitably defeats all definition. But we can, at any rate, make a list of the measures by which the policy of Napoleon transformed Europe.

These methods differed in the three regions into which the continent was then divided. There was, first of all, the French empire, which included Belgium, the Rhineland, Piedmont, and Liguria. At the moment of its greatest extent it even included Holland and the German North Sea coast at the one end, and, at the other, Rome, which was to become its second capital. The social changes brought about by the Revolution and the Napo-leonic system of administration were introduced in all these territories, which were divided into departments controlled by vigorous prefects. The peoples of the foreign countries thus incorporated in France found that the opening of the French market was favourable to the development of their industry and the rise of their middle class. On the other hand the continental blockade was harmful to their agriculture and ruined their ports. National resentment was strong against the invader, but it did not take the form of active resistance. In the Rhineland the French régime won supporters and had a lasting influence.

Beyond the French empire stretched a 'great empire' formed of satellite states. At their head the emperor placed members of his family and some of his principal officers. Sometimes he left the legitimate sovereigns on their thrones. But in reality he ruled himself under different disguises. The rest of the continent formed the third region, and consisted of countries which were his allies—Austria, Prussia, and Russia. Napoleon forced his alliance upon them: it was for them to be his associates in his fight against England.

The tempo and the extent of the reforms which introduced French institutions into the states of the 'great empire' differed according to the exigencies of Bonaparte's general policy. They were pushed farthest and fastest in Italy, already conquered by the Revolutionary armies and the first scene of Napoleon's victories.

In the north the kingdom of Italy (the Milanese, Venice, and the Marches), where Bonaparte himself assumed the crown, was strongly centralized and subject to the system of the Civil Code, which was administered by tribunals organized on the French model. Taxes were the same as in France. Public works, public assistance, and education were administered uniformly by numerous officials, and priests were compelled, under the terms of the Concordat, to teach the imperial catechism. In the states of the Holy See, divided into departments, French laws and administration were imposed on the inhabitants, who regretted the flight of the papal court and the disappearance of the convents. In the kingdom of Naples Joseph Bonaparte, followed later by Murat, carried out a similar policy, in conditions made more difficult by the constant menace of the English fleet; and here 'intendants' discharged the duties of prefects. The abolition of feudal rights and the distribution of waste land began an agrarian revolution. The government, it is true, had to seek the advice of a consultative assembly; but it reserved to itself the right of appointing the members. On the other side of the Adriatic the policy of assimilation was extended to the Illyrian provinces, which consisted of territories annexed from Venice and Austria. Here Marmont was entrusted with the task of introducing French laws and taxes, and of abolishing feudalism.

Holland and Germany underwent changes that were less rapid and less profound. When Napoleon expelled his brother Louis from Holland and made it part of the empire, he still left it outside the French customs borders; French law was only enforced there in 1810, and the introduction of French taxation was planned only for 1813. The action of France in western Germany was on a larger scale. The kingdom of Westphalia, under King Jerome Bonaparte, adopted the French legal and administrative system, and abolished feudal dues on the payment of compensation. The same methods were tried, but more gradually, in the duchy of Berg. In the states where the German rulers had become vassals of the French empire, the result was not so much an infiltration of French ideas and institutions as a continuation of the work of enlightened despotism.

By administrative centralization, a better distribution of taxes, and the control of the Church by the state, the rulers hoped to strengthen their governments, which now took under their charge the services of education, public assistance, and health. On the other hand they did not attempt to transform society by agrarian reforms, and they continued to make use of the services of the aristocracy, which they treated with respect. These were the methods followed by Dalberg, who exchanged the arch-bishopric of Mainz for the grand duchy of Frankfurt, by the king of Bavaria, and by the grand duke of Baden. Napoleon asked for no more. When the sovereign was not an enlightened despot, and when, like the king of Württemberg, he was only concerned to strengthen his administration, or even, like the king of Saxony, was not interested in any sort of reform, Napoleon did not interfere to force a different policy upon him.

His restraint was explained by the proximity of states, on the frontiers of the great 'empire', which though they were allied to it were still independent. Before taking further steps he had to wait for the result of the campaign against Russia which he had been preparing since 1810. This is why he acted with great circumspection in the Polish provinces which had been formed after the treaty of Tilsit into the grand duchy of Warsaw. He wished to introduce in them the Civil Code and to abolish serfdom, but he left the diet still dominated by nobles and only admitted a small minority of commoners.

Napoleon's work was thus incomplete; and he did more to reform the state than he did to alter social conditions. It was nevertheless a considerable achievement, and it did not disappear with the fall of the empire; the sovereigns restored after 1815 in the Italian states had to reckon with its results. Even a reactionary like Ferdinand of Naples did not restore the feudal régime and could not abolish the Civil Code. Germany, with a new and simplified system of political geography which was to be permanent, was henceforth divided into the western states, where the bourgeoisie and the peasantry had benefited from French rule, and the eastern states where the aristocracy had retained its privileges and power.

In another respect also Napoleon stopped short. To ensure the success of the Napoleonic programme, France should have given to a united Europe the economic equipment which was necessary for its development. What actually happened was the opposite: the economic system of Europe was forced to adapt itself to the exigencies of war and the needs of France. The emperor did not attempt to create a system of economic regions in Europe which might have made it prosperous by their very diversity. The idea of a German Zollverein, which had been suggested at the time, awoke no echo in his mind. Nor had he any idea of creating an Italian economy: his only thought was to deprive the English of their markets in the peninsula, and he would not allow Holland to be included within the customs barriers of the empire.

The most striking expression of a policy which subordinated the whole economic life of the continent to the interests of France was the continental blockade. We shall see later the causes and the consequences so far as they affected England. Its effects on the economy of the continent were complicated, and are still imperfectly understood. The disappearance of the formidable competition of English industry was of great advantage to continental industry. The cotton trade, in spite of the difficulty of obtaining raw cotton, woollen manufactures, mining, and the sugar-beet industry, all benefited, and the blockade stimulated the development of European capitalism. But it ruined the ports and greatly diminished the amount of trade done in the great fairs of Europe. The continent was deprived of colonial supplies, and agriculture was severely affected by the ban placed on exports.

France wished to make the conquered countries pay for the cost of war, and she taxed them heavily. Any advantage they might have gained from the economic and social reforms carried out under her impulse was more than outweighed by double and treble taxation, and a great part of their productive strength was devoted to the military programme insisted on by the emperor. Napoleon wished the conquered countries to supply him with soldiers. His demands became more exacting when the Spanish war engaged the 'Grande Armée' which had fought his campaigns until Tilsit. For the invasion of Russia he demanded a large contingent from each of his satellites. He plunged into the plains of Russia with an army of 700,000 men, only one-third of whom were French. Almost all his soldiers perished there. Thus Russia became the grave not only of the emperor's ambitions but, almost literally, of Napoleonic Europe.

His fall brought a new Europe suddenly to light, a Europe of nationalities throwing off the tyrant's yoke. The Spanish rising of 1808 had been the first expression of their discontent, and the capitulation of the French troops at Baylen struck the first blow at the foundations of the emperor's continental structure. But although Spain and Portugal, the scene of the campaigns of Wellington's army, played a very great part in the defeat of the emperor, it was in Germany, and after the Russian disaster, that national feeling really showed its strength.

German nationalism pinned its hopes of recovery on Prussia. The Austrian reaction after Austerlitz had been only a short-lived movement, and after Wagram the Austrian régime became once more, like the emperor Francis himself, conservative and humdrum. How could the Habsburgs have encouraged any national movement when they saw the awakening of Czech national consciousness, with its centre in the university of Prague, and the simultaneous growth of a Magyar nationalism which was a still greater menace to their authority? The czar Alexander, too, had soon abandoned the programme of liberal reform formed after Tilsit, and the part played by national feeling in the Russian resistance of 1812 must not be exaggerated. The case was different in Prussia. Here a constellation of bold counsellors had surrounded Frederick William III since 1807 and induced him to undertake a series of reforms. The majority of these counsellors were not Prussians; but they saw in Prussia the instrument of German revenge. They were not revolutionaries; but after seeing how the Revolution had inspired the French armies they wanted the king of Prussia to base himself similarly on his people. They believed it possible to do this without bringing about a revolution in Prussia like that which had overturned French society.

The policy of agrarian reform carried out by Stein and Hardenberg enabled the peasants to leave their holdings, or to escape from *corvées* and feudal dues by surrendering a part of their holding to their landlord. The landlord retained his rights of jurisdiction and his power of evicting his tenants, and he continued to administer the villages. The power of the 'Junkers' was hardly affected by this reform. In the towns, however, the municipal bodies, which had previously been controlled by the guilds, were now elected by all the inhabitants. The chief work of the Prussian ministers was the reorganization of the army by Scharnhorst and Gneisenau. They re-formed the regiments: they organized large reserves by the use of 'Krumpers', soldiers who had been given a rapid preliminary training and discipline by short periods of service. General Yorke's Prussian contingent, which Napoleon had taken to Russia, went over to the enemy immediately after the French defeat. Yorke placed himself under the czar's command, and the king of Prussia, who was at first terrified, decided to ally himself with the Russians and call up the *Landwehr*. Prussia, like France in 1793, had recourse to a *levée en masse*.

She was thus prepared to defend the cause of German natio- nalism, which had found a rallying-point in the university of Berlin, recently founded by Humboldt. German nationalism, as we have already seen, had long been an active force in the ranks of the intellectuals, though it had not prevented a number of Germans from giving a warm welcome to the French Revolution. The Terror, followed by the dictatorship of Napo- leon, had been a great disappointment for them. Beethoven removed the name of Bonaparte from the first page of his *Eroica*. At Heidelberg, which in the words of Stein was 'the heart of the conflagration', the romantic movement, with its zest for legends and folk-tales, had become a nursery of patriot- ism and German national pride. The German language, the *Ursprache*, was pitted against the Romance languages, which were only the debris of a dead language. German literature claimed that it alone was truly original.

Romanticism, allying itself with enlightened despotism, led German philosophers also to develop a new conception of the state, as a being with a life of its own, distinct from that of the individuals who composed it, and with its own mode of growth. These were the ideas current in Germany when the 'Tugend- bund' was formed at Königsberg, a society for the promotion of civic virtues which aimed at a national rising. It was to the 'Tugendbund' that Fichte addressed his 'Speeches to the Ger- man nation' from his chair in Berlin in 1810.

Napoleon's victories had finally created a Europe which national aspirations directed into new paths.

§ 3. *England and Napoleon*

The war had also increased the strength of national feeling in England. From 1793 to 1814, with a brief truce after the peace of Amiens, England had carried on a bitter struggle against the France of the Revolution and the empire. She had thus set a great example to Europe. It was not her kings who inspired her to such efforts. After 1788, George III was haunted by the madness which overcame him in 1810. His son the regent made himself very unpopular by his frivolous character and dissolute life. But England was led by great ministers, and above all by the great minister who had governed with such authority ever since 1784. Pitt died on the eve of the battle of Austerlitz, and Fox, his successor, only survived him by a year. But two of Pitt's followers, Canning and Castlereagh, played a great part in the later years of the war.

It is true that English statesmen were far from agreeing with one another. The rivalry of Pitt and Fox lasted all their lives; Canning and Castlereagh quarrelled bitterly. The government made serious mistakes in the conduct of operations, and Pitt himself, torn between the supporters of a naval war and those who demanded attacks on the continent, showed less sagacity in war than he had done in peace. Without underestimating the part which ministers played in the victory, we must pay a large tribute to the spirit of the people. John Bull, made into a traditional figure by English cartoonists of the period, was the chief architect of his own salvation.

The English victory was first and foremost a naval victory. After defeating Bonaparte's eastern schemes at Aboukir, Nelson put a stop at Trafalgar to the attempts to invade Great Britain. The English navy blockaded the coasts of France, and after the Spanish rising the French fleet gave up the attempt to break the blockade. Its ships confined themselves to privateering, for which the conditions of navigation at that time were unfavourable.

Could the British gain a foothold on the continent besides holding the seas? During the revolutionary wars their armies had suffered a series of defeats in the Low Countries, and again in 1809 a landing at Walcheren was a disastrous failure. But the Spanish rising provided an opportunity which Canning and Castlereagh after him resolved to seize. Wellington's deter-

mination enabled him to establish himself in Portugal, and then
to carry on a long campaign which took his armies as far as the
Pyrenees at the moment when his allies reached the Rhine. The
English army thus took part in the invasion of France in 1814,
and it was on that army that Napoleon first hurled himself at
Waterloo.

During the war Britain used to the full the great advantage
which the Industrial Revolution had given her capitalists over
their competitors. The war also made her a place of refuge for
European capital. The abundance of specie and credit favoured
economic expansion. But the costs of the war, and the enormous
increase in the number of exchequer bills accepted by the bank,
endangered the position of sterling in 1797. The prompt action
of Pitt and the good discipline of the public succeeded in preserving its value. During the wars of the Revolution, trade
continued to expand; England increased sixfold her exports to
the Hanseatic ports, and doubled those to the United States.
During the Napoleonic wars, however, the position was drasti-
cally altered, and Europe was barred and bolted against English
trade. In 1806 Napoleon declared a blockade of the British Isles;
then he announced that neutral ships touching at a British port
would be treated as British ships. He could not hope to starve
out a country which was mistress of the seas, and whose agricultural production was still high, but he believed he could
deal her a blow severe enough to undermine the complicated
and delicate structure, as yet unknown to the rest of Europe,
which the British economy and system of credit appeared to be.
The disastrous fall in British exports in 1808 was enough to
show that his plan was not wholly fantastic. But the Spanish
rising in the following year, followed by the defection of Turkey,
made the first breaches in the European blockade. The English
depots in Heligoland and Sicily served as a basis for the opening
of others. Napoleon finally came to regard the European blockade less as an instrument of war than as a commercial device,
and its character was transformed by the multiplication of
licences. England eventually emerged victorious from this
ordeal.

She had also borne successfully the very heavy burden of a
war which eventually cost more than £800,000,000. Half this
sum was met by loans and the rest by increased taxation, proportions similar to those which were followed in the financing of

the last world war. Pitt had not hesitated to triple the rates of the
principal taxes, and in 1798 he had introduced an income tax,
an innovation which was to have so many imitators in Europe.
At the end of the war England's national debt was increased by
£400,000,000. But at any rate fiscal policy had not hindered
commercial development, or impeded the progress of an expansion which was to enable England to make important contributions to the inheritance of Europe.

The wars with France had not led to changes in English
political institutions. They had only cooled the sympathy which
had at first been felt for the early stages of the French Revolution. In 1795 Pitt had been able to secure the support of a
majority of the Whigs, whose leaders joined his government, and
Fox was left almost alone to uphold the independence of his
party. But the victorious Tories abandoned the reforms which
Pitt, before the crisis, had hoped to carry out. In 1800 the Prime
Minister thought it necessary to strengthen the links which
bound his country to Ireland, where the flame of rebellion was
fanned by France. He succeeded in suppressing the Dublin
parliament, and promised in return to allow the Catholics access
to public office in England; but the opposition of the king forced
him to resign, and in order to regain power he had to abandon
the plan. England thus escaped the influence of the Revolution,
and under the Tory régime became still more conservative.
There was a general reaction of opinion, among nonconformists
and Anglicans alike, as well as among business men, many of
whom had joined the ranks of the landed aristocracy in the
House of Lords. But the English did not surrender their liberties. When the government prosecuted the leaders of popular
societies, the jury found them not guilty, and public opinion
rejoiced in the verdict.

The campaign for parliamentary reform continued, and was
even intensified. It was not only waged in the press and in
public meetings by tireless agitators like Cobbett and Burdett;
it found support in the principles of utilitarian philosophy, as
enunciated by Bentham; and parliamentary reform thus came
to be regarded as the means whereby a democratic state could
achieve a host of administrative reforms. Side by side with the
followers of Bentham, the disciples of Adam Smith addressed
themselves to the problems of property and population, in the
attempt to show that economics could dispense with the inter-

PLATE 35

The English Parliament in 1742. From a print in the British Museum

vention of the state. These two trends, far from contradicting one another, were united in the common conception of an economic society progressing by 'spontaneous adaptation' and a political society achieving the necessary democratic reforms by 'deliberate adaptation'. The forces which led England in the nineteenth century to electoral reform and free trade were thus taking shape and beginning to unite. She was preparing to show Europe how a free country could develop gradually into a democracy and could thus attain, through freedom, the fullest development of her economy.

§ 4. *European Expansion in the World*

During the eighteenth century the development of European civilization was accompanied by a remarkable movement of expansion. Europe exercised a much greater influence than before upon other continents. Not only was colonization growing in scale: it tended to shed its original character of a commercial enterprise and to become a policy of imperial conquest. The capture of trading depots and naval bases was succeeded by the occupation of vast territories whose inhabitants sought to model their institutions on those of the mother country.

It will be shown later, in the second part of this section, what interest was taken by Europeans at the end of the century in some of the regions overseas. The great response awakened in Europe by the American Declaration of Independence was the most striking example. But the attention of the Old World was also drawn to other continents, partly by the accounts of explorers who brought the Islands of the Pacific into general vogue, partly by the discovery of Chinese art, and partly, too, by the seductive spectacle of the riches of India. The highly cultured civilization of Europe was interested all the more because it believed that, old and infirm, it had discovered the secret of a new youth in primitive societies.

At the same time centres of European life had grown up outside Europe, and particularly in the New World. The English colonists of North America were governed by assemblies which gradually developed into little parliaments, in rivalry with the parliament at Westminster; and the popularity among them of Blackstone's picture of English institutions is indicative of their ideas and aims. The selfish authoritarian policy of Madrid did not prevent the Spaniards who had settled in Latin

America from setting up similar centres of political and economic life, which were capable of achieving self-sufficiency.

The immigration of negro slaves imported from Africa gave a peculiar character to colonial societies. But the conscience of Europe was already troubled by the problem of slavery. Wilberforce had persistently pressed for its abolition in the British House of Commons from 1787 onwards: his efforts were supported by Pitt and Fox, and in 1807, just after his death, the zeal of Fox was at length rewarded by an act for the legal prohibition of the slave-trade. England proposed the abolition of slavery to the European powers assembled at the congress of Vienna. The proposal was not accepted, but the opposition to it was weakening. The resistance of their colonists in the French West Indies prevented the French, in spite of the Revolution, from proclaiming the emancipation of slaves; but they too were concerned with the problem of slavery.

English liberties and the principles of the French Revolution were the two great moral forces through which Europe exerted an influence on the world, apart from trade connexions. But the colonial disputes which plunged France and England in war during the eighteenth century had the effect of making England the best fitted of all the countries of Europe to spread European ideas and to introduce European ways of life in the world outside.

England's naval superiority had enabled her after the treaty of Utrecht to make Holland follow in her wake, and when the United Provinces tried to assert their independence, as they did during the war of American Independence, the attempt met with complete failure. Little was left to them of their former colonial power beyond the opportunity for trading on a large scale with the support of their considerable financial resources. During the revolutionary wars Pitt could not save them from a French invasion, and later, when Holland was under the yoke of Napoleon, England seized their colonies at the Cape and in Ceylon. In 1815 the need for protection against the possibility of French revenge again made the Low Countries dependent on England.

Throughout the century England had coveted the trade of the vast Spanish empire. In the trade with America from Spanish ports English merchants had had a considerable share; but their ships had not succeeded in securing direct entry to the ports of Latin America, which was inaccessible to European influence except through Spain and the Spanish monarchy.

On the other hand the decisive victory of England in the course of the wars with France which ended in 1763 gave her the opportunity of building, on the ruins of the French empire, a new empire which might one day become the chief instrument of European expansion in the world.

It must be admitted, however, that up to that time England had shown very little sign of wishing to play such a role. Her government remained faithful to the old 'Colonial system', under which the navigation laws reserved a monopoly of foreign trade for her merchant fleet, and commercial profit was her dominating motive. It was without the help of the mother country, and even against her will, that the English colonists settled on the Atlantic coasts of North America had established there organized European communities which adopted the laws and ideas of the mother country, and preserved its manners and ways of life in the new conditions of their environment. In fact it was France rather than England who had tried to set up European communities in the New World, by creating in Canada a new France governed like a French province, and by settling large numbers of colonists in the rich West Indian islands which she held.

The victory of 1763 brought England face to face with new imperial problems. She was unable to find an immediate solution. It was natural that after the conclusion of peace the British government, which had borne almost all the cost of the American war, should expect the colonies to bear part of the cost of their own defence; nor did it wish to leave in their hands, without any control, the immense territories in the Mississippi valley from which it had driven the French. But George III's ministers did not understand that they laid the way open to a dangerous conflict when they sought to oppose an irresistible movement and attempted to impose on British settlers taxes which had not been voted by their representatives. In spite of the warnings of the elder Pitt, who had now become Lord Chatham, they persisted in a policy which after twelve years led the colonies to combine in order to proclaim the independence of the United States. The War of American Independence, in which French intervention greatly contributed to the English defeat, forced George III to recognize the loss of his American colonies by the treaty of Versailles in 1783.

This treaty was, and still remains, one of the most important landmarks in European history. It is true that the United States was to be populated by European immigrants, and that, in spite of its diverse origins, it was still to retain the character of an Anglo-Saxon country. It is true that eighteenth-century French writers were the most popular in North America, and that the American Revolution exercised a profound influence on France and also on Germany. But the fact remains that these American communities, although they were the offspring of Europe, were henceforth to live and grow in absolute independence, outside and apart from Europe. The more prosperous they became, the greater became the magnitude of the loss which Europe suffered at that moment.

On the other hand England succeeded in preventing any revolt which might have been anticipated from the French Canadians. They remained loyal, and Canada even became a sanctuary for the American loyalists who had been unwilling to join in resistance to the British government. The government had wisdom enough to respect the Catholic sympathies of the Canadians, and to leave French civil law intact. In 1791 the younger Pitt created a government under which Canadians played their part in the exercise of power. This was the first stage of an evolution which led Great Britain, in the end, to recognize the independence of Canada without any severance of the association between her and the mother country.

The defeat of France had left the English a clear field in India, and Robert Clive, by the conquest of Bengal, had immediately begun to realize the ambitions of Dupleix, to his country's great advantage. The English East India Company soon became the master of regions whose rich treasures it could not be allowed to exploit unchecked. The appearance in Parliament of rich traders or officials from India—the 'nabobs'—already showed the danger which threatened English institutions from such riches. The problem forced itself on the attention of statesmen just at the time when the American war was ending. One of the first acts of the younger Pitt's ministry was to pass a law which, without abolishing the Company, put it under the control of a ministerial department.

The work of Clive was, however, continued, first by Warren Hastings and then by Lord Wellesley, who extended British dominion into the Punjab and even into Afghanistan. In the Deccan England was able to suppress the revolt of Tippoo Sahib, by which France had attempted to regain a foothold in the peninsula. During the Napoleonic wars the English attacked the French in Madagascar and seized the island of Reunion. But the famous impeachment of Warren Hastings, to whose prosecution Pitt had agreed under pressure from Burke, had the advantage of showing, in spite of the prejudice and bigotry of the enemies of the great governor, that England would not allow her colonial peoples to be unscrupulously exploited. At that time there could be no question for her of teaching the immense population of that great peninsula to understand or to imitate European civilization. She could only hope to maintain order and create the material conditions favourable to the development of India's resources. This was the work of a small group of soldiers and administrators of integrity, who between them formed a society acting in strict conformity with British ideas and practices and planted in the midst of peoples with whom it preferred not to mix for fear of diminishing its prestige.

Still farther afield, at the very end of the eighteenth century, England had sent a first ship-load of emigrants to Australia. It was only a colony of convicts that Captain Philip founded in 1798 at Sydney, but it grew rapidly, attracted immigrants, and after a century this settlement in the Antipodes finally developed into the most British of all the dominions.

The wars against the French Revolution and Napoleon also hastened the fall of the Spanish empire. Latin America became more accessible to European influences, and England, who had been watching her chance throughout the eighteenth century, was the first to take advantage of the opening. English merchants were long unsuccessful in establishing any trading connexions. Spain steadily tried to prevent other European countries from having dealings with her viceroyalties, which stretched in a long line from California to the Argentine. Portugal followed the same policy with Brazil, an enormous colony which had gradually developed along the banks of the Amazon and on the plateaux in the interior, and which was growing prosperous on the produce of its new coffee-plantations.

The government of Madrid had, nevertheless, realized the necessity of improving the administration of its viceroys and the officials who assisted them. It had at once exploited the mines and developed agriculture; and European undertakings now prospered. But the government had not been able to stop European ideas from spreading into its empire. The *Encyclopédie* and Raynal's famous book *Histoire des Établissements Européens dans les deux Indes* had an enthusiastic public. Mexico, now a town of 130,000 inhabitants, possessed scholarly and scientific institutions of repute. The three million whites and the five million inhabitants of mixed blood who formed half the population of Latin America bore their servile position and their isolation with growing impatience. The success of the North American revolt set them a dangerous example, and the Spanish minister Arunda proposed that Charles III should transform his colonies into independent kingdoms, with Infantes to rule over them.

The French Revolution had profound repercussions in Latin America. It encouraged the future leaders of the American rebellion; Miranda went to France and served in Dumouriez's army; Bolivar was present at the crowning of Napoleon in Notre-Dame. It was, nevertheless, to the English that they first looked for help. When Napoleon persuaded Spain to declare war on England, Miranda led English forces from the Cape to attack Buenos Aires. A French *émigré* Liniers, in the service of Spain, prevented his attempt.

But Napoleon's conquest of Spain and Portugal brought England and Latin America face to face with a new situation. The Portuguese house of Braganza fled to Brazil, whose ports were now opened to the English. The Braganzas immediately carried out reforms, which it is true they tried to revoke when they returned to Lisbon at the end of the Napoleonic wars; but this did not prevent Brazil from proclaiming her independence early in the nineteenth century. On the other hand, the English could not support his rebellious subjects in America against King Ferdinand VII of Spain, who had become Napoleon's prisoner and was now their own ally. For this reason the first attempt of Miranda and Bolivar failed. It was forcibly suppressed by the Spanish officials, and when the king returned to Madrid after the defeat of Napoleon he was still in possession of almost all his colonies. He did not keep them long. It was already possible to foresee the imminent development of independent Latin American states, bound to France and England by the closest economic and intellectual links.

These were the chief signs which heralded the world expansion of European civilization, which reached its peak during the nineteenth century.

§ 5. *Conclusion*

The Europe of 1815 was very different from that of 1715. This was the result, first and foremost, of her experiences during the twenty-five terrible years which had just ended. The extraordinary figure who now left her shores, after involving her in the vicissitudes of his meteoric career, had left his mark upon her. His image still lingered in men's minds, exciting their imagination or awakening their fears. His memory, distorted by legend, appeared to Frenchmen of the nineteenth century as the incarnation of their Revolution, and to foreigners as tyranny personified. In fact Napoleon bequeathed to Europe not only a stupendous epic but also an instructive example of a democracy enslaved by a dictatorship. He had taught his enemies to know both the weakness of coalition and the strength of patriotism in the defence of national independence.

It is true that in the last stage of the conflict the nations had been forced to submit to the oppressive authority of their old sovereigns. Metternich's Austria, alarmed by the forces which Prussia had aroused to fling into the battle, desired the defeat of Napoleon not by a league of the peoples he had conquered but by a coalition of their rightful sovereigns. The czar held the same views; and the holy alliance brought about by Alexander only united the victorious allies against any French attempt at revenge and the princes against any demands of their subjects. It aimed at guaranteeing the peace of Europe, and England believed that it might succeed in its aim. But this attempted organization of Europe, made at the dawn of the nineteenth century, realized none of the pacific ideals formed a century earlier by the Abbé de St. Pierre. Nor did it follow the project of perpetual peace, founded on international law, which had just been propounded by Kant. The peoples eventually rebelled against it.

How could they ever have succeeded in forgetting the principles of the French Revolution? Napoleon's armies had helped to implant them over a part of the continent; and Europe was now more than ever divided into two regions, two types of society, one of which preserved the feudal system while the other had overthrown it. But apart from that, and in themselves, the principles of the Revolution carried an impulse to freedom which had by no means spent itself. On the contrary, as the remembrance of the Terror gradually faded, the ideals of 1789 recovered their old power of inspiration. The nineteenth century began to cherish the idea of a legendary revolution which would have culminated in a social revolution if it had not been turned aside from its aims by the influence of war.

This explains the reverence paid to it by the armies of want, the immense proletariat created by large-scale industry. After 1815 industrialization spread from England, where it had been so highly developed, to the countries of the continent. The growth of capitalism in turn gave rise to socialism, and socialistic theories began to emerge in France and England.

In a Europe which had survived such great upheavals, and which was destined to undergo new strains, memories of the eighteenth century proper—the century which ended in 1789— receded into an already distant past. They had the charm of an age that had disappeared for ever, of a sort of antiquity. The eighteenth century fascinated men by the brilliant and delicate images which it had left behind in their minds. Its witty and lively society still lived in the works of art which it had created. Men loved to think of the dream-like canvases of French painters, of English portraits, of Venetian ornaments, of the characters of Italian comedy; they loved to listen to the music of which the great German composers had shown themselves to be masters, the symphony whose first chords had been struck by Bach and Handel and whose final enchantment had been achieved by Mozart. But already the charm of the eighteenth century was being challenged by painters of the school of David, who opposed to it an art inspired by ancient Rome and the Napoleonic legend; and music began to reveal the grand harmonies of Beethoven's symphonies. In a temper of nostalgic regret the greatness of the eighteenth century was forgotten in favour of its elegance.

The eighteenth century led European thought from the age of Cartesian reason and Newtonian science to that of the metaphysics and the ethics of Kant. Scientific progress gave it its first impetus, opening up new views of society and the universe. The discoveries of mathematicians such as Euler and D'Alembert, and those of astronomers such as Clairault and Herschel, led to a new conception of a *système du monde* for which Laplace could offer his *Exposition*. Physics, with the work of Monge and Black, discovered the relations between light and heat. Priestley and Lavoisier founded modern chemistry. The long labours of Buffon, which took forty years, painted a picture of the *Époques de la Nature* which prepared the way for the theory of the origin of species. The work of the scientists was closely linked with that of the writers who constantly brought their discoveries within reach of a very wide public.

The following pages trace the development of this intense intellectual activity. It is important to consider it in relation to the political, economic, and social development which we have described. In order to understand both developments, and to see them in relation to one another, we may recall, with Valéry, the famous meeting of Goethe and Napoleon in 1809: 'The one certainly the wisest, the other perhaps the maddest of mankind'; Bonaparte 'running riot in the actual . . . conducting with furious gestures the orchestra of facts'; Goethe 'convinced, and as it were enamoured, of the maternal deliberation of the movement of nature'.

POLITICAL, ECONOMICAL, AND SOCIAL DEVELOPMENT IN THE EIGHTEENTH CENTURY

DOCUMENTS

I

Rousseau on the Social Contract, Civil Liberty, and Sovereignty

1. *The Social Contract*

'Some form of association must be found as a result of which the whole strength of the community will be enlisted for the protection of the person and property of each constituent member, in such a way that each, when united to his fellows, renders obedience to his own will, and remains as free as he was before.' That is the basic problem of which the Social Contract provides the solution.

The clauses of this Contract are determined by the Act of Association in such a way that the least modification must render them null and void.

.   .   .   .

It must be clearly understood that the clauses in question can be reduced, in the last analysis, to one only, to wit, the complete alienation by each associate member to the community of *all his rights*. For, in the first place, since each has made surrender of himself without reservation, the resultant conditions are the same for all; and, because they are the same for all, it is in the interest of none to make them onerous to his fellows.

Furthermore, this alienation having been made unreservedly, the union of individuals is as perfect as it well can be, none of the associated members having any claim against the community. For should there be any rights left to individuals, and no common authority be empowered to pronounce as between them and the public, then each, being in some things his own judge, would soon claim to be so in all. Were that so, a state of Nature would still remain in being, the conditions of association becoming either despotic or ineffective.

In short, whoso gives himself to all gives himself to none. And, since there is no member of the social group over whom we do not acquire precisely the same rights as those over ourselves which we have surrendered to him, it follows that we gain the exact equivalent of what we lose, as well as an added power to conserve what we already have.

If, then, we take from the social pact everything which is not essential to it, we shall find it to be reduced to the following terms: 'Each of us contributes to the group his person and the powers which he wields as a person, and we receive into the body politic each individual as forming an indivisible part of the whole.'

J.-J. ROUSSEAU, *The Social Contract* (1762), Book I, chap. vi (from the translation by Gerard Hopkins in *The Social Contract*, World's Classics).

2. *Liberty in the Civil State*

What a man loses as a result of the Social Contract is his natural liberty and his unqualified right to lay hands on all that tempts him, provided only that he can compass its possession. What he gains is civil liberty and the ownership of what belongs to him. That we may labour under no illusion concerning these compensations, it is well that we distinguish between natural liberty which the individual enjoys so long as he is strong enough to maintain it, and civil liberty which is curtailed by the general will; between possessions which derive from physical strength and the right of the first-comer, and ownership which can be based only on a positive title.

Ibid., Book I, chap. viii.

3. *Sovereignty*

I maintain, therefore, that sovereignty, being no more than the exercise of the general will, can never be alienated, and that the sovereign, who is a collective being only, can be represented by no one but himself. Power can be transmitted, but not will.

Ibid., Book II, chap. i.

For the same reason that sovereignty is inalienable, so, too, is it indivisible. For either the will is general or it is not.[1] Either it is the will of the whole body of the People, or it is the will merely of one section. In the first case, this declared will is an act of sovereignty, and has the force of law. In the second, it is partial only, or, in other words, an act imposed by Government; and then, the most that can be said of it is that it is a decree.

Ibid., Book II, chap. ii.

[1] That Will be general, it is not always necessary that it be unanimous, though it is necessary that every vote cast should be counted. Any deliberate exclusion breaks the general nature of the decision.

II

Catherine II on Freedom and Order

So extensive an Empire naturally presupposes unlimited power in the hand of its ruler. Swiftness in deciding problems that reach the ruler from distant places must compensate for their slowness in coming to hand, an inevitable consequence of that distance.

Any other form of government would not only be harmful to Russia; it would eventually involve its total destruction.

Another reason is, that it is more desirable to obey the laws under a single master than to have to submit to the will of several.

Now, what is the object of an absolute government? It is certainly not to deprive men of their natural liberty, but to direct all their actions towards the greatest amount of happiness. . . .

Thus the form of government which tends more than any other towards that object, while at the same time restricting natural liberty less than any other, will best fulfil the aims which must be attributed to beings endowed with reason, and will most naturally achieve the object which men have hitherto sought in the formation of civil societies. . . .

General or political freedom does not consist in every individual being allowed to do whatever he likes. In a State, that is to say a society having laws, freedom can only consist in being able to do what one ought to wish to do, and in not being obliged to do what one ought not to wish to do.

We must form a clear idea of what is meant by freedom. Freedom is the right to do everything that the laws allow; and if a citizen were able to do what they forbid, there would be no more freedom, because others would also be able to do so. Political freedom, for a citizen, is that tranquillity of mind derived from the individual's knowledge of his own security; and in order to have this freedom, the Government must be such that one citizen cannot fear another citizen, but all together fear the Law.

CATHERINE II: *Instructions given to the Commission established for drawing up a new Code of Laws in 1767* (published by F. Grasser, Lausanne, 1769).

III

Frederic II on Enlightened Despotism (1781)

We have observed that citizens have only granted pre-eminence to one of their fellows in consideration of the services they expect from him; these services consist in maintaining the laws, in seeing that justice is strictly observed, in opposing the corruption of morals to

the utmost of his power, in defending the State against its enemies.
. . . Princes, sovereigns and kings are not, therefore, invested with
supreme authority in order to plunge with impunity into debauchery
and luxury; they are not raised above their fellow citizens in order
to satisfy their pride by ostentatious display, thus contemptuously
insulting those who live in simplicity of manners, poverty, or destitution; they are not at the head of the State in order to maintain
around themselves a crowd of hangers-on, whose idleness and use-
lessness will beget all manner of vices. . . .

The sovereign is bound by indissoluble bonds to the body of the
State; in consequence, he suffers the repercussion of all the ills that
afflict his subjects, and society in its turn suffers from the misfortunes
that affect its sovereign. There exists only one welfare, which is that
of the State in general. If the prince loses provinces, he is no longer
in a condition to assist his subjects as heretofore, and if misfortune
has obliged him to incur debts, his poor citizens will have to dis-
charge them; on the other hand if his people are few in number and
sunk in destitution, the sovereign is debarred from all renown. These
are truths so incontestable that it is needless to dwell further on them.

I repeat, then, the sovereign represents the State; he and his
people form one single body, which can only be happy in so far as it
is harmoniously united. The prince stands in relation to the society
over which he rules as the head stands to the body; he must see,
think, and act for the community, in order to procure for it all the
advantages which it is capable of enjoying. If the monarchical form
of government is to prevail over the republican, the sovereign's duty
is clear; he must be active and upright, and gather together all his
strength to follow the path that is prescribed for him. This is the
view I take of his duties. . . . That he may never swerve from them,
he must remember that he is a man, like the humblest of his servants;
if he is the first judge, the first general, the first financier and the
first minister of society, it is not in order that he should represent it,
but that he may fulfil its duties. He is merely the first servant of
the State, obliged to act with probity, wisdom and complete dis-
interestedness, as though at any moment he might be called upon
to give an account of his administration to his fellow citizens.

FREDERIC II: 'Essay on the Forms of Government and on the Duties of
Sovereigns' (*Works*, IX, p. 198).

IV

Bentham's Hope of Reformation in the Moral World

The age we live in is a busy age; in which knowledge is rapidly advancing towards perfection. In the natural world, in particular, everything teems with discovery and with improvement. The most distant and recondite regions of the earth traversed and explored—the all-vivifying and subtle element of the air so recently analysed and made known to us, —are striking evidences, were all others wanting, of this pleasing truth.

Correspondent to *discovery* and *improvement* in the natural world, is *reformation* in the moral; if that which seems a common notion be, indeed, a true one, that in the moral world there no longer remains any matter for *discovery*. Perhaps, however, this may not be the case: perhaps among such observations as would be best calculated to serve as grounds for reformation, are some which, being observations of matters of fact hitherto either incompletely noticed, or not at all, would, when produced, appear capable of bearing the name of discoveries: with so little method and precision have the consequences of this fundamental axiom, *it is the greatest happiness of the greatest number that is the measure of right and wrong*, been as yet developed.

Be this as it may, if there be room for making, and if there be use in publishing, *discoveries* in the *natural* world, surely there is not much less room for making, nor much less use in proposing, *reformation* in the *moral*. If it be a matter of importance and of use to us to be made acquainted with *distant* countries, surely it is not a matter of much less importance, nor of much less use to us, to be made better and better acquainted with the chief means of living happily in our *own*. If it be of importance and of use to us to know the principles of the element we breathe, surely it is not of much less importance nor of much less use to comprehend the principles, and endeavour at the improvement of those *laws*, by which alone we breathe it in security.

The Preface of BENTHAM's *Fragment on Government* (1776).

V

The Declaration of Independence 1776
The Unanimous Declaration of the Thirteen United States of America

We hold these truths to be self-evident, that all men are created equal, that they are endowed by their Creator with certain unalienable Rights, that among these are Life, Liberty and the pursuit of

Happiness. That to secure these rights, Governments are instituted among Men, deriving their just powers from the consent of the governed. That whenever any Form of Government becomes destructive of these ends, it is the Right of the People to alter or to abolish it, and to institute new Government, laying its foundation on such principles and organizing its powers in such form, as to them shall seem most likely to effect their Safety and Happiness. Prudence, indeed, will dictate that Governments long established should not be changed for light and transient causes; and accordingly all experience hath shown, that mankind are more disposed to suffer, while evils are sufferable, than to right themselves by abolishing the forms to which they are accustomed. But when a long train of abuses and usurpations, pursuing invariably the same Object, evinces a design to reduce them under absolute Despotism, it is their right, it is their duty, to throw off such Government, and to provide new Guards for their future security. Such has been the patient sufferance of these Colonies; and such is now the necessity which constrains them to alter their former Systems of Government.

Note. The text will be found on p. 157 of s. e. morison's *Sources and Documents illustrating the American Revolution*, published by the Clarendon Press, Oxford, 1923.

VI

Declaration of the Rights of Man and of Citizens, by the National Assembly of France (1789), Prefixed to the French Constitution of 1791

The representatives of the people of France, formed into a National Assembly, considering that ignorance, neglect, or contempt of human rights, are the sole causes of public misfortunes and corruptions of Government, have resolved to set forth in a solemn declaration, these natural, imprescriptible, and inalienable rights: that this declaration being constantly present to the minds of the members of the body social, they may be for ever kept attentive to their rights and their duties; that the acts of the legislative and executive powers of government, being capable of being every moment compared with the end of political institutions, may be more respected; and also, that the future claims of the citizens, being directed by simple and incontestable principles, may always tend to the maintenance of the Constitution, and the general happiness.

For these reasons, the National Assembly doth recognize and declare, in the presence of the Supreme Being, and with the hope of his blessing and favour, the following *sacred* rights of men and of citizens:

I. Men are born, and always continue, free and equal in respect of their rights. Civil distinctions, therefore, can be founded only on public utility.

II. The end of all political associations is the preservation of the natural and imprescriptible rights of man; and these rights are liberty, property, security, and resistance of oppression.

III. The nation is essentially the source of all sovereignty; nor can any individual, or any body of men, be entitled to any authority which is not expressly derived from it.

IV. Political liberty consists in the power of doing whatever does not injure another. The exercise of the natural rights of every man has no other limits than those which are necessary to secure to every *other* man the free exercise of the same rights; and these limits are determinable only by the law.

V. The law ought to prohibit only actions hurtful to society. What is not prohibited by the law should not be hindered; nor should any one be compelled to that which the law does not require.

VI. The law is an expression of the will of the community. All citizens have a right to concur, either personally or by their representatives, in its formation. It should be the same to all, whether it protects or punishes; and all being equal in its sight, are equally eligible to all honours, places, and employments, according to their different abilities, without any other distinction than that created by their virtues and talents.

VII. No man should be accused, arrested, or held in confinement, except in cases determined by the law, and according to the forms which it has prescribed. All who promote, solicit, execute, or cause to be executed, arbitrary orders, ought to be punished, and every citizen called upon, or apprehended by virtue of the law, ought immediately to obey, and renders himself culpable by resistance.

VIII. The law ought to impose no other penalties but such as are absolutely and evidently necessary; and no one ought to be punished, but in virtue of a law promulgated before the offence, and legally applied.

IX. Every man being presumed innocent till he has been convicted, whenever his detention becomes indispensable, all rigour to him, more than is necessary to secure his person, ought to be provided against by the law.

X. No man ought to be molested on account of his opinions, not even on account of his *religious* opinions, provided his avowal of them does not disturb the public order established by the law.

XI. The unrestrained communication of thoughts and opinions being one of the most precious rights of man, every citizen may speak, write, and publish freely, provided he is responsible for the abuse of this liberty, in cases determined by the law.

From the translation in THOMAS PAINE's *Rights of Man* (1791).

VII

Edmund Burke
On Liberties as an Entailed Inheritance (1790)

You will observe, that from Magna Charta to the Declaration of Right, it has been the uniform policy of our constitution to claim and assert our liberties as an *entailed inheritance* derived to us from our forefathers and to be transmitted to our posterity; as an estate specially belonging to the people of this kingdom, without any reference whatever to any other more general or prior right. By this means our constitution preserves a unity in so great a diversity of its parts. We have an inheritable Crown; an inheritable peerage; and a House of Commons and a people inheriting privileges, franchises and liberties from a long line of ancestors.

This policy appears to me to be the result of profound reflection; or rather the happy effect of following nature, which is wisdom without reflection, and above it. A spirit of innovation is generally the result of a selfish temper and confined views. People will not look forward to posterity, who never look backward to their ancestors. Besides, the people of England well know that the idea of inheritance furnishes a sure principle of conservation, and a sure principle of transmission; without at all excluding a principle of improvement. It leaves acquisition free; but it secures what it acquires. Whatever advantages are obtained by a state proceeding on these maxims, are locked fast as in a sort of family settlement; grasped as in a kind of mortmain for ever. By a constitutional policy, working after the pattern of nature, we receive, we hold, we transmit our government and our privileges in the same manner in which we enjoy and transmit our property and our lives. . . . Our political system is placed in a just correspondence and symmetry with the order of the world and with the mode of existence decreed to a permanent body composed of transitory parts; wherein, by the disposition of a stupendous wisdom, moulding together the great mysterious incorporation of the human race, the whole, at one time, is never old, or middle-aged, or young, but, in a condition of unchangeable constancy, moves on through the varied tenor of perpetual decay, fall, renovation and progression . . . . By adhering in this manner and on those principles to our forefathers, we are guided, not by the superstition of antiquarians, but by the spirit of philosophic analogy. In this choice of inheritance we have given to our frame of polity the image of a relation in blood; binding up the constitution of our country with our dearest domestic ties; adopting our fundamental laws into the bosom of our family affections; keeping inseparable, and cherishing with the warmth of all their combined and mutually reflected charities, our state, our hearths, our sepulchres and our altars. . . .

This idea of a liberal descent inspires us with a sense of habitual native dignity, which prevents that upstart insolence almost inevitably adhering to and disgracing those who are the first acquirers of any distinction. By this means our liberty becomes a noble freedom. It carries an imposing and majestic aspect.

> From BURKE's *Reflections on the Revolution in France*, in the World's Classics edition, vol. iv, pp. 35–37.

VIII

Thomas Paine on Opposite Forms of Government (*1791*)

The two modes of Government which prevail in the world are, *first*, Government by election and representation; *secondly*, Government by hereditary succession. The former is generally known by the name of republic; the latter by that of monarchy and aristocracy.

Those two distinct and opposite forms erect themselves on the two distinct and opposite bases of Reason and Ignorance. As the exercise of government requires talents and abilities, and as talents and abilities cannot have hereditary descent, it is evident that hereditary succession requires a belief from man to which his reason cannot subscribe, and which can only be established upon his ignorance; and the more ignorant any country is, the better it is fitted for this species of Government.

On the contrary, Government, in a well constituted Republic, requires no belief from man beyond what his reason can give. He sees the *rationale* of the system, its origin and its operation; and as it is best supported when best understood, the human faculties act with boldness and acquire under this form of government a gigantic manliness.

As, therefore, each of those forms acts on a different base, the one moving freely by the aid of reason, the other by ignorance, we have next to consider what it is that gives motion to that species of Government which is called mixed Government, or as it is sometimes ludicrously stiled, a Government of *this*, *that* and *t'other*.

The moving power in this species of Government is of necessity Corruption. However imperfect election and representation may be in mixed Governments, they still give exercise to a greater portion of reason than is convenient to the hereditary part; and therefore it becomes necessary to buy the reason up. A mixed Government is an imperfect everything, cementing and soldering the discordant parts together by corruption, to act as a whole. . . .

What is Government more than the management of the affairs of a Nation? It is not, and from its nature cannot be, the property of any particular man or family, but of the whole community at whose expense it is supported. . . . Sovereignty, as a matter of right, appertains to the Nation only, and not to any individual; and a Nation has at all times an inherent indefeasible right to abolish any form of government it finds inconvenient, and establish such as accords with its interest, disposition and happiness.

> From PAINE's *Rights of Man*, Part I, Conclusion, pp. 161–6 of the 3rd edition of 1791. The text is also given in A. COBBAN, *The Debate on the French Revolution* (1950), pp. 200–2.

IX

Goethe on Germany and the Revolution

(a) The 'Cannonade of Valmy'

So the day had passed; the French had not budged; Kellermann had even taken up a more advantageous position. Our men were now withdrawn out of range, and everything was exactly as though nothing had happened. Consternation spread over the army. Only that morning everyone had assumed we should make a couple of mouthfuls of the French. I myself had had complete confidence in this fine army and in the Duke of Brunswick; otherwise I should not have been led astray into joining so dangerous an undertaking. But now everyone went around with his own thoughts, avoiding his fellows; or if he spoke, it was only to swear or to curse. Just as night was falling we had come together by chance into a circle, in the middle of which we could not even make our accustomed fire. Most were silent; some spoke, but really no one knew what to think or say. Finally someone called on me to say what I thought about it, for I had often cheered and amused the company with brief comments. This time I said: 'From this place and moment a new epoch of world history begins, and you all can say that you were there.'

> From GOETHE's *Campagne in Frankreich* (translated for the editors by C. H. Trevelyan), 19 September 1792, night (near the end).

(b) Hermann and Dorothea

For who would deny that his heart leapt up and the blood coursed freer and purer in his breast as the first gleam of the new sun shone out? For we heard of the rights of man that are the heritage of all, of inspiring liberty and of praiseworthy equality. Then in each arose the hope to live his own life; the toils in which so many nations lay entangled seemed now to be dissolving out of the hands of idleness and greed, which held them. Did not all peoples, in those stirring days, turn their eyes to the capital of the world, which so long had borne that glorious name and now more than ever deserved it? Were not the names of those men who first cried the glad tidings, held equal to the greatest of the great immortals? Did not courage and understanding and gifts of speech grow greatly in each of us?

And we first of all, their next neighbours, were quickly set on fire. Then the war began, and the hosts of Frenchmen in arms drew nearer; yet they seemed to bring only friendship. And indeed they did bring it; for the hearts of all of them beat more nobly. Eagerly they planted the gay trees of liberty, promising to each man his due and to each his own government. What joy then filled the hearts of youth, and of old age too! Gaily we danced about the new banner. So they soon won the minds of the men, these forceful Frenchmen, with their fiery, restless activity, and then the hearts of our women-folk with their irresistible charm. Even the burden of greedy war seemed to us not hard to bear. For in the distance we saw Hope circling, enticing our gaze into new paths, till then close barred. Ah, how blissful are the days when the bride and bridegroom whirl in the dance; for the hour of their union is not far! But still more wonderful was that time when the noblest life that man can dream of seemed near and in our grasp. Then each man's tongue was loosened; greybeards, grown men and youths all spoke clear words of lofty sense and feeling.

But soon the sky was darkened. A graceless tribe, unworthy to build a better world, struggled for the spoils of power. They slaughtered each other and oppressed their new-found neighbours and brothers, and visited them with a grasping rabble. The great ones robbed us largely and squandered our wealth, and the underlings robbed and squandered down to the meanest. Their only care it seemed that something should still be left for the morrow's plunder. Then great was our distress and daily the oppression grew. No one heard our cry; for they were our masters. Then anger and bitterness consumed even the unwarlike heart; and all bethought them and swore to avenge the injury and the bitter loss of hope, now doubly deceived.

From GOETHE's *Hermann und Dorothea* (*Klio*, or *Das Zeitalter*, at the beginning, 1797, translated for the editors by C. H. Trevelyan).

X

Kant on Perpetual Peace

1.

Nations, as states, may be judged like individuals who, living in the natural state of society—that is to say, uncontrolled by external law—injure one another through their very proximity. Every state, for the sake of its own security, may—and ought to—demand that its neighbour should submit itself to conditions, similar to those of the civil society where the right of every individual is guaranteed. This would give rise to a federation of nations which, however, would not have to be a State of nations.

.   .   .   .   .   .

The attachment of savages to their lawless liberty, the fact that they would rather be at hopeless variance with one another than sub-mit themselves to a legal authority constituted by themselves, that they therefore prefer their senseless freedom to a reason-governed liberty, is regarded by us with profound contempt as barbarism and uncivilisation and the brutal degradation of humanity. So one would think that civilised races, each formed into a state by itself, must come out of such an abandoned condition as soon as they possibly can. On the contrary, however, every state thinks rather that its majesty (the 'majesty' of a people is an absurd expression) lies just in the very fact that it is subject to no external legal authority: and the glory of the ruler consists in this, that, without his requiring to expose himself to danger, thousands stand at his command ready to let themselves be sacrificed for a matter of no concern to them.

IMMANUEL KANT: *Perpetual Peace*, second section, Second Definitive Article (from the translation by N. CAMPBELL SMITH, Allen & Unwin, 1903).

2.

The practical man, however, for whom morals is mere theory, even while admitting that what ought to be can be, bases his dreary verdict against our well-meant hopes really on this: he pretends that he can foresee from his observation of human nature, that men will never be willing to do what is required in order to bring about the wished-for results leading to perpetual peace. It is true that the will of all individual men to live under a legal constitution according to the principles of liberty—that is to say, the distributive unity of the wills of all—is not sufficient to attain this end. We must have the collective unity of their united will: all as a body must deter-mine these new conditions. The solution of this difficult problem is required in order that civil society should be a whole. To all this diversity of individual wills there must come a uniting cause, in order to produce a common will which no distributive will is able to give. Hence, in the practical realization of that idea, no other beginning of a law-governed society can be counted upon than one that is brought about by force: upon this force, too, public law afterwards rests.

.   .   .   .   .   .

A state which enjoys an independence of the control of external law will not submit to the judgment of the tribunals of other states, when it has to consider how to obtain its rights against them. And even a continent, when it feels its superiority to another, whether this be in its way or not, will not fail to take advantage of an opportunity offered of strengthening its power by the spoliation or even conquest of this territory. Hence all theoretical schemes, connected with constitutional, international or cosmopolitan law, crumble away into empty impracticable ideals.

.   .   .   .   .   .

Now certainly, if there is neither freedom nor a moral law founded upon it, and every actual or possible event happens in the mere mechanical course of nature, then politics, as the art of making use of this physical necessity in things for the government of men, is the whole of practical wisdom, and the idea of right is an empty concept. If, on the other hand, we find that this idea of right is necessarily to be conjoined with politics and even to be raised to the position of a limiting condition of that science, then the possibility of reconciling them must be admitted. I can thus imagine a moral politician, that is to say, one who understands the principles of statesmanship to be such as do not conflict with morals; but I cannot conceive of a political moralist who fashions for himself such a system of ethics as may serve the interest of statesmen.

> Ibid., Appendix I, On the Disagreement between Morals and Politics with reference to Perpetual Peace.

XI

Napoleon on the Civil Code

My glory does not lie in forty victories, or in the fact of having imposed my will on kings. Waterloo will wipe out the memory of many victories. The last act makes the first forgotten. But there are some things that will never disappear: my Civil Code, the reports of the sessions of the State Council, my correspondence with my ministers. . . . My Code alone, by reason of its simplicity, has done more good in France than the whole mass of laws that came before me. My schools, my system of mutual instruction, are preparing generations as yet unknown. . . . I wanted to found a European system, a European code, a Supreme Court of Appeal for all Europe; there would have been a single European people. . . .

Nothing can henceforth destroy or obliterate the great principles of our revolution; those great and noble truths will endure for ever, for we have interwoven with them a multitude of illustrious actions and prodigies of achievement; we have drowned in floods of glory the blots that at first defiled them; they are henceforward immortal! They were first uttered by French orators, they were sealed with the blood of our soldiers, crowned with the laurels of victory, acclaimed by nations, sanctioned by treaties and by alliances with sovereigns; they sound familiarly in the ears and on the lips of kings; nothing now can make them retreat! . . . All peoples will find in them a faith, a religion, a moral code; and this memorable era will be connected, whatever men may say, with my person; because after all I made the torch blaze, I consecrated the principles and, to-day, persecution brings it about that I am their Messiah. Friends and enemies, all will call me the first soldier of this era, its great representative. And even when I shall have ceased to be, I shall still remain for the nations the lodestar of their rights; my name will be the battle-cry of their endeavours, the watchword of their hopes.

NAPOLEON: *Mémorial de Sainte-Hélène* (in Las Cases, op. cit., ed. Garnier, vol. i, p. 306).

Note. Documents II, III, and XI have been translated from the French by one of the editors (E. B.).

V. 11

THE DEVELOPMENT OF LITERATURE AND CULTURE IN THE EIGHTEENTH CENTURY

By

PROFESSOR DANIEL MORNET
of the University of Paris

I

THE SUPREMACY OF FRENCH CULTURE

THE BEGINNINGS OF ITS DECLINE AND THE DEVELOPMENT OF ENGLISH INFLUENCE

§1. *New Confidence of Reason: Dogmatic Religions on Trial: Atheism and Deism in England: Religion beyond the Dogmas: Pope: Voltaire*

The most violent conflict of ideas in Europe in the first half of the eighteenth century was provoked by religious problems. The battle really began with the Renaissance; but it is not our business here to go back to its origin. Towards the end of the seventeenth century it becomes more violent, and above all it begins to engage the attention of a much wider public. Let us briefly recall its different aspects. In France, scholarly and sceptical free-thinkers were a more or less secret and closed order, and by about 1660 their influence had almost completely disappeared. But there were many other free-thinkers who did not concern themselves about logic or philosophy. They too have their place in the great struggle which, at varying times and with varying fortunes, is joined in all the countries of Europe, and which may be described as the 'Battle of the Passions'. The whole of Christianity is founded on a dogma, that of original sin. Ever since that first sin, human nature has been utterly corrupt, and can only go the way of sin. The coming of Christ was needed before sin could be resisted and salvation achieved. Grace, bestowed by God, was still a necessity; and a fight must constantly be waged against nature. But what is nature, human nature? In the view of the 'rigorists'—the Puritans, Quakers, Wesleyans, and the like in England, and the Jansenists and many others in France—there are two kinds of action open to man. The first is the actions decided upon by our intelligence and our will, because they seem good to us; these actions, in themselves, neither give us nor are meant to give us any pleasure, except that of a duty performed. The second kind of actions consists in obedience to a natural inclination and to any form of desire. No effort of will is required to persuade us to perform them; we just seek to gratify our wants. But in the view of the 'rigorists' any seeking after pleasure, no matter how innocent it may seem, is guilty, or at any rate leads us down a slope where we fall inevitably into sin. To Bossuet, there is serious guilt in going to the opera or a comedy, and in reading novels or poetry; even those who study history, physics, mathematics, and the like, are on the path of wrong-doing. Those who want religion to be 'human and reasonable', as Molière says in *Tartuffe*, oppose themselves to these 'rigorists'. But besides men of this stamp, who wish to find a compromise between religion and the reasonable enjoyment of the senses in artistic and social pleasures, there are those who have no intention of controlling or resisting nature, who declare that nature is everywhere and always good, and that the object of our being is to enjoy the pleasures she offers on the one condition of avoiding excess and its penalty of ill health. In England this was the temper of the elegant and cynical society of the Restoration, and of what was left of that society after the fall of James II. In France, in the eighteenth century, it was the temper of the social world of the *châteaux*; after the death of Louis XIV it was that of the regency, which was sometimes simply elegant and fastidious, at other times openly debauched.

None of this was a serious menace to religious faith. But faith had faced, and was destined to face, more dangerous attacks. It matters little whether a religion is strict, or how strict it is, if only people believe in its truth. But attempts had been made, and were again to be made, to show that the Christian religion was not true, and that there was nothing to prove its truth. In France, Fontenelle, Bayle, and others had consciously or unconsciously undertaken this task. Developing the critical faculty by their works, they had encouraged it to deny and doubt the traditional proofs of revelation.

Bayle's dictionary was famous. Out of 500 private libraries in France, these weighty volumes were to be found in 288. Extracts from his dictionary and other writings were translated into German in 1741. But neither he nor anyone else had written anything that could be classed as a complete, methodical, and critical examination of the Christian faith. The great attack on the whole body of Christian revelation came from England.

Here, between 1696 and 1760, a dozen deist or atheist writers published more than fifty works which, directly or indirectly, undermined all the foundations of Christianity.

First, between 1696 and about 1730, come Toland, Woolston,

Collins, Tindal; a little later came Chubb, Gordon, Middle-ton, Annet, Trenchard, and some less-known authors. Their polemic was often very violent. It used complicated arguments, which varied, at any rate in the importance attached to them, from author to author. But all, or almost all, of the arguments had common features. They were to the effect that rational criticism cannot accept the proofs of Christianity drawn from the Old and New Testaments, and that there is no more proof of the miracles they record than there is of the wonders alleged by any superstition. These English atheists and deists tackled the actual texts and based their criticisms upon them. They employed methodical arguments which no one had ever dared to use before. Not only, in their view, are the beliefs contained in the Old Testament contrary to reason, but its ethics are also completely unethical; they are based on violence, injustice, fanaticism, and fear. Moreover, everything in these ancient books shows the work of man and not that of divine revelation.

What was their influence, in England and in Europe? They had a real influence, but in England it was rather weak. Only a few of their works ran into two or three editions; and it was not the most violent that were most often read. In France their influence was also weak until about 1760. They certainly did not circulate outside groups of the initiated, who because of their position were more or less safe from police inquiries. The situation was different after 1760, thanks to d'Holbach, whose works, many of them translations or adaptations from the English, went into some seventy-five editions, and thanks also to Voltaire, whose 'rational' and anti-religious philosophy was propagated in a hundred works and pamphlets of a vigour and incisive lucidity which profoundly influenced public opinion not only in France but also in other countries.

At first Voltaire was more in agreement with Locke and with Pope, who were convinced Christians. Then, as he became more and more embroiled in the war against 'the infamous' (*l'infâme*), that is to say, against fanaticism and intolerance, he developed a lively interest in writers who supplied him with more precise arguments. Thus he gradually became the follower of Toland, Collins, Tindal, Annet, &c., especially in his *Dictionnaire philosophique* and his *Questions sur l'Encyclopédie*.

In spite of the avowed unbelievers in England, and in spite of Voltaire, d'Holbach, and some others in France, the war engaged against Christianity in Europe did not end in victory, or even in a partial victory. What tended to win the day was rather a form of deism, at once vague and accommodating, which claimed to rise above dogma. You must believe that a God exists distinct from the universe; that He has given us an immortal soul, and a conscience capable of distinguishing Good from Evil; that He will punish the wicked and reward the good; and finally that He is good. This optimistic deism was partly derived from Leibnitz; but his philosophy was too general, too abstract, and too subtle to reach the average mind except through intermediaries, and in distorted and debased versions. It owed even more to English writers. The two English philosophers who, after Locke, were most influential in Europe, and especially in France, in the first half of the eighteenth century, were Shaftesbury and Bolingbroke. Shaftesbury (in his *Inquiry concerning Virtue or Merit*) is certainly not a believer, and he is the enemy of any fanatical or intolerant religion. All dogmatic religions leave him unmoved. But in defence of his deism he appeals to arguments which have nothing to do with the rationalist and critical reason. He believes that everything fine and noble in man and his works springs from a mysterious faculty, divine in essence, which is called 'enthusiasm'. 'Enthusiasm' gives no reasons, and need give none, for its inspiration. We know, with conviction, that what it implants in us is true, just, noble, and beautiful. The influence of Bolingbroke only made itself felt after 1750. It was limited to smaller and more aristocratic circles. But the prestige of the man, his French connexions, and the combination in him and his works of a certain elegant scepticism with a shrewd distrust of all sceptical reasoning, served rather to confirm than contradict the 'enthusiasm' of Shaftesbury.

It was, however, neither Shaftesbury nor Bolingbroke, nor the other English writers of their stamp, who were responsible for the signal success of a deism so broad and so tolerant that it attracted both believers and unbelievers. It was first and foremost the work of Pope, in his *Essay on Man* (1732–4) and his *Universal Prayer*. Pope believed that God has implanted in man's soul the desire for happiness. It is useless for men to puzzle over the nature of God and the universe, or to trouble about finding reasons for God and the universe. Problems such as these are insoluble, and their pursuit can only lead us into folly and useless anxiety. We must be content to understand two self-evident truths. The first is that we are not the ultimate aim of the universe, and that the creation was not made solely for man's convenience; the second is that we cannot find happiness by means of egoism. Our happiness and our chances of happiness increase in proportion to the general happiness of the human race. We work for ourselves when we work for the good of all. Egoism is calculating and detestable. On the other hand, God has not inflicted upon us a life of austerity and expiation. In the 'Battle of the Passions' of which we have spoken, Pope is really on the side of the passions. They can of course constantly lead us into fatal excesses; they must be controlled by reason and knowledge; but in themselves they are good or indifferent, and it is they that make of our life something which is vital and happy.

These works of Pope (and in fact all his work) met with considerable success. In France alone du Reusel's translation of the *Essay on Man* had run into twenty-eight editions by 1788; by the same date there were also twenty-seven editions of the translation by Silhouette. In 1767 there appeared a revised translation into four languages (French, Latin, Italian, German, along with the English). Voltaire in particular helped to disseminate Pope's teaching still more rapidly and more widely.

Voltaire's *Discours en vers sur l'homme* (which appeared between 1734 and 1745) is undoubtedly an original work. Voltaire's polemics are mainly levelled against pious hypocrisy and blind and bitter fanaticism. His *Discours*, even more obviously than the writings of Pope, is a declaration of war on the enemies of the 'passions'; on those who believe that man cannot attain virtue or salvation without renouncing all pleasure. In the first six discourses the right to prudent and wise pleasure appears as a selfish right; the wise man orders his life for the satisfaction of himself. Only in the seventh and last discourse does he acknowledge the necessity of the virtues of 'humanity' and 'benevolence'.

§ 2. *The New Reasons for Thought*

In spite of the importance attached by some thinkers to enthusiasm and the truths of the heart, almost all modes of thought and trends of opinion are inspired by Cartesian principles; the only truths are those which our reason really accepts as true after a methodical examination. These Cartesian principles spread like wildfire across the whole of Europe after the end of the seventeenth and the beginning of the eighteenth century. But towards the end of the seventeenth and throughout all the eighteenth century the system of Descartes met a formidable enemy which captured most of the territories where he had claimed to be master. In all the natural sciences experimental rationalism begins to take the place of logical rationalism.

Let us outline the essential arguments which were to challenge Cartesianism. Descartes tried to give all human sciences the same exactitude that is to be found in mathematics. If one proposition follows necessarily from another proposition already recognized as necessarily true, that proposition is itself true. In this way, by deduction after deduction, we may explain the universe, the nature of man, and life. Descartes thus maintains that there are only two substances or realities, the soul which is without extension and matter which is simply extension. In discussing extension, or space, Descartes seeks to prove that it constitutes a universe in the nature of a *plenum*. In this *plenum* only one kind of movement is logically possible, and this is circular movement. Thus Descartes builds up his system of vortices. Here Newton intervenes, and shows that in reality the movements of the stars do not correspond with Descartes's system. To explain them, we must have recourse to the principle of gravitation. This causes great confusion in the Cartesian camp. 'Your gravity', the Cartesians argue, 'is only an empty word, logically without any meaning. Logically, there is no reason why bodies should not repel one another instead of attracting one another.' 'I agree', Newton replies: 'I do not know what is the nature of gravity; I can only say this is how things are. . . . And my supposition is correct, because it is confirmed by the facts, because all the movements of the stars agree with my calculations, and because I can forecast the return of comets. I cannot say exactly what is the nature of light; but my experiments prove that white light may be decomposed into seven coloured lights.' Briefly, we may say that Descartes claims that he can give a deep explanation that shows us the very reason of things. 'I do not know the deep reason of things', Newton replies, 'but from observation and experiment I can show you how things happen and how they obey unvarying laws constantly verifiable by experiment. Science, as I understand it, will not perhaps explain the reasons for the universe, but it will show how it is ordered.'

The conflict between logical and mathematical reason and reason based on experiment does not, of course, date from the clash between Descartes and Newton. It exists throughout the whole of the seventeenth century, and it exists not only as between different philosophers or thinkers, but often in the mind of one and the same philosopher or thinker, as it does, for instance, in Père Mersenne, Descartes, and Pascal in France. Gradually, however, the experimental method gains ground. By about 1750 its victory is complete and decisive.

It was in England and Holland that the victory was won. Other nations of course also played their part: France, for example, with the Academy of Sciences and scholars like Roberval or Mariotte, and Italy, with the works of a physiologist such as Malpighi, in the seventeenth century, and later the *Mémoires* of the Accademia del Cimento in Florence. But it was Newton's fame, and the teaching and writings of his Dutch disciples, that finally defeated and routed Cartesian rationalism in the field of the natural sciences. Everyone, in short, became Newtonian, not only in the Royal Society, of which he was the president, but also outside it. But it was mainly through Dutch scholars, teaching in the universities, that the Newtonian method gained its hold on European thought. All of them became the followers of Newton. Leuwenhoeck submitted all his work to the Royal Society before publishing it. 's Gravenzande worked in London under Desaguliers and Newton. All their published works acknowledged Newton as their master; and in the European scientific world these works had a tremendous success (Boerhaave, *De comparando certo in physicis*, 1715; 's Gravenzande, *Physices elementa . . . sive introductio ad philosophiam newtonianam*, 1720–1, and *Discours sur l'évidence*, 1724; Musschenbroek, *De methodo instituendi experimenta physica*, 1730; &c.). The works of these Dutch scholars were translated into English or French. Their courses drew students from all the countries of Europe. It was owing to French students that the *Experimenta et institutiones chemiae* of Boerhaave was first published in Paris in 1724.

All these scholars agree with one another completely. No more 'systems'; no more science, or pseudo-science, which makes itself the slave of a general philosophy that claims to explain nature by reasoning derived from a so-called logic itself unproven and contradicted by the facts. The only true explanations are those given by the facts. These facts are presented by observation or constructed by means of experiments. Experiments are valid whenever the same causes are followed by the same effects with the necessary precision. These explanations and laws are, of course, always limited. But all the apparently reliable general systems have collapsed, one after another, and any similar systems that may succeed them are doomed to the same fate.

In England and Holland the Newtonian, or experimental, method triumphed practically without opposition. In Germany Leibniz's high reputation as a philosopher and mathematician, and the renown of his follower Wolff, enabled general philosophies to resist the slow and careful methods of experimental philosophy. In France there was a vigorous struggle between Cartesians and Newtonians; but by 1750 the experimental method had won a complete and decisive victory. Experimental philosophy won its victories everywhere through the visible evidence of facts and through teaching. Instead of abstract speculations and melancholy meditations, it introduced a picturesque note—the tangible evidence of experiments, scales, air pumps, and electrical machines. The abbé Nollet instituted laboratory instruction. He was a pupil of the English, during his travels in England in 1754, and of the Dutch. In 1738 a chair of experimental physics was founded for him, and in 1753 it became a chair at the college of Navarre in the university of Paris. More than 600 students attended his lectures. His works (*Leçons de physique expérimentale*, 1743, 8th ed. in 1775) were translated into English, Dutch, Italian, Spanish, German, and Latin. In England Benjamin Martin had published a *Grammar of the philosophical sciences, or short analysis of modern philosophy, based on experiments*. It too was a most scholarly work, couched in the form of questions and answers. It was translated into French in 1749, and republished afterwards.

By the second half of the century it may be said that Newton's theories and the experimental method in the natural sciences have ceased to be challenged except by a few diehards. The *Encyclopédie*, with its large circulation, was entirely Newtonian. Everyone was against speculative systems, particularly in England, Holland, and France.[1]

---

[1] In connexion with this study of the influence of Newton and his followers mention should also be made of the lively curiosity shown in all English works

During the same half of the century another field of know-ledge had also claimed and won independence. The philoso-phies of Descartes and Leibniz did not distinguish the study of psychology from a general explanation of the universe. But in 1690 Locke published in England a small work with the unassuming title: *An Essay Concerning Human Understanding*. The immediate effects of this essay were revolutionary. Locke admits that he understands little or nothing of the vast systems which explain the whole nature of the soul and that of the universe together, and for which no explanation is valid unless it forms part of a general explanation of everything. But real life sets us, he argues, all kinds of immediate problems which may be easily answered by observation of the facts. For instance, an infant does not think; we might even say that he does not see; he cannot at first grasp any object; later he puts out his hand to grasp an object far away from it. Then gradually his thought takes shape; he learns not to touch things that might burn him; he learns to talk; he does not at first learn to reason, but he learns to asso-ciate ideas, and so on. Now Descartes taught that all ideas were innate and developed of themselves in the course of time, just as a whole ear of corn is contained in a grain of wheat. 'Purely hypothetical', says Locke. Observation shows us, he argues, that the mind of a child is constantly coming into contact with facts which consist in sensations. These contacts and their effects may be constantly and everywhere seen. It is possible to observe the history of the development of thought. This history will not reveal to us the mysteries of matter and the soul, or the nature of matter, or the reasons of life and death. For the present at least all that is insoluble. But we can know with certainty how our thought develops, and what it receives and what it creates.

Locke had a European reputation. He was in touch with scholars and philosophers all over the world. But it was in France especially that he became a sort of symbol of the true philosopher who discards laborious and contradictory systems to put men in constant contact with reality. Translations of the *Essay Concerning Human Understanding*, and an abridged version of its argument, went into more than a dozen editions.

A place must be found for Montesquieu in this great movement

dealing with various sciences of a less rigorous nature. Information on this may be found in the valuable work of G. Bouno, *La Culture et la civilisation britanniques devant l'opinion française, de la paix d'Utrecht aux Lettres Philosophiques*, 1948.

of thought which everywhere tends to replace the fashion for rational systems by a method based on facts and experiment. He was certainly not alone in exploring the field which is covered by his *L'Esprit des Lois*. In 1764 Beccaria was to publish in Italy a *Treatise on Crime and Punishment* which had a European reputation, was translated into almost every language, and was studied by nearly all the French philosophers. Like Montesquieu, Beccaria stated facts, and argued only from the realities which common sense approved. But it was after all Montesquieu who paved the way in 1748, and his book had great vogue throughout Europe.

To understand the true originality and influence of Montesquieu, we must remember what were the great European books that dealt with legal principles before the appearance of *L'Esprit des Lois*. They were chiefly the *Law of War and Peace* by the Dutchman Grotius, published in 1624, and the German Pufendorf's work, of the year 1672, on *The Law of Nature and Nations, or a general system of the principles of jurisprudence and politics*. Between 1747 and 1774 the Genevan Burlamaqui published his *Principles of Natural Law* and *Principles of Political Law*, which were celebrated works. All three, even Grotius, who was before Descartes, were Cartesians. We must ask ourselves, according to them, not what are the laws of a country or how to understand them and put them into practice, but what laws ought to be. To understand this we must ask ourselves what is the nature of man, man as he is in all ages and all countries, and what is required by the conscience of this universal man. When we have agreed on these requirements we shall establish, by a series of deductions, what the laws of war and peace ought to be, or what ought to be the nature of a general system of the principles of jurisprudence and politics.

Montesquieu reacted violently against this method, but less violently than has been alleged. In what may be called the first part of *L'Esprit des Lois*, he is still under the influence of Descartes. He bases his study of the three kinds of government—despotism, monarchy, and democracy—much more on logical distinctions than on the truth of facts, which he draws almost entirely from Greek and Roman history. But when he begins to discuss the influence of climate, soil, and the general trend of thought upon laws, his method becomes totally different: it is based on the spirit of experimental philosophy, and this explains his influence. It is no longer for him a question of knowing what laws ought to be, and how they can give satisfaction to the conscience of man in every age and country where a certain standard of culture and reflection has been attained. It is only necessary to prove what laws actually are. Such proof must, it is true, enable us to form a judgement, but this judgement will be based on an absolutely different principle from that of the previous method. No law is good or bad in itself. Those laws are good which are successful, in the sense that they bring greater happiness to those for whom they are made; laws are bad when they fail, and bring about distress and disorder. But men differ fundamentally according to climate, soil, and the general trend of thought; what is suitable for some is not suitable for others; polygamy or even polyandry may possibly be good laws. It is useless and even dangerous to believe in a universal reason which is capable of building a universal system of law. There are only facts, which are always various and even contradictory, and the consequences or experience of facts. Social observation must continue to be the permanent and necessary condition of what may be called social science.

§ 3. *The New Reasons for Life*

Do not deism, and *a fortiori* atheism, which only allow a vague hope, or deny altogether the prospect, of a future life which will recompense us for the misfortunes of this, condemn us to pessimism and even despair? This question prompted the eighteenth century to address itself still more eagerly to the old problem of optimism versus pessimism.

The philosophers, such as Leibniz or Shaftesbury, argue the problem in philosophic terms. But philosophic arguments were hardly likely to prove to the world, or at any rate to those who wished to have some proof, that life is worth living when you know what it is, and that a man may be a deist without renouncing the reasons for being happy. A whole host of writers undertook to provide some proof for the general public.

The Englishman Pope was certainly the most popular of these optimists. From him we learn to give up useless metaphysical problems and the feverish pursuit of an impossible solution. He teaches us that man can no more be regarded as the sole object of the universe, and that the universe was not created for his sake alone; that one man is not the reason for the existence of all other men, and that if each of us tries to achieve happiness regardless of others, we shall all be miserable; finally, that happiness is not to be found in the illusory pleasures of ambition, pride, riches, or riotous living, but in the sure and simple joys which may be shared by all. The French translations of Pope's *Essay on Man* ran into fifty-five editions. There were eighteen editions of German translations, not to mention three translations of his complete works, a translation of his poems, and a translation of extracts.

To Pope's influence must be added, in France, the influence of Voltaire, who was at first Pope's most ardent disciple. We have already noted that his *Discours en vers sur l'homme* is often an adaptation of the *Essay of Man*. Like the *Essay*, it preaches not only natural religion and hatred of fanaticism but also an optimistic acceptance of life. We must take life as it comes; give up trying to understand the world's insoluble mysteries; give up, too, thinking ourselves lords of creation. But we must also cherish the belief that we can find all the means of happiness here on earth. This philosophy of Voltaire is, of course, superficial, but the lucidity and good humour of the *Discours* made it instantly popular, at any rate in France.

Even more than through the works of Pope and Voltaire the cult of optimism was spread by a broad movement of European opinion which one may call by the name of 'providentialism'. Its astonishingly rapid spread may be explained by the fact that it combined ancient beliefs with new curiosities and tastes—the curiosity of experimental science and the taste for optimism. The discovery of the sciences of observation revealed, particularly in natural history, the complex and subtle secrets governing the processes of nature and particularly of life. Only a divine intelligence could have conceived and created all this. Thus a broad theology was born, based on the discoveries of physicists and naturalists who were expected, whether they wished it or not, to demonstrate the existence of God. Such a theology may be found in scores of writers: among them are many Dutch, English, German, Swiss, and French names. For instance, the *Spectacle de la Nature* by the Abbé Pluche (nine volumes, from 1732 onwards; at least fifteen French editions; translations into English, Italian, and Spanish) extols in the last volume the goodness of God, who created the various shades of green in nature, so that our eyes might not be tired, and who invented tides, so that ships might be able to sail into harbour.

This first chapter is entitled 'The Supremacy of French Culture', but hitherto we have given first place to philosophers, polemists, moralists, and scholars belonging to England and Holland. Yet however important a part may be played in the development of thought and customs by works of philosophy, or of religious polemic, or even more of natural science, such works reach directly only a small minority of readers. France, though surpassed by others in these fields, was still regarded by European opinion as pre-eminent. There were two reasons for this. The first was her literature and art, which will be discussed later; the second and main reason was the prestige of her social life, where optimism and the pleasures of life seemed to have more flavour, and to be more assured, than in any other country.

It is true that this social life, and the charm of the French 'salons', do not begin with the eighteenth century. But it is during the first third of the eighteenth century that they begin to influence the whole of Europe, if not towards imitation, at any rate towards admiration and envy.

What was the life of the 'salons', and what was it foreigners came to seek there? Let us first take, as an example, Madame de Tencin's salon (about 1730), where Fontenelle, Marivaux, and scholars like Mairan shone. This 'salon' was open every day. People did not meet there for the kind of pleasures that might degenerate into sins; they did not drink, and they did not gamble. They went there to please themselves and others; they went for the pleasure of company—but of an intelligent and cultured company. They passed the time in conversation, free from all constraint and pedantry; men could be silent during its course, or even think of other things. They talked of literature, art, and philosophy, provided that the philosophy did not bury itself in obscurities. Men endeavoured to be subtle and witty: this was why foreigners not only visited Madame de Tencin, but were eager to return. An introduction was necessary to gain an entry to this 'realm of the rue St. Honoré'. To gain admission for a Mrs. Cleland, Chesterfield wrote a long letter full of oratorical assurances and almost of humility.

Béal-Louis de Muralt, of Berne, published in 1725 one of his *Lettres sur les Anglais et les Français et sur les voyages* which was very successful (eight editions in French and two editions of an

English translation). This intelligent and honest traveller is far from being a friend of France; he loathes society life. Quite frankly, and at length, he states his preference for the sober, thoughtful temperament of the English and their view of life. Nevertheless, he feels bound to acknowledge all the charm of French society and the reputation which it commands. 'Many people are delighted with it, and consider France the leading country in the world . . . it is certainly true that we foreigners find in France everything that the traveller could desire of a country which he is visiting'—and in which (we may add), as will appear later, people even settle or wish to settle.

There were even attempts at a sort of apology, on social if not on moral grounds, for this life of fashionable pleasure. In 1714 the Dutchman Mandeville, English by adoption, published (with additions and annotations down to 1728) a verse allegory called *The Grumbling Hive*, translated into French under the title *La Fable des Abeilles*. In it he explains and justifies a complicated doctrine. He is not really either a sceptic or a cynic. He even inclines towards a 'rigorist' interpretation of goodness —if it is really worth the name. But he argues that in practice no society has ever been built, nor could be built, on this rigid foundation. In practice he thinks that we ought to believe that a state can only be prosperous through the vices of individuals; and his motto is 'private vices, public benefits'. It is private vices that create luxury: luxury creates luxury industries, and makes money circulate; a number of workers are thus saved from poverty, and the coffers of the state are filled. His work had a tremendous success all over Europe. In the eighteenth century there were a dozen English editions, two or three French translations and one into German (followed by others in the nineteenth century). In France this 'defence of luxury' was adopted by Melon (*Essai politique sur le commerce*, 1734, of which there were at least four editions). He believed that prosperity depends on the circulation of wealth and that luxury is one of its essential features; it should therefore be encouraged rather than attacked. Finally Voltaire brought to the argument the charm of his wit and his elegant scepticism. In the *Mondain* (1736) and the *Défense du Mondain* (1737) he proclaimed: 'Away with these ascetic sermonizers who would like to drag us back to the slime and bestiality of primitive man: the earthly paradise is where I am'—that is to say, anywhere where there are fine carriages,

good dinners, and pretty women, elegantly dressed and per-
fumed.

§4. *The Old and the New Reasons for Art*

The discreet and considered elegance, the moderation and
the charm of French social life are matched by the characteristic features of French literature in the second half of the seventeenth century. When the life attracted everyone, the literature
was bound to please. Thus there developed in Europe a classical
age of literature in which French influence predominated.

It is easy to trace, as indeed has often been done, the characteristic features of this classical age in France. We have only to
compare the English literary works which preceded the vogue
of classicism, or those which followed it afterwards and were
independent of it. On the one hand we have freedom of inspiration, with its violences, its whims, its contradictions, its
disorder, and its prolixities, but also with its power, its pro-
fundity, and its flashes of imagination. On the other hand
we have the constant control of reason and of a discriminating
and selective taste which rejects everything in the nature of
impulsive digression or adventurous fancy. The famous rules of
style are only the outward expression of this desire for order and
deliberation. Besides, we must not forget that this love of reason
and rules in France is only one of the two forces which deter-
mine the shape of our classical literature, as I have tried to
show in my *Histoire de la littérature française classique*. Almost all
of us know that in order to make a masterpiece something else
is needed besides a knowledge and exact application of rules.
There is also needed, in addition, *agrément*: there are needed
délicatesses; and often there is even needed a certain *je ne sais
quoi*. But outside France the followers, direct or indirect, of our
Boileau, Racine, Molière, and La Bruyère did not breathe the
atmosphere of our salons. They were necessarily much less sensitive to this *je ne sais quoi*. If most of the classical works which
came from the literary schools of other countries were very soon
antiquated, it was not only because they were more or less
imitations, but also because they could not imitate the inimi-
table.

However this may be, the literary influence of France was at
first considerable. In England and Germany even more than
France, where the moderns were against him, Boileau was still

the 'legislator of Parnassus'. Dryden found him 'admirable':
Addison visited him. Finally Pope, in his works of criticism and
satire, was by his own confession his disciple, although he protested against the abuse of reason and rules.

French drama had just as great a reputation. Harvey-Jellic
has made a list of the sources of English drama at the time of the
Restoration. The list of plays which derived their plot from
English literature fills two and a half pages; that of plays which
drew on French literature takes up three pages (a third of a
page is enough for borrowings from the Italian, and the same
for borrowings from Spanish and from classical sources). French
influence on the English novel was less marked. This was because
there were no particular principles and no classical school among
French novelists.

French classical art and taste had an even greater reputation
in those countries where there was as yet no truly national literature, or where the characteristics of national literature were still
more or less vague and contradictory. This was true of Germany,
where down to 1760 literature and culture were deeply indebted
to French influence. Under the influence of Gottsched, drama
was closely modelled on the drama of France. Voltaire was also
popular: not, it is true, Voltaire the philosopher, who led the
attack on 'superstition', or in other words on Christianity, but
Voltaire the dramatist, poet, storyteller, the stylish and witty
man of letters. During the eighteenth century there were 51
German translations of his tragedies, 24 of his comedies, 17 of
his stories, and 34 of selections (but none of the *Dictionnaire
philosophique* or of the *Questions sur l'Encyclopédie*). It is scarcely
necessary to recall that Frederic II spoke and wrote French as
readily as German, that almost all his prolific work was composed in French, and that the most honoured members of his
Berlin Academy were Frenchmen like Maupertuis and Voltaire.
In 1753 Grimm began his famous *Correspondance littéraire*, which
kept readers informed about all the novelties of literature,
philosophy, and art then under discussion in the salons of Paris.
His subscribers included Catherine II, the queen of Sweden,
the king of Poland, and a score of petty German sovereigns,
whose principal ambition was to think like the French, to copy
French taste, and to be on 'record'—that is to say, on record in
France.

From the beginning to the end of the century Italy also was

completely under French influence. Translations and imitations of French works abounded. Critics, at least until about 1770, considered Racine and Molière to be the perfect dramatists. Voltaire was equally popular; there were fifteen translations of *Zaïre* into Italian. There were also printed in Italy editions of many French writers in the original French, among them Bossuet, Fénelon, Montesquieu. In Bologna it could be said that among the aristocracy, the Church, and even in the middle class, all culture was the culture of France. It was the same at Parma.

French cultural supremacy extended its sway also to Spain. In the second half of the century there was a conflict of influences; England, with Young, 'Ossian', and other writers, often through the medium of French translations, began to take the place of French classicism. But the classicism of France held the field in the first half of the century. Boileau was honoured as a master. Molière in particular (in whose tracks Moratín followed step by step) was translated and imitated, together with Racine and the sentimental comedies of Nivelle de la Chaussée.

While French scientific thought was dominated by the influence of the scholars of the Netherlands, Dutch literature and culture was modelled on the French. Everyone prided himself on knowing French. The companies of French actors which travelled in Holland met with great success. The profit motive was wedded to the fashion for things French by the printing in Holland of a large number of French works (either by agreement with the authors or in pirated editions). Mlle ter Meulen has counted the number of French works printed in Holland which are to be found in the Amsterdam University library: there are 4,500. In Dutch private libraries whose catalogues have been studied there are more French works than Dutch.

Switzerland still retained her intellectual independence. In spite of complaints about the relaxation of moral standards, the Genevese still believed, at any rate overtly, in a rigid Calvinism which frowned on the theatre, dancing, and even light reading. In French-speaking Switzerland generally men were less strict, and more addicted to pleasures which, if not altogether serious, were of an intellectual order. In 1733 the *Swiss Mercury* was founded at Neuchâtel; like its French model it tried to mingle the pleasant and the useful, the amusing and the serious. German-speaking Switzerland looked towards

Germany: it played no small part in the revival of German literature, and it also asserted its Swiss independence by opposing
its own tastes and habits to any suggestion of change. In 1729
the famous physiologist Haller published his poem on the Alps,
translated several times into French, which contained some
praise of the Swiss landscape, but much more of the simple,
contented, and patriarchal life of the inhabitants of the Swiss
mountains.

But it must be admitted that even in the field of literature,
manners, and good taste French influence met with some opposition, all the more as it discouraged an interest in other literatures. In the first half of the eighteenth century there grew up
in France, and even more in England and elsewhere, the idea
that there is no universal and immutable standard of taste, or
any universal or immutable rules, but that, on the contrary,
every country and even epoch has its own standards, and therefore any attempt to judge and assess literary works on the basis
of absolute principles is doomed to failure. A battle was joined
between what may be called the school of French classicism and
those who wished to throw off its yoke (a battle in which classicism was doomed to defeat in the second half of the century).
Paul Hazard has shown how treatises on 'the poetic art', or
critical essays in the same style, increased at this time in every
European literature. Almost all of them followed the classical
model; but their tone was no longer that of deferential homage.
The rule of reason is now no more than a very limited and rather
fainéant form of monarchy, which leaves a large scope for
fancy and imagination, and for all the diversities, and even the
irregularities, which may be involved in their play.

It is easier to understand this conflict between the discipline
of a strict classical tradition and the need for the infusion of new
blood if one examines the influence of English writers like
Milton, Pope, Swift, and Shakespeare in France. On the whole,
Milton's *Paradise Lost* could easily take its place in the temple
raised by the classical age of reason to house the epics which
deserved a place. But there were also many things in his epic
that might shock the judgement of reason and cause it to
denounce the errors of a taste which ignored the principles of
selection and measure. It was not Milton's naïve use of anthropo-
morphism, in his descriptions of the supernatural, that was

here in question. Milton, like all the other writers of his day, could only represent the supernatural by means of human symbols; the art of leading thought beyond reality without the aid of terms belonging to reality was an unknown art. The real matter in question was the tedious disquisitions and the theological descriptive digressions in Milton's poem. Faced with these, Boileau would have gone on repeating:

The man who knows not when to stop does not know how to write.

But there was also at issue the quality which constituted the genius and greatness of Milton: the power of an inexhaustible imagination which could conjure up (or, in the language of that age, 'paint to the mind') both the terrible splendours of Hell and the harmonious vision of Heaven, the dread cohorts of the army of Satan as well as the army of God, and the almost ineffable ecstasies of Paradise before it was lost.

During the eighteenth century, and already in its first half, Milton's poem had none the less a large general vogue. In the seventeenth century it was unknown. Dupré de St. Maur made the first translation in 1729. This translation ran into twenty editions down to 1800; there were also translations by Louis Racine (1755), Le Roy, and others. There were, too, numerous partial translations. But this popularity did not mean unqualified acceptance. All the translators were well-meaning 'traitors'[1] who sought to rectify English 'bad taste' by means of French 'good taste'. In the case of Pope there were fewer reservations; but even here there were some. Clearly, Pope was more classical than Milton. Voltaire said of him, in an obviously risky metaphor: 'He has tuned down the harsh blasts of the English trumpet into the sweet notes of the flute.' But this flute still played a music that was ill suited to French ears. So De Resnel thought, in the preface to his translation. But he also admitted— and in 1736 this marks an advance which is worthy of note— that he could not decide whether the French or the English were right.

English liberty, or licence, was still more in evidence in the work of Swift. He was extremely popular with French readers. There were ten editions of translations of *Gulliver* before 1750, and seven more before the Revolution. There were fifteen editions of

---

[1] The author refers to the Italian saying, 'traduttore traditore'.

the *Tale of a Tub* (in translations or adaptations) between 1721
and 1757; which proves once more how strong French love of
religious argument still was. But were Frenchmen able to enjoy
the peculiarly English flavour of these works? Voltaire, who had
personal relations with Swift, and who was then at the height of
his love for England, had no doubts when he wrote in his
Lettres Anglaises: 'Swift possesses all the finesse, the intellect, the
discrimination and good taste which are lacking in our priest of
Meudon (Rabelais)'; but the translator Desfontaines believed
just the opposite. In one particular respect, however, Swift's
work exercised an important influence. This was at a point
where the genius of England and that of France, or, as may
already be said in advance, that of the north and that of the
south, once more confront one another. What is the meaning of
French 'wit' and English 'humour', and how do they differ or
agree? The Bernese Muralt introduced the word 'humour' into
the French language to describe a form of wit that did not seem
to be French. But it was easier to accept the word than to define
its exact meaning. Actually humour, at least in an attenuated
form, already existed in French literature. It is to be found in
St-Évremond's *Contes d'Hamilton*; in a heavier and more laboured
form it may be found in the *Chef-d'œuvre d'un inconnu* by the
Franco-Dutch journalist Thémiseul de St-Hyacinthe (1714,
with at least ten editions before 1750, and later editions down to
the nineteenth century). Humour cannot thus be said to be 'in
great measure the peculiar province of the English nation', as
the English critic Blair maintained. Nevertheless, it was Swift
who revealed its most characteristically English form.

There is no doubt that during this first half of the century
English and Dutch philosophy and science were dominant in
Europe, while the classical culture and aesthetics of France were
always accepted as models, though with a growing amount of
qualification. But other nations, who had dominated the scene a
century earlier, still held their ground. The influence of Spain
had certainly declined. But during the seventeenth century *Don
Quixote* was known throughout Europe; and its fame lasted into
the eighteenth century. Italy stood her ground more firmly.
The memory of her scientists, Torricelli and Malpighi, was still
fresh. Ariosto, and Tasso's *Jerusalem delivered*, were still read;
and the latter, although debated, remained a model of epic

poetry. Italy still enjoyed the glory of her ancient ruins, her
museums, and her atmosphere of light and harmony. The Italian
tour was still the ambition, not only of painters, sculptors, and
architects, but also of men of letters. It was taken by President
de Brosses, Montesquieu, Chesterfield, Smollett, and Fielding.
Italian comedy held a high place in France, and rivalled the
plays of the Comédie Française. Italian music, in particular,
had a long succession of triumphs in Europe. There was some
French music, of course, and German music too was already
beginning. But Lully was an Italian; and though the genius of
Rameau, evident alike in his theory and his compositions, had
produced a new music which was wholly French, the musical
genius of Italy always found its enthusiastic admirers. Pergolesi's
Serva padrona, performed in 1746 at the Italian theatre and in
1752 at the Opéra, provoked the famous 'Querelle des bouffons',
which lasted for two years. In its course the 'Corner of the King',
with the help of d'Alembert and Fréron, upheld the cause of
French music in a hundred leaflets, pamphlets, articles, epigrams,
and songs, against the 'Corner of the Queen', which took the side
of Italian music with the aid of Grimm, Diderot, d'Holbach, and
Rousseau. The lyric tragedies of Metastasio achieved European
fame; he enjoyed in Vienna the title of 'Poeta cesareo' and
a pension of 3,000 florins. Rousseau fell wholly under the influence of his works.

II

(1750 *circa*—1789)

THE DIMINUTION OF FRENCH INFLUENCE

PREDOMINANCE OF ENGLISH OR 'NORTHERN' INFLUENCE: BEGINNINGS OF GERMAN INFLUENCE

§ 1. *The 'Cosmopolitans'*

In the second half of the century 'cosmopolitanism' and the craze for travel began to spread. The word 'cosmopolitan' had existed in France since the sixteenth century, but was not to be found in any dictionary until Trévoux's appeared in 1721, and it did not enter into common usage, in a good sense, until about 1760. Actual cosmopolitans, or those who wished to be counted as such, were already growing in number. In 1715 the *Annales de la Cour et de la Ville* recorded that there were 15,000 foreigners in the Faubourg Saint-Germain: a year later the figure reached 36,000. More than ever the French 'salons' opened their doors to foreigners, who were greeted, not only with courtesy and eager curiosity, but also with a warm friendliness. There was Mme d'Épinay's salon, lorded over by the German Grimm and the Italian Galiani; there was Mme Necker's, where the future Mme de Staël was preparing herself, in the most cosmopolitan of atmospheres, to write her Italian *Corinne* and her German *De l'Allemagne*; there was Suard's, closely in touch with the Englishmen Wilkes and Robertson. Horace Walpole was the lion of all the salons. Hume was almost overwhelmed by the warmth of the welcome extended to him. Gibbon, Franklin, and Jefferson were equally well received. Franklin came so much under the spell that at eighty he proposed marriage to Mme Helvétius, who was sixty-five. Mme Brillon, who was not yet forty, called him 'papa'; and he called her 'daughter'. Jefferson, less paternal but no less proper, enjoyed the friendship of Mme de Bréhan, Mme de Tessé, and Mme de Corny.

Many crowned heads were also cosmopolitan. Peter the Great had been; Frederic II and Catherine the Great continued to be, if not at the bottom of their hearts and in their conception of authority, at any rate in their tastes and their expression of their tastes. But others gave more convincing proof of their cosmopolitanism: they longed to see the world. Gustavus III, first heir to the throne and then king of Sweden, wished to tour Europe. But it was in Paris that he found his anchorage, in 1770, with Mme de Soufflers, and with her he contracted that close friendship of which their letters remain to give eloquent testimony. In 1768 the king of Denmark was in Paris. He gave audience to eighteen scholars or philosophers. In 1777 Joseph II of Austria stayed in Paris under the name of the count of Falkenstein. The chroniclers of the day refer to him in tones of admiration. His journey 'was worthy of being described by a historian such as Plutarch'. The academies held grand receptions in his honour. Crowds waited for him at the door of the Austrian embassy. At the theatre the audience applauded him vigorously. He was the philosopher-king.

The creation and diffusion of journals is a further evidence of the growth of cosmopolitanism; and we have to remember that these journals correspond more or less to our modern reviews. The Dutch journals of the beginning of the century were followed in three or four countries by about a dozen publications devoted to foreign affairs. As an Italian journal wrote, 'men who used to be Romans, Florentines, Genoese or Lombards are now more or less all Europeans'.

§ 2. *The Survivals of French Prestige*

We shall presently have reason to note, during the second half of the eighteenth century, how the seeds of a vigorous growth of English and 'northern' genius were planted and began to flourish. In its shade French culture seemed to wither. But nevertheless it survived, and there still remained broad and spacious fields in which it was always prosperous. France and Paris kept their faithful and enthusiastic admirers. It was often, of course, the trivial and even the ridiculous that was imitated. But it was also the beauty and grandeur of French architecture, French parks, French painting, and French sculpture. It is enough to recall the lists drawn up, and the figures given, by Louis Réau. All the attempts made anywhere to attain sublimity and grandeur were inspired by the sublimity and grandeur of French style. The Place Royal in Paris inspired imitations in London, Brussels, Lisbon, Madrid, Berlin, Vienna, and St. Petersburg. The palace and the park of Versailles inspired some twenty-five royal or princely residences in England, Germany, Russia, Italy, and even in Spain and Portugal; at Hampton

Court, Coblenz, Mannheim, Bonn, Potsdam, Peterhof, Tsarkoie-Selo, Caserta, La Granga, and elsewhere. From the end of the seventeenth century until 1815 a list can be made of the names of more than two hundred French artists working abroad, often for a regular salary, and of nearly two hundred foreign artists studying in Paris.

The French language, and the art of expression which is the attribute of France, were held in equal esteem. Frederic II, Catherine II, the Dutch Justus van Effen, the Bernese Muralt, and the Italian Casanova wrote in French; Gibbon published his *Essay on the Study of Literature* in French (1761). In 1753 the Berlin Academy set in French a subject for a prize essay on Pope, and the winning essay was written in French. In 1784 the same academy set another subject: 'Why is French the universal language of Europe? What has earned it this prerogative? Are we justified in assuming that it will retain its position?' It was not, of course, agreed by all at the time that French deserved to be the universal language. However, Rivarol won the prize, and he considered the prerogative deserved and secure for years to come.

It was not only by her prestige in fashion, in social life and elegance, in the fine arts, and in language that France maintained her position in the eyes of the world outside. French literature, French philosophers, French playwrights, and French novelists had many readers, and even a number of imitators.

In England, to give only a few examples, there were five translations of the abbé Prévost's *Cleveland* between 1731–8 and 1780, five of his *Mémoires d'un homme de qualité*, four of his *Doyen de Killerine* (but only two of *Manon Lescaut*). In drama, translations or adaptations of Voltaire's plays were very popular, especially between 1750 and 1775. There were imitations of French sentimental comedies and other plays. Between 1780 and 1788 there were eighteen adaptations of Marmontel, Sedaine, and Beaumarchais, and of plots drawn from Rousseau's *La Nouvelle Héloïse* and from Laclos, Florian, and others.

For a long time Holland had been intellectually half French. This was still true throughout the second half of the eighteenth century. French was widely known among cultivated people. In 1766 we find Juliana Cornelia de Lannoy asking: 'Can people who do not know French be considered as rational beings?' Here again the figures, for all their dryness, speak for themselves. At about this date there were fifty-six teachers of French at the university of Leyden. In the catalogues of a hundred private libraries M. Dubosq reckons that French books amount to eleven and a half per cent., and that eleven and a half per cent. are Dutch (the rest being religious and Latin books, with only a few Spanish, Italian, English, and German works).

There were numerous translations of Voltaire's *Henriade* and of his tragedies, and of works by Marmontel, Baculard d'Arnaud, and L. S. Mercier. (Generally, however, during the period between 1760 and the French Revolution English writers such as Gray, Hervey, Young, 'Ossian', Richardson and Goldsmith were taking the place of Racine, Voltaire, and Boileau.)

French influence was considerable in Italy and Spain. But it was French manners, good breeding, and art which were held in especial honour. Switzerland remained predominantly Swiss. French Switzerland naturally looked towards Paris and the fame of the Paris salons, and tried to imitate them, with something of a time-lag. The salons of Mme Curchod and Mme de Charrière were precious as well as philosophical in tone. J. J. Rousseau made furious enemies, but he also had all kinds of admirers, even to the point of fanaticism. Besides, he was Swiss, and what he contributed had nothing in common with the classicism of Racine, Boileau, and Voltaire. German Switzerland looked towards Germany, and may be even be said to have taken the lead in the movement for liberating German literature from the influence of France.

On the other hand, and in spite of other influences by which it was crossed, French influence was strong in Russia, Hungary, and Poland. Catherine II prided herself on being a philosopher in the French style; she bought the libraries of Diderot and Voltaire. French fashions were followed in dress and food. French tutors were in demand. There was a flood of books by French authors, such as Mably, Raynal, and more especially Voltaire, of whose works some 140 translations, more or less partial and incomplete, way be traced during the period from 1780 to 1790. Polish comedies were all drawn from Molière; and after 1772 there flourishes a sort of French school, represented by Messenyer and Baroczy. Austria and Hungary were equally under the spell of French taste and wit: German influence was hardly perceptible in Vienna, and at least five French journals appeared between 1768 and 1785. Theatres produced the plays of Voltaire, Destouches, and Marivaux: people read Voltaire and the *Encyclopédie* (and also the works of Rousseau). In Hungary, Voltaire (*Zaïre, Alzire, Nanine, L'Écossaise*) and La Chaussée held the stage: people read Dorat and Colardeau, and everybody read Baculard d'Arnaud, who nowadays seems so ridiculous to us, but whose success spread none the less throughout Europe.

It was in Germany that the most lively and systematic reaction arose against the influence of France fashions and literary aesthetics. Admiration and slavish imitations of French works produced violent protests. But the protests were not always heeded, at any rate when they were first made. The prestige of France did not begin to decline until about 1770. The German writer Grimm, established in luxury at Mme d'Epinay's, began his *Correspondance littéraire* which, with the collaboration of Diderot and Meister, lasted until 1793 and kept the courts of Bayreuth, Anspach, Brunswick, Gotha, &c., informed of all the events, great or small, in the world of French literature and philosophy. In all these little courts, with their tangle of protocols and German traditions, the means which they used to convince themselves that they were enjoying a French style of life was a succession of galas, masquerades, and French (or Italian) comic operas.

But there were other and often invisible means by which French influence persisted, with a secret and hidden power. Indeed, European readers often found themselves in greater sympathy with the temper of the French translators than with that of the English writers translated. One reason was that French was better known than English; another was that French order was preferred to the disorder of the English genius. In Italy Young's *Night Thoughts* was always translated from the French translation of Letourneur. It was the same in Spain.[1] In Germany *George Barnwell*[2] was a great success, but adaptations of it were not drawn from Lillo's text but from three French translations and adaptations. Swift was read in an expurgated French translation. Shakespeare was often known through Ducis and Letourneur. Even the first German trans-

[1] On Spanish translations of French translations of Shakespeare see Sir Henry Thomas, 'Shakespeare in Spain', in the *Proceedings of the British Academy*, vol. xxxiv (Editor's note).

[2] A play, written by George Lillo and produced in 1731, which was based on an old English ballad. Lessing based one of his plays upon it (Editor's note).

lation of the prudent Pope, who could at any rate think with point if he could not give his thoughts order, was based on a French translation. Gessner, a Swiss of Zürich, was not in the least a romantic: his writings were perfectly clear, and the nature of his genius familiar: he could be read in the original by anyone who knew German. Yet it was in Hüber's French translation that Gessner's works were known all over Europe, in Italy, Spain, Portugal, England, Holland, Sweden, Hungary, Poland. Before anyone would walk in the 'dark' forests of romanticism the paths had nearly always to be cleared by French gardeners.

§ 3. *The Continuation and Expansion of Old Themes*

We shall presently see new tastes and a new spirit of inquiry emerging, and beginning to grow with astonishing strength; but this does not mean that the past was obliterated by the new growth. Except in Germany (and even there reservations must be made), there was no real literary revolution in Europe in the eighteenth century.

It is scarcely necessary to say that experimental science continued its dazzling career in Europe. Here it was useless to maintain that all beauty is 'dark', and that the real truths are those of the heart, which cannot be proved, but only felt; when physics, chemistry, or natural history is in question men will trust only the evidence of the scales, retorts, or microscopes. The same is true, in large measure, also of philosophy. Cartesianism, in its axioms if not in its deductions, was extinct. The system of Leibniz was antiquated. The philosophy of Kant began to exert its influence only after the Revolution. All general systems were carefully avoided. The spirit of Locke was still dominant, revived by the work of his French disciple Condillac, whose *Traité des sensations* (1754) attempted, not to discover the nature of the soul and its metaphysical substance, but to trace its history, and to show how the soul of a child acquires one by one through the medium of experience the different ideas which constitute the essence of the thought of a normal man. But the works of Condillac, in spite of their popularity, had not such a wide public as those of Locke.

There was, however, a revival of the discussion of metaphysical problems on a more restricted and less general plane. Men were anxious and eager to prove that the God of the Deists, whatever He was, was a Providence which was benevolent to man. There was, indeed, opposition to that view; and the opposition of Voltaire was violent. In his *Candide* (1759) he set himself to prove that everything is for the worst in this distracted world, and that no man can count on anyone but himself for help in getting to land across an inevitable sea of troubles. He was at one time a follower of Pope, but he rejects his ideas contemptuously in some manuscript notes in a copy of the *Essay on Man* in the library at Lenigrad: 'I said that forty years ago.' *Candide* met with considerable success; and it threw the optimism of Leibniz and Pope into the shade. But Voltaire's pessimism was matched by the optimism of Rousseau, who was a pessimist for himself but strove to teach men easy ways to the discovery of happiness under the wings of God. This is also the optimism of Bernardin de St-Pierre, who believed that melons were made polygonal so that they might the more easily be eaten by a family, and that fleas are black so that they may the more easily be seen on white skins. In England there was the optimism of Goldsmith's *Vicar of Wakefield*, which had a great and durable success all over Europe, and which preached the doctrine that the just are finally rewarded, in spite of the direst tribulations, if only they have faith in Providence. There is also the Arcadian or Biblical optimism of Gessner, to which we shall return later. This optimism is more or less bound up with the idea of progress. But we must first define the word 'progress'. In the view of men like Rousseau, Bernardin de St-Pierre, and Gessner, material progress, or increase of luxury and comfort, is useless or dangerous. For the rationalists the mental progress which comes from the development of intellect and knowledge inevitably brings material progress: for Rousseau and Bernardin de St-Pierre there is always a conflict between the two. The more civilized man becomes, the less chance he has of finding happiness. A savage is better and happier than a civilized man. There is no doubt that this paradox had a great vogue. Actually, however, the antithesis between a return to nature and the improvement of nature by the civilizing power of the human intellect is merely a subject for disputation. Rousseau himself had no wish to see man return to the simple life. He realized that this would be a ridiculous undertaking. In their idyllic life at Clarens, as depicted in the *Nouvelle Héloïse*, Monsieur and Madame Wolmar had no intention, when they helped

PLATE 36

FRONTISPICE DE L'ENCYCLOPEDIE.

Frontispiece of the French *Encyclopédie*, after Cochin fils (1770)

their servants with the grape harvest, of discarding the wine-
press on the ground that it was an invention of civilization. It
was the same with all other writers. The final result of endless
discussions was to establish a universal conviction that progress
is the law and the *raison d'être* of human life. In France the *Encyclopédie* is a memorial raised to the glory of civilization. This
work emerged victorious from fifteen years of controversy, and
escaped all the traps set for it by its enemies. People soon ceased
even to dream that it could trouble the conscience or threaten
the very foundations of the Christian faith. In spite of its size
and its high price it was in everybody's hands, and might be
found in the libraries of all academies and societies of readers.
The success of the dictionary spread all across Europe. New
editions, which involved considerable outlay on the part of pub-
lishers, were successfully issued at Geneva, Lucca, Leghorn,
Berne, Lausanne, and Yverdon. England believed even more
strongly in the idea of progress. It was the *Cyclopaedia* of Chambers, at the end of the seventeenth century,[1] which suggested the
idea of Diderot's dictionary. Other encyclopaedias were later
published in Edinburgh and London. In the second half of the
eighteenth century the idea of progress was an integral part of
English life. But the English were also aware of its dangers, and
a strict religious discipline was constantly there to remind them
that it is heaven which really matters, and that neither mathematics nor physics lead men directly to heaven. But neither do
they lead men away from heaven: indeed, it is they that produce
the inventions and build the machines which enable England
to develop into the most powerful of all industrial countries.

At the same time we may also observe the continuous development in Europe of a general movement of reflection and discussion which is directed to discovering what is the right or the
wrong sort of progress in the social order, and which sort does
good and which harm. First of all it has to be shown, and
this is now done more vigorously than it had been in the first
half of the century, that some sort of revision of the general code
of morality is needed. According to the traditional code the great
thing was, in effect, that each individual should cultivate the
virtues and avoid the vices. We have shown in our first chapter
how this idea of personal salvation came to be amplified by

---

[1] The *Cyclopaedia* of Ephraim Chambers was published in two volumes in 1728.
It has no connexion with the modern *Chambers's Encyclopaedia* (Editor's note).

altruistic ideas. The happiness of each is bound up with the happiness of all: progress can only be collective progress. A new social code of morality must accordingly be developed. This was the aim, particularly in France, of all the philosophers who followed, in a greater or less degree, the tenets of the *Encyclopédie*. England, more firmly rooted in her traditions and her religious code of ethics, was less ready to acknowledge the necessity of a complete revision of the moral code; but even there the same tendency is to be found, and it is summed up in Bentham's formula: 'The greatest happiness of the greatest number.'

It is necessary, however (and many will hold that it is especially and peculiarly necessary), to turn from these broad generalities and to come down to particulars. Is this or that particular society organized for the greatest happiness of the greatest number? If not, what are its errors, and what are their remedies? All kinds of works accordingly appeared, claiming to expose errors and to suggest remedies. First there are works on social reform.[1] Montesquieu's *L'Esprit des Lois* had challenged the dangerous illusion that there was any reason for reliance on a natural and universal conscience of mankind. The goodness or badness of laws, and even their justice or injustice, could only be decided by experience, an experience that was constantly shifting and changing its nature. Montesquieu's influence was strengthened by the writings of the Italian Beccaria. His treatise on *Crimes and Punishments* (1764) clearly showed the influence of the French philosophers of the *Encyclopédie*. He was still a follower of reason and system. But at any rate the problem he raised was a definite problem, capable of suggesting definite and immediate reforms and arousing public opinion. To see a man hanged for a trivial domestic theft, to hear the cries of men condemned to torture and to know that accused men could be tortured before their crime was proved, was enough to make men wonder whether justice was not cruel, and indeed uselessly or dangerously cruel. Beccaria's book was translated several times into French, notably by the abbé Morellet (the translations ran into many editions); commentaries were written by Voltaire, Diderot, Mirabeau, Brissot, Franklin, and others. It was

---

[1] The term 'social' is here used for anything that can be altered without affecting the fundamental constitution of the government; the term 'political' for anything that implies a change in that constitution.

also translated into the other main European languages. In
England it had a great influence upon the teaching of Bentham.
From a practical point of view it was influential in suppressing
the preliminary examination of accused persons. It is possible,
after all, to discover some common characteristics in this confused mass of ideas.

In the first place despotism was hated and despised. From
north to south and from east to west, men treated it with contempt. Everyone saw it through Montesquieu's eyes. They held
that it could only survive for a time, based as it was on the
terror, the degradation, and the misery of peoples. But it is easy
to see that this is a conventional picture of a despot, which
corresponds only, in its measure, to the sultans of Turkey or the
shahs of Teheran. It is true that Frederic II, Catherine II, and
even Maria Theresa and Joseph II, were actually absolute monarchs; but who would insult them by calling them despots?
They were 'philosopher kings', or queens. In them their people
had the good fortune to be ruled by philosophers who governed
according to reason and for the public good. This was the justification for their power; and the French philosophers (except
Voltaire, in his attitude to Frederic II) toiled indefatigably
and in all sincerity to create a legend, which made them the
opposite of despots. In the second place it is true to say that
hardly anybody was a republican (except in democratic countries) or thought of revolution. Before 1787 no one in France
wanted revolution; any suggestion of it is infrequent, and is only
made by fits and starts. The impatient pages or phrases of so-
called revolutionary writers are amply contradicted by many
other pages, and above all by the general conclusions which
clearly emerge from their works. Reforms were wanted, but not
upheavals.

And reforms were actually achieved. In the second half of the
century the whole of Europe was stirred by a great movement
of reform. The movement sprang from the philosophy of the
Enlightenment, and was inspired by the rational arguments, de-
ductive and inductive, of French and English philosophers such
as Voltaire, Diderot, the *Encyclopédie*, Locke, Hume, &c. Yet it
is obvious that rulers like Frederic II, Joseph II, Catherine II,
the king of Denmark and the king of Sweden are not democrats. What then do they borrow from the philosophers, or what
do the philosophers tell them? Briefly, that they are absolute

monarchs, and that it is all the better for their subjects if they are at the same time enlightened monarchs. It is also in their own interest to be so. They wish to be assured of their thrones; they wish to have power. The more prosperous their country, and the more contented their subjects, the more powerful will they be. Happiness and prosperity are not at the mercy of chance or blind forces; they are the results of sensible organization and the lessons which the wise, that is to say the philosophers, are able to provide.

In the narrow limits to which this study is confined we cannot attempt to give a detailed account of the enlightened reforms attempted in the various European monarchies, or to explain their merits and their mistakes. It is sufficient just to recall the fact that reform was not a matter merely of a few timid impulses, but a question of far-reaching plans which involved a complete reorganization of the state. Take only a few examples. In France the criminal laws were intolerably harsh: a maid-servant could be hanged for stealing a few of her mistress's towels; an accused man could be subjected to a preliminary examination and tortured in order to make him confess a crime which sometimes he had not committed. There were no such abuses in England; and everybody in France admired the English criminal law. The academy of Châlons-sur-Marne set the question for a prize essay: 'How can the French penal law be reformed?' 'Copy England' was the answer of Brissot (1781) and of Bernardi. There was a problem still more urgent, for the simple reason that it concerned the very existence of a nation: the problem of the famines which ravaged almost every country in Europe. A sound agricultural policy was needed. In France the philosophers of the Physiocrat school showed the importance of the problem and offered their solution with resounding success. We are all familiar with the general tenor of the doctrine expounded by Quesnay, Gournay, Forbonnais, and the other followers of the 'Physiocratic sect', which indeed deserved the title of sect by virtue of its industry, its tenacity, and its intolerance. A country's true wealth does not consist in its trade, as the mercantilists or 'Colbertists' believed, or even in industry or in financial riches. It consists in the land which produces and multiplies the primary necessaries of life: it consists in agriculture. The Physiocrats were able to study, and they actually studied, the abundant earlier English literature on economic subjects which runs from Locke to Mandeville, from Child to Tucker, and so on. But they were the first thinkers in Europe to form a school, to multiply works which developed the principles of that school, and to publish a periodical of their school, the *Éphémérides du Citoyen*. This is not the place to trace the history of the Physiocratic controversy, which ended in the discredit of the system in France. But the prestige of the Physiocrats created and fostered the fruitful idea that the prosperity of its rural workers is necessary to a nation, and that agriculture (a new word which now began to appear in the French language) is something which can be improved and transformed by human progress. After 1755 agricultural associations sprang up everywhere, at the rate of several a year. Later, Adam Smith exercised a considerable influence in France and in Europe by his writings: in philosophy by his *Theory of Moral Sentiments* (first translated into French in 1764) and in economics by his *Inquiry into the Nature and Causes of the Wealth of Nations* (more than once translated into French, the first time in 1781), in which he found a happy medium between the Mercantilist theories and the doctrines of the Physiocrats.

§ 4. *New Themes: Sentimental and Pastoral Moralizings; the Drama*

All the efforts of the philosophers of reason to create a benevolent secular code of morality were met by an apparently reasonable objection, the cynical objection, for instance, of Diderot's *Neveu de Rameau*: 'Only one thing interests me, and that is my own well-being: if I know how to get that I shall be happy, in my own ego, without bothering about virtue and vice.' It was for this reason that there began to flourish a system of ethics which no longer made any appeal to reason, but based itself on the needs of the heart and the demands of conscience. This largely explains the astonishing success of works which were, it is true, as we shall have reason to notice later, a new type of poetry, but were also long and verbose sermons: Hervey's *Meditations*, Young's *Night Thoughts*, or, in a more sober style, Gray's *Elegy* and Goldsmith's *Deserted Village*; or again the latter's *Vicar of Wakefield*, in which humour and a rather childish romanticism are made to serve the cause of the most pious form of morality.

In France this fashion for moralizing had a curious history, for it had a much longer road to travel, on the journey from cynicism or scepticism to virtue, than in Holland, Switzerland, Germany, and elsewhere. The period before 1750 was still the heyday of the sensual novel, in spite of much opposition and reaction. After 1760 the reverse is the case: hardly any novels or literary works of any kind appeared which pandered to the reader's sensuality, or which approved, or at any rate viewed with indifference, ways of life which any standard of piety would condemn. In this respect Rousseau's *Nouvelle Héloïse* marked the decisive turning-point. The work met with unprecedented success (there were more than seventy-five editions between 1761 and the end of the century). The whole life-story of the heroine, Julie, is her need of goodness and her need of love. She lives only with her heart; but her heart is not only hungry for human love, it also feels that it cannot be satisfied if it is not filled with the love of God. Rousseau's work touched many more hearts than did Richardson's novels. All sorts and conditions of readers wrote to tell him how he had moved them and how he had revealed to their eyes the meaning and the value of life.

But the moral English novel had also considerable prestige. All sorts of English novels, both famous and unknown, were translated indefatigably between 1750 and the end of the century. A considerable number of them were certainly not English. But the English novel was so fashionable that in order to gain popularity it was necessary to add to the title the words 'translated' or 'adapted' from the English, even when there was nothing English about it but the name.

The fashion for the countryside, and for the wholesome, inexpensive pleasures to be found there, does not date from the eighteenth century. It has existed in almost every age and almost every country. In any case it was widespread in France in the seventeenth century. The one thing which must be admitted is that there was as yet no love for nature in too wild or irregular a state, the nature of marshes or barren moors; that mountains and the sea were ignored; and that nature was never a subject of literature. In this last respect Thomson's *Seasons* had a considerable influence.

Thomson's poem appeared between 1726 and 1730. It is not at all a romantic work. In part it was inspired by the keen interest in natural history which spread through Europe in the first half of the eighteenth century, in part by the equally keen interest in travel. The reader is never made to feel that Thomson relives his memories in his imagination. When he speaks in the first person, his *I* is not so much himself as the wise man displaying his wisdom. He shows us what might be the lot of any good man who decided to live a simple, secure, and pious life. The secret of happiness is to choose the joys of a country life above all others. The secret of love for God and obedience to His commandments is to contemplate and worship Him in His works. Thomson had a great influence. The first translation of the *Seasons* in France appeared in 1759. It immediately inspired imitations: Saint-Lambert's *Saisons*, Rosset's *Agriculture*, Roucher's *Mois*. In the French poets, as in Thomson, there was the same excessive use of descriptive passages (which gave to the genre the name of descriptive poetry); the same habit of describing things which they had never seen; the same taste for moralizing and for preaching a rustic philosophy, but with less of a Christian belief in providence and with more reliance on a secular and deist code of morality; the same lack, not of sincerity, but of any appeal to true personal emotion. Thomson was translated into French at least half-a-dozen times in the eighteenth century (and still more often in the first third of the nineteenth). There were also many translations in Germany, Sweden, Italy, &c.

The influence of Gessner ranks with that of Thomson: his *Daphnis*, *Death of Abel*, *Idylls*, and *New Idylls*, which appeared in German (from 1751 to 1772), soon attained an incredible success in Europe. His style is Greco-Latin and his taste fundamentally classical. His models are Theocritus and Virgil. His moralizing is in the style of Thomson or Rousseau. In his rather heavy Swiss fashion he has a certain grace, and a feeling for harmony of actions and attitudes; but all this is no revelation. He has, however, something new to offer. Through the popularity of his works he introduces a sort of compromise into the pastoral. He knows that his Daphnis and his Menalcas, his Phyllis and Myrtilus, are not real and were perhaps never real, and that the golden age in which they live is certainly only a legend. But he sets them in a framework of reality. The poetry of the countryside, which is part of the charm of their loves and endearments, is something more than a dream. Anyone who wants may enjoy it. He upholds the pastoral convention, but he brings it into touch with real life by a strength of conviction which makes him one with Rousseau and the moralist poets and novelists of Germany and England. Men can no longer be born in Arcadia, but they can return to a much simpler and more secure life. This ideal received an enthusiastic welcome everywhere, and particularly in France and Italy. Gessner was translated into nine languages. In France, besides the translations, there were more than a hundred imitations of his *Idylls*. His poems had a great vogue in Italy (they were particularly admired in the French translations of Hüber and Turgot). They achieved the same success in the Scandinavian countries; but there was more opposition (for instance from Goethe and especially Schiller), or more indifference, in England and in Germany. But all in all there were more than seventy translations, or new editions of translations, of his works in Europe at large between 1762 and 1846.

A place must be found here, in conclusion, for the history of a form of literature in which relics of the past are mixed with the need of novelty, though it is not often easy to distinguish what is old and what is new. We come to the history of the drama, or, if you will, to the history of the difference between the drama of Shakespeare and that of Corneille and Racine. The argument continued throughout the century without any definite victory for either side. Voltaire could not at first make up his mind. He admitted that tragedy ought to be revived, and that the stage should be given its rightful place. Then, as Shakespeare grew more popular, he denied what he had once admired, and turned against Shakespeare with insults and gibes. Down to the end of the century the critics who rallied round him, whether philosophers or no, persistently excluded Shakespeare from the temple of taste. But gradually, after 1770, admiration of Shakespeare defeated the critics, at least among the reading public. The splendid edition of Letourneur's translation gives a comparatively faithful version. On the stage, at least in France, the case is very different. In the name of 'good taste' the plays of Shakespeare were censored, cut, and transposed, until they were turned into sorry tragedies decked in timid romantic fripperies. In Ducis's version of *Hamlet* the prince does not talk with his father's ghost: he addresses the urn which contains his ashes. Instead of suffocating Desdemona with a pillow, a vulgar method of murder, Othello stabs her with a dagger, and so on.

The really bold ventures of the theatre of the eighteenth century were made in a new genre, that of the 'drama'. 'Drama', as Diderot understood it, was a form of art which was certainly influenced by English plays such as Lillo's *London Merchant* (1731) and Edward Moore's *Player* (1753). Diderot was familiar with them: they were translated into French and frequently imitated. But it was Diderot who constructed a fuller and clearer doctrine of 'drama', and who thereby exerted a great influence in Germany. 'Bourgeois drama' was indebted to many sources. From the classical tradition it took over not only unity of action but often—especially in the works of Diderot—unity of place and time. From English drama it borrowed the taste for rather declamatory pathos; but its pathos was less crude than the English, and in Diderot it showed a psychological quality. There had to be scenery, and there was; but the scenery used was intended to give an impression of real family life, and not to dazzle the eyes by strange and dramatic effects. Fine speeches and even dialogue played a less important part; the effect was often meant to be produced by the attitudes of the characters, and even by their silences. Naturally the object of the whole play was to point a moral: the aim of the theatre must always be to teach men to hate vice and love virtue. But after Diderot's time drama moved farther and farther away from his conception of its character. The influence of Shakespeare and the 'tragic genre' began to make itself felt, and that influence, which will be discussed in the next section, was strongly entrenched towards 1770. Murders and suicides abound; all the frenzy of violence and horror which characterizes romantic melodrama is already to be found in the dramas of Baculard d'Arnaud and Louis-Sébastien Mercier. Beaumarchais kept much more in line with Diderot. We must mention, however, his play *Eugénie*, where the scene is placed in England, and where Beaumarchais is at pains to describe in detail the English costumes to be worn by the actors. It is this French drama which, more than Shakespeare, Lillo, or Moore, influences drama and dramatic comedy in Germany. Lessing translated the plays of Diderot with an enthusiasic introduction. There were five German translations of Mercier's *Déserteur*. His *Nouvel essai sur l'art dramatique* was also translated, and it was warmly received by the Stürmers. German drama, however, is very various and constantly in transition.

§ 5. *New Themes: the 'Sombre Style'; the Romantic Feeling for Nature*

1740 in England and 1760 in France saw the beginning of what was regarded, at any rate in France, as a new style of literature—the 'sombre style'. Ruins and tombs were a familiar theme of this style, as they were to be later of romantic literature. With few exceptions, the English novel, in spite of its variety, was not influenced by this fashion for horror and misery. But French novels were full of it, and they almost seemed written expressly to inflict horror upon horror on the reader. We may cite as examples Baculard d'Arnaud's *Épreuves du sentiment* and his *Délassements de l'homme sensible* (1772 and afterwards); L. S. Mercier's *Jezennemours* (1776); Loaisel de Trégate's *Soirées de mélancolie* and his *Dolbreuse* (1783), which are full of all the horrors and catastrophes dear to the romantic novel.

At this time, too, still another funereal colour is added, though as yet only timidly, to the palette of the sombre style. This is the colour of the diabolical mysteries of the supernatural world: phantoms, and ghosts, and the old castles which they were supposed to haunt. Walpole, an Englishman in whose composition there was nothing diabolical or any form of obsession, set the fashion. His *Castle of Otranto* (translated in 1761, and running into several editions) unrolls before the reader's eye a whole series of disasters, enacted in a Gothic castle and brought about by spectres acting under the influence of a power which spreads horror and dismay. The *Castle of Otranto* did not, however, at once set a fashion; and it was not until the end of the century that Ann Radcliffe and Lewis in England, and the German novelists on the continent, started a taste, which lasted for thirty or forty years, for phantoms, devils, wizards, witches, massacres, and atrocities.

We have already said that there was always a certain feeling for nature, even in France, although for a century it was almost entirely absent from literature. In the second half of the century another form of nature was discovered. The change to this new form is translated into material terms when one studies the process of development which sets the English garden over

PLATE 37

LE DESERT

Parc d'Ermenonville: the 'Desert'

against the French. Lenôtre's French gardens at Versailles, Marly, and elsewhere were, as is generally known, a collaboration of man with nature. Lenôtre meant the plan of a garden to be a continuation of that of a *château*: he wanted the lines of the park to be determined by the same attention to harmony and balance which had determined the architecture of the *château*. But might not nature be equally beautiful when she followed her own devices and not those of a landscape gardener? Wild woodlands, groups of trees growing at random, winding brooks and rushing streams, flowers which nobody has attempted to arrange—are all these not as good as the ruler and pair of compasses which set bounds to the freedom of nature? The English, it began to be said in France, understood this. Kent and Brown designed parks which copied the freedom and fancy of nature, and where everything seemed to grow and flow at the pleasure of God. Soon English gardens were on everybody's lips. Scores of books were written in every country to give instruction in the practice of this delicate art, and some were adorned with beautiful engravings. In practice, as well as in theory, the fashion of the English garden became the rage. Fortunes were spent in the attempt to achieve them. Rich bankers spent ten or sixteen million francs on having valleys dug, hills built, and streams diverted. A hundred gardens in the English style can be counted in France. The parc Monceau in Paris, the remains of an older park, was created in 1774 by Carmontelle for the duke of Orleans. The parc de Bagatelle, in the Bois de Boulogne, follows in its general lines (and its buildings) the design of the 'folie d'Artois' laid out for the comte d'Artois. The parc d'Ermenonville, along with the 'desert' which today has another owner (the Institut de France), is still much as it was when the marquis of Girardin designed it and offered it as a sanctuary to Rousseau, who finally died there. The fashion, indeed, was not only French, but European.

In these gardens the aim was not only to give a different aspect of nature, but to give nature itself a new form. This new form of nature, to be found in these parks, was to be the inspiration of dreams, melancholy, gloomy apprehension, and mysterious shivers, everything, in a word, that was dear to the romantics. Nature was also to be improved by being associated with all sorts of buildings, which were also to be romantic: ruins, for example, which had to be erected at great expense when there was no real ruin to be had, and 'Gothic' ruins above all others; Young's cave; Ossian's tomb; and so on.

After 1760 the feeling for nature took another and still more romantic form, both in literature and in life. It became a passion for mountains. Before 1750 mountains were completely ignored. It was Rousseau's *Nouvelle Héloïse*, of the year 1762, which opened men's eyes in France, Switzerland, and Germany to the poetry of mountains. Rousseau's novel would lose its essential character if it were not set in the scenery and steeped in the atmosphere of the lake of Geneva, the Bernese Alps, and the Alps of Savoy. All the moving passages of the book seem transfigured by a secret association between the soul of the characters and the great soul of nature. Suddenly, with recollections of Rousseau fresh in their minds, men crowded to the places where Julie and Saint-Preux had lived, loved, and suffered. To the mountains, hitherto forgotten and neglected, there now flocked crowds of travellers, eager to experience emotions or simply anxious to be in the fashion. Switzerland became the fashionable honeymoon resort. There were times when it was impossible to find a villa to let on the shores of the lake of Geneva. To visit the Lauterbrunnen valley or Grindelwald the 'beaux' of the fashionable world had the first 'Alpinist' suits made for them. There were innumerable guides for all these tourists.

Rousseau, as a matter of fact, had only enjoyed and described in his book green and pastoral hills of moderate height. High mountains, with their wild icebound solitudes and their 'sublime horrors', did not attract him. We owe the discovery of the eternal snows to a sort of collaboration between the Swiss, the English, and the Frenchman Ramond. English literature had gradually discovered the English mountains; it does not appear to have felt the Alpine influence of the *Nouvelle Héloise*. For a long time the English had visited the Swiss Alps, both as travellers moved by pure curiosity and as scholars studying the geography of the country or collecting botanical and geological information. Among the Swiss, too, there are some notable forerunners of Alpine mountaineering, such as the brothers de Luc (whose works appeared in 1772, 1776, 1780) and Saussure, who made the first ascent of Mont Blanc (and whose works appeared in 1779–96, 1787, &c.). There were at least four French translations of W. Coxe's *Letters from Switzerland*. The Swiss and the English were men of science, more given to practical observation than to dreaming. Only those who were already of a romantic temper aspired to reverie and meditation. Like the old *motifs* of night and tombs and caves, the solitude and austere grandeur of high mountains provided such men with the atmosphere they needed. It was Ramond who, in his notes on the translation of Coxe's letters (1782), initiated sensitive souls into the sense of 'the sublime' which overwhelmed the climber when he reached the eternal snows.

§ 6.   *The Cult of the Primitive and the 'Northern'*

Rousseau was not exactly the first to put civilization in the dock. The idea of the good and happy primitive savage, which appears in his *Discours sur l'origine de l'inégalité parmi les hommes*, was not a figment of his imagination. G. Chinard has shown in a series of excellent works that he had informed himself of the facts and was fully supported by the evidence. A considerable number of travellers, generally missionaries, had described their visits to the natives of the West Indies and North America. They were almost all agreed in declaring that on the whole these savages were happier and less corrupt than civilized Europeans. It was, however, Rousseau's works which helped more than anything else to disseminate the idea that the progress of civilization was only superficial, and had done more harm than good. Not that Rousseau for one minute wished to preach a return to primitive nature; he stated quite clearly that this would be a ridiculous paradox; and none of his followers was deceived on this point. What Rousseau did try to teach was that actually we can all seek and find happiness in the simple life and the simple pleasures which Providence never denies us. In England the belief that simplicity was essential to happiness owed nothing to the influence of Rousseau: the novelists of the moral school and the Protestant sects were a sufficient warrant. But in France and Switzerland, and to some extent in Germany, the ideal of Rousseau had a prestige and influence of the first order.

The influence of Rousseau was reinforced by Daniel Defoe's *Robinson Crusoe*. This novel was indeed long anterior to Rousseau. It was published in 1719, and the first French translation appeared in 1720. What people enjoyed most, to begin with, was the romantic side of the story. They were just as much, or even more, attracted by the series of adventures which Crusoe met with after leaving his island as they were by his struggle with loneliness and the material necessities of life and by the happy relations which he achieved with nature. It was Rousseau, in his *Émile*, who emphasized this latter aspect, perhaps unconscious on Defoe's part, of the moral of *Robinson Crusoe*. From this time onward translations were published which included only the stay on the island (one of these was Feutry's French translation of 1767); and from this time, too, there began to appear numerous imitations ('robinsonnades') all over Europe.

The trial and condemnation of civilization had a further result, which was purely literary but still of some importance. It introduced a complete revolution in the conception of poetry. For one or two generations, with the reservations which have already been made, French classicism had been the rule. Genius was held to be useless unless it was controlled by reason, which confined it within rigid rules. But it now begins to be argued that true poetry can only spring from instinctive forces and mysterious powers which lie dormant in the depth of human nature, but awake to life in privileged beings to lift them above themselves. From the first half of the eighteenth century onwards it is to these forces, as opposed to the classical ideal, that men begin to appeal. Vico does so in Italy, in his *Scienza Nuova* (1725, 1730); and Shaftesbury does so in England, in his *Essay on Merit and Virtue*, translated into French by Diderot (1745). Later, in the second half of the century, Young makes the same appeal in his *Conjectures on Original Composition* (1759), which had a definite influence in Germany and in France (notably on Chénier). Lessing, in Germany, strikes a balance between the reasoning intellect and the free inspiration of genius; Herder deliberately chooses 'the poetry of Nature' and 'the spirit of Nature.'

Examples were to be found of this 'true' poetry which springs of itself into life among the peoples to whom real civilization is still unknown. There were, first of all, the poems of Ossian, or pseudo-Ossian, revealed to the world by Macpherson (1760 to 1763). As soon as the *Fragments of Ancient Poetry collected in the Highlands of Scotland and translated from the Gaelic or Erse language* appeared, their authenticity was in dispute. But authentic or not, they were almost universally admired. They contained everything for which 'sensibility' craved: the melancholy and the gloom of landscapes bathed in solitude, mist, winds, and

PLATE 38

OSSIAN

Frontispiece to Letourneur's translation of Ossian's Poems (1810)

raging seas, the tragedy of death and desperate grief, the mystery of ghosts and gods wandering on wild moors and in sunless mists; heroic valour, desperate and inconsolable love, the whole life of beings who were at once rude and refined. The success of Ossian spread throughout Europe (it was actually less in England than on the continent). There were many translations in France, Germany, and Italy.

But it was not only the people of Caledonia who could give the world admirable examples of primitive or 'true' poetry. There were also other masterpieces, which had the additional advantage of being truly authentic. In particular, the Frenchman Mallet (who was primarily an historian and a philosopher) discovered in his *Histoire du Danemark* (1758), and in his subsequent works, the greatness of the primitive races of Scandinavia. The works of Mallet were translated into German and English; and the day now began of the poets who could write verse with the inspiration of the 'scald' or the 'bard'. There was, of course, no attempt at scholarly accuracy. Celts, Germans, and Scandinavians were deliberately confused. In order to be one of these bards or scalds, it was enough to invoke some god or goddess from any mythology, to steep oneself in the mists, storms, and gloom of a land where the wild seas were breaking, to people it with phantoms of the dead, and to be convinced that these so-called primitive peoples had in them more grandeur than the 'ancient' Greeks or Romans, revered in 'classical' literatures.

§ 7. *The Beginnings of German Influence*

Three stages may be clearly distinguished in the history of the liberation of German literature from foreign influences. As we have already said, French classical influence predominated before 1750. Its place was then taken by English influence, which was strongly felt almost to the end of the century. For instance, Thomson's *Seasons* had been translated eleven times by the end of the century. Thomson was still half classical in character; Shakespeare was not classical at all, and his work was soon read with enthusiasm. Lessing was not unreservedly Shakespearian, but it was nevertheless to the English drama that he looked for inspiration in writing some of his plays. English novelists were equally popular; the realistic novels of Smollett (of which there were thirteen translations before 1789), the humorous works of Sterne (there were some forty-six editions of German translations of his writings), the works of Swift (also with forty-six editions, of which eight were of *Gulliver's Travels*), the sentimental and moral novels of Richardson—all were widely read. B. L. Morgan has made a bibliography of German translations of English works in the eighteenth century; it includes 1,165 items.

English influence was equally strong in the other Germanic countries. From the first half of the century onward, English works were being translated in German Switzerland in some numbers. Swift, Thomson, and Hume were translated in the second half of the century. It was in Switzerland, at Zürich, in 1762–6, that Wieland published a translation of Shakespeare in eight volumes.

The lingering influence of French and Italian classicism, the infatuation for English and 'Northern' literature, and the attempt to develop a spirit of true German originality, long combined to produce a great confusion in German literary theories and writing. Then came a movement of general revolt against reason and all its rules. Men must clear away every obstacle which encumbered thier paths, and refresh themselves at the primitive springs which arise in the depths of the soul. With this object the Bible, Ossian, the Eddas, Shakespeare—and even scholarship and philology as guides to the truths of antiquity— were indiscriminately pressed into service.

It is not necessary here to pursue this history in detail. There can be no doubt that after 1760 all German writers were increasingly anxious to be leaders instead of followers, and to create a literature which should be primarily and essentially German. It was at about this date that German writers were discovered and began to be translated abroad. Until the appearance of Goethe's *Werther* these translations made no great stir, and the selection was indiscriminate, with little attempt to draw any distinction beweent writings which were imitative and those which struck an original note. The works of Winckelmann, notably his *Geschichte der Kunst des Alterthums* (1764), resulted in a new conception of art. Winckelmann believed, it is true, that the finest masterpieces of art were the works of the Greeks and Romans; but he added the qualification that admiration of their works must be reasonable, and that it should not take the form of servile imitations or be disfigured by embellishments. Art, like all human creations, has a life of its own: nothing about it is fixed and a rule for all eternity. We may love the masterpieces of antiquity passionately, but we must paint and sculpt and build as our own spirit moves us. 'O Germania', cried the French poet Dorat, in 1769, in his *Idée de la poésie allemande*, 'our best days have vanished; yours are just beginning!' But Dorat, who was a weathercock to every wind of fashion, was rather premature. The European heyday of German literature was not to begin until after the French Revolution.

Many German works were translated into English, but Schiller did not achieve a reputation in Great Britain until 1789, with H. Mackenzie's report to the Royal Society of Edinburgh. Almost the only work of Goethe that was known was his *Werther*. It was not until after 1790 that German works were found in any numbers in English libraries. In Holland the influence of France, and above all English and 'northern' influences, still largely predominated.

This was not true of *Werther*, which exercised a deep and immediate influence over the whole of Europe. 'The Sorrows of Werther' introduced an entirely new note. It is the one clear expression, in the last third of the eighteenth century, of the sense of *mal du siècle*, or *Weltschmerz*. There had been, it is true, a taste for gloom and night and tombs. But the stirring emotions of the soul which were solicited by such means were wholly literary emotions, which might even lend a sharper edge to the pleasure of life. Even Rousseau counts for nothing in the matter of *mal du siècle*. It is true that he was a pessimist, but only about himself. He was, or believed himself to be, persecuted; but he does not inflict the same fate upon humanity at large. On the contrary, he believes—and we may believe him—that happiness is easy for the world in general. *Werther* was entirely different. To begin with, the plot which is there unfolded does not consist of exceptional circumstances, which the odds are one in ten thousand that we should ever encounter. It is set in peaceful and sensible middle-class surroundings; and fate never strikes those unforeseen blows which make one believe in the existence of a mysterious and terrible power. We feel throughout the book that the trouble, or rather the danger, is in the soul of Werther himself; that he is not made to be happy; and that he is under a sort of compulsion which sooner or later will bring him into mortal conflict with the normal realities of life.

The teaching of *Werther* produced a dangerous intoxication which led to the malady of *mal du siècle*.

§8. *Intellectual Relations between North America and Europe; the Beginnings of European Curiosity about Australasia*

Throughout the eighteenth century, North America (and the West Indies) played an important role as an object of European curiosity, but chiefly in the realm of the novel and philosophy. Men were far less interested in the Europeans who had settled there than they were in the savages with whom the settlers came into conflict. They persuaded themselves that these natives were normally more sensible, just, and contented than so-called civilized man. For instance, in spite of some vigorous criticism, *Les Dialogues et les Mémoires de l'Amérique septentrionale* by the Baron de Lahontan had a considerable vogue. In France as well as in England the work produced a whole family of good and happy savages, whose story G. Chinard has told. America thus served, in the main, as an excuse for philosophic and moral observations put in the mouth of its savages. Otherwise it continued to remain a country among many countries, and a colony among other colonies. The *Encyclopédie* devotes some articles to America, naturally at second or third hand, and occasionally full of startling inaccuracies. It tells, for instance, of 'a large and navigable stream, called the Hudson river' (article on New Jersey), and does not mention New York. But important events were soon destined to draw the eyes of the European world to these Americans, and to teach it that they were not only thinkers, but might even be regarded as harbingers of the future.

In the first place, Canada and the United States served to prove, by an actual and living example, that it was possible without being a savage to find the true secret of happiness by pursuing the healthy activity of agriculture far away from any city. This is the explanation of the astonishing success of Saint-John de Crèvecœur's book, *Letters from an American Farmer . . . by J. Hector St.-John, a farmer in Pennsylvania* (1782), which ran into five editions by 1793, was translated into French (the translation too ran into five editions) by de Crèvecœur himself, and was twice translated into German and once into Dutch. The book was everywhere received with enthusiasm and even emotion. People forgot all the things that could make life in

Pennsylvania, like life anywhere else, anything but idyllic: floods, fires, hard winters, sanguinary Indian raids, epidemics, and the internal strife which set one faction against another. Crèvecœur himself forgot them, particularly in the French translation of the *Letters*, which only too frequently substituted a sentimental and humanitarian philosophy for a realistic description of life.

Saint-John de Crèvecœur's success owes much to the fact that when his book appeared Americans had for many years held the first place in world affairs. Opinion in Europe was passionately in favour of the American 'rebels'. In England, of course, they were generally regarded merely as rebels against their country, and men only thought of them to condemn them. In Germany and Italy the struggle was followed from a greater distance; and public opinion, in principle, was not on the side of a people which was engaged in revolt. But everybody in France was soon on the American side. The minister Vergennes knew how to act with energy and address. He sent secret agents to America; he dictated the policy of all the newspapers which authority could either control or bribe. Private initiative, welcomed and aided by Vergennes, made up for the vacillation shown by the government. Beaumarchais enthusiastically financed a scheme, by which he was ruined, for the supply of arms to the rebels. Lafayette, the son-in-law of Louis de Noailles, duc d'Ayen and head of one of the most powerful families in France, embarked for America at the head of a group of officers, with the tacit support of the government, and with the open and enthusiastic support of public opinion.

Franklin, the American envoy to France, played a role of the first importance, not only in virtue of his intelligence, character, and diplomacy, but also owing to the happy chance which made him the hero whom public opinion had dreamed of and for whom it was waiting. Here, in very deed, was 'the philosopher'. He was wise; what he said was always sense, and good sense; he did not lose himself in clouds of speculation; he was a teacher of life who taught from actual experience of life. He was simple, he was of the people, he was country-bred. He had 'sensibility'; he had ideals and a religion—not a fanatical and dogmatic religion, but a religion which sprang from the heart—a religion which meant belief in God and in the dignity of a moral life. No doubt there was something of pose along with much that was genuine in Franklin's personality. But the public believed him to be perfectly sincere. It received him at first with sympathy, then with affection, and then with devotion. He was the ornament and the glory of the most fashionable salons. When he took his grandson to the death-bed of Voltaire to ask for his blessing, and Voltaire pronounced over the child the words *Dieu, liberté*, it seemed as if here the best in the thought and spirit of France was blended with the spirit of America. Those who frequented neither salons nor academies knew Franklin from his *Poor Richard's Almanack*, which had been translated by 1773 in the edition of his complete works, was published separately in 1777, and achieved a great success.

The American Declaration of Independence crowned Franklin's work. His own aims were practical; he was after all only human. The Declaration, on the other hand, gave to the American cause the majesty of principles and the dignity of an ideal. Whatever the sources that had inspired Jefferson, and whether or no he had drawn on France, French readers could not fail to recognize in him the ideas of their own philosophers and the social and political ideals which were the secret or avowed inspiration of their own creed. Natural law and natural rights; the God to be found in nature and in the goodness of man, and not in dogmas and theologians; self-evident truths proceeding from the reason common to all men; the inalienable rights of men to liberty and happiness; a consequent scorn of rights based merely on prescription and force, a hatred of all that savoured of despotism and fanaticism, and a contempt for an ethics of resignation and renunciation—these were the ideas which had been hinted, suggested, and then openly preached in a hundred works by Voltaire, Rousseau, Diderot, Helvétius, Raynal, and many others. The one difference was that almost all the French philosophers had been content with abstract speculations. The American Declaration had another bearing; it justified a revolution and laid the foundations of a society; it proved that a basis for government might be found in an appeal to nature and reason, and not to the grace of God and prerogatives imposed by force and established by tradition.

A whole body of literature soon sprang up and flourished in celebration of America, the virtues of America, and particularly her civic and political virtues. M. Faÿ has catalogued them; there are about a hundred works between 1776 and 1778, to

which may be added all the newspaper articles, the commentaries, and the encomiums interspersed in the pages of
works which were not directly devoted to the United States.
Other evidence might be added to the very ample data collected
by M. Faÿ. But the quantity is of itself the most convincing
proof of the extent and the strength of American influence.
Even those who regretted the influence recognized its strength
and its essential role. Morellet believed that the French people
'enjoyed the best constitution known to the world', and yet
they suffered from a dangerous infirmity: they 'wished to drink
toasts to the freedom of America, freedom of conscience, freedom of trade'. Many writers of memoirs recalled the enthusiasm which carried away the young aristocracy and 'the
hot-heads of all ages, who were enamoured of the theories of
Penn and Franklin'. The abbé de Véri persuaded Franklin to let
Greuze paint his portrait. His opinion of the American Constitution was that no other in the world had 'foundations so just, so
simple, and so strong'. Count Mollien reports the same obsession
in the judicial world: 'I never meet a magistrate who is not
more preoccupied with American affairs than with the case
which I have to plead, or a soldier who is not discussing the
Constitution of the United States.' The viscountess of Pars-
Fausselandry speaks for the women of her class: 'The cause of
America seemed our own; we were proud of their victories, we
wept at their defeats; we seized the bulletins and read them in
every house, and none of us stopped to think of the danger of
the example which the New World set to the Old.' In the provinces, the town of Clermont ordered public rejoicings to celebrate the independence of the United States in 1783. The good
Lamare, secretary to the Benedictine Dom Goujet, though he
had very little interest in politics and seemed to know nothing
outside the affairs of his diocese, noted nevertheless in his *Mémorial* the victory of 'the English colonies', by which he meant the
victory of the Americans.

   The political consequences and the practical results of this
spiritual unity between French opinion and American objec-
tives are known to all. The period of moral support and of
La Fayette's expedition was followed by an alliance between
the two peoples and by the courage and self-sacrifice of the
French volunteers; and after the peace treaty the ties still
remained, if they were not so close. When the Revolution broke

out in France in 1789 those who were most active in its direction were, at any rate in the beginning, imbued with the
lessons of American experience. The Declaration of the Rights
of Man, on the night of 4 August, certainly owed something to
the ideas of Washington, Franklin, and Jefferson.

The happy savage of earlier days had not fallen from favour
by the end of the century. But the Hurons, the Iroquois, and
the other red men now had rivals, and rivals whose happiness
seemed even more authentic. During the last quarter of the
eighteenth century the Gardens of Eden in the Pacific began to
arouse the interest of the public, and first made their appearance in European literature. From the time of the first great
voyages round Africa and America a vision of the 'lands of the
south' fired the imagination of the authors of imaginary voyages. In reality no 'land of the south' was discovered except
impassable ice barriers. But Australasia was discovered on the
way to the south, and these actual discoveries stirred men's imagination almost as vividly as the dreams of imaginary voyages
had done. The first explorer was the Frenchman Bougainville. In 1771 he published his *Voyage autour du monde par la
frégate du roi la Boudeuse et la flûte l'Étoile en 1766, 1767, 1768 et 1769*.
He was anxious above everything else to give a true account of
his voyages; and his description of Tahiti was therefore all the
more telling. He had indeed found in the Antipodes 'the freedom of the Golden Age' and the 'Garden of Eden'. The earth
and the water provided in profusion, under a gentle sky, all
that man had elsewhere to wrest from the grudging soil by the
sweat of his brow. All was peace and harmony, from the scenery
to the natives. There were no dangerous animals, and no violence or cruelty. Diderot, filled with enthusiasm, wrote a
Supplément au voyage de Bougainville (which only appeared in
1796) in which the discussion between A and B, and the conversation of the Almoner and Orou, showed that the Tahitians, in
their religion and their moral customs, were far more sensible
than the Europeans, and were happier for that very reason. In
England the same importance does not appear to have been
attached to the Tahitian idyll. But the glorious voyages of Cook
none the less opened a new world, a world with its own splendours and its own excellences. A nation of sailors, the English had
a passion for these great voyages which discovered so many

curious countries. The copious and scholarly writings of Cook (first voyage 1773; second voyage 1777; third voyage, partly by Captain King, 1784) were translated into French in 1774, 1778, and 1785; and the three voyages were combined and published in eighteen volumes in 1785. Henceforth people were aware of a fifth part of the world.

III

THE PERIOD FROM 1789 TO 1815[1]

WE may begin by noting that the French Revolution left a manifold and deep imprint on the literature of ideas, though the changes which it brought about in literary art only made themselves felt after the fall of the empire.

The disruption of the material, intellectual, religious, and social life of France, in the space of a few years, had a number of obvious consequences. The literary world of the old régime disappeared; it never returned, even under the restoration of the Bourbons after 1815. Emigration, which, after 1789, and especially after 1792, drove so many Frenchmen, many of them writers, to England, Germany, and other foreign countries, had a decisive influence on the two most important writers of this period, Chateaubriand and Madame de Staël.

In countries other than France, literary developments due to political conditions made themselves felt in various degrees, and at different times, in each different nation. It was in Italy that the political events which had originated in France affected literature most forcibly. The intellectual and moral *rinnovamento* which, under the influence of a philosophy of enlightenment derived from English and French sources, had fostered progress among the *élite* of society during the last fifty years, was in full course of development when the news from Paris, in 1789, came first to inspire enthusiasm and then to fill men with horror. From 1796 to 1815, from Napoleon's first advance beyond the Alps down to the return of the old régime, everything of any importance in literature is connected, directly or indirectly, with the military and political events which aroused such love and hate, so many hopes of early liberation, and so much disillusion. Literature became more and more permeated with the idea of *risorgimento*; and this was to be the inspiration of the romantic movement which began definitely in 1816.

The influence of historical events on literature is less marked in countries other than Italy, though they too were directly concerned in the consequences of the French Revolution. In

[1] This part was treated much more fully in a first draft written by the late Paul Van Tirghem, which has been adapted for the present work by Professor Mornet.

Great Britain there was a short-lived enthusiasm among poets after 1789, and there was some advance in liberal ideas; but the reaction against the Revolution and a dislike of France and Napoleon were uppermost. Germany felt the armed shock of the Revolution and Napoleon more violently than any other country. The ordeal through which she went left her literature untouched, except after 1812, when a flood of patriotic and martial poetry summoned the nation to arms against the invader.

What are the chief works of this period, considered in themselves and regarded purely from the point of view of literary appreciation, that is to say in terms of their intellectual or aesthetic significance and their artistic value? The mediocrity of French literature during the decade of the Revolution—and also, with the two brilliant exceptions of Madame de Staël and Chateaubriand, during the consulate and the empire—has often been remarked. It is noteworthy that these two writers, like all their French contemporaries whose works have any value, are prose writers; poetry only revived with Lamartine after the end of this period.

In England, on the other hand, there was no writer of eminence in the field of ideas during the course of this period; but there was a poetical revival which attained an exceptional height. This brilliant flowering of poetry began after 1789 and did not fade until after 1830. These are the years of the English Romantic movement, a movement which was mainly poetical and which was remarkably independent of the other branches of the great international movement of Romanticism in Europe. Of the four principal pre-Romantic poets who are prior to 1789, Cowper's early powers had now spent themselves, Burns died in 1796, and Crabbe and Blake (more especially Blake) were continuing to write in an unchanged vein. After 1789 the Lakeland poets appeared, Wordsworth, Coleridge, and Southey; and soon after them came Walter Scott with his narrative poems. Byron's brilliant career did not begin until the last years just before 1815.

German poetry, which reached the age of maturity in the history of modern western literature much later than English or French, attained during this period (1789–1815) a richness and power which placed it undeniably in the first rank. Wieland and Herder continued their work until the beginning of the nineteenth century; the writings of Jean Paul covered the whole period under consideration; Hölderlin, Novalis, and Kleist, whose careers were to be cut short untimely by madness or death, were writing between 1797 and 1811. The brothers Schlegel and Tieck founded the Romantic school, along with their friend Novalis, a little before 1800; and the Romantic group gathered round Arnim and Brentano appeared about 1808. But the forefront of the scene is occupied by the figures of Goethe and Schiller. The former, who had returned from his fruitful visit to Italy in 1788, now entered on his second period, a period of intensive production, which lasted until his death in 1832. Schiller, who had outgrown his youthful period of dramatic writing, did his best work in the fifteen years which preceded his untimely death in 1805. It is remarkable that France was unaware of these riches—with the exception of Goethe's *Werther* and a few ballads and other poems—until the very end of this period, when they became known through the medium of Madame de Staël's book, which was only published in 1811. In England, they were unknown for much longer.

What general impression emerges from this diverse and changing international panorama? Primarily it is an impression of disorder and confusion, more pronounced, for instance, than in the middle of the eighteenth or of the nineteenth century; of a literary chaos, in which opposing elements are to be found side by side, often jostling each other without mingling or attaining any harmony. And yet it is also a period in which a number of pre-Romantic tendencies show themselves most clearly in countries differing widely from one another—tendencies such as the taste for Ossian, the passion for Scandinavian literature, the appetite for German ballads, the poetic preoccupation with 'tombs', and above all the cult of Shakespeare, whose plays had just been discovered. To these must be added some tendencies more peculiarly characteristic of this quarter of a century—the development of a literature dealing with childhood or the family; the vogue of the mystery or 'horror' novel, and of stories of brigands; and a passion for the Middle Ages which runs to the sentimental rather than the picturesque.

But the influence of the past was still strong. The classical tradition in literature, unchallenged since the Renaissance, and still dominant almost everywhere for most forms of poetry, was nowhere more rigidly enforced than in lyric poetry proper. The ode, the dithyramb, and the hymn—forms consecrated by the example of the ancients and the usage of modern poets ever since the sixteenth century—were still at the end of the eighteenth and the beginning of the nineteenth century the vehicles in most literatures of the religious, patriotic, and political emotions aroused by the historic events which filled those troubled years. In France and Italy, and even in England and Sweden, lyrical poetry of a lofty flight and dealing with general or sublime subjects was still almost always objective: the personality of the poet is not intruded, or only appears discreetly. The style is purely classical; always elevated; generally abstract; full of periphrases, similes, allegories, and mythology; violent and sometimes declamatory in its search for pathetic effects.

Subjective lyric poetry, in which the poet's personal emotions are the main theme, was to be brilliantly developed by the Romantics, but it played at this stage a very small part in countries still dominated by the classical tradition. With them it took the humble and commonplace form of the elegy, which had been adopted since the Renaissance on the model of Latin elegiac poetry.

The most striking feature of European literature during this period is the scarcity or even the absence of any great poetry of love. Poets of the day, like all other men, must have known as much of the passion of love as their predecessors or their successors; but they could not, or dared not, let their heart speak in their poetry with the freedom and warmth which awaken an echo in the soul of the reader. This is no doubt the reason why poetry which is impersonal and objective, or at any rate appears to be so, is much more characteristic of the period. Didactic poems were common, in the tradition of the classical ages; there were also descriptive poems, a form which became the fashion after the appearance of Thomson's *Seasons*; but what we most often find is a combination of the two. We may cite as an example of this combination the products of the fertile pen of the abbé Delille, 'the French Virgil', who followed up the brilliant success of his *Les Jardins* of 1782 with *L'Homme des Champs*, *L'Imagination*, *La Conversation*, and *Les Trois Règnes de la Nature*, a long series of poems which only ended in 1812. He was imitated almost everywhere in Europe, but most successfully in Holland and Sweden. A third great type of impersonal poetry derived from antiquity was the epic. This tradition was unbroken from the sixteenth century onward; it was still followed in many countries at the beginning of the nineteenth. But it always gives the impression of a survival, with little in it which is likely to become a permanent heritage of posterity. It is not until the time of the Romantics that narrative poetry, throwing off the well-worn and outmoded robes of the ancient Muse, takes on new forms in the work of Scott, Byron, and some of the German and Swedish poets.

It is in the realm of the drama that we can particularly trace this conventional clinging to outworn traditions, traditions which in most countries prevented literature from recovering originality and vigour by new experiments. Conventional tragedy in the French style, which dominated all Europe from the end of the seventeenth century (sometimes inaugurating a period of serious literary plays, as was the case in Sweden, Russia, and Hungary, but sometimes ousting national forms of free dramatic art, as was the case in Spain and England), continued to hold the stage, even where plays in an original style were published and occasionally acted. The great majority of the public had not changed its tastes. Most playwrights continued to use plots drawn from the Greek or Latin, and often the most hackneyed of these plots. People never seemed to tire of those old friends *Agamemnon*, *Oedipus at Colonus*, and *Ajax*, accompanied by *Idomeneus*, *Polyxenus*, and *Timoleon*. Comedy was not bound by such strict rules; it had shown a variety and fertility of forms in France well before 1789. But during the following quarter of a century it was lacking in originality, whether, in the old style, it was written in verse or took the form of prose.

The novel was still less restricted by traditional forms, and the sixty years before 1789 had seen the birth of novels of the highest order, alike in France and England and the Germany of Goethe's *Werther*. During the period here under consideration, both men and women novelists (for in the field of the novel women now played an increasingly important part) continued to follow the old lines without any perceptible innovation either in form or substance. The 'novel of terror' paraded its haunted castles and its mysterious villains in Lewis's *Monk* and in *The Mysteries of Udolpho* and other tales of Ann Radcliffe, which today are chiefly interesting for their suggestive descriptions of landscapes, streams, skies, and forests. In Germany the impersonal biographical novel, or at any rate what professed to be such, readily assumed the character of the 'novel of development' (*Bildungsroman*), which described the growth of mind and heart from earliest youth: Moritz's *Anton Reiser* is an example at the very beginning of the period, and a little later there is Goethe's *Wilhelm Meister*, though this largely belongs to the period before 1789. Other categories of prose writing more often than not still clung, unconsciously rather than of set purpose, to the literary *status quo* of the end of the classical period. Literary criticism, prolific in most countries during this period, remained for the most part classical in temper, not only in France and southern Europe, but also in England, Scotland, Holland, and Sweden. Professional critics ridiculed or attacked the early poems of Wordsworth and Byron and those of the Swedish Romantics, the ideas of Mme de Staël, and sometimes even the art of Chateaubriand.

But the future was already in train. The first striking fact in this connexion is the profusion of new literary ideas (which had often, it is true, been sketched here and there in advance by the pre-Romantics before 1789), ideas which in some countries prepared, and in others accompanied, the appearance of Romantic literature. The common basis of these ideas was a reaction against the rationalism of the age of enlightenment. A need was felt for giving weight to national and legendary elements, the supernatural, and mystery; for giving freer expression to emotions, faith, imagination, and dreams; and even for making the ineffable speak. There were some who felt that above all things literature should be up to date; there were many others who felt that it should evoke the past, a past which was often legendary; but both these schools were agreed in thinking that it must be national. In opposition to the traditional conception of one single and continuous literature, developing in accordance with the same principles from Homer to the present day, August Wilhelm Schlegel and Mme de Staël, both in 1800–1, but each separately from the other, preached the need for an art perpetually engaged in the process of renewal.

It was poetry above all else which the men of the age desired to transform, some of them by their theories, and others by their example; and each man put the accent on this or that particular feature. But whatever the particular feature—the nation, the Middle Ages, chivalry, fairyland, the people, or the modern world—poetry, drawing inspiration from Christianity and not from pagan antiquity, will no longer speak the language of mythology, and no longer be didactic or intellectual. It will be personal, direct, sincere; it will be generally serious, and even melancholy; it will be an outpouring of the soul, and no longer a matter of abstract thoughts wrapped in conventional language. Tragedy on the French model, according to the rules, is considered to have had its day; even the most timid reformers are ready to turn away from it to a tragedy which draws on modern life, preferably with a national tinge, and which sheds the unities of time and place, providing more interest for a modern audience by presenting a richer variety of scenes and actions and characters. The example of Shakespeare—and also, for some of the German play-writers, that of the Spanish dramatists—suggests the idea of an even freer form of drama, which can find room for the appearance of fairies, fancies, and music, and in which different styles and tones are all mixed. These ideas of dramatic art make their appearance here and there before 1815.

This new form of literature, which was the aspiration of the keenest critics and the most gifted poets, and which was already beginning to appear in some countries by the turn of the century, was still for the most part only a seed or at most a seedling. Italy, the home of humanism, remained faithful to the ideal and art-forms of strict classicism through all the successive phases of the *Seicento* and Arcadianism. The three great poets who flourished there about 1800—Alfieri, Monti, and Foscolo—if they often chose modern or contemporary subjects, still handled them in a purely classical spirit and style, and still used classical ornaments. Even Foscolo's novel in letter form, which in 1800 seemed to open the floodgates of Romanticism, was really derived (by way of Goethe's *Werther*, which was its direct inspiration) from the sentimental novels—'novels of sensibility', as they were then called—of which there were so many in England, France, and Germany after 1740. In Spain, Holland, Hungary, Poland, Russia, and Portugal few signs of new literary tendencies appeared.

We have seen that cultured society in France—or what remained of it during the Revolution, and grew up again under the consulate and the empire—along with the general public and the critics, was little accessible to new ideas from abroad, and showed little interest in new literary tendencies. The literary works which prepared or inaugurated a period of change came mostly from travellers, or from authors who were isolated or had come back to France after living abroad.

These works, full of promise and some of them heralding a new literary movement, only appeared after 1800. Sénancour, that solitary dreamer who took his melancholy and his meditations with him among the mountains of Switzerland, produced in his *Obermann*, which is rather the history of a soul than a novel, a counterpart to Chateaubriand's *René*. It is a worthy counterpart, though less romantic and less cunningly orchestrated. *René* itself did not attain fame before the age of the Romantics; but it came to be increasingly enjoyed for its intimate understanding of nature and the deep echoes it awoke in every heart.

The years 1800–15 are especially important in French literature because they cover most of the creative period of Mme de Staël and Chateaubriand, who, almost exact contemporaries, appeared at the opening of the century as the prophets of a new literary age in their country. Though widely differing from one another in the country of their origin, in religion, in political and philosophical ideas, and in taste and style, they were fellow workers, if on different grounds, in the cause of liberation from the classical tradition and the inauguration of a new form of literature. In *Delphine* Mme de Staël continues, though she also enriches, the eighteenth-century tradition of the epistolary novel; but in *Corinne ou l'Italie* she introduces a new note of national characteristics. Her *De la Littérature* and her *De l'Allemagne* represent an important advance in the history of literary ideas in France; the first of these works raised clearly, for the first time, the problem of the connexion between literature and historical, political, and social conditions; the second, widely read in the original and in translations, did much to introduce the public, not only in France but throughout all Europe, to German ways, philosophy, and literature. The revelation thus made was fruitful; and it gave the book the name of the 'Bible of the French Romantics'.

Mme de Staël was a child of the eighteenth century in her feeling for society, her philosophic attitude, and her analytical treatment of the emotions. Chateaubriand resolutely turned his back upon it. He was afterwards to be called the 'Enchanter', and he adorned his works with a new form of prose at once harmonious, full of colour, brilliant and moving. His Indian novel *Atala* had an exotic character which, even after *Paul et*

Virginie, appeared as a revelation. *René*, semi-autobiographical, was full of restless passion; the *Génie du Christianisme* revived belief in the Middle Ages and the Catholic faith, whose aesthetic, literary, social, and moral value it sought to prove; and in addition to these there is also his prose epic *Les Martyrs*, the 'basement', as it may be called, of his *Itinéraire de Paris à Jérusalem*. He introduced men to a new climate of magnificent or mysterious landscapes, to the surge of passions, to romantic melancholy, and to a style of rich images and orchestration.

English literature, as we have noted, was particularly rich in poets at this time. The *Lyrical Ballads* of Wordsworth and Coleridge (1798) may be regarded as introducing a new period of English poetry. The contributions of the two friends were not only unequal in quantity: they also showed differing characteristics, all of which were, however, important in the revival of European poetry. Wordsworth had begun, in 1793, the long series of poems of nature, in which he sought to evoke her more picturesque or her purely rural aspects. In the *Lyrical Ballads* of 1798 he took humble subjects of the simple and homely countryside and commonplace scenes of daily life, and sought to distil the deep and true poetry which they could offer to the soul and the art of a poet resolved to discard the whole classical tradition and any idea of 'poetic style'. But the most enduring beauty of his poetry was in his own personal reflections, stirred by an emotion which stirs also the reader, and in his meditations based on religious philosophy, as, for instance, in his *Tintern Abbey*. This was the path to be followed later by Lamartine and Victor Hugo; and Sainte-Beuve also was to love Wordsworth as the initiator of that poetry of homely and simple life which was his dream. Coleridge, much more romantic in the sense in which the word is often used by the Anglo-Saxons (a sense which implies the charm of legends, the Middle Ages, and the play of fancy), and on the whole more essentially a poet, contributed to the collection *The Rime of the Ancient Mariner*, one of the most typical works of European romantic poetry.

Another innovation in the romantic field was Walter Scott's long series of metrical romances, *Marmion*, *The Lady of the Lake*, &c., which was begun in 1805 and was to last till after 1815. These narratives in an epic style, with their chivalry and sentiment, recalling as they did the manners and the legends of the Scotland of the past, and full as they were of picturesque scenery and local colour, renewed the ancient epic on a more limited canvas but in a less restricted form. They were popular because of their romantic attraction; but they have been sadly antiquated by time. With *Waverley*, in 1814, Scott created the genuine historical novel in prose, the romantic form *par excellence*, in which he was to become the undisputed master.

It was not until the end of this period that the first poems of Byron and Shelley appeared. In Germany, Goethe returned from his grand tour of Italy; he began a new period in his career; his heart was still susceptible to the passion of love— indeed, it remained so almost to the end of his long life—but his literary taste and his art underwent a change. His detailed study of natural history, and his contact with the Mediterranean world and especially with Greek art, turned him from the enthusiastic and impassioned advocate of liberty and nature in art, and in the emotions and social life, which he had been in 1770, into the conscious artist who felt the charm of measure and harmony, and whose Hellenic ideal made him a 'classic' of a new order. But he began work again on the theme of Faust, already handled in an early version with which he had made considerable progress before he established himself at Weimar in 1774, and in 1790 he published *Faust, ein Fragment*, which contained the essentials of the First Part. He returned to the theme at the beginning of the nineteenth century, and in 1810 he published *Faust, Part One of the Tragedy*. This was one of the most important works produced during this period, not only in itself but also for its influence—an influence most marked after 1830—and for the works derived from that influence in Europe generally. Goethe's friendship with Schiller, and their life together at Weimar until Schiller's early death, must not be forgotten; it drew them both together in the pursuit of Greek aesthetic ideas and a new form of classicism. From 1795 to 1805, the year of his death, most of Schiller's work was done in the field of tragedy. The period of the plays of his youth was long since over; and his finest tragedies now appeared in quick succession—the *Wallenstein* trilogy, *Maria Stuart*, *Wilhelm Tell*, and the rest.

During this time the romantic school in Germany (which may be dated about 1795 to 1805) pushed to its farthest verge the revolution against the traditions of the age of enlightenment (*Aufklärung*). Tieck joined with Wackenroder to begin the attack: after Wackenroder's early death he continued the fight first with Novalis (who also died prematurely) and then with the brothers Schlegel, who were in close touch with the philosopher Schelling. This romantic school, which rejected Schiller, and combined a respectful admiration for Goethe's work with a lack of genuine appreciation, formed a very compact group. It threw up in abundance new ideas, or busied itself in reviving, though with considerable modifications, the ideas of Herder and the *Sturm und Drang* period. Its themes were the relativity of art; the unity of true poetry, in a thousand different forms, through all ages and in all places; the intuitive, spontaneous, mysterious, and even mystical nature of the poetic art; the absolute freedom of the drama; the search for sources of inspiration in popular tales and legends; and so on. But although they produced endless prefaces, articles, and symbolical stories or poems, its members left hardly any masterpieces, with the exception of Novalis's *Hymns to the Night* and his *Fragments*.

The second half of the period, beginning in 1802, was similarly marked by a notable revival of imaginative literature in Scandinavian countries. Denmark gave the signal, but Sweden played the most important part. The Danish poet Oelenschlaeger came into contact with Steffans, a scholar and traveller returning from a visit to Germany, and in a conversation which lasted sixteen hours was converted by him to the ideas of the German romantic school. He imitated Tieck in his *Nordic Poems* and in a fanciful play called *Aladdin*, and became the herald of a Romantic theory of aesthetics based on the legends of the north: his influence served as the medium through which these new conceptions of poetry made their way into Sweden.

THE DEVELOPMENT OF LITERATURE AND CULTURE IN THE EIGHTEENTH CENTURY

DOCUMENTS

I

Extracts from Benjamin Martin's 'Philosophical Grammar',
1738

Rule IV. Propositions and Conclusions, deduced from actual Experiments, must be esteemed true and accurate, notwithstanding any *Hypotheses*, or received *Suppositions*, to the contrary; and must be insisted on, till some other *Phoenomena* either render them more accurate, or liable to Exception.

.   .   .   .   .

A. Indeed the Reason of the last *Rule* is so obvious, that, I think, none can doubt it; no Person being so perverse and preposterous, as to affirm there is more Reason in a bare *Hypothesis*, than in *Facts* or *Experiments*.

B. Yet, it is strange, you'll say, that, by this very *Rule*, the System of the *Cartesian Philosophy* must fall; that *Burnet's* theory of the *World* and *Deluge* must be valued at no greater Estimation, than an ingenious *Romance*: And thus must Mr. *Whiston's*, and all other *World-mongers* Systems and Theories, dissolve into a philosophical Nothing, which want actual and repeated Experiments to support them.[1]

.   .   .   .   .

B. They who have reduced experimental Philosophy to Method, and make it their Business to teach it others, prepare a large *Apparatus* of Instruments of all Kinds, to the value of five or six hundred Pounds; and at stated Times, in a very large Room, there is an Operator appointed to perform a Course of Experiments therewith, in all the various Parts of natural Philosophy, in the open View of all who are present to see and learn the Manner thereof.

A. Cannot you give me some particular Account of those Instruments and the manner of using them?

[1] ... *Monsieur des Cartes*, the great Master and Deliverer of the Philosophers from the Tyranny of *Aristotle*, is to be blamed for all this, for he has encouraged so very much the presumptuous Pride of Philosophers, that they think they understand all the Works of Nature, and are able to give a good Account of them; whereas neither He, nor any of his Followers, have given us a right Explication of any one Thing.— His great Fault was, that he made no use at all of Geometry in Philosophy. (*Keil's* Introduction to his Examination of Dr. *Burnet's Theory of the Earth.*)

B. It is the Subject of a large volume to describe them with their uses in particular: However, of such as are most common, to be had in the easiest Manner, and which you yourself may understand, and use if you please, you may take the following Account.

The *Telescope* is an optic Instrument, wherewith to view distant Objects, which it greatly enlargeth, and makes them seem near us; by which Means the Astronomers and Philosophers have made wonderful Discoveries in the Sun, Moon, and Planets.

The *Microscope* is contrived to augment and render visible very minute and small Objects, which otherwise escape the Sight.

The *Helioscope* is a Sort of *Telescope*, fitted so, as to look on the Body of the Sun without Offence to the Eyes.

The *Barometer*, or *Baroscope*, is contrived to estimate the small variations of the Weight or Pressure of the Air.

The *Anemoscope* is an Instrument invented to foreshew the Change of the Air or Wind.

The *Æolipyle* is contrived to shew the Nature and Force of pent-up Air, rarefied and breaking forth, resembling a Tempest, etc.

The *Areometer* is an Instrument to measure the specific Gravity of Liquids.

The *Hygroscope* is an Instrument to shew the Moisture and Dryness of the Air.

The *Thermometer* measureth the Degrees of Heat and Cold in the Air.

The *Hydrostatic* Balance is an exceeding exact fine Pair of Scales for making Experiments, relating to the Gravity of Fluids.

Dioptric Instruments of various Sorts explain the Nature of refracted Rays of Light through various Mediums.

Catoptric Instruments are also manifold, which shew the Nature of Reflected Rays of Light.

The *Pneumatic* Engine, called the *Air-Pump*, is the most universal of all others; it is the very Basis of the Philosophy of the Air, and hath opened a greater Door to the Secrets of Nature, than any Thing that was ever invented besides.

. . . . .

Note. MARTIN's *Philosophical Grammar* is one of the European books of the eighteenth century. The first edition appeared in 1738: the eighteenth appeared in 1778. There was a French translation by de Puisieux in 1749 which ran through at least three editions. There was at least one Italian translation (based on the French) and one in Greek. It is an educational book, proceeding by questions and answers, which shows the diffusion of experimental philosophy. Along with it should be mentioned MARTIN's *The Young Gentleman and Lady's Philosophy*, of which there were several editions.

II

Extracts from Letourneur's Preface to his translation of Young's 'Night Thoughts' (1769)

Si les Anglois s'égarent souvent par trop de licence & de témérité, les François pourroient bien être accusés quelquefois de lâcheté dans le champ du génie; souvent ils étouffent leur talent à force de goût & de servitude. Le vrai goût, c'est-à-dire, ce tact naturel qui fait sentir les vraies beautés, perfectionné par l'habitude de comparer, est peut-être aussi rare que le génie. Mais il en est un fort commun. C'est le goût de tous ceux qui n'ont ni imagination, ni sensibilité, ou qui n'en ont reçu qu'une mesure foible, qu'ils prennent encore soin d'affoiblir tous les jours. Ceux-là ne vantent dans un ouvrage que deux qualités; c'est qu'il soit *bien écrit*, & *bien fait*. Mais qu'entendent-ils par *bien fait*? Un plan exact, mais étroit; une forme élégante, mais commune & petite. Pénétrez dans l'intérieur. Qu'y trouvez-vous? Trop souvent des idées communes, empruntées des ouvrages d'autrui, revêtues peut-être d'autres termes ou développées un peu davantage. Au lieu de méditer soi-même chaque partie de son sujet, de le féconder en l'échauffant long-tems au feu de sa propre imagination, on recueille froidement tout ce que les autres ont écrit qui peut s'y rapporter: on s'environne de cette multitude de lambeaux mal assortis; on offusque, on masque son âme sous l'amas de ces décombres. Elle ne sçait plus voir l'original qui est en elle, & ne se regarde que dans toutes ces images qui ne sont point la sienne. On n'ose pas écrire un instant seul & libre: c'est toujours sous les yeux de mille témoins, sous la dictée de tous ces maîtres, dont la présence gêne votre âme & tient l'imagination dans les entraves. L'ouvrage est fini; le style en est pur; il est même élégant: mais vous le saviez par cœur avant de l'avoir lu. Vous n'y trouvez point de ces idées qui interrompent le lecteur, donnent une secousse à l'âme, & l'avertissent de penser. Rien qui vous étonne, rien qui inonde tout à coup votre âme de lumière, en éclaire un coin nouveau que vous n'aviez pas observé, ou l'affecte d'émotions vives & durables.

. . . . . .

Le défaut le plus général & celui qui m'a paru le plus propre à inspirer le dégoût, c'est une abondance stérile, une reproduction des mêmes pensées sous mille formes presque semblables, un retour perpétuel de l'Auteur aux idées qu'il a déjà épuisées. Les Anglois en ont porté le meme jugement. 'Au milieu de ces vols de pensée presque au-dessus de la portée de l'esprit humain, dit un de leurs Journalistes, tels que la* description de la mort, qui, cachée dans un coin du

---

* J'ai jugé autrement de cet episode bizarre. L'idée est ingénieuse, & la morale en est belle. Mais la mort faisant sa toilette, passant une robe de satin par dessus

bal, note les folies & les excès d'une troupe de jeunes débauchés, l'épitaphe de l'univers détruit, Satan sortant de sa prison au jour du jugement, on rencontre un mélange de mauvais jeux de mots qui dégoûtent le lecteur. Souvent une belle pensée qui s'annonçoit avec éclat, finit par une pointe insipide. Young ne sçavoit pas s'arrêter : il épuisoit son sujet & fatiguoit ses idées : comme Ovide il ne quitte point une métaphore qu'il ne l'ait tourmentée en tout sens, & exténuée à force de la décomposer.' J'ai élagué toutes ces superfluités, & je les ai rassemblées à la fin de chaque Nuit sous le titre de *Notes*, qui ne sont point mes remarques, mais l'amas de ces fragmens que j'ai mis au rebut, & de tout ce qui m'a paru bisarre, trivial, mauvais, répété & déjà présenté sous des images beaucoup plus belles. Mon intention a été de tirer de l'Young anglois, un Young françois qui pût plaire à ma nation, & qu'on pût lire avec intérêt, sans songer s'il est original ou copie. Il me semble que c'est la méthode qu'on devroit suivre en traduisant les Auteurs des langues étrangères, qui avec un mérite supérieur, ne sont pas des modèles de goût. Par là, tout ce qu'il y a de bon chez nos voisins nous deviendroit propre, & nous laisserions le mauvais, que nous n'avons aucun besoin de lire ni de connoître.

Note. The method here described was almost universally followed by French translators of English works during the whole of the eighteenth century.

The extracts given show clearly both the novelties which Young's work revealed and the reservations which French taste none the less made.

III

Extracts from the announcement of Mme d'Arconville's translation (1770) of James Hervey's 'Meditations among the Tombs'

Il est à propos d'avertir aussi que pour mettre plus d'ordre dans ces Méditations, on a cru devoir les diviser suivant les différents sujets qui en font la matière. Cette forme, d'ailleurs, sert à soulager la mémoire du Lecteur, & lui procure la facilité de choisir la Méditation qui pourra l'affecter davantage. Cette division n'est point marquée dans l'original ; mais du reste, on a suivi le plan de l'Auteur.

M. Hervey se représente comme un homme qui voyage, & qui rend à une Dame de ses amies un compte exact & fidèle des Réflexions Philosophiques & Chrétiennes, que lui font naître les monumens qu'il a trouvés dans une Eglise de la Province de Cornouaille.

son drap mortuaire, & prenant le bras d'un Médecin pour aller au bal, m'a paru une mascarade burlesque & peu digne du ton noble & sérieux de l'ouvrage. Je l'ai retiré dans les notes.

PLATE 39

The two frontispieces to Young's *Night Thoughts*, 1769

On prévient seulement qu'on a beaucoup abrégé la morale de
M. Hervey, pour s'attacher davantage aux idées, aux images & aux
sentimens, sur-tout dans les endroits où la morale se présentoit
d'elle-même. On avoue de plus, que pour conserver la pureté & la
clarté de l'expression françoise, on a été quelquefois obligé de sacri-
fier & d'affoiblir des idées trop métaphysiques, qu'il n'appartient
qu'à la Langue Angloise de bien rendre.

On s'est permis aussi d'étendre, & de développer certaines pensées,
pour les mieux faire sentir en notre langue, d'aggrandir certains
tableaux, & d'ajouter quelques traits que l'imagination même désire
à la lecture de cet Ouvrage.

Note. This extract corroborates the previous extract from Letourneur's
preface.

IV

Description of the ideal of an English Garden

A travers les ombrages noirâtres des sapins et les amphithéâtres
de rochers, la rivière limpide descend de cascades en cascades jusque
dans la vallée tranquille; c'est là qu'elle semble s'étendre avec
plaisir, pour former un lac entre la chaîne des rochers majestueux,
dont les intervalles laissent apercevoir dans le lointain ces respec-
tables montagnes, dont les cimes couvertes de glaces et de neiges
éternelles ressemblent, à cette distance, à d'énormes masses d'agate
et d'albâtre, qui réfléchissent, comme autant de prismes, toutes les
couleurs de la lumière. Les eaux du lac sont d'une couleur bleu
céleste tel que l'azur du plus beau jour, et transparentes comme le
cristal le plus pur; l'œil y peut suivre jusqu'au fond les jeux de la
truite sur des marbres de toutes les couleurs. Une île s'élève au milieu des eaux, comme pour servir de théâtre aux plaisirs champêtres;
cette île charmante est entremêlée de vignes et de prairies, et de
distance en distance des ombrages variés y forment d'agréables
bocages.

La rivière, en sortant du lac, s'enfonce dans un vallon resserré
et profond; de hautes montagnes et des rochers sourcilleux sem-
blent séparer cet asile du reste de l'univers. Les cimes en sont
couronnées de sapins où ne toucha jamais la cognée; sur les pelouses
de thym et de serpolet, des chèvres blanches s'élancent gaiement de
rochers en rochers. . . . Après quelques chutes précipitées par l'opposition des rochers qui se croisent sur son cours, la rivière trouve enfin
dans ce vallon étroit un petit espace où ses eaux écumantes et con-
trariées peuvent jouir d'un moment de repos. Un bois de chênes verts
antiques s'avance sur les rives adoucies: sous leurs ombrages mysté-
rieux est un tapis d'une mousse fine. Les eaux limpides et peu

profondes s'entremêlent avec les tiges tortueuses, et leurs ondes qui
se jouent sur un gravier de toutes les couleurs invitent à s'y rafraîchir;
les simples aromatiques, les herbes salutaires, et la résine des pins
odorants y parfument l'air d'une odeur balsamique qui dilate les
poumons. A l'extrémité du bois de chênes, à travers un verger dont
les arbres sont entortillés de vignes et chargés de fruits de toutes
espèces, on entrevoit une cabane; son toit de chaume y met à l'abri,
sous une grande saillie, tous les ustensiles du ménage rustique. . . .

C'est dans de semblables situations que l'on éprouve toute la
force de cette analogie entre les charmes physiques et les impressions
morales. On se plaît à y rêver, de cette rêverie si douce, besoin pres-
sant pour celui qui connaît la valeur des choses et les sentiments
tendres; on voudrait y rester toujours, parce que le cœur y sent
toute la vérité de la nature.

> From the MARQUIS DE GIRARDIN's *Traité de l'art des jardins*, originally
> published in 1771: the passage appears on pp. 151–5 of the 4th
> edition, of 1809. [*Note*. The Marquis was the creator of the Parc
> d'Ermenonville, which is in the environs of Paris, and where J.-J.
> Rousseau died.]

V

Extracts from Letourneur's translation of Ossian (1777)

(a) *Temora. Chant VII*

Quand les portes de l'occident se sont fermées sur le soleil, et
cachent le monde à son œil perçant, de sombres vapeurs s'élèvent
des eaux du Légo, et des bois qui couvrent ses bords: l'épaisse fumée
s'étend au loin sur le torrent de Lara: la lune, comme un obscur
bouclier, nage dans les flots de ces noires exhalaisons. C'est de ces
vapeurs que les ombres des morts s'enveloppent quand elles mar-
chent dans l'espace, et qu'elles effraient les mortels par leurs gestes
terribles. Souvent elles se mêlent avec les vents de la nuit, et soufflent
sur la tombe de quelque guerrier le brouillard où son âme doit
rester captive, jusqu'à ce que les bardes aient chanté sa gloire. Un
bruit soudain part du désert; c'est l'ombre de Conar qui vole sur
l'aile des vents, et va souffler sur le corps de Fillan le brouillard qui
enveloppait son ombre. L'âme du jeune guerrier se penche tristement du sein de son épaisse vapeur; les tourbillons l'emportent
quelquefois; mais l'aimable fantôme revient sans cesse; il revient les
yeux baissés, et sa chevelure aérienne flotte sur les vents.

Les ténèbres régnaient sur la plaine: les armées tranquilles
dormaient sous les voiles de la nuit; la flamme s'éteignait sur le
rocher où Fingal appuyé sur son bouclier reposait à l'écart. Ses

yeux étaient à demi fermés par le sommeil. La voix de Fillan vint
frapper l'oreille du roi. 'Il dort, l'époux de Clatho, le père du
guerrier qui n'est plus! Tranquille et solitaire dans les ombres de la
nuit, tu m'oublies donc, ô mon père, au milieu de tes songes!'

'Pourquoi viens-tu troubler mon sommeil?' dit Fingal en se levant.
'Puis-je t'oublier, ô mon fils? Puis-je oublier ta course glorieuse dans
le champ de bataille? Non, les actions des braves ne s'effacent point
de l'âme de Fingal, comme l'éclair qui brille et n'est plus; je me
souviens de toi, ô Fillan! et je sens ma fureur s'enflammer.'

A ces mots Fingal saisit sa lance homicide. Dans les ténèbres il
frappe son bouclier, funeste signal du combat. De tous côtés les
ombres épouvantées fuient dans les airs. Leurs formes fantastiques
roulent l'une sur l'autre au milieu des vents. Trois fois du fond des
vallons s'élèvent les voix de la mort; les harpes des bardes roulent
d'elles-mêmes un son lugubre et plaintif.

(b) Description d'une nuit du mois d'Octobre[1]

PREMIER BARDE

La nuit est triste et sombre, les nuages reposent amoncelés sur
les collines: la lune ne paraît point dans les cieux: pas une étoile qui
brille. J'entends le bruit sourd et confus des vents dans la forêt loin-
taine: le torrent murmure tristement au fond du vallon: la chouette
glapissante crie au haut de l'arbre qui est auprès de la tombe des
morts. J'aperçois un fantôme dans la plaine; c'est l'ombre d'un guerrier qui n'est plus. Elle se dissipe: elle s'est évanouie. On portera par
ce chemin quelqu'un dans la tombe: ce fantôme lui a tracé sa route.

J'entends un chien aboyer dans une cabane éloignée; le cerf est
couché sur la mousse de la montagne; sa biche repose à ses côtés;
elle a entendu le vent résonner dans son bois, je la vois qui se dresse
avec effroi: elle se rassure et se couche sur la bruyère. Le chevreuil
dort dans le creux d'un rocher, la tête du coq de bruyère est cachée
sous son aile. Nul animal, nul oiseau dans la plaine que le renard et
la chouette. L'une est perchée sur un arbre sans feuilles, l'autre
paraît dans un nuage sur la cime du coteau.

Le voyageur triste, haletant, tremblant dans les ténèbres a perdu
sa route: il avance au travers des épines et des buissons, et suit avec
inquiétude le gazouillement du ruisseau: il craint les rochers et les
marécages: il redoute les fantômes de la nuit. Le vieux arbre gémit
sous l'effort des vents; la branche tombe, retentit sur la terre, et le
vent chasse devant lui sur le gazon les glouterons flétris et enchaînés
ensemble: il croit entendre les pas légers d'un fantôme; il frissonne
dans l'obscurité.

---

[1] Ce poème n'est point d'Ossian: il a même été composé plus de mille ans après
lui; mais comme l'auteur de cette pièce a beaucoup de la manière du barde
écossais, nous croyons faire plaisir à nos lecteurs en la joignant ici.

La nuit est sombre, nébuleuse, orageuse: les vents, les fantômes, les morts sont dans la plaine: mes amis, recevez-moi, sauvez-moi de la nuit.

Note. These extracts show the contribution made by this 'Nordic' poetry to the imagination of France and Europe. It may be noted that the translations of Letourneur were the medium by which Young and Ossian became known in Europe.

INDEX

Dates of monarchs are those of the years during which they reigned; dates of other persons are those of birth and death.

abacus, 124.

Abbas I, shah of Persia (1585–1628), 82.

Aboukir, 254.

academies, beginnings of, mid 15th c., 13; scientific, 17th c., 110.

Academy of Châlons-sur-Marne, 314.

Academy of Sciences, Russia, 223; France, 289.

Accademia del Cimento, Florence, 289.

Addison, Joseph (1672–1719), English writer, 298.

administration: by German princes, 16th c., 92; science and, 17th c., 111; central governmental, 15th c., 20; in Austria, 18th c., 209–10; centralization of, in Spain, 18th c., 218; under Napoleon, 19th c., 246, 250; in Germany, 19th c., 250.

administrative decree, Russian (1775), 225.

Adriatic, the, 129.

Afghanistan, 18th c., 260.

Africa: slave-trade, 63–64, 258.

African languages, study of, 17th c., 120.

aggression, policy of, 18th c., 206.

agrarian reform: Denmark, 18th c., 222; Prussia, 19th c., 252.

agricultural associations, creation of, 315.

agriculture, 15th c., 4, 75; decline of, in Spain, 16th c., 92; science and, 17th c., 111; increase in English production, 18th c., 227; France, 18th c., 191, 233–5, 314, 328; Italy, 18th c., 220; Milanese, 18th c., 221; Naples, 18th c., 221; Tuscany, 18th c., 221; European, severely affected by Napoleon's ban on exports, 251.

aide, French indirect tax, 18th c., 190.

Aix-la-Chapelle, peace of (1748), 201.

Albania, 33.

Alberoni, Giulio (1664–1752), Spanish minister, 188.

Albert of Hohenzollern (1490–1568), 104.

Alberti, Leon Battista (1404–72), 12.

Albuquerque, Alfonso (1453–1515), Portuguese viceroy, 65–66.

alchemy in the Middle Ages, 108, 112.

Alembert, Jean le Rond d' (1717–83), French philosopher and writer, 264, 303.

Alexander I, tsar of Russia (1801–1825), 252, 263.

Alexander VI, pope (1492–1503), the Spanish Rodrigo Borgia, 26, 71.

Alexis, tsar of Russia, code of laws (1649), 150.

Alfieri, Vittorio (1749–1803), Italian tragic poet, 340.

Alfonso, his 'Highness', chief of the Congo (16th c.), 65.

Algiers, 28, 50–51.

Algoa, 66.

Alkazar-el-Kebir, battle of, 16th c., 91.

Allgemeine Deutsche Bibliothek, 216.

alliances, 15th c., 24.

Alpine mountaineering, development of, 322.

'Alpinist' suits, 322.

Alps: roads across, 18th c., 221; Swiss, 322; in literature, 322.

Alsace: won by France, 17th c., 96, 97; German princes owning lands in, and the French Revolution, 244.

Alva, duke of (1508–83), Spanish general, 49, 85, 91.

ambassadors, 15th c., 23; rise of power, 17th c., 100; and trade treaties, 16th–17th cc., 129.

America and Columbus, 68; gold and silver from, 16th c., 79; witch-hunting in North, 17th–18th cc., 118; Spaniards in Latin, 18th c., 257–8; French secret agents in North, 329; intellectual relations between Europe and, 328–32.

American Constitution, 331; Germany in favour of independence, 18th c., 217; — Independence, Declaration of, 257, 271–2, 330–1; — Independence, War of, 259; — languages, study of, 17th c., 120; — Revolution, Europe and, 329.

Amiens, 248; peace of (1802), 254.

Amsterdam, the great money market, 17th c., 132.

Anabaptists, 52.

Analects of Confucius, 121.

anatomy and renaissance artists, 107; new era in, 17th c., 110.

ancien régime, 189, 202–3, 235, 239, 334.

Andalusia, 218.

Andean range, 69.

Anglo-Dutch rivalry, 17th c., 136; — wars, 17th c., 141.

Anglo-French alliance, 18th c., 188; — struggles, 199.

Angola, Portuguese conquest of, 16th c., 65.

Melon, 18th-c. French writer, 296.

Mendelssohn, Moses (1739–86), German philosopher, 214.

mercantilism (mercantile system), 17th c., 132–4; in Austria, 18th c., 212; Dutch, 17th c., 133; English, 18th c., 194.

mercantilist principles, Frederic the Great and, 211.

mercenary soldiers, 15th c., 3, 20; 17th–18th cc., 128; hired by the Dutch, 16th c., 88; in imperial army, 17th c., 94; Swiss, 15th–16th cc., 25, 28, 75.

merchants, capitalist in France, 18th c., 191, 234; as captains, English, 17th c., 135; class in Russia, 18th c., 225, 226; marine, naval recruitment and, 17th c., 128.

merchantmen, armed, 16th c., 128.

Mercier, Louis Sébastien (1740–1814), French writer, 307, 319, 320.

Mersenne, le Père, French 18th-c. philosopher, 289.

Messenyer, Polish 18th-c. playwright, 307.

metal industry, 16th–18th cc., 127; English, 18th c., 228; Russian, 18th c., 197.

metallic money, 15th and 16th cc., 77, 79.

metaphysical problems, revival of discussion of, 309.

Metastasio, Pietro (1698–1782), Italian poet, 303.

métayer system abolished in Piedmont-Sardinia, 18th c., 221.

Methodism, 18th c., 229.

metrical romances, 342–3.

Metternich, Prince von (1773–1859), 263.

Metz, 49, 85, 97.

Meulen, Mlle ter, 299.

Mexico: Aztecs of, 16th c., 72; discovery and conquest of, 16th c., 68–69; Europeans in, small number of, 16th c., 72; printing-press in, 16th c., 70.

Michelangelo (1475–1564), 60.

Middle Ages, idea of, 13; and science, 107; 18th-c. passion for, 336.

Middleton, Conyers (1683–1750), English divine, 285.

migration, 15th c., 3.

Milan: agriculture in 18th c., 221; and system of ambassadors, 15th c., 23; and Austria, 17th c., 143; Council of, 16th c., 30; duchy of, 15th c., 25, 18th c., 49; and France, 15th–16th cc., 29, 30; Habsburg colony, 18th c., 209; principality of, 15th c., 22; and Spain, 17th c., 143.

Milanese, and Napoleon, 248.

military organization, Swedish, 17th c., 143.

military strength, diplomacy and, 206.

Milton, John (1608–74), English poet, 300–1.

mines, pumping water out of, 17th c., 111; Swedish, 16th–17th cc., 102.

mining, European, 19th c., 251.

ministers, increased powers of, 17th c., 100.

Minorca, 18th c., 145, 201.

Mirabeau, Honoré Gabriel (1749–91), French statesman, and Bentham, 243.

miracles, belief in, shaken, 118.

'miraculous year' (1759), 200.

missionaries, and colonization, 16th c., 67.

missions, Christian, 17th c., 120.

Mohacs, battle of (1526), 51, 93.

Moldavia, and Turkey, 16th c., 34.

Molière (Jean Baptiste Poquelin de), French dramatist (1622–73), 138, 297, 299, 307.

Mollien, Nicolas François (1758–1850), count, 331.

Moluccas, the, 16th c., 66.

Mombasa, 16th c., 72.

monarchy: 15th c., 22; new conception of, 18th c., 206; Descartes and, 292; Aragon, 16th c., 84; Castile, 16th c., 84; France, 16th–18th cc., 84, 85, 208, 232, 241; Great Britain, 17th c., 99, 144; Muscovy, 15th c., 17; Spain, 16th c., 84.

monasteries: in Austria, 18th c., 213; in England, 16th c., 89.

Monceau, Parc, Paris, 321.

money: growth of bargaining power of, 77; wages instead of service, 17th c., 133; - managers, 18th c., French, 234.

— metallic, 15th–16th cc., 77, 79.

— paper, 15th c., 77; 18th c., 190, 219.

Monge, Gaspard (1746–1818), physicist, 265.

monopolies, 66, 129, 131.

monopoly, 15th c., 64; of office, French, 18th c., 235; treaties, 16th–17th cc., 129.

Mont Blanc, 322.

Montenegro, 33; printing in, 15th c., 37.

Montesquieu, Charles Louis de Secondat de (1641–1707), French lawyer and political philosopher, 206, 224, 291–3, 299, 303, 312, 313.

Monti, Vincenzo (1754–1828), Italian poet, 340.

Moore, Edward (1712–57), English dramatist, 319.

Moors, the, 15th c., 27, 28.

state, the, and trade, 130; changing conception of, 144; civil, liberty in, Rousseau on, 268; the guardian of civilization, 16th–17th cc., 161; new conception of, 18th c., 200; power of wealth of, 126–39; sovereign, rise of the, 17th c., 133.
state management, 131.
state-system, European, 19–34; western, 15th–16th cc., 34, 17th–18th cc., 147.
state trading, 131.
States-General, French, 17th c., 85; Assembly of the, 18th c., 238–40.
statesmen, co-operation with business men, 16th–17th cc., 129; work of, 16th–17th cc., 160; English, Elizabethan, 16th c., 90.
statistics, 15th c., 20; of population, interest in, 16th–18th cc., 127; science and, 17th–18th cc., 111.
steam-engine, first, 17th c., 111; invention of, 18th c., 145; Watts (1769), 228.
steel, manufacture of iron and, English, 18th c., 228.
Steffans, 18th-c. Danish scholar, 344.
Stein, Heinrich Friedrich Karl (1757–1831), Prussian statesman, 252, 253.
Sterne, Laurence (1713–68), English writer, 325–6.
Stockholm, 18th c., 236.
Stoics, beliefs of, 122.
stone, for building, 15th c., 7.
Stowe, duke of Newcastle's palace at, 18th c., 232.
Strassburg, 18th c., 214.
strikes, industrial, 17th c., 134–5.
Struensee, Johann Friedrich (1737–72), Danish statesman, 221.
Stuart, James (1688–1766), the Old Pretender, 193.
Stuarts, the, 18th c., 193.
students, wandering, after 15th c., 159.
Sturm und Drang, 215, 344.
Stürmers, the, 18th c., 320.
Suard's salon, 304.
succession, Austrian laws of, 18th c., 213.
Suez Canal, idea of, 15th c., 78.
suffrage, universal (male), French, 18th c., 244.
sugar from Brazil, 16th c., 78; -beet industry, European, 19th c., 251; -cane from Madeira, 16th c., 71.
Sully, Maximilien de Béthune (1560–1641), duc de, French statesman, 137.
Sunday schools, English, 18th c., 229.
supernatural, the, in literature, 18th c., 320.
Surbatov, Russian prince, 18th c., 226.

surgeons, and science, 17th c., 109.
surveying, science and, 17th c., 111.
Swabia, 18th c., 215.
Sweden, 16th–17th cc., 102; 18th c., 197; and the Baltic, 16th–17th cc., 102, 148; and Baltic wars, 16th c., 104; and Catholic reformation, late 16th c., 105; and Charles Gustavus (Charles X), 148; and Congress of Westphalia, 101; and the Danes in the Baltic, 17th c., 148; and Dutch, 148; and France, 17th c., 140, 148; and Russia's 'Troubled Times', 17th c., 105–6; and the Turkish alliance against Russia, 17th c., 152–3; conquests from Germany, 16th–17th cc., 97; drama, at close of the 18th c., 338; great soldier kings of, 18th c., 148; literary criticism in, at close of the 18th c., 339; literature, close of the 18th c., 344; Lutheranism in, 53; lyrical poetry in, late 18th c., 337; military organization in, 17th c., 143; monarchy in, 15th c., 22; partition of, projected, 18th c., 206, defeated, 18th c., 222; printing in, 15th c., 37; reforms in, 18th c., 222–3; toleration, Lutheran, in, 120; treaty with Russia, 17th c., 106; war with the emperor, 17th c., 94.
Swedish landlords, 104; -Polish peace, France and, 17th c., 95; Romantics, literary critics and, 339; townsmen, 104.
Swift, Jonathan (1667–1745), English author, 300–2, 308, 326.
Swiss, the, the French and, 16th c., 30; cantons, 87; mercenary soldiers, 15th–16th cc., 75; mercenaries in French army, late 15th c., 26, 78.
Switzerland, 18th c., 299–300; as fashionable honeymoon resort in late 18th c., 322; culture in, 307; fall in death-rate in, 16th–18th cc., 127; growth of power of towns in, 79; in time of Charles the Bold, 87; influence of French Revolution on, 242; rising and riots in, 17th c., 134; witch-hunting in, 18th c., 119.
— German, literature, English influence on, 18th c., 326.
Sydney (Australia), founded (1798), 261.
Syria, decline of, 16th c., 78; Turkish conquest of, 16th c., 34.

Tahiti, Bougainville's description of, 332.
taille, 18th c., 190.
Tanucci, 18th-c. Neapolitan minister, 221.

PRINTED IN
GREAT BRITAIN
AT THE
UNIVERSITY PRESS
OXFORD
BY
CHARLES BATEY
PRINTER
TO THE
UNIVERSITY